Lecture Notes in Computer Science 12803

Founding Editors

Gerhard Goos
Karlsruhe Institute of Technology, Karlsruhe, Germany
Juris Hartmanis
Cornell University, Ithaca, NY, USA

More information about this subseries at http://www.springer.com/series/7407

Sebastian Maneth (Ed.)

Implementation and Application of Automata

25th International Conference, CIAA 2021
Virtual Event, July 19–22, 2021
Proceedings

 Springer

Editor
Sebastian Maneth
University of Bremen
Bremen, Germany

ISSN 0302-9743   ISSN 1611-3349   (electronic)
Lecture Notes in Computer Science
ISBN 978-3-030-79120-9   ISBN 978-3-030-79121-6   (eBook)
https://doi.org/10.1007/978-3-030-79121-6

LNCS Sublibrary: SL1 – Theoretical Computer Science and General Issues

This Springer imprint is published by the registered company Springer Nature Switzerland AG
The registered company address is: Gewerbestrasse 11, 6330 Cham, Switzerland

Preface

The 25th International Conference on Implementation and Application of Automata (CIAA 2021) was organized by the Database Group of the Faculty of Mathematics and Informatics of the University of Bremen. The conference took place during July 19–22, 2021, and was held online, due to the COVID-19 pandemic.

This volume of *Lecture Notes in Computer Science* contains the scientific papers presented at CIAA 2021. The volume also includes extended abstracts of the three invited talks presented by *Mikołaj Bojańczyk* on "Polyregular Functions", by *Javier Esparza* on "Back to the Future: A Fresh Look at Linear Temporal Logic", and by *Jeffrey Shallit* on "Say No to Case Analysis: Automating the Drudgery of Case-Based Proofs".

The 13 regular papers were selected from 20 submissions covering various fields in the application, implementation, and theory of automata and related structures. Each paper was reviewed by at least three Program Committee members, with the assistance of external referees. Papers were submitted by authors from the following countries: Bulgaria, Canada, France, Germany, Israel, Italy, Japan, Portugal, Russia, South Africa, and South Korea.

I wish to thank everybody who contributed to the success of this conference: the authors for submitting their carefully prepared manuscripts, the Program Committee members and external referees for their valuable judgment of the submitted manuscripts, and the invited speakers for their excellent presentations of topics related to the theme of the conference. Last but not least, I would like to express my sincere thanks to the local organizers Peter Leupold, Kathryn Lorenz, and Martin Vu, to the University of Bremen for sponsoring the event, and to the editors of *Lecture Notes in Computer Science*, in particular to Anna Kramer, for their help in publishing this volume in a timely manner.

July 2021   Sebastian Maneth

Organization

Program Committee Chair

Sebastian Maneth   Universität Bremen, Germany

Program Committee

Marie-Pierre Béal	Université Paris-Est Marne-la-Vallée, France
Francine Blanchet-Sadri	University of North Carolina at Chapel Hill, USA
Cezar Câmpeanu	University of Prince Edward Island, Canada
Jan Daciuk	Gdańsk University of Technology, Poland
Mike Domaratzki	University of Manitoba, Canada
Emmanuel Filiot	Université libre de Bruxelles, Belgium
Yo-Sub Han	Yonsei University, South Korea
Jan Holub	Czech Technical University in Prague, Czech Republic
Markus Holzer	Justus Liebig University Giessen, Germany
Oscar Ibarra	University of California, Santa Barbara, USA
Christos Kapoutsis	Carnegie Mellon University in Qatar, Qatar
Jarkko Kari	University of Turku, Finland
Markus Lohrey	University of Siegen, Germany
Sylvain Lombardy	Université de Bordeaux, France
Andreas Maletti	University of Leipzig, Germany
Brink van der Merwe	Stellenbosch University, South Africa
Nelma Moreira	University of Porto, Portugal
Cyril Nicaud	Université Paris-Est Marne-la-Vallée, France
Dirk Nowotka	University of Kiel, Germany
Alexander Okhotin	St. Petersburg State University, Russia
Giovanni Pighizzini	University of Milan, Italy
Bala Ravikumar	Sonoma State University, USA
Daniel Reidenbach	Loughborough University, UK
Rogério Reis	University of Porto, Portugal
Kai Salomaa	Queen's University, Canada
Hiroyuki Seki	Nagoya University, Japan
Shinnosuke Seki	University of Electro-Communications, Japan
Helmut Seidl	Technical University of Munich, Germany
Jean-Marc Talbot	Aix-Marseille University, France
Bruce Watson	Stellenbosch University, South Africa
Hsu-Chun Yen	National Taiwan University, Taiwan

Steering Committee

Markus Holzer (Chair)	Justus Liebig University Giessen, Germany
Oscar Ibarra	University of California, Santa Barbara, USA
Sylvain Lombardy	Université de Bordeaux, France
Nelma Moreira	Universidade do Porto, Portugal
Kai T. Salomaa (Co-chair)	Queen's University, Canada
Hsu-Chun Yen	National Taiwan University, Taiwan

External Referees

Kenji Hashimoto
Ian McQuillan
Christian Rauch

Andrew Ryzhikov
Martin Viet Vu
Jianxin Wei

Abstract of Invited Lecture

Polyregular Functions

Mikołaj Bojańczyk [ID]

University of Warsaw, Poland

The class of polyregular functions is a class of string-to-string transducers, which extends the class of regular string-to-string transducers. The difference is that regular functions have linear size outputs, while polyregular functions have polynomial size outputs.

Regular functions. The class of regular string-to-string functions is currently one of the main topics of transducer theory. The allure of the class is that it has many equivalent definitions:

1. two-way deterministic automata with output [11]
2. monadic second-order string-to-string transductions [7];
3. streaming string transducers [1];
4. regular expressions for transducers [2, 6];
5. a combinatory functional programming language [4]

Also, the class is shares many similarities with the regular languages of words, explaining its name, in particular: (a) it is decidable if a given word belongs to the range of a regular function, more generally the class of regular word languages is effectively closed under taking inverse images of regular functions; and (b) it is decidable if two regular functions (represented by any of the formalisms described above) are actually the same string-to-string function [8].

Polyregular functions. The output of a regular function is at most linear in the input size. This is easily seen if we think of regular functions as deterministic two-way automata with output: if such an automaton has k states, then it can visit each position at most k times (otherwise it will enter a loop), and therefore the length of the output word is at most k times the length of the input word. The idea behind polyregular functions is to find a class of functions that has the good theoretical properties of regular functions, and yet allows outputs of polynomial, but not necessarily linear, size. For example, consider the *squaring* function which inputs a word w, and outputs $|w|$ copies of w, as in the following example:

$$1234 \quad \mapsto \quad 1234123412341234.$$

If the length of the input word is n, then the length of the output is n^2, and therefore the squaring function is not a regular function. It is, however, polyregular, as we will see below.

Supported by ERC Consolidator grant LIPA 683080.

The study of polyregular functions was proposed in [3], building on deterministic k-pebble transducers with stack discipline [10]. If an input word has length n, then k pebbles can be placed in at most n^k ways on its positions, and therefore the length of a run of a k-pebble transducer (and also the length of the output) are going to be at most polynomial in the length of the input word. The degree of the polynomial is the number of pebbles, which is fixed for each transducer. For example, the squaring function is computed by a 2-pebble transducer, which runs the first pebble through all positions in the input word, and for each position uses the second pebble (which can be viewed as the head of the transducer) to copy the entire input word to the output. When the number of pebbles is equal to $k = 1$, then pebble transducers are the same thing as two-way automata with output, thus corresponding to the regular functions.

It turns out that the functions computed by pebble transducers can be described in many different ways, just like the regular functions:

1. pebble transducers;
2. a restricted variant of pebble transducers, called for programs, where each pebble has an assigned direction (left-to-right, or right-to-left), and therefore pebbles cannot move both ways;
3. a higher-order functional programming language, which is built on basic list operations such as "reverse" or "head", using basic mechanisms of functional programming such as λ-abstraction;
4. the smallest class of string-to-string functions that is closed under function composition, contains all regular functions, plus one extra function, which extends squaring with an "underline" as explained in the following example:

$$1234 \quad \mapsto \quad \underline{1234}1\underline{23}41\underline{2}341\underline{234}.$$

5. an extension of monadic second-order transductions, where each output position is represented not by a single input position, but by a k-tuple of input positions.

The models in items 2, 3 and 4 were introduced in [3]; the same paper also proved that they are equivalent to each other and to pebble transducers. The model in item 5 was shown to be equivalent to the previous ones in [5].

If we think of the regular functions as a fragment of the polyregular functions, then this fragment is very clean: a function is regular if and only if it is polyregular and it has linear size outputs [9]. Furthermore, since having linear size outputs is a decidable property of polyregular functions, it follows that one can decide if a polyregular function is already regular.

Like regular functions, polyregular functions effectively preserve regularity when taking inverse images. An important outstanding open problem about polyregular functions is decidability of equivalence: is there an algorithm which decides if two polyregular functions, represented using any one of the many equivalent formalisms, are actually the same string-to-string function?

References

1. Alur, R., Černý, P.: Expressiveness of streaming string transducers. In: Foundations of Software Technology and Theoretical Computer Science, FSTTCS 2010, Chennai, India, LIPIcs, vol. 8, pp. 1–12. Schloss Dagstuhl - Leibniz-Zentrum fuer Informatik (2010)
2. Alur, R., Freilich, A., Raghothaman, M.: Regular combinators for string transformations. In: Proceedings of the Joint Meeting of the Twenty-Third EACSL Annual Conference on Computer Science Logic (CSL) and the Twenty-Ninth Annual ACM/IEEE Symposium on Logic in Computer Science (LICS), p. 9. ACM (2014)
3. Bojańczyk, M.: Polyregular functions. CoRR, abs/1810.08760 (2018)
4. Bojańczyk, M., Daviaud, L., Krishna, S.N.: Regular and first-order list functions. In: Proceedings of the 33rd Annual ACM/IEEE Symposium on Logic in Computer Science, LICS 2018, Oxford, UK, 09–12 July 2018, pp. 125–134 (2018)
5. Bojanczyk, M., Kiefer, S., Lhote, N.: String-to-string interpretations with polynomial-size output. In: 46th International Colloquium on Automata, Languages, and Programming, ICALP 2019, 9–12 July 2019, Patras, Greece, pp. 106:1–106:14 (2019)
6. Dave, V., Gastin, P., Krishna, S.N.: Regular transducer expressions for regular transformations. In: Proceedings of the 33rd Annual ACM/IEEE Symposium on Logic in Computer Science, LICS 2018, Oxford, UK, 09–12 July 2018, pp. 315–324 (2018)
7. Engelfriet, J., Hoogeboom, H.J.: Mso definable string transductions and two-way finite-state transducers. ACM Trans. Comput. Log. (TOCL) 2(2), 216–254 (2001)
8. Gurari, E.M.: The equivalence problem for deterministic two-way sequential transducers is decidable. SIAM J. Comput. 11(3), 448–452 (1982)
9. Lhote, N.: Pebble minimization of polyregular functions. In: LICS 2020: 35th Annual ACM/IEEE Symposium on Logic in Computer Science, Saarbrücken, Germany, 8–11 July 2020, pp. 703–712 (2020)
10. Milo, T., Suciu, D., Vianu, V.: Typechecking for xml transformers. J. Comput. Syst. Sci. 66(1), 66–97 (2003)
11. Shepherdson, J.C.: The reduction of two-way automata to one-way automata. IBM J. Res. Dev. 3(2), 198–200 (1959)

Contents

Invited Lectures

Back to the Future: A Fresh Look at Linear Temporal Logic

Javier Esparza[✉][iD]

Technical University of Munich, Munich, Germany
esparza@in.tum.de

Abstract. This note tells the story of how I came to understand that my work with Křetínský and Sickert on translating LTL into ω-automata was deeply connected to a normal form for LTL, obtained 35 years ago by Lichtenstein, Pnueli and Zuck.

Keywords: Linear Temporal Logic · ω-Automata · Formal verification

In the last 10 years, Jan Křetínský, Salomon Sickert, and myself have investigated novel algorithms for translating formulas of Linear Temporal Logic (LTL) into ω-automata (i.e., automata on infinite words) that are either deterministic or only exhibit a limited form of non-determinism. I have only recently understood that our work is deeply connected to a normal form for LTL, obtained 35 years ago by Lichtenstein, Pnueli and Zuck in [18]. THis normal form plays a central role in Manna and Pnueli's books on specification and verification of reactive systems using temporal logic [23, 24]. The complexity of normalizing a given LTL formula remains an open but forgotten problem, to which Sickert and myself have recently made a contribution in [33] using results from [7]. Since space constraints on regular conference papers usually prevent one from exposing the history behind one's research in any detail, I am using the kind invitation of the PC Chairs of CIAA 2021 to explain the problem, why I think it became forgotten, why it should not have, and why our solution is relevant for probabilistic verification and reactive synthesis.

1 Manna and Pnueli's Safety-Progress Hierarchy

In the late 1970s, Amir Pnueli introduced Linear Temporal Logic (LTL) into computer science as a framework for specifying and formally verifying concurrent

The work surveyed in this note was partially supported by the DFG projects 183790222 "Computer-Aided Verification of Automata Constructions for Model Checking" and 317422601 "Verified Model Checkers", and by the European Research Council (ERC) under the European Union's Horizon 2020 research and innovation programme under grant agreement No 787367 "Parameterized Verification and Synthesis" (PaVeS). This paper was written while the author was participating in a program at the Simons Institute for the Theory of Computing.

S. Maneth (Ed.): CIAA 2021, LNCS 12803, pp. 3–13, 2021.
https://doi.org/10.1007/978-3-030-79121-6_1

programs [28, 29], a contribution that earned him the 1996 Turing Award. LTL extends propositional logic with temporal operators like the unary *next* operator $\mathbf{X}$, where $\mathbf{X}\varphi$ means that φ holds at the next point in time (i.e., that φ "holds tomorrow"), and the binary *until* operator $\mathbf{U}$, where $\varphi \, \mathbf{U} \, \psi$ means that ψ holds at some point in the future and φ holds until ψ holds, i.e., at every point before ψ holds for the first time.

During the 1980s and the early 1990s, in collaboration with other researchers, Pnueli proceeded to study the properties expressible in LTL. In 1985, Lichtenstein, Pnueli and Zuck introduced a classification of LTL properties, later refined and described in detail by Manna and Pnueli in [21, 22], who also gave it its current name, the *safety-progress* hierarchy. These works deal with an extended version of LTL including past operators, called Past LTL, and introduce a hierarchy of six classes: a *safety* class of formulas expressing requirements that must hold at all times, and five *progress* classes, called *guarantee, obligation, response, persistence*, and *reactivity*, whose formulas specify that some requirement should eventually be fulfilled. The inclusions between these classes are shown in Fig. 1a. The progress classes differ in the conditions and frequency at which the requirement is to be fulfilled. The papers prove that each class corresponds to a syntactically defined set of LTL formulas. In particular, the reactivity class, which contains all others, corresponds to the formulas of the form

$$\bigwedge_{i=1}^{n} (\mathbf{GF}\varphi_i \vee \mathbf{FG}\psi_i)$$

where $\mathbf{F}\varphi$ and $\mathbf{G}\varphi$ mean that φ holds at some and at every point in the future, respectively, and $\varphi_1, \ldots, \varphi_n, \psi_1, \ldots, \psi_n$ are formulas containing only past operators.

In 1992, Chang, Manna, and Pnueli presented a different and very elegant characterization of the hierarchy in terms of standard LTL formulas without past operators [1] (see also [27]). The characterization uses the until operator and the *weak until* operator $\varphi \, \mathbf{W} \, \psi$, meaning that either $\varphi \, \mathbf{U} \, \psi$ holds, or φ holds at every point in the future. Every formula is equivalent to another one in negation normal form (i.e., with negations only in front of propositional variables) containing only $\mathbf{X}$, $\mathbf{W}$, and $\mathbf{X}$. In particular, we have $\mathbf{F}\varphi \equiv \mathbf{true} \, \mathbf{U} \, \varphi$ and $\mathbf{G}\varphi \equiv \varphi \, \mathbf{W} \, \mathbf{false}$. Chang, Manna, and Pnueli show that every reactivity formula is equivalent to a Boolean combination of formulas exhibiting at most one alternation of these two operators. More precisely, consider the following classes of LTL formulas:

- The class $\Sigma_0 = \Pi_0 = \Delta_0$ is the closure under conjunction and disjunction of the atomic propositions and their negations.
- The class Σ_{i+1} is the closure of Π_i under conjunction, disjunction, and the $\mathbf{X}$, and $\mathbf{U}$ operators.
- The class Π_{i+1} is the closure Σ_i under conjunction, disjunction, and the $\mathbf{X}$, and $\mathbf{W}$ operators.
- The class Δ_{i+1} is the closure of Σ_{i+1} and Π_{i+1} under conjunction and disjunction.

The inclusions between these classes are shown in Fig. 1b. It is shown in [1] that this alternation hierarchy coincides with the safety-progress hierarchy of Fig. 1a.

(a) The safety-progress hierarchy   (b) The **U-W** alternation hierarchy

Fig. 1. Two hierarchies of LTL properties

In the first half of the 90s, Manna and Pnueli condensed their work into two books [23, 24]. They should have been followed by a third one, which unfortunately was never completed; a little part of it can be found in [25]. The trilogy is structured around the safety-progress hierarchy; the first volume introduces it, and the second volume describes proof techniques for properties in the safety class, plus a model-checking algorithm for arbitrary properties. The incomplete third volume should have described proof techniques for properties in the progress classes.

The safety-progress hierarchy hinges on a fundamental *Normalization Theorem* stating that every LTL formula is equivalent to a reactivity formula, its largest class, and so that the hierarchy indeed covers all properties expressible in LTL. In terms of the characterization of [1], the theorem states that every LTL formula is equivalent to a Δ_2-formula, i.e., to a formula in which every path through the syntax tree contains at most one alternation of the **U** and **W** operators. Despite its relevannce, is not very easy to find a proof in the literature. The Normalization Theorem is announced in passing in [18], as a corollary of another theorem, and the proof of this theorem is said to be based on many previous results, including papers by Büchi; McNaughton and Papert; Choueka; Thomas; and Gabbay, Pnueli, Shelah, and Stavi, which "when combined, yield the theorem almost immediately". Although the theorem features prominently in [21–24], all of them declare its proof out of the scope of the publication. Finally, [1] does not provide a proof either, since it only shows the equivalence between the safety-progress and the **U-W** alternation hierarchies, but not the completeness of the Δ_2 class. To the best of my knowledge, a complete proof can only be found in Zuck's PhD Thesis [38]. The proof starts in Sect. 4, where Zuck, relying on previous results by other authors, shows how to translate a Past LTL formula into a counter-free semi-automaton. In a second step, Zuck invokes the Krohn-Rhodes cascade decomposition theorem to translate this semi-automaton into a star-free regular expression. Finally, in Sect. 5 she presents a procedure to translate this regular expression into a reactivity formula, and remarks that the complete translation may cause a non-elementary blow-up in the length of the formula.

The Normalization Theorem is a cornerstone of Manna and Pnueli's books, one of the most remarkable achievements of theoretical computer science during the 1980s, to wit: one year after the publication of the second book, Pnueli received the Turing Award for introducing temporal logic into computer science. It is remarkable that, despite this prominence, no subsequent work tried to improve Zuck's non-elementary normalization procedure, even though no lower bound was known. To the best of my knowledge, the only exception is a paper on the Krohn-Rhodes theorem, published twenty years later in a volume of essays in memory of Pnueli, in which Maler, based on former work with Pnueli, sketches a triple exponential construction [20]. In a discipline that routinely devotes papers to the investigation of much smaller complexity gaps, why was there no subsequent work on this question? I don't know, but my conjecture is that it had to do with the rise of the automata-theoretic approach to LTL verification, which brings us to the next section.

2   The Automata-Theoretic Approach to LTL Verification

Manna and Pnueli's books present a methodology to specify requirements of concurrent and reactive program in temporal logic, and to *prove* that a given program satisfies them. Their approach was geared towards actually producing a correctness *proof*, and for this purpose they produced axiom systems, and sound and complete proof rules. Their work can be seen as an extension to the realm of reactive and concurrent programs of well-know proof systems like Hoare logic, Dijkstra's weakest preconditions, or the Owicki-Gries system.

Constructing a proof of a program required a lot of human intervention in the 1980s (and still does), which made the techniques only applicable to very small programs. Since the beginning of the 1980s, a new approach, pioneered by Clarke, Emerson, and Sifakis, proposed to substitute proofs by *computation* [2]. Under the name *model checking*, it dispensed with axioms and proof rules, and directly verified that the program satisfies its LTL specification by exhaustively exploring its set of reachable states, which only required to know the syntax and semantics of LTL. A few years later Vardi and Wolper formulated the *automata-theoretic approach* to model checking [36,37]. They showed that LTL formulas could be translated into equivalent non-deterministic automata on infinite words, or ω-automata, thus reducing the LTL verification problem to an automata-theoretic question.

Model Checking gave an enormous impulse to formal verification, and its success earned Vardi and Wolper the 2000 Gödel Prize, and Clarke, Emerson, and Sifakis the 2007 Turing Award. In particular, the automata-theoretic approach was implemented by Holzmann in SPIN, a verification tool that has passed the test of time [9]. However, the success of model checking also decreased the interest of the formal verification community in logical proof techniques. Translating LTL formulas into non-deterministic automata did not depend on axiom systems, proof rules, or on formulas belonging to particular classes, and it is telling that Manna and Pnueli included it as a final chapter of their second book, emphasizing that it provided a universal verification algorithm, valid for any formula. By the 1990s most researchers were using LTL as little more than a more human-readable syntax for ω-automata. I think this shift in interest is the most likely explanation for the "fall into oblivion" of the open questions around the Normalization Theorem. But the new approach also brought with it a new challenge.

3   A New Challenge

In 1988, Safra famously showed that ω-automata could be determinized in single exponential time [31]. This led to two new applications of the automata-theoretic approach, which have become two of the most intensely studied areas in formal verification: Probabilistic model checking [35], and reactive synthesis (also pioneered by Pnueli [30]). Instead of "does every run of the program satisfy the property?", probabilistic model checking investigates the questions "is the probability of the runs of the program satisfying the property equal to 1?" (qualitative model checking) or "does the probability of the runs of the program exceed a given bound?" (quantitative model checking).

Reactive synthesis goes beyond verification, by investigating how to automatically construct systems that are correct by construction. More precisely, the reactive synthesis problem consist of synthesizing a reactive system that produces an output for every given input in such a way that every infinite sequence of alternating inputs and outputs satisfies a given LTL property. The automata-theoretic approach reduces the synthesis problem to finding a winning strategy in an infinite two-player game. The players, which correspond to the inputs and outputs, take turns in moving a pebble along the edges of a given graph, and the output player wins if the infinite path followed by the pebble satisfies a given LTL property.

Probabilistic model checking and reactive synthesis can be solved by translating the LTL property into a deterministic ω-automaton. This stands in contrast to non-probabilistic model checking, for which a non-deterministic ω-automaton suffices (see Chapter 3 of [16] for a nice explanation of why this is the case). By concatenating a translation from LTL into a nondeterministic automaton with Safra's construction, the automata-theoretic approach could be applied to the new problems. Safra's construction was implemented in tools like LTL2DSTAR [10], and used in the PRISM probabilistic model checker [17].

While Safra's construction was a breakthrough, it also raised an important challenge. First, the translation of LTL to deterministic ω-automata induces a double exponential blow-up (one exponential for the translation of LTL to non-deterministic ω-automata, and a second exponential for determinization), which is asymptotically optimal. Moreover, Safra's construction is "monolithic", meaning that it directly defines the states and transitions of the deterministic automaton. A state of Safra's automaton consists of a tree of sets of states of the original automaton, each of them with an additional bit "flagging" it or not, satisfying certain conditions. Naive algorithms for the construction of the automaton can be easily affected by combinatorial explosion, and produce many redundant or useless states (but see [10,11] for techniques to palliate this problem). About 10 years ago, Jan Křetínský, at the time a PhD student bothered by the very large automata the tools produced for very small formulas, initiated a research program based on two observations:

- It is well known that ω-automata are more expressive than LTL. They recognize all ω-regular languages, which correspond to the languages expressible in S1S, the monadic second-order theory of one successor, while LTL only expresses the languages expressible in the first-order fragment of the theory. Traditionally, this has been seen as an additional point in favor of the automata-theoretic approach: One gets extra expressive power "for free". However, perhaps it is not for free when the target is a deterministic automaton? Since there is ample evidence that LTL is a sufficiently expressive specification language for many applications, can *direct* translations from LTL to deterministic ω-automata prove more efficient than indirect translations whose starting point is an arbitrary nondeterministic ω-automaton?
- LTL formulas are by their very nature defined compositionally, larger formulas are obtained by applying Boolean or temporal operators to smaller ones. Is it possible to use this information to obtain a compositional translation, in which the final deterministic ω-automaton is the result of combining smaller automata?

4   Closing the Circle

Křetínský's first paper (in which I played a small part) studied the fragment of LTL containing only the **F** and **G** operators [12]. We showed how to directly construct deterministic ω-automata whose states were Boolean combinations of subformulas of the original formula. This made the construction very suitable for applying reductions based on logical equivalences; indeed, many states did not need to be constructed because their associated formulas were equivalent to the ones of previously constructed states. While the experimental results were good, even the inclusion of the next operator **X** seemed challenging at that time. In [8,13] the construction was extended to larger fragments containing **X** and restricted appearances of the until operator **U**, but a general translation remained elusive.

We obtained a first breakthrough in [4], where we presented a novel approach in which the deterministic automaton was obtained as the intersection of a primary automaton and an array of secondary automata, one for each **G**ψ-subformula of the original formula, in charge of recognizing whether **FG**ψ. However, the paper contained two mistakes. First, it wrongly claimed that the construction could be extended to the alternation-free linear-time μ-calculus; this was a classical error of the form "it is easy to see that ...". The second error was a very subtle mistake in an induction proof. The error was found by

Salomon Sickert in the course of his Master's Thesis, whose topic was checking the correctness of the proof of [4] in the Isabelle theorem prover. Sickert got stuck proving a technical lemma by structural induction. An inspection of the failed proof showed that the smallest formula for which the construction would have produced a wrong result is $\mathbf{G}(\mathbf{X}a \vee \mathbf{G}\mathbf{X}b)$, which would have probably survived a large amount of experimental testing. Fortunately, the error could be corrected, and the repaired construction, now mechanically checked in Isabelle, was published in [5].

The construction of [4], once corrected, also led to a new development, which has proved to be particularly relevant in practice. While deterministic automata are *sufficient* for probabilistic model checking, one can ask whether they are *necessary*. The answer was known to be negative. Already in the 1990s, Courcoubetis and Yannakakis showed that qualitative probabilistic model checking of Markov Decision Processes (MDPs) could be carried out using *limit-deterministic ω-automata*, which only need to behave deterministically after reaching an accepting state for the first time [3] (see also [31,35] for similar results). In particular, they showed that every nondeterministic ω-automaton could be translated into an equivalent limit-deterministic one. We observed that our construction provided a simpler direct translation from LTL into limit-deterministic ω-automata, again without any detour through non-deterministic automata. Moreover, our automata could be applied not only to qualitative model checking, but also to quantitative problems. Sickert and Křetínský presented in [34] an extension of PRISM for LTL model checking based on this construction.

At this point the experimental results were already very satisfactory, and one could have declared the research program concluded. However, our direct translation was still unsatisfactory from a theoretical point of view. While the translation from LTL to deterministic ω automata that takes the detour through Safra's construction had a worst-case double exponential blow-up, ours had a triple exponential one. This was not relevant in practice, but it made us continue.

In 2018 we obtained our second breakthrough. We were able to design a unified translation of LTL formulas into deterministic Rabin automata, limit-deterministic Büchi automata, and nondeterministic Büchi automata [6,7] (see also Sickert's PhD thesis [32]). All translations yielded automata of asymptotically optimal size (double or single exponential, respectively). Moreover, all three translations were derived from one single Master Theorem, which decomposes the language of the sequences satisfying an LTL formula into a positive boolean combination of languages, each of which can be translated into ω-automata by elementary means [7]. As in the first paper of the series [12], the states of these automata are boolean combinations of subformulas of the original formula. The constructions were implemented in RABINIZER 4.0 [15] and in the OWL library [14]. They were also integrated in the STRIX tool for LTL synthesis [19,26], which won the LTL category of the SYNTCOMP competition in 2018, 2019, and 2020.

We were finally done. Or were we? The Master Theorem stated that an ω-word w satisfies an LTL formula φ iff there exists two sets M and N of subformulas of φ satisfying three conditions. The last two, put together, state that w must satisfy a formula of the form

$$\bigwedge_{\psi \in M} \mathbf{GF}\psi_N \wedge \bigwedge_{\psi \in N} \mathbf{FG}\psi_M,$$

where the formulas ψ_M and ψ_N are obtained from φ, M, and N by means of a purely syntactic procedure. This formula was oddly similar to the original normal form of Lichtenstein, Pnueli and Zuck. However, the analogy did not extend to the first of the three conditions, which had a different shape. It did not require that w satisfies a formula, but that *some suffix w'* of w satisfies a formula $\psi_{M,w'}$, dependent not only of M but also of the suffix w'. From a practical point of view this did not constitute a problem, because it was easy to construct an automaton recognizing the words satisfying the condition. However, this immediately raised the question whether the first condition could be replaced by another one of the same kind as the last two. I kept asking this question to Salomon Sickert, my PhD student at the time, until he found a solution that leads to a new normal form for LTL [33]. It states that for every formula φ of LTL:

$$\varphi \equiv \bigvee_{N,M} \left(\varphi_M \wedge \bigwedge_{\psi \in M} \mathbf{GF}\psi_N \wedge \bigwedge_{\psi \in N} \mathbf{GF}\psi_M \right)$$

where the disjunction is over all sets M, N of $\mathbf{U}$ and $\mathbf{W}$-subformulas of φ, respectively, the φ_M are formulas of Δ_2, the ψ_N do not contain any occurrence of $\mathbf{W}$, and the ψ_M do not contain any occurrence of $\mathbf{U}$. The formulas ψ_N and ψ_M depend on N and M, respectively, but can be easily constructed from the corresponding ψ by a simple and purely syntactic procedure[1].

Taking into account $\mathbf{F}\varphi \equiv \mathbf{true} \; \mathbf{U} \; \varphi$ and $\mathbf{G}\varphi \equiv \varphi \; \mathbf{W} \; \mathbf{false}$, this shows that every formula is equivalent to a Δ_2-formula. Moreover, if φ has length n, then $\varphi_M, \psi_N, \psi_M$ have length $2^{O(n)}$, $O(n)$, and $O(n)$, respectively. Since there are $2^{O(n)}$ choices for M and N, the total length of the equivalent formula is also $2^{O(n)}$, improving on the non-elementary bound of [38] and on the (likely) triple exponential bound of [20].

Thanks to this result I think I finally understand the goal of our nearly 10 years of work on LTL and ω-automata: Develop translations that (1) put the formula into Δ_2 form; (2) translate these formulas into automata of the desired type, exploiting the fact that they exhibit only one alternation; and (3) combine these automata into an automaton for the full formula.

5   Conclusions: Back to the Future

Ironically, in our ten year investigation of translations of LTL into ω-automata all developments seem to have occurred in the wrong temporal order. If Chang, Manna, and Pnueli (or other researchers) would have tried to improve on the

---

[1] For readers familiar with LTL, the result of [33] can also be used to normalize into formulas containing also the operators $\mathbf{R}$ and $\mathbf{M}$. This has relevance, because the normal form with these operators can be exponentially more compact than the normal form with only the $\mathbf{U}$ and $\mathbf{W}$ operators.

non-elementary upper bound of the translation, by perhaps 1995 it would have already been shown that the Δ_2 normal form only incurs in at most a single exponential blow-up, and that normalization is efficient in practice. This would have led to an interest into efficiently translating *normalized* formulas into automata, and such translations would have probably already been in place by the early 2000s. This was the time at which the first tools for probabilistic model checking appeared, followed a few years later by the first tools for reactive synthesis of arbitrary LTL specifications. Sometimes I wish I could travel back in time to 1992, like Marty McFly in the movie "Back to the Future", to suggest Amir Pnueli to work on the complexity of normalization, and return to the present to see how much better our probabilistic model checkers and tools for reactive synthesis have become.

Acknowledgment. I thank Jan Křetínský and Salomon Sickert for sharing their insights with me in countless conversations, for all our joint work, and for their comments on a draft of this note.

References

1. Chang, E., Manna, Z., Pnueli, A.: Characterization of temporal property classes. In: Kuich, W. (ed.) ICALP 1992. LNCS, vol. 623, pp. 474–486. Springer, Heidelberg (1992). https://doi.org/10.1007/3-540-55719-9_97
2. Clarke, E.M., Henzinger, T.A., Veith, H., Bloem, R. (eds.): Handbook of Model Checking. Springer, Heidelberg (2018)
3. Courcoubetis, C., Yannakakis, M.: The complexity of probabilistic verification. J. ACM **42**(4), 857–907 (1995)
4. Esparza, J., Křetínský, J.: From LTL to deterministic automata: a safraless compositional approach. In: Biere, A., Bloem, R. (eds.) CAV 2014. LNCS, vol. 8559, pp. 192–208. Springer, Cham (2014). https://doi.org/10.1007/978-3-319-08867-9_13
5. Esparza, J., Kretínský, J., Sickert, S.: From LTL to deterministic automata - a safraless compositional approach. Formal Methods Syst. Des. **49**(3), 219–271 (2016)
6. Esparza, J., Kretínský, J., Sickert, S.: One theorem to rule them all: a unified translation of LTL into ω-automata. In: LICS, pp. 384–393. ACM (2018)
7. Esparza, J., Kretínský, J., Sickert, S.: A unified translation of linear temporal logic to ω-automata. J. ACM **67**(6), 33:1–33:61 (2020)
8. Gaiser, A., Křetínský, J., Esparza, J.: Rabinizer: small deterministic automata for LTL(**F**, **G**). In: Chakraborty, S., Mukund, M. (eds.) ATVA 2012. LNCS, pp. 72–76. Springer, Heidelberg (2012). https://doi.org/10.1007/978-3-642-33386-6_7
9. Holzmann, G.J.: The SPIN Model Checker - Primer and Reference Manual. Addison-Wesley, Boston (2004)
10. Klein, J., Baier, C.: Experiments with deterministic omega-automata for formulas of linear temporal logic. Theor. Comput. Sci. **363**(2), 182–195 (2006)
11. Klein, J., Baier, C.: On-the-fly stuttering in the construction of deterministic ω-automata. In: Holub, J., Žd'árek, J. (eds.) CIAA 2007. LNCS, vol. 4783, pp. 51–61. Springer, Heidelberg (2007). https://doi.org/10.1007/978-3-540-76336-9_7
12. Křetínský, J., Esparza, J.: Deterministic automata for the (F,G)-fragment of LTL. In: Madhusudan, P., Seshia, S.A. (eds.) CAV 2012. LNCS, vol. 7358, pp. 7–22. Springer, Heidelberg (2012). https://doi.org/10.1007/978-3-642-31424-7_7

13. Křetínský, J., Garza, R.L.: Rabinizer 2: small deterministic automata for LTL$_{\backslash GU}$. In: Van Hung, D., Ogawa, M. (eds.) ATVA 2013. LNCS, vol. 8172, pp. 446–450. Springer, Cham (2013). https://doi.org/10.1007/978-3-319-02444-8_32

14. Křetínský, J., Meggendorfer, T., Sickert, S.: Owl: a library for ω-words, automata, and LTL. In: Lahiri, S.K., Wang, C. (eds.) ATVA 2018. LNCS, vol. 11138, pp. 543–550. Springer, Cham (2018). https://doi.org/10.1007/978-3-030-01090-4_34

15. Křetínský, J., Meggendorfer, T., Sickert, S., Ziegler, C.: Rabinizer 4: from LTL to your favourite deterministic automaton. In: Chockler, H., Weissenbacher, G. (eds.) CAV 2018. LNCS, vol. 10981, pp. 567–577. Springer, Cham (2018). https://doi.org/10.1007/978-3-319-96145-3_30

16. Křetínský, J.: Verification of Discrete- and Continuous-Time Non-Deterministic Markovian Systems. Ph.D. thesis, Technical University of Munich, Germany (2013). https://www.in.tum.de/en/research/publications/dissertations/

17. Kwiatkowska, M., Norman, G., Parker, D.: PRISM 4.0: verification of probabilistic real-time systems. In: Gopalakrishnan, G., Qadeer, S. (eds.) CAV 2011. LNCS, vol. 6806, pp. 585–591. Springer, Heidelberg (2011). https://doi.org/10.1007/978-3-642-22110-1_47

18. Lichtenstein, O., Pnueli, A., Zuck, L.: The glory of the past. In: Parikh, R. (ed.) Logic of Programs 1985. LNCS, vol. 193, pp. 196–218. Springer, Heidelberg (1985). https://doi.org/10.1007/3-540-15648-8_16

19. Luttenberger, M., Meyer, P.J., Sickert, S.: Practical synthesis of reactive systems from LTL specifications via parity games. Acta Informatica **57**(1–2), 3–36 (2020)

20. Maler, O.: On the Krohn-Rhodes cascaded decomposition theorem. In: Manna, Z., Peled, D.A. (eds.) Time for Verification. LNCS, vol. 6200, pp. 260–278. Springer, Heidelberg (2010). https://doi.org/10.1007/978-3-642-13754-9_12

21. Manna, Z., Pnueli, A.: A hierarchy of temporal properties. In: PODC, pp. 377–410. ACM (1990)

22. Manna, Z., Pnueli, A.: Completing the temporal picture. Theor. Comput. Sci. **83**(1), 91–130 (1991)

23. Manna, Z., Pnueli, A.: The Temporal Logic of Reactive and Concurrent Systems - Specification. Springer, Heidelberg (1992)

24. Manna, Z., Pnueli, A.: Temporal Verification of Reactive Systems - Safety. Springer, Heidelberg (1995)

25. Manna, Z., Pnueli, A.: Temporal verification of reactive systems - progress (1996). https://theory.stanford.edu/~zm/tvors3.html

26. Meyer, P.J., Sickert, S., Luttenberger, M.: Strix: explicit reactive synthesis strikes back!. In: Chockler, H., Weissenbacher, G. (eds.) CAV 2018. LNCS, vol. 10981, pp. 578–586. Springer, Cham (2018). https://doi.org/10.1007/978-3-319-96145-3_31

27. Pelánek, R., Strejček, J.: Deeper connections between LTL and alternating automata. In: Farré, J., Litovsky, I., Schmitz, S. (eds.) CIAA 2005. LNCS, vol. 3845, pp. 238–249. Springer, Heidelberg (2006). https://doi.org/10.1007/11605157_20

28. Pnueli, A.: The temporal logic of programs. In: FOCS, pp. 46–57. IEEE Computer Society (1977)

29. Pnueli, A.: The temporal semantics of concurrent programs. Theor. Comput. Sci. **13**, 45–60 (1981)

30. Pnueli, A., Rosner, R.: On the synthesis of an asynchronous reactive module. In: Ausiello, G., Dezani-Ciancaglini, M., Della Rocca, S.R. (eds.) ICALP 1989. LNCS, vol. 372, pp. 652–671. Springer, Heidelberg (1989). https://doi.org/10.1007/BFb0035790

31. Safra, S.: On the complexity of omega-automata. In: FOCS, pp. 319–327. IEEE Computer Society (1988)

32. Sickert, S.: A unified translation of linear temporal logic to ω-automata. Ph.D. thesis, Technical University of Munich, Germany (2019). https://www.in.tum.de/en/research/publications/dissertations/

33. Sickert, S., Esparza, J.: An efficient normalisation procedure for linear temporal logic and very weak alternating automata. In: LICS, pp. 831–844. ACM (2020)

34. Sickert, S., Křetínský, J.: MoChiBA: probabilistic LTL model checking using limit-deterministic Büchi automata. In: Artho, C., Legay, A., Peled, D. (eds.) ATVA 2016. LNCS, vol. 9938, pp. 130–137. Springer, Cham (2016). https://doi.org/10.1007/978-3-319-46520-3_9

35. Vardi, M.Y.: Automatic verification of probabilistic concurrent finite-state programs. In: FOCS, pp. 327–338. IEEE Computer Society (1985)

36. Vardi, M.Y., Wolper, P.: An automata-theoretic approach to automatic program verification (preliminary report). In: LICS, pp. 332–344. IEEE Computer Society (1986)

37. Vardi, M.Y., Wolper, P.: Automata-theoretic techniques for modal logics of programs. J. Comput. Syst. Sci. **32**(2), 183–221 (1986)

38. Zuck, L.D.: Past temporal logic. Ph.D. thesis, The Weizmann Institute of Science, Israel, August 1986

Say No to Case Analysis: Automating the Drudgery of Case-Based Proofs

Jeffrey Shallit$^{(\boxtimes)}$ (ID)

School of Computer Science, University of Waterloo, Waterloo, ON N2L 3G1, Canada
`shallit@uwaterloo.ca`

Abstract. I present an argument that long, tedious proofs requiring a human to check many cases should be replaced by an algorithm, so a computer can do the work instead.

Keywords: Decision procedure · Automata · Case-based proof · Algorithm

1 Introduction

My talk can be briefly summarized as follows: *Long, tedious proofs that require a human to check many cases should be replaced by an algorithm, so a computer can do the work instead.*

Doing so offers a number of advantages:

- An algorithm replaces valuable human time with what a computer does best: tedious examination of a large number of cases.
- Implementing an algorithm allows one to test whether all cases have in fact been considered, and correct any errors in the analysis.
- An algorithm is often more general than the specific problem at hand, and can easily be modified to explore generalizations of the original problem.
- If a conjecture can be phrased in a logical language that is algorithmically decidable, then one can use a decision procedure instead of a case-based proof.
- By combining a decision procedure with heuristics, one can algorithmically "guess" possible solutions to a problem, and then prove the guess is correct. So one can "guess" the correct routes to a proof, and then complete it.

Furthermore, automata and formal languages provide a framework that can replace case analysis for a diverse set of problems.

2 Why We Need Cases: Some Things Are True for No Good Reason

As mathematicians and theoretical computer scientists, we are conditioned to believe that most of the true statements we are interested in have proofs. For

© Springer Nature Switzerland AG 2021
S. Maneth (Ed.): CIAA 2021, LNCS 12803, pp. 14–24, 2021.
https://doi.org/10.1007/978-3-030-79121-6_2

hundreds of years, nearly everyone believed that Fermat's "Last Theorem" was true and that a proof would be found someday. And our intuition was confirmed when Andrew Wiles succeeded in finding a proof.

Yet we know from Gödel that, in a sufficiently powerful consistent formal system, there are true statements that have no proof in the system. Furthermore, some of these assertions will be very simple to state (at least conceptually), such as "This statement has no proof in Peano arithmetic". But there may be other, more "natural" true statements that are simple, lack obvious self-reference, and still have no proof. Here is a possible example:

Numbers that are exact powers of two are 2, 4, 8, 16, 32, 64, 128 and so on. Numbers that are exact powers of five are 5, 25, 125, 625 and so on. Given any number such as 131072 (which happens to be a power of two), the reverse of it is 270131, with the same digits taken in the opposite order. Now my statement is: it never happens that the reverse of a power of two is a power of five.

– Freeman Dyson [9]

Dyson's conjecture is plausible because of some "randomness" in the decimal digits of powers, together with the lack of small counterexamples. But it is that very "randomness" that makes it hard to find a route to a proof.

We are also conditioned to believe that the true statements we are interested in not only have proofs, but also have *simple* proofs, if only we are clever enough to find them. Consider, for example, the attraction of "proofs from the Book"— an Erdős fantasy that there exists a celestial Book containing *the* optimal proofs for all important theorems [1].

While it is certainly desirable to find short proofs that give insight into a problem, we also know that in any sufficiently powerful consistent system there are true statements that are provable, but whose shortest proof is astronomically long in comparison to the length of the statement.[1] We might say these are statements that are *true, but for no good reason.*

So, a priori, we should not be at all surprised that some simple statements like the Four-Color Conjecture (4CC) might end up having no simple proof. The original proof of 4CC by Appel and Haken [2] involved finding an "unavoidable set of reducible configurations", reducing the problem to checking 1,834 individual cases by a computer. To date there is still no really simple proof of this theorem.

This is an automata theory conference, so let's look at an example from automata theory. Suppose we conjecture that all strings satisfy some property. If this property can be represented by an NFA $M = (Q, \Sigma, \delta, q_0, F)$, then this conjecture becomes the *universality problem*: does M recognize Σ^*? Unfortunately, the universality problem for NFA's is PSPACE-complete [18], so probably there is no efficient algorithm to check universality. Even worse, we may not

---

[1] An example is "This statement has no proof in Peano arithmetic with less than 10^{100} symbols.".

even be able to check a possible counterexample in polynomial time, since there are $O(n)$-state NFA's where the shortest string *not* accepted is of length $\geq 2^n$. An example is provided by the language

$$L_n = \{0, 1, \#\}^* - \{ [0]\#[1]\# \cdots \#[2^n - 1] \},$$

where $[a]$ is the binary representation of a, padded on the left to make it n bits long. It is not hard to construct an NFA M_n for L_n that has $O(n)$ states, while the shortest (and only) string M_n does not accept is clearly of length $(n+1)2^n - 1$.

Hence short conjectures about universality, represented by NFA's, might have exponentially long counterexamples, and we might need to examine exponentially many cases to rule them out.

3   Let a Computer Do the Work

In a classic paper of Entringer, Jackson, and Schatz [10], the authors proved that every binary word containing no squares xx with $|x| \geq 2$ is of length ≤ 18. They do so by a case-based analysis that is displayed in a large diagram that takes up an entire page of their paper.

But why do this? One can check each case tediously by hand, but do we get any real insight this way? And after doing so, does the reader feel sure that every case has been covered?

Instead, one can recognize this as a classic avoidance problem that can be solved almost trivially with breadth-first or depth first search. Let P be a set of patterns one wants to avoid over some alphabet Σ. Construct a (potentially) infinite tree T, with nodes labeled by Σ^*. The root is labeled with the empty string ϵ. If a node is labeled x and does not end in a pattern in P, then its children are xa for $a \in \Sigma$. Otherwise the node is a leaf. Then T is finite iff the set P cannot be avoided. Furthermore, if the node at greatest depth is xa for $a \in \Sigma$, then x is a longest word avoiding P.

By reporting statistics obtained by breadth-first or depth-first search, one can provide enough information that anyone else can easily check the results with a simple program. For the Entringer et al. problem, one can provide the number of leaves in the tree (478) and the leaves at greatest depth, which are

$$0100110001110011010, 0100110001110011011,$$

and their binary complements.

4   Algorithmic Case Analysis Prevents Errors

One of the advantages of automating case-based proofs is increased certainty in the correctness of the proof. Once all the cases have been expressed algorithmically, one can then test a large number of randomly-chosen examples (or try to exercise all paths in the case analysis) to make sure all cases have been covered.

As an example, consider a recent theorem by Cilleruelo and Luca [5]: for every integer base $b \geq 5$, every natural number is the sum of three natural numbers whose base-b representations are palindromes. Their 30-page proof required examining a very large number of cases (one case was labeled IV.5.v.b), and would be rather challenging to verify. As it turns out, however, the initial proof had some small, easily-repaired flaws that were only discovered when the case analysis was programmed up in Python by Baxter [6].

5   Replacing a Large Number of Cases with a General Argument

Returning to the sum-of-palindromes problem, Cilleruelo et al. were not able to handle the case of bases $b = 2, 3, 4$ in their analysis. I wondered if a more general approach might work to solve this problem. We want to show that every integer can be represented as a sum of numbers with a certain easily-describable base-b representation. If we can use some flavor of automata to check these representations, then this becomes a universality problem for nondeterministic machines: for every natural number N, we "guess" a representation as a sum of palindromes, and then check it. Even though universality problems are hard in general, we might "luck out" and get one that runs in a reasonable length of time.

We were able to solve the sum-of-palindromes problem for the remaining cases $b = 2, 3, 4$ using two different approaches:

- "guess" a representation of N as a sum of terms and use a visibly-pushdown automaton to verify that the guessed representations are palindromes;
- "guess" only the first half of the representations of the terms to be summed with an NFA, and then verify that the full representations sum to a "folded" version of the representation of N.

Using these ideas, we were able to prove

Theorem 1. *For base 2, every natural number is the sum of four palindromes. For bases 3 and 4, every natural number is the sum of three palindromes.*

For the details, see [21, 22].

Furthermore, now that we have the idea that computational models such as visibly-pushdown automata and NFA's can be used this way, it suggests a large number of related problems that are easily solved. For example, instead of palindromes, we could consider sums of *generalized palindromes*: these are numbers, like 1100, that have palindromic base-k representations if one allows insertion of leading zeroes. We also obtained results about sums of generalized palindromes with only minor modifications.

Or we could look at "squares" instead of palindromes: these are numbers whose base-b representation consists of two consecutive identical blocks. For this, see [17].

Let's look at another example: words avoiding various sets of palindromes. Let x be a finite or infinite word. The set of all of its factors (that is, contiguous blocks appearing in x) is written $\mathrm{Fac}(x)$, and the set of its factors that are palindromes is written $\mathrm{PalFac}(x)$. In [12], we proved the following result:

Theorem 2. *Let S be a finite set of palindromes over an alphabet Σ. Then the language*

$$C_\Sigma(S) := \{x \in \Sigma^* \ : \ \mathrm{PalFac}(x) \subseteq S\}$$

is regular.

Proof. Let ℓ be the length of the longest palindrome in S. We claim that $\overline{C_\Sigma(S)} = L$, where

$$L = \bigcup_{t \in P_{\leq \ell+2} - S} \Sigma^* t \, \Sigma^*.$$

$\overline{C_\Sigma(S)} \subseteq L$: If $x \in \overline{C_\Sigma(S)}$, then x must have some palindromic factor y such that $y \notin S$. If $|y| \leq \ell + 2$, then $y \in P_{\leq \ell+2} - S$. If $|y| > \ell + 2$, we can write $y = uvu^R$ for some palindrome v such that $|v| \in \{\ell + 1, \ell + 2\}$. Hence x has the palindromic factor v and $v \in P_{\leq \ell+2} - S$. In both cases $x \in L$.

$L \subseteq \overline{C_\Sigma(S)}$: Let $x \in L$. Then $x \in \Sigma^* t \, \Sigma^*$ for some $t \in P_{\leq \ell+2} - S$. Hence x has a palindromic factor outside the set S and so $x \notin C_\Sigma(S)$.

Thus we have written $\overline{C_\Sigma(S)}$ as the finite union of regular languages, and so $C_\Sigma(S)$ is also regular. ∎

Not only does this theorem show that the language of words avoiding palindromes is regular, it also gives a method to actually construct a DFA recognizing the language of all such words. With this theorem, then, we can replace much of the case analysis in [11, 23] with a calculation based on automata. As an example of the power of the method, we just mention one result from [12]:

Theorem 3. *The sequence $(e_{2,5}(n))_{n \geq 0}$ counting the number of binary words of length n containing no palindromes of length > 5 satisfies the recurrence*

$$e_{2,5}(n) = 3e_{2,5}(n-6) + 2e_{2,5}(n-7) + 2e_{2,5}(n-8) + 2e_{2,5}(n-9) + e_{2,5}(n-10)$$

for $n \geq 20$. Asymptotically $e_{2,5}(n) \sim c\alpha^n$ where $\alpha \doteq 1.36927381628918060784\cdots$ is the positive real zero of the equation $X^{10} - 3X^4 - 2X^3 - 2X^2 - 2X - 1$, and $c = 9.8315779\cdots$.

6   Heuristics Plus Algorithms Can Create Proofs

One of the most useful examples of these ideas is the following: use heuristics to find possible routes to a proof, and then use an algorithm to complete the proof itself.

Consider the following problem: choose a finite set of unary operations on languages, such as $S = \{$ Kleene closure, complement $\}$. Start with a language L, and apply the operations of S to L as many times as you like, and in any order. (This is the *orbit* of L under the set S.) How many different languages can you get?

For the particular S above, the answer is 14; this is a version of the Kuratowski 14-theorem from topology.

We can then try different sets of operations. In 2012, we proved the following result [4].

Theorem 4. *For the set of eight operations*

$$S = \{\text{Kleeneclosure, positiveclosure, complement, prefix, suffix,}$$
$$\text{factor, subword, andreverse}\}$$

the size of the orbit of every language is at most 5676.

The simple idea behind the proof is that certain finite sequences of composed operations generate the same language as shorter sequences. For example, if k denotes Kleene closure and c denotes complement, then $kckckck$ has the same effect as kck. By generating an extensive list of identities like $kckckck \equiv kck$, we can do a breadth-first search over the tree of all sequences of operations, demonstrating that there is a finite set of sequences that covers all possibilities.

But which identities are true? Here is where heuristics can help us. We can model all languages with the class of regular languages. To find an identity, we can apply one list of operations to some randomly-generated set of regular languages and compare it to the result of some other list. If the results agree everywhere, we have a candidate identity we can try to prove.

When implemented, our procedure generated dozens of identities, most of which had trivial proofs. Once we had these identities, we used the breadth-first search to prove that the size of the orbit was finite. I'd be very surprised if there is a simple proof of Theorem 4.

7   Decision Procedures

Let us continue with the theme of the previous section. The best possible example of what I'm talking about involves a *decision procedure*. If the statement you're trying to prove can be phrased in a logical theory that is recursively decidable (an algorithm exists to find proofs of all true statements), you can replace a case-based proof with running the decision procedure.

One domain where this has been very successful is the combinatorics of automatic sequences. (For us, "sequence" is synonymous with "infinite word"). A sequence $(s_n)_{n\geq0}$ over a finite alphabet is *automatic* if, roughly speaking, there is a deterministic finite automaton with output (DFAO) that, on input the representation of the natural number n in some form, ends in a state with output s_n. A typical example of the kind of representation we are talking about is base-2 representation. For automatic sequences, thanks to Büchi and others (see [3]) there is a decision procedure to answer questions about these sequences that are phrased in first-order logic.

Let's look at a specific example. The *Thue-Morse sequence*

$$\mathbf{t} = (t_n)_{n \geq 0} = 0110100110010110 \cdots$$

is an automatic sequence and is generated by the following very simple automaton. Here the label a/b on a state means that the state is numbered a and the output associated with the state is b.

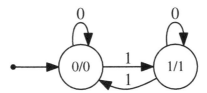

A word x has period $p \geq 1$ if $x[i] = x[i+p]$ for all indices i that make sense. Currie and Saari [7] proved that $\mathbf{t}$ has a factor of least period p for all integers $p \geq 1$. Their proof required 3 lemmas, 6 cases, and 3 pages.

However, their claim can be phrased in a certain logical system that is algorithmically decidable, and there is a decision procedure for it. This procedure has been implemented in the **Walnut** theorem prover [19] written by Hamoon Mousavi, and so we can enter the commands

```
def tmperi "(p>0) & (p<=n) & Aj (j>=i & j+p<i+n) => T[j]=T[j+p]":
def tmlper "$tmperi(i,n,p) & (Aq (q>=1 & q<p) => ~$tmperi(i,n,q))":
eval currie_conj "Ap (p>=1) => Ei,n (n>=1) & $tmlper(i,n,p)":
```

which returns **TRUE** in a matter of .062 s of CPU time. Here **tmperi** asserts that $\mathbf{t}[i..i+n-1]$ has period p, and **tmlper** asserts that the least period of $\mathbf{t}[i..i+n-1]$ is p.

A factor is said to be *bordered* if it begins and ends with the same word in a nontrivial way, like the English word **entanglement**. If it is not bordered, we call it *unbordered*. Currie and Saari [7] were also interested in determining all lengths of unbordered factors in $\mathbf{t}$. They proved that $\mathbf{t}$ has a length-n unbordered factor if $n \not\equiv 1 \pmod 6$, but were unable to find a necessary condition. We can do this with **Walnut** by writing

```
def tmfactoreq "At (t<n) => T[i+t]=T[j+t]":
def tmbord "(m>=1) & (m<n) & At (t<m) => $tmfactoreq(i,(i+n)-m,m)":
def tmunbordlength "Ei Am ~$tmbord(i,m,n)":
```

Running this in **Walnut** produces the following automaton, which recognizes the base-2 representation of all n for which $\mathbf{t}$ has a length-n unbordered factor:

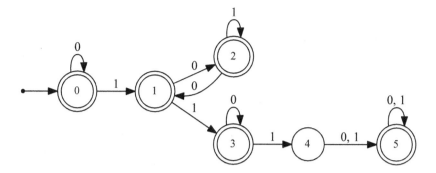

By inspection, we get the following theorem:

Theorem 5. *The Thue-Morse sequence* **t** *has an unbordered factor of length n if and only if* $(n)_2 \notin 1(01^*0)^*10^*1$.

Finally, let's look at one more problem from additive number theory. The *upper Wythoff set* $U = \{2, 5, 7, 10, 13, \ldots\}$ is defined to be $\{\lfloor \alpha^2 n \rfloor : n \geq 1\}$, where $\alpha = (1 + \sqrt{5})/2$ is the golden ratio. Recently Kawsumarng et al. [16] studied the sumset $U + U = \{x + y : x, y \in U\}$. Using a case-based argument, they constructed a rather complicated description of this set, noting that it "has some kinds of fractal and palindromic patterns".

However, it turns out that the assertion $n \in U + U$ is first-order expressible in a decidable logical theory; this allows us to give a complete description of $U + U$ as the set of natural numbers whose Fibonacci representation[2] is recognized by the following automaton:

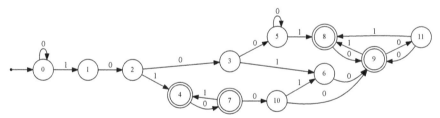

Here no explicit breakdown into cases was necessary; instead, the decision procedure "automatically" constructs the automaton from a description of U. The fact that this automaton has so many states and a complicated structure partially explains why the set $U + U$ is difficult to describe explicitly. See [24].

In the next two subsections I mention some other examples of this approach that don't quite rise to the status of a decision procedure, but are still enormously useful.

---

[2] The Fibonacci representation of a natural number n is a finite binary string $a_1 a_2 \cdots a_t$ such that $n = \sum_{1 \leq i \leq t} a_i F_{t+2-i}$, and $a_i a_{i+1} = 0$ for $1 \leq i < t$.

7.1   SAT Solvers

The *boolean Pythagorean triples problem* is the following: are there infinite binary words $\mathbf{a} = a_1 a_2 \cdots$ with the property that if $i^2 + j^2 = k^2$, then $a_i = a_j = a_k$ never holds? This was finally resolved negatively by Heule, Kullmann, and Marek [15], who proved that the longest such word is of length 7824. The really interesting thing about their proof is how it was achieved: they coded the avoidance conditions as a SAT instance and then applied a general-purpose tool—a SAT solver—to check if this instance is satisfiable. Even though, as is well-known, SAT is an NP-complete problem, modern SAT solvers can often determine if particular instances are satisfiable or not, even if they have thousands of variables and clauses.

For another interesting application of SAT solvers, see [14].

7.2   The W-Z Method

The W-Z method (developed by Gosper [13] and Wilf, Zeilberger, and Petkovšek [20]) is a decision procedure that allows verification of general combinatorial identities involving polynomials, exponentials, binomial coefficients, and similar quantities. It has been implemented in Maple, and hence automatically proving identities like

$$\sum_{-n \leq k \leq n} (-1)^k \binom{2n}{n+k}^3 = \frac{(3n)!}{n!^3}$$

is now almost trivial [25].

8   Heuristics Plus Decision Procedures Provide Proofs

Finally, we can combine the ideas of depth-first or breadth-first search over a space with a decision procedure to (a) figure out a good candidate for a solution and then (b) prove it is correct.

As an example, let's return to automatic sequences. In 1965, Dean [8] studied the *Dean words*: squarefree words over $\{x, y, x^{-1}, y^{-1}\}$ that are not reducible (that is, there are no occurrences of $xx^{-1}, x^{-1}x, yy^{-1}, y^{-1}y$) [8]. Let us use the coding $0 \leftrightarrow x$, $1 \leftrightarrow y$, $2 \leftrightarrow x^{-1}$, $3 \leftrightarrow y^{-1}$. We can use breadth-first search to find a candidate for an infinite Dean word that is automatic.

When implemented, breadth-first search quickly converges on the sequence

$$0121032101230321 \cdots,$$

which (using the Myhill-Nerode theorem) we can guess as the fixed point of the morphism

$$0 \to 01, \ 1 \to 21, \ 2 \to 03, \ 3 \to 23.$$

Now the decision procedure kicks in. We make a DFAO for this sequence and store it under the name `DE.txt` in the `Word Automata` library of `Walnut`.

Then we carry out the following commands:

```
eval dean1 "Ei,n (n>=1) & At (t<n) => DE[i+t]=DE[i+n+t]":
# check if there's a square
eval dean02 "Ei DE[i]=@0 & DE[i+1]=@2":
eval dean20 "Ei DE[i]=@2 & DE[i+1]=@0":
eval dean13 "Ei DE[i]=@1 & DE[i+1]=@3":
eval dean31 "Ei DE[i]=@3 & DE[i+1]=@1":
# check for existence of factors 02, 20, 13, 31
```

All of these return **FALSE**, so this word is a Dean word. We have thus proved the existence of Dean words with essentially no human intervention.

9   Objections

- You've replaced a case-based proof with an algorithm, but how do you know the algorithm is correct?
  Answer: Sometimes an implementation will be much simpler than the record of the cases it examines, so it will actually be *easier* to verify the program than the case-based argument.
  In other cases, the algorithm can produce a *certificate* that another, simpler program can easily verify.
  Finally, in addition to formal correctness, there is also empirical correctness.[3] With a program in hand, we can test it on a wide variety of different inputs to look for oversights and omissions.
- Running a program provides no insight as to *why* a result is true.
  Answer: Sometimes, as I've argued above, there just *won't be* a simple reason why a result is true. In situations like this, it's better just to accept the result and move on.
- Some of the decision procedures you've talked about have astronomical worst-case running times.
  Answer: Don't pay much attention to the worst-case running time of decision procedures! They often run in a reasonable length of time for the instances we are interested in.

References

1. Aigner, M., Ziegler, G.M.: Proofs from THE BOOK, 5th edn. Springer, Heidelberg (2014). https://doi.org/10.1007/978-3-662-44205-0
2. Appel, K., Haken, W.: Every Planar Map is Four-Colorable. Contemporary Mathematics, vol. 98. American Mathematical Society (1989)
3. Bruyère, V., Hansel, G., Michaux, C., Villemaire, R.: Logic and p-recognizable sets of integers. Bull. Belg. Math. Soc. **1**,191–238 (1994), corrigendum, Bull. Belg. Math. Soc. **1** (1994), 577

---

[3] For example, "Beware of bugs in the above code; I have only proved it correct, not tried it."– Donald Knuth.

4. Charlier, E., Domaratzki, M., Harju, T., Shallit, J.: Composition and orbits of language operations: finiteness and upper bounds. Int. J. Comput. Math. **90**, 1171–1196 (2013)
5. Cilleruelo, J., Luca, F.: Every positive integer is a sum of three palindromes (2016). preprint available at https://arxiv.org/abs/1602.06208v1
6. Cilleruelo, J., Luca, F., Baxter, L.: Every positive integer is a sum of three palindromes. Math. Comp. **87**, 3023–3055 (2018)
7. Currie, J.D., Saari, K.: Least periods of factors of infinite words. RAIRO Info. Theor. Appl. **43**, 165–178 (2009)
8. Dean, R.A.: A sequence without repeats on x, x^{-1}, y, y^{-1}. Amer. Math. Monthly **72**, 383–385 (1965)
9. Dyson, F.: What do you believe is true even though you cannot prove it? (2005). https://www.edge.org/response-detail/11675
10. Entringer, R.C., Jackson, D.E., Schatz, J.A.: On nonrepetitive sequences. J. Combin. Theory Ser. A **16**, 159–164 (1974)
11. Fici, G., Zamboni, L.Q.: On the least number of palindromes contained in an infinite word. Theoret. Comput. Sci. **481**, 1–8 (2013)
12. Fleischer, L., Shallit, J.: Automata, palindromes, and reversed subwords (2020). Manuscript under submission
13. Gosper Jr., R.W.: Decision procedure for indefinite hypergeometric summation. Proc. Natl. Acad. Sci. U.S.A. **75**, 40–42 (1978)
14. Heule, M.: Schur number five. In: Thirty-Second AAAI Conference on Artificial Intelligence (AAAI-18), pp. 6598–6606. AAAI Press (2018)
15. Heule, M.J.H., Kullmann, O., Marek, V.W.: Solving and verifying the boolean Pythagorean triples problem via cube-and-conquer. In: Creignou, N., Le Berre, D. (eds.) SAT 2016. LNCS, vol. 9710, pp. 228–245. Springer, Cham (2016). https://doi.org/10.1007/978-3-319-40970-2_15
16. Kawsumarng, S., Khemaratchatakumthorn, T., Noppakaew, P., Pongsriiam, P.: Sumsets associated with Wythoff sequences and Fibonacci numbers. Period. Math. Hung. **82**(1), 98–113 (2020). https://doi.org/10.1007/s10998-020-00343-0
17. Madhusudan, P., Nowotka, D., Rajasekaran, A., Shallit, J.: Lagrange's theorem for binary squares. In: Potapov, I., Spirakis, P., Worrell, J. (eds.) 43rd International Symposium on Mathematical Foundations of Computer Science (MFCS 2018), pp. 18:1–18:14. Schloss Dagstuhl–Leibniz-Zentrum für Informatik (2018)
18. Meyer, A.R., Stockmeyer, L.J.: The equivalence problem for regular expressions with squaring requires exponential space. In: Symposium on Switching and Automata Theory (SWAT), pp. 125–129. IEEE Computer Society (1972)
19. Mousavi, H.: Automatic theorem proving in Walnut (2016). arxiv preprint. http://arxiv.org/abs/1603.06017
20. Petkovšek, M., Wilf, H., Zeilberger, D.: $A = B$. A. K. Peters (1996)
21. Rajasekaran, A., Shallit, J., Smith, T.: Additive number theory via automata theory. Theor. Comput. Syst. **64**, 542–567 (2020)
22. Rajasekaran, A., Smith, T., Shallit, J.: Sums of palindromes: an approach via automata. In: Niedermeier, R., Vallée, B. (eds.) 35th Symposium on Theoretical Aspects of Computer Science (STACS 2018), pp. 54:1–54:12. Leibniz International Proceedings in Informatics, Schloss Dagstuhl–Leibniz-Zentrum für Informatik (2018)
23. Rampersad, N., Shallit, J.: Words avoiding reversed subwords. J. Combin. Math. Combin. Comput. **54**, 157–164 (2005)
24. Shallit, J.: Sumsets of Wythoff sequences, Fibonacci representation, andbeyond (2021). Period. Math. Hung., to appear
25. Tefera, A.: What is a Wilf-Zeilberger pair? Not. Am. Math. Soc. **57**, 508–509 (2010)

Technical Contributions

Regularity Conditions for Iterated Shuffle on Commutative Regular Languages

Stefan Hoffmann$^{(\boxtimes)}$ (iD)

Informatikwissenschaften, FB IV, Universität Trier,
Universitätsring 15, 54296 Trier, Germany
hoffmanns@informatik.uni-trier.de

Abstract. We identify a subclass of the regular commutative languages that is closed under the iterated shuffle, or shuffle closure. In particular, it is regularity-preserving on this subclass. This subclass contains the commutative group languages and, for every alphabet Σ, the class $\mathbf{Com}^+(\Sigma^*)$ given by the ordered variety $\mathbf{Com}^+$. Then, we state a simple characterization when the iterated shuffle on finite commutative languages gives a regular language again and state partial results for aperiodic commutative languages. We also show that the aperiodic, or star-free, commutative languages and the commutative group languages are closed under projection.

Keywords: Finite automata · Commutative languages · Closure properties · Iterated shuffle · Shuffle closure · Regularity-preserving operations

1 Introduction

The shuffle and iterated shuffle have been introduced and studied to understand, or specify, the semantics of parallel programs. This was undertaken, as it appears to be, independently by Campbell and Habermann [3], by Mazurkiewicz [15] and by Shaw [26]. They introduced *flow expressions*, which allow for sequential operators (catenation and iterated catenation) as well as for parallel operators (shuffle and iterated shuffle) to specify sequential and parallel execution traces.

For illustration, let us reproduce the following very simple Reader-Writer Problem from [26], as an example involving the iterated shuffle. In this problem, a set of cyclic processes may be in read-mode, but only one process at a time is allowed to be in write-mode, and read and write operations may not proceed concurrently. Additionally, we impose that the processes have to come to an end, in [26] they are allowed to run indefinitely. This constraint could be specified, using our notation, by

$$((\text{StartRead} \cdot \text{Read} \cdot \text{EndRead})^{\sqcup,*} \cup \text{Write})^*,$$

where "$\sqcup,*$" denotes the iterated shuffle and "$*$" the Kleene star.

© Springer Nature Switzerland AG 2021
S. Maneth (Ed.): CIAA 2021, LNCS 12803, pp. 27–38, 2021.
https://doi.org/10.1007/978-3-030-79121-6_3

Let us note that in [26] additional lock and signal instructions were allowed. Also in [23] similar expressions for process modeling were investigated, allowing the binary shuffle operation, but without inclusion of the iterated shuffle.

The shuffle operation as a binary operation, but not the iterated shuffle, is regularity-preserving on all regular languages. However, already the iterated shuffle of very simple languages can give non-regular languages. Hence, it is interesting to know, and to identify, quite rich classes for which this operation is regularity-preserving. Here, we give such a class which includes the commutative group languages and the languages described by the positive variety **Com**$^+$. Additionally, we give a characterization for the regularity of the iterated shuffle when applied to finite commutative languages and state some partial results for aperiodic (or star-free) commutative languages.

We mention that subregular language classes closed under the binary shuffle operation were investigated previously [1,2,4,9,18,22].

We also show that the commutative star-free languages and the commutative group languages are closed under projections. For further connections on regularity conditions and closure properties, in particular for the star-free languages, see the recent survey [21].

2   Preliminaries and Definitions

2.1   General Notions

Let Σ be a finite set of symbols called an *alphabet*. The set Σ^* denotes the set of all finite sequences, i.e., of all *words*. The finite sequence of length zero, or the *empty word*, is denoted by ε. For a given word we denote by $|w|$ its length, and for $a \in \Sigma$ by $|w|_a$ the number of occurrences of the symbol a in w. A *language* is a subset of Σ^*. If $L \subseteq \Sigma^*$ and $u \in \Sigma^*$, then the *quotients* are the languages $u^{-1}L = \{v \in \Sigma^* \mid uv \in L\}$ and $Lu^{-1} = \{v \in \Sigma^* \mid vu \in L\}$.

We assume the reader to have some basic knowledge in formal language theory, as contained, e.g., in [12,14]. For instance, we make use of regular expressions to describe languages.

Let $\Gamma \subseteq \Sigma$. Then, we define *projection homomorphisms* $\pi_\Gamma : \Sigma^* \to \Gamma^*$ onto Γ^* by $\pi_\Gamma(x) = x$ for $x \in \Gamma$ and $\pi_\Gamma(x) = \varepsilon$ for $x \notin \Gamma$.

By $\mathbb{N}_0 = \{0, 1, 2, \ldots\}$, we denote the set of natural numbers, including zero. We will also consider the ordered set $\mathbb{N}_0 \cup \{\infty\}$ with $\mathbb{N}_0$ having the usual order and setting $n < \infty$ for any $n \in \mathbb{N}_0$.

A quintuple $\mathcal{A} = (\Sigma, Q, \delta, q_0, F)$ is a finite *(incomplete) deterministic automaton*, where $\delta : Q \times \Sigma \to S$ is a partial transition function, Q a finite set of states, $q_0 \in S$ the start state and $F \subseteq Q$ the set of final states. The automaton $\mathcal{A}$ is said to be *complete* if δ is a total function. The transition function $\delta : Q \times \Sigma \to S$ could be extended to a transition function on words $\delta^* : Q \times \Sigma^* \to S$ by setting $\delta^*(q, \varepsilon) = q$ and $\delta^*(q, wa) := \delta(\delta^*(q, w), a)$ for $q \in Q$, $a \in \Sigma$ and $w \in \Sigma^*$. In the remainder, we drop the distinction between both functions and will also denote this extension by δ. The language *recognized* by an automaton $\mathcal{A} = (\Sigma, Q, \delta, q_0, F)$ is $L(\mathcal{A}) = \{w \in \Sigma^* \mid \delta(q_0, w) \in F\}$. A language $L \subseteq \Sigma^*$ is called *regular* if $L = L(\mathcal{A})$ for some finite automaton $\mathcal{A}$.

The following classic result will also be needed later.

Theorem 1 (Generalized Chinese Remainder Theorem [24]). *The system of linear congruences*

$$x \equiv r_i \pmod{m_i} \quad (i = 1, 2, \ldots, k)$$

has integral solutions x if and only if $\gcd(m_i, m_j)$ divides $(r_i - r_j)$ for all pairs $i \neq j$ and all solutions are congruent modulo $\operatorname{lcm}(m_1, \ldots, m_k)$.

2.2 Commutative Languages and the Shuffle Operation

For a given word $w \in \Sigma^*$, we define $\operatorname{perm}(w) := \{u \in \Sigma^* \mid \forall a \in \Sigma : |u|_a = |w|_a\}$. If $L \subseteq \Sigma^*$, then we set $\operatorname{perm}(L) := \bigcup_{w \in L} \operatorname{perm}(w)$. A language is called *commutative*, if $\operatorname{perm}(L) = L$. Let $\Sigma = \{a_1, \ldots, a_k\}$. The *Parikh mapping* is $\psi : \Sigma^* \to \mathbb{N}_0^k$ given by $\psi(u) = (|u|_{a_1}, \ldots, |u|_{a_k})$ for $u \in \Sigma^*$. We have $\operatorname{perm}(L) = \psi^{-1}(\psi(L))$.

The *shuffle operation*, denoted by $\shuffle$, is defined by

$$u \shuffle v = \{w \in \Sigma^* \mid w = x_1 y_1 x_2 y_2 \cdots x_n y_n \text{ for some words}$$
$$x_1, \ldots, x_n, y_1, \ldots, y_n \in \Sigma^* \text{ such that } u = x_1 x_2 \cdots x_n \text{ and } v = y_1 y_2 \cdots y_n\},$$

for $u, v \in \Sigma^*$ and $L_1 \shuffle L_2 := \bigcup_{x \in L_1, y \in L_2} (x \shuffle y)$ for $L_1, L_2 \subseteq \Sigma^*$.

In writing formulas without brackets, we suppose that the shuffle operation binds stronger than the set operations, and the concatenation operator has the strongest binding.

If $L_1, \ldots, L_n \subseteq \Sigma^*$, we set $\shuffle_{i=1}^n L_i = L_1 \shuffle \ldots \shuffle L_n$. The *iterated shuffle* of $L \subseteq \Sigma^*$ is $L^{\shuffle,*} = \bigcup_{n \geq 0} \shuffle_{i=1}^n L$. We also set $L^{\shuffle,+} = \bigcup_{n \geq 1} \shuffle_{i=1}^n L$.

Theorem 2 (Fernau et al. [6]). *Let $U, V, W \subseteq \Sigma^*$. Then,*

1. *$U \shuffle V = V \shuffle U$ (commutative law);*
2. *$(U \shuffle V) \shuffle W = U \shuffle (V \shuffle W)$ (associative law);*
3. *$U \shuffle (V \cup W) = (U \shuffle V) \cup (U \shuffle W)$ (distributive over union);*
4. *$(U^{\shuffle,*})^{\shuffle,*} = U^{\shuffle,*}$;*
5. *$(U \cup V)^{\shuffle,*} = U^{\shuffle,*} \shuffle V^{\shuffle,*}$;*
6. *$(U \shuffle V^{\shuffle,*})^{\shuffle,*} = (U \shuffle (U \cup V)^{\shuffle,*}) \cup \{\varepsilon\}$.*

The next result is taken from [6] and gives equations like $\operatorname{perm}(UV) = \operatorname{perm}(U) \shuffle \operatorname{perm}(V)$ or $\operatorname{perm}(U^*) = \operatorname{perm}(U)^{\shuffle,*}$ for $U, V \subseteq \Sigma^*$. A *semiring* is an algebraic structure $(S, +, \cdot, 0, 1)$ such that $(S, +, 0)$ forms a commutative monoid, $(S, \cdot, 1)$ is a monoid and we have $a \cdot (b + c) = a \cdot b + a \cdot c$, $(b + c) \cdot a = b \cdot a + c \cdot a$ and $0 \cdot a = a \cdot 0 = 0$.

Theorem 3 (Fernau et al. [6]). $\operatorname{perm} : \mathcal{P}(\Sigma^*) \to \mathcal{P}(\Sigma^*)$ *is a semiring morphism from the semiring $(\mathcal{P}(\Sigma^*), \cup, \cdot, \varnothing, \{\varepsilon\})$, that also respects the iterated catenation resp. iterated shuffle operation, to the semiring $(\mathcal{P}(\Sigma^*), \cup, \shuffle, \varnothing, \{\varepsilon\})$.*

The class of commutative languages obeys the following closure properties.

Theorem 4 ([10,11,19,20]).   *The class of commutative languages is closed under union, intersection, complement, projections, the shuffle operation and the iterated shuffle.*

2.3   Aperiodic and Group Languages

The class of aperiodic languages was introduced in [17] and admits a wealth of other characterizations.

Definition 5. *An automaton* $\mathcal{A} = (\Sigma, Q, \delta, q_0, F)$ *is* aperiodic, *if there exists* $n \geq 0$ *such that, for all states* $q \in Q$ *and any word* $w \in \Sigma^*$, *we have* $\delta(q, w^n) = \delta(q, w^{n+1})$.

We define the class of aperiodic languages.

Definition 6. *A regular language is called* aperiodic *if there exists an aperiodic automaton recognizing it.*

The class of *star-free regular languages* is the smallest class containing $\{\varepsilon\}$, Σ^* and $\{a\}$ for any $a \in \Sigma$ and closed under the boolean operations and concatenation. Let us state the following, due to [25].

Theorem 7 (Schützenberger [17,25]**).** *The class of star-free languages equals the class of aperiodic languages.*

Next, we introduce the group languages.

Definition 8 (McNaughton [16]**).**   *A* (pure-)group language[1] *is a language recognized by an automaton* $\mathcal{A} = (\Sigma, Q, \delta, q_0, F)$ *where every letter acts as a permutation on the state set*[2], *i.e., if* $a \in \Sigma$, *then the map* $\delta_a : Q \to Q$ *given by* $\delta_a(q) = \delta(a, q)$ *for* $q \in Q$ *is total and a permutation of* Q. *Such an automaton is called a* permutation automaton.

Observe that a permutation automaton, as defined here, is always complete[3].

Remark 1. Note some ambiguity here in the sense that if $\Sigma = \{a, b\}$, then $(aa)^*$ is not a group language over this alphabet, but it is over the unary alphabet $\{a\}$. Hence we mean the existence of an alphabet such that the language is recognized by a permutation automaton over this alphabet. By definition, $\{\varepsilon\}$ is considered to be a group language[4]. Also, group languages are closed under the boolean operations if viewed over a common alphabet, but not over different alphabets. For instance, $L = (aa)^* \cup (bbb)^*$ is not a group language.

---

[1] These were introduced in [16] under the name of pure-group events.
[2] Such automata are also called *permutation automata*, and the name stems from the fact that the transformation monoid of such an automaton forms a group.
[3] Another way would be, to allow incomplete automata, to insist that every letter either gives a permutation or labels no transition.
[4] It is not possible to give such an automaton for $|\Sigma| \geq 1$, but allowing $\Sigma = \emptyset$ the single-state automaton will do, or similarly as $\Sigma^* = \{\varepsilon\}$ in this case.

2.4   Commutative Aperiodic and Group Languages

The next definitions and results are taken from [19,20]. For $a \in \Sigma$ and $n, r \geq 0$ set

$$F(a, r, n) = \{u \in \Sigma^* \mid |u|_a \equiv r \pmod{n}\},$$

and, for $a \in \Sigma$ and $t \geq 0$,

$$F(a, t) = \{u \in \Sigma^+ \mid |u|_a \geq t\}.$$

Note that these sets are defined relative to an alphabet Σ.

Example 1. Let Σ be a non-empty alphabet, $a \in \Sigma$ and $\Gamma \subseteq \Sigma$.

1. $F(a, 0, 1) = \Sigma^*$.
2. $F(a, 0, 2) \cap F(a, 3, 4) = \varnothing$.
3. $F(a, 1) = \Sigma^* a \Sigma^*$.
4. $\Gamma^* = \Sigma^* \setminus \left(\bigcup_{b \in \Sigma \setminus \Gamma} F(b, 1) \right)$.

Theorem 9 ([19,20]). *Let Σ be an non-empty[5] alphabet.*

1. *The class of commutative group languages over Σ is the boolean algebra generated by the languages of the form $F(a, r, n)$, where $a \in \Sigma$ and $0 \leq r < n$.*
2. *The class of commutative aperiodic languages over Σ is the boolean algebra generated by the languages of the form $F(a, t)$, where $a \in \Sigma$ and $t \geq 0$.*
3. *The class of all commutative regular languages over Σ is the boolean algebra generated by the languages of the form $F(a, t)$ or $F(a, r, n)$, where $t \geq 0$, $0 \leq r < n$ and $a \in \Sigma$.*

A *positive boolean algebra* is a class of sets closed under union and intersection. In [20], the positive variety **Com**$^+$ was introduced. A *positive variety* [19,20] $\mathcal{V}$ of languages maps any alphabet Σ to a subclass $\mathcal{V}(\Sigma^*)$ of languages over this alphabet that is closed under union, intersection, quotients and inverse homomorphisms. I only mention in passing that there is a rich theory between positive varieties of languages and so called pseudovarieties of finite ordered semigroups [19]. Originally, **Com**$^+$ was defined in terms of certain ordered semigroups, but here, as we do not introduce these notions, we introduce it with an equivalent characterization from [20].

Definition 10 ([20]). *For every alphabet Σ, the class **Com**$^+(\Sigma^*)$ is the positive boolean algebra generated by the languages of the form $F(a, t)$ and $F(a, r, n)$, where $a \in \Sigma$ and $t \geq 0$, $0 \leq r < n$.*

Lemma 11. *Let Σ be a non-empty set[6] and $\Gamma \subseteq \Sigma$ be a proper subset. Then, $\{\Gamma^*, \Gamma^+\} \cap **Com**^+(\Sigma^*) = \varnothing$.*

Note that the previous lemma, by choosing $\Gamma = \varnothing$, implies for $\Sigma \neq \varnothing$ that $\{\varepsilon\} \notin **Com**^+(\Sigma^*)$. The sets $F(a, t)$ were defined as subsets of Σ^+ [20], not Σ^*. However, this makes no difference as $\Sigma^+ = F(a, 0) = \bigcup_{b \in \Sigma} F(b, 1)$ and $F(a, 0, 1) = \Sigma^*$ and so $\{\Sigma^+, \Sigma^*\} \subseteq **Com**^+(\Sigma^*)$.

---

[5] For $\Sigma = \varnothing$, we set all these classes to equal $\{\varnothing, \{\varepsilon\}\}$.
[6] For $\Sigma = \varnothing$, we set **Com**$^+(\Sigma^*) = \{\varnothing, \{\varepsilon\}\}$.

3   Commutative Aperiodic and Group Languages Under Projection

First, we strengthen Theorem 9 for commutative group languages.

Theorem 12. *A commutative language $L \subseteq \Sigma^*$ is a group language if and only if it could be written as a finite union of languages of the form*

$$\bigcap_{i=1}^{m} F(a_i, k_i, n_i),$$

where $a_i \in \Sigma$ and $0 \le k_i < n_i$ for $i \in \{1, \ldots, m\}$ with $m \ge 0$.

A similar statement holds for the star-free languages. But we cannot use the languages $F(a, t)$ introduced earlier. Set, for $a \in \Sigma$ and $k_1, k_2 \in \mathbb{N}_0 \cup \{\infty\}$,

$$I(a, k_1, k_2) = \{u \in \Sigma^* \mid k_1 \le |u|_a < k_2\}.$$

Theorem 13. *A commutative language $L \subseteq \Sigma^*$ is aperiodic if and only if it could be written as a finite union of sets of the form*

$$\bigcap_{i=1}^{n} I(a_i, r_i, s_i),$$

where $0 \le r_i < s_i$ and $a_i \in \Sigma$ for $i \in \{1, \ldots, n\}$ with $n \ge 0$.

Next, we state how these languages behave under projection.

Lemma 14. *Let $\Gamma \subseteq \Sigma$, $n \ge 0$, $a_i \in \Sigma$ and $0 \le r_i < s_i$ for $i \in \{1, \ldots, n\}$. Then,*

$$\pi_\Gamma \left(\bigcap_{i=1}^{n} I(a_i, r_i, s_i) \right) = \left(\bigcap_{\substack{i \in \{1, \ldots, n\} \\ a_i \in \Gamma}} I(a_i, r_i, s_i) \right) \cap \Gamma^*.$$

With Lemma 14, we can prove that the star-free commutative languages are closed under projections.

Proposition 15. *Let $L \subseteq \Sigma^*$ be commutative and star-free. Then, for any $\Gamma \subseteq \Sigma$, the language $\pi_\Gamma(L)$ is commutative star-free.*

In general, for homomorphic mappings, this is not true, as a^* could be mapped homomorphically onto $(aa)^*$, and $(aa)^*$ is not star-free [17]. Also, more specifically, there exist non-commutative star-free languages with a non-star-free projection language. For example, the language $L = (aba)^*$ is star-free, as

$$L = \{\varepsilon\} \cup (aba\Sigma^* \cap \Sigma^* aba) \setminus (\Sigma^* \cdot \{aaa, bba, bab, abb\} \cdot \Sigma^*),$$

but $\pi_{\{a\}}(L) = (aa)^*$. Similarly, with Theorem 12, we can show the next result.

Proposition 16. *Let $L \subseteq \Sigma^*$ be a commutative group language. Then, for any $\Gamma \subseteq \Sigma$, the language $\pi_\Gamma(L)$ is a commutative group language.*

However, also here, this is false for general group languages. The language $(aa)^*$ could be mapped homomorphically onto $L = (abab)^*$, which is not a group language. Also, for projections, consider the group language given by the permutation automaton $\mathcal{A} = (\{a, b\}, \{0, 1, 2\}, \delta, 0, \{2\})$ with $\delta(0, a) = 1$, $\delta(1, a) = 0$, $\delta(2, a) = 2$ and $\delta(0, b) = 1$, $\delta(1, b) = 2$, $\delta(2, b) = 0$. Then, $\pi_{\{b\}}(L(\mathcal{A})) = bb^*$, which is not a group language. For example, b is the projection of $ab \in L(\mathcal{A})$, or bbb the projection of $abbab \in L(\mathcal{A})$.

4   A Class of Regular Languages Closed Under Iterated Shuffle

Here, we introduce a subclass of commutative regular languages, which contains the commutative group languages, that is closed under iterated shuffle. In Definition 17, we introduce the *diagonal periodic* languages, and first establish that the iterated shuffle of such a language gives a language that is a union of diagonal periodic languages. We then use this result to show closure under this operation of our subclass, which either could be described as the positive boolean algebra generated by languages of the form $F(a, n, k)$, $F(a, k)$, Γ^* and Γ^+ for $\Gamma \subseteq \Sigma$, $a \in \Sigma$, $0 \le k < n$, or as finite unions of diagonal periodic languages.

Note that, for already very simple languages, the iterated shuffle can give non-regular languages, for example $(a \sqcup b)^{\sqcup,*} = \{ab, ba\}^{\sqcup,*} = \{u \in \{a, b\}^* \mid |u|_a = |u|_b\}$, or $(a \sqcup \{b, bb\})^{\sqcup,*} = \{u \in \{a, b\}^* \mid |u|_b \le |u|_a \le 2|u|_b\}$.

Definition 17. *A* diagonal periodic *language over $\Gamma \subseteq \Sigma$ is a language of the form*

$$\sqcup\!\!\!\sqcup_{a \in \Gamma} a^{k_a}(a^{p_a})^*,$$

where $k_a \ge 0$ and $p_a > 0$ for $a \in \Gamma$ when $\Gamma \ne \varnothing$, or the language $\{\varepsilon\}$.

Remark 2. Let $\Sigma = \{a_1, \ldots, a_k\}$ In [5] a sequence of vectors $\rho = v_0, v_1, \ldots, v_k$ from $\mathbb{N}_0^k$ was called a *base* if $v_i(j) = 0$ for[7] $i, j \in \{1, \ldots, k\}$ such that $i \ne j$. The ρ-set was defined as $\Theta(\rho) = \{v \in \mathbb{N}^k : v = v_0 + l_1 v_1 + \ldots + l_k v_k \text{ for some } l_1, \ldots, l_k \in \mathbb{N}_0\}$. Then, in [5], a language $L \subseteq \Sigma^*$ was called *periodic* if, for some fixed order $\Sigma = \{a_1, \ldots, a_k\}$, there exists a base ρ such that $L = \psi^{-1}(\Theta(\rho))$. With this geometric view, the diagonal periodic languages are those periodic languages such that, for $i, j \in \{1, \ldots, k\}$, either

$$v_i(j) \ne 0 \text{ or } v_i(j) = v_0(j) = 0.$$

Intuitively, and very roughly, the vector $\sum_{a_i \in \Gamma} v_i$ points diagonally in the subspace corresponding to the letters in Γ, or more precisely, the dimension of the subspace spanned by $v_1, \ldots, v_k$ is precisely $|\Gamma|$. Hence, the name diagonal periodic.

---

[7] Note that the entries of $v \in \mathbb{N}_0^k$ are numbered by 1 to k, i.e., $v = (v(1), \ldots, v(k))$.

As the languages $a^{k_a}(a^{p_a})^*$, $a \in \Gamma$, are regular and the binary shuffle operation is regularity-preserving [13], we get the next result. But it was also established in [5,10,11] for the more general class of periodic languages.

Proposition 18. *The diagonal periodic languages are regular and commutative.*

Remark 3. Suppose, for each $a \in \Sigma$, we have a unary language $L_a \subseteq a^*$ and $\Gamma \subseteq \Sigma$. Then, $\pi_\Gamma(\bigsqcup_{a \in \Sigma} L_a) = \bigsqcup_{a \in \Gamma} L_a$ and $\pi_\Sigma^{-1}(\bigsqcup_{a \in \Gamma} L_a) = \bigsqcup_{a \in \Gamma} L_a \sqcup (\Sigma \backslash \Gamma)^*$.
This could be worked out to give a different proofs for the results from Subsect. 3.

Remark 4. The reason a subalphabet $\Gamma \subseteq \Sigma$ is included in Definition 17, and
later in the statements, is due to Lemma 11, i.e., to have a larger class as given
by $\mathbf{Com}^+$.

Next, we investigate what languages we get if we apply the iterated shuffle
to diagonal periodic languages.

Proposition 19. *The iterated shuffle of a diagonal periodic language $L \subseteq \Sigma^*$
over $\Gamma \subseteq \Sigma^*$ is a finite union of diagonal periodic languages. In particular, it is
regular.*

The next lemma is the link between the languages $F(a,t)$, $t \geq 0$, and
$F(a,r,n)$, $0 \leq r < n$, and the diagonal periodic languages.

Lemma 20. *Let $\Sigma_1, \Sigma_2 \subseteq \Sigma$. Suppose we have numbers t_a for $a \in \Sigma_1$ and
$0 \leq r_a < n_a$ for $a \in \Sigma_2$. Then,*

$$\bigcap_{a \in \Sigma_1} F(a, t_a) \cap \bigcap_{a \in \Sigma_2} F(a, r_a, n_a) = \bigsqcup_{a \in \Sigma} a^{k_a}(a^{p_a})^*,$$

where[8]

$$k_a = \begin{cases} t_a + (n_a - ((t_a - r_a) \bmod n_a)) & \text{if } a \in \Sigma_1 \cap \Sigma_2, t_a > r_a; \\ r_a & \text{if } a \in \Sigma_1 \cap \Sigma_2, t_a \leq r_a; \\ r_a & \text{if } a \in \Sigma_2 \backslash \Sigma_1; \\ t_a & \text{if } a \in \Sigma_1 \backslash \Sigma_2; \\ 0 & \text{if } a \notin \Sigma_1 \cup \Sigma_2. \end{cases}$$

and $p_a = \begin{cases} n_a & \text{if } a \in \Sigma_2; \\ 1 & \text{if } a \notin \Sigma_2. \end{cases}$

Now, we have everything together to prove our main theorem of this subsection.

Theorem 21. *Let $L \subseteq \Sigma^*$ be in the positive boolean algebra generated by languages of the form $F(a,k)$, $F(a,k,n)$, Γ^+ and Γ^* for $\Gamma \subseteq \Sigma$. Then, the iterated
shuffle of L is contained in this positive boolean algebra. In particular, the iterated
shuffle is regular.*

---

[8] For $x, n \in \mathbb{N}$, by $x \bmod n$ we denote the unique number $r \in \{0, \dots, n-1\}$ such that
$r \equiv x \pmod{n}$.

Proof (sketch). As intersection distributes over union, L could be written as an intersection over the generating languages. Now,

$$F(a, k_1) \cap F(a, k_2) = F(a, \max\{k_1, k_2\})$$

and, by the generalized Chinese Remainder Theorem, Theorem 1, every intersection $\bigcap_{i=1}^{m} F(a, r_i, n_i)$ is either the empty set, or also a set of the form $F(a, r, n)$. So, every such intersection could be written in the form

$$\left(\bigcap_{a \in \Sigma_1} F(a, t_a) \right) \cap \left(\bigcap_{a \in \Sigma_2} F(a, r_a, n_a) \right) \cap L$$

where $L \in \{\Gamma^+, \Gamma^*\}$ for some $\Gamma \subseteq \Sigma$ and $\Sigma_1, \Sigma_2 \subseteq \Sigma$. By Lemma 20, these language are diagonal periodic over Γ. By Theorem 2, the iterated shuffle of L is a finite shuffle product of iterated shuffles of these languages, which are regular by Proposition 19. Hence, they are a finite shuffle product of regular languages and as the binary shuffle product is a regularity-preserving operation [13], the language L is regular. More precisely, as the iterated shuffles are finite unions of diagonal periodic languages, the result could be written as a finite union of diagonal periodic languages, which, by Lemma 20, are contained in this class. □

The method of proof of Theorem 21 also gives the next result.

Proposition 22. *The positive boolean algebra generated by languages of the form $F(a, k)$, $F(a, k, n)$, $0 \leq k < n$, Γ^+ and Γ^*, $\Gamma \subseteq \Sigma$, is precisely the language class of finite unions of the diagonal periodic languages.*

Corollary 23. *The iterated shuffle of a commutative group language is regular.*

Proof. By Theorem 12, the class introduced in Theorem 21 contains the group languages.   □

Corollary 24. *The variety $\mathbf{Com}^+$ is closed under iterated shuffle.*

Proof. By Definition 10, the class introduced in Theorem 21 contains $\mathbf{Com}^+(\Sigma^*)$ for any alphabet Σ. Furthermore, by the method of proof of Theorem 21 and as the iterated shuffle does not introduce new letters, and does not remove old letters, we do not leave the class $\mathbf{Com}^+(\Sigma^*)$.   □

Also, as, for $U_a, V_a \subseteq \{a\}^*$, $a \in \Sigma$, we have $(\bigsqcup_{a \in \Sigma} U_a) \sqcup (\bigsqcup_{a \in \Sigma} V_a) = (\bigsqcup_{a \in \Sigma} (U_a \cdot V_a))$, and with Theorem 2, we can deduce, by Proposition 22, the next result. This extends an old result by J.F. Perrot [18] stating that the star-free commutative language are closed under binary shuffle.

Proposition 25. *The positive boolean algebra generated by the languages $F(a, k)$, $F(a, k, n)$, $0 \leq k < n$, Γ^+ and Γ^* for $\Gamma \subseteq \Sigma$ is closed under binary shuffle.*

5   Characterizing Regularity of the Iterated Shuffle

First, in Subsect. 5.1, we will give a necessary and sufficient condition when the iterated shuffle of a commutative finite language is regular. Then, in Subsect. 2.3, we will present partial results for aperiodic commutative language. Lastly, in Subsect. 5.3, we discuss decision procedures related to regularity, the commutative closure and the iterated shuffle.

5.1   Finite Commutative Languages

Here, we investigate finite commutative languages.

Theorem 26. *Let $L \subseteq \Sigma^*$ be a finite language. Then, $\mathrm{perm}(L)^{\sqcup,*}$ is regular if and only if for any $a \in \Sigma$ with $\Sigma^* a \Sigma^* \cap L \neq \varnothing$ we have $a^+ \cap L \neq \varnothing$.*

By the next corollary, we find that we can characterize regularity of expressions, for instance, of the form

$$\mathrm{perm}(u_1^+) \sqcup \ldots \sqcup \mathrm{perm}(u_n^+) = \mathrm{perm}(u_1 \cdots u_n) \sqcup \mathrm{perm}(u_1^*) \sqcup \mathrm{perm}(u_1^*)$$
$$= \mathrm{perm}(u_1 \cdots u_n) \sqcup \mathrm{perm}(\{u_1, \ldots, u_n\})^{\sqcup,*}$$

with Theorem 26, where the above equalities are implied by Theorem 2 and Theorem 3.

Corollary 27. *Let $u \in \Sigma$ and $L \subseteq \Sigma^*$ be a finite language. Then, $\mathrm{perm}(u) \sqcup \mathrm{perm}(L)^{\sqcup,*}$ is regular if and only if for any $a \in \Sigma$ with $\Sigma^* a \Sigma^* \cap L \neq \varnothing$, we have $a^+ \cap L \neq \varnothing$.*

5.2   Aperiodic Commutative Languages

Here, we investigate aperiodic commutative languages.

Proposition 28. *Every aperiodic commutative language could be written as a finite union of languages of the form $\mathrm{perm}(u) \sqcup \Gamma^*$ for $u \in \Sigma^*$ and $\Gamma \subseteq \Sigma$.*

Remark 5. By a result from [13, Page 9], it follows that a letter which permutes with every other letter has to permute the states of every strongly connected component. This could be used to prove that the minimal automaton of an aperiodic commutative language cannot have non-trivial loops, i.e., every loop must be a self-loop, which could also be used to give a proof of Proposition 28.

With Theorem 26 we get the next result.

Proposition 29. *Let $u \in \Sigma^*$ and $\Gamma \subseteq \Sigma$. The iterated shuffle of $\mathrm{perm}(u) \sqcup \Gamma^*$ is regular if and only if there exists $a \in \Sigma$ such that $u \subseteq a^+$ or when $u \in \Gamma^*$.*

Next, we give a simple sufficient criterion of regularity for a binary alphabet.

Lemma 30. *Let $\Sigma = \{a, b\}$ and $L \subseteq \Sigma^*$ be regular. Then, if there exists $u \in \Sigma^*$ such that $\mathrm{perm}(u) \sqcup \Sigma^* \subseteq \mathrm{perm}(L)$, then $\mathrm{perm}(L)$ is regular.*

Lastly, a few examples of aperiodic commutative languages, some of them yielding non-regular languages and some of them regular languages when applying the iterated shuffle.

Example 2. Let $\Sigma = \{a, b, c\}$.

1. The iterated shuffle of $\{ab, ba\} \cup \{c\} \amalg \{a, b\}^*$ is not regular.
2. The iterated shuffle of $\{ab, ba\} \amalg \{c\}^* \cup \{ac\} \amalg \{a, b\}^*$ is not regular.
3. The iterated shuffle of $\{ab, ba\} \cup \{c\} \amalg \{a, b\}^* \cup \mathrm{perm}(abb) \amalg \{a, b\}^*$ is regular.
4. The iterated shuffle of $\{ab, ba\} \cup \{c\} \amalg \{a, b\}^* \cup \mathrm{perm}(abb) \amalg \{a\}^* \cup \{bb\}$ is regular.

5.3   Decision Procedures

In [7,8] it was shown that for regular $L \subseteq \Sigma^*$, it is decidable if $\mathrm{perm}(L)$ is regular. As $\mathrm{perm}(L)^{\amalg,*} = \mathrm{perm}(L^*)$, also the regularity of the iterated shuffle on commutative regular languages is decidable. This result was also shown directly, without citing [7,8], in [13]. However, the precise computational complexity was not clear, and by a statement given in [6, Theorem 45] it follows that for a regular language given by a regular expression it is NP-hard to decide if the commutative closure is regular. On the contrary, the conditions stated in Theorem 26 could be tested in polynomial time for a finite commutative language given by a deterministic, a non-deterministic or a regular expression as input. This follows as non-emptiness of intersection with the fixed languages $\Sigma^* a \Sigma^*$ and a^+, $a \in \Sigma$, could be done in polynomial time by the product automaton construction.

6   Conclusion

A general criterion as given for finite (commutative) languages in Theorem 26, which gives a polynomial time decision procedure, for general commutative regular languages is an open problem. For the subclass closed under iterated shuffle identified in Subsect. 4, a sharp bound for the size of a recognizing automaton of the iterated shuffle is unknown.

Acknowledgement. I thank the anonymous reviewers for careful reading, pointing out typos and unclear formulations and providing additional references.

References

1. Almeida, J., Ésik, Z., Pin, J.: Commutative positive varieties of languages. Acta Cybern. **23**(1), 91–111 (2017)
2. Berstel, J., Boasson, L., Carton, O., Pin, J., Restivo, A.: The expressive power of the shuffle product. Inf. Comput. **208**(11), 1258–1272 (2010)
3. Campbell, R.H., Habermann, A.N.: The specification of process synchronization by path expressions. In: Gelenbe, E., Kaiser, C. (eds.) OS 1974. LNCS, vol. 16, pp. 89–102. Springer, Heidelberg (1974). https://doi.org/10.1007/BFb0029355

4. Castiglione, G., Restivo, A.: On the shuffle of star-free languages. Fundam. Inf. **116**(1–4), 35–44 (2012)
5. Ehrenfeucht, A., Haussler, D., Rozenberg, G.: On regularity of context-free languages. Theor. Comput. Sci. **27**, 311–332 (1983)
6. Fernau, H., Paramasivan, M., Schmid, M.L., Vorel, V.: Characterization and complexity results on jumping finite automata. Theor. Comput. Sci. **679**, 31–52 (2017)
7. Ginsburg, S., Spanier, E.H.: Bounded regular sets. Proc. Am. Math. Soc. **17**, 1043–1049 (1966)
8. Gohon, P.: An algorithm to decide whether a rational subset of n̂k is recognizable. Theor. Comput. Sci. **41**, 51–59 (1985)
9. Gómez, A.C., Pin, J.: Shuffle on positive varieties of languages. Theor. Comput. Sci. **312**(2–3), 433–461 (2004)
10. Hoffmann, S.: Commutative regular languages - properties, state complexity and generalizations. Inf. Comput. (submitted)
11. Hoffmann, S.: Commutative regular languages – properties and state complexity. In: Ćirić, M., Droste, M., Pin, J.É. (eds.) CAI 2019. LNCS, vol. 11545, pp. 151–163. Springer, Cham (2019). https://doi.org/10.1007/978-3-030-21363-3_13
12. Hopcroft, J.E., Ullman, J.D.: Introduction to Automata Theory, Languages, and Computation. Addison-Wesley Publishing Company (1979)
13. Ito, M.: Algebraic Theory of Automata and Languages. World Scientific (2004)
14. Kozen, D.: Automata and Computability. Undergraduate Texts in Computer Science. Springer, Heidelberg (1997). https://doi.org/10.1007/978-1-4612-1844-9
15. Mazurkiewicz, A.: Parallel recursive program schemes. In: Bečvář, J. (ed.) MFCS 1975. LNCS, vol. 32, pp. 75–87. Springer, Heidelberg (1975). https://doi.org/10.1007/3-540-07389-2_183
16. McNaughton, R.: The loop complexity of pure-group events. Inf. Control **11**(1/2), 167–176 (1967)
17. McNaughton, R., Papert, S.A.: Counter-Free Automata (M.I.T. Research Monograph No. 65). The MIT Press (1971)
18. Perrot, J.: Varietes de langages et operations. Theor. Comput. Sci. **7**, 197–210 (1978)
19. Pin, J.: Varieties of Formal Languages. Plenum Publishing Co. (1986)
20. Pin, J.: Syntactic semigroups. In: Rozenberg, G., Salomaa, A. (eds.) Handbook of Formal Languages, vol. 1, pp. 679–746. Springer, Heidelberg (1997). https://doi.org/10.1007/978-3-642-59136-5_10
21. Pin, J.É.: How to prove that a language is regular or star-free? In: Leporati, A., Martín-Vide, C., Shapira, D., Zandron, C. (eds.) LATA 2020. LNCS, vol. 12038, pp. 68–88. Springer, Cham (2020). https://doi.org/10.1007/978-3-030-40608-0_5
22. Restivo, A.: The shuffle product: new research directions. In: Dediu, A.-H., Formenti, E., Martín-Vide, C., Truthe, B. (eds.) LATA 2015. LNCS, vol. 8977, pp. 70–81. Springer, Cham (2015). https://doi.org/10.1007/978-3-319-15579-1_5
23. Riddle, W.E.: An approach to software system behavior description. Comput. Lang. **4**(1), 29–47 (1979). https://doi.org/10.1016/0096-0551(79)90008-0
24. Schmid, H.L., Mahler, K.: On the Chinese remainder theorem. Math. Nachrichten **18**(1–6), 120–122 (1958)
25. Schützenberger, M.P.: On finite monoids having only trivial subgroups. Inf. Control. **8**(2), 190–194 (1965)
26. Shaw, A.C.: Software descriptions with flow expressions. IEEE Trans. Softw. Eng. **4**, 242–254 (1978)

Memoized Regular Expressions

Brink van der Merwe[1], Jacobie Mouton[1], Steyn van Litsenborgh[1],
and Martin Berglund[2(✉)]

[1] Department of Computer Science, Stellenbosch University,
Stellenbosch, South Africa
[2] Department of Information Science, Stellenbosch University,
Stellenbosch, South Africa
pmberglund@sun.ac.za

Abstract. We extend non-deterministic finite automata (NFAs) and
regular expressions (regexes) by adding memoization to these formalisms.
These extensions are aimed at improving the matching time of backtracking regex matchers. Additionally, we discuss how to extend the concept
of ambiguity in order to be applicable to memoized extensions of regexes
and NFAs. These more general notions of ambiguity can be used to ana-
lyze the matching time of backtracking regex matchers enhanced with
memoization.

Keywords: Ambiguity · Regular expression matching · Memoization

1 Introduction

Regular expressions (regexes) provide a convenient way to describe the class
of regular languages and are frequently used as textual pattern descriptors in
practical string-matching tasks. The backtracking algorithm used by many regex
matchers can however become very slow under conditions identifiable by ambiguity considerations. This exposes a vulnerability in applications making use of
backtracking regex matchers which can be exploited in a denial of service attack,
known as a regular expression denial of service (ReDoS) attack [1]. A ReDoS
attack occurs when a malicious user provides input that will cause the backtracking algorithm to take superlinear time when performing an input-directed
depth-first search required to match the input with a given regex, or determine
that no such match is possible. It has been established empirically that software engineers often use ReDoS-vulnerable regexes and thus thousands of web
services are exploitable [2].

As pointed out by Davis in his PhD dissertation [2], the proportion of
regexes that exhibit exponential or non-linear polynomial worst-case matching
time varies widely by language. According to Davis, regex engines can be cat-
egorized into the following categories, based on worst-case matching time: (i)
Slow (JavaScript, Java, Python, Ruby), (ii) Medium (PHP, Perl), and (iii) Fast
(Go, Rust). A Thompson-style regex engine, employing an on-the-fly subset construction, is used by Go and Rust, but these matching engines do not support,

© Springer Nature Switzerland AG 2021
S. Maneth (Ed.): CIAA 2021, LNCS 12803, pp. 39–52, 2021.
https://doi.org/10.1007/978-3-030-79121-6_4

amongst others, lookahead assertions. The six remaining languages employ a Spencer-style backtracking regex engine [3], performing an input-directed depth-first search on a Thompson (or similar) constructed NFA. In PHP and Perl, runtime caps short circuit long-running evaluations. Davis et al. considered in [1], mostly from an empirical point of view, the effectiveness of memoization to curb the occurrence of worst-case superlinear matching time. It is easy to reason (as done by Davis) that when keeping track of the combination of an NFA state and input string position from where matching is not possible, that the resulting backtracking regex engine (without backreferences) will have a worst case linear matching time in the length of input strings. This form of memoization comes at the cost of a significant increase in space usage. Davis therefore also proposes two more memoization schemes to reduce space usage, and refer to these schemes as being selective, since they memoize only some (and often significantly fewer) of the Thompson NFA states.

A form of memoization has been added to the Java 14 regex matcher, as can be established when inspecting the source code. In Java 14 we observed the following behaviour on a few sample regexes that could potentially have bad matching time, based on ambiguity considerations as discussed in [4]. We used input strings of the form "a... ab", which are rejected by all three regexes discussed next. As expected, $\hat{}(a|a)\{0,100\}\$$ and $\hat{}(((a+)+)+)\$$ takes an excessive amount of time to reject the input, but $\hat{}(a|a)*\$$ does not trigger catastrophic backtracking (whereas it does in Java 8). By analysing the source code of the Java matcher, we concluded that ReDoS protection was added to the Java regex matcher that protects the matcher in some situations, but not others. The $\hat{}$ and \$ anchors in the regex examples above, indicate that the matcher should start matching from the start and match all the way to the end of the input string if possible, instead of doing substring matching. Since we only consider full matching in this paper, we do not indicate the anchors $\hat{}$ and \$, and assume that they are always implicitly present. An overview of regex notation is given in the next section.

It should be pointed out that memoization is not the only way to address excessive backtracking in regex matchers, but atomic operators, designed specifically to reduce backtracking, may also change the language accepted in difficult to determine ways [5].

It was shown in [4] that algorithms identifying infinite or exponential ambiguity in NFAs, are well-suited to identify regexes with bad matching time. Our contribution is to show how to extend these ambiguity concepts to regexes and NFAs enhanced with memoization. This can then be used again to analyse matching time when using backtracking regex matchers enhanced with memoization.

The outline of this paper is as follows. We start by giving the required definitions. This is followed by a section in which we generalize some ambiguity results from [6,7] to memoized NFAs. Next we investigate the hardness of determining the minimal number of NFA states required to memoize in order to achieve finite ambiguity. Then we discuss selective memoization schemes that can be used to turn regexes and NFAs into memoized regexes and NFAs having much lower ambiguity. Some of these schemes guarantee finite ambiguity and thus ensure linear matching time in the length of input strings. Finally, we list future work.

2 Notation and Definitions

We extend the standard definition of strong ambiguity on regexes in this section. Strong ambiguity is studied and compared to weak ambiguity in [8], and we refer to our extended version simply as ambiguity. We first introduce some required preliminary notation and concepts, we then consider ambiguity concepts for NFAs, before finally considering regexes.

By $\mathbb{N}$ we denote the natural numbers including 0. For a finite alphabet Σ, we denote the set of all strings or finite sequences over Σ, by Σ^*, with Σ^* containing the empty string ε. To avoid confusion, it is assumed that $\varepsilon \notin \Sigma$, and $\Sigma_\varepsilon = \Sigma \cup \{\varepsilon\}$. We denote by Σ^+ the set of strings $\Sigma^* \setminus \{\varepsilon\}$. Similar notation is used in regexes, for example E^* (and E^+), defined shortly, and by Σ^* (and Σ^+) we in fact denote the language defined by the regexes F^* (and F^+), with F being constructed using the union operator over all subexpressions representing each of the individual symbols in the set Σ.

For $\Sigma' \subseteq \Sigma$ and $w = a_1 \ldots a_n \in \Sigma^*$ (or $w = \varepsilon$), with $a_i \in \Sigma$, we let $\pi_{\Sigma'}(w)$ be the word $b_1 \ldots b_n$ over Σ', with $b_i = a_i$ if $a_i \in \Sigma'$, and $b_i = \varepsilon$ otherwise (and $\pi_{\Sigma'}(\varepsilon) = \varepsilon$). Also, by $|w|$ we denote the number of symbols (from Σ) in w. The cardinality of a set A is denoted by $|A|$ (always finite in our setting), and $\mathcal{P}(A)$ denotes the powerset of A.

2.1 Memoized NFA

Next we define memoized non-deterministic finite automata, where a subset of the states are distinguished as memoized. The choice of memoized states never changes the language accepted by the automaton.

Definition 1 (see [1]). *A memoized non-deterministic finite automaton (mNFA) is a tuple $A = (\mathcal{M}, Q, \Sigma, \delta, q_0, F)$ where: (i) Q is a non-empty finite set of states; (ii) $\mathcal{M} \subseteq Q$ is a set of memoized states; (iii) Σ is the input alphabet; (iii) the function $\delta : Q \times \Sigma_\varepsilon \to \mathcal{P}(Q)$ is the transition function; (iv) $q_0 \in Q$ is the initial state; and (v) $F \subseteq Q$ is the set of final states.*

Also, $|A|_\delta := \sum_{q \in Q, a \in \Sigma_\varepsilon} |\delta(q, a)|$ is the transition size of A.

When $\mathcal{M} = \varnothing$, the mNFA is an NFA. Next we define (accepting) runs of an mNFA.

Definition 2. *For an mNFA $A = (\mathcal{M}, Q, \Sigma, \delta, q_0, F)$ and $w \in \Sigma^*$, a run on w is a string $r = s_0 \alpha_1 s_1 \cdots s_{n-1} \alpha_n s_n$, with $s_0 = q_0$, $s_i \in Q$ and $\alpha_i \in \Sigma_\varepsilon$ such that $s_{i+1} \in \delta(s_i, \alpha_{i+1})$, $\pi_\Sigma(r) = w$, and r is not allowed to contain a substring from Q^* with more than one instance of any specific $qq' \in Q^2$, i.e. no ε-transition is allowed to be repeated without reading an intermediate symbol from Σ. A run is accepting if $s_n \in F$. The set of accepting runs on w and all accepting runs are denoted by $\mathcal{R}_A(w)$ and $\mathcal{R}_A$ respectively. The language accepted by A, denoted by $\mathcal{L}(A)$, is $\{\pi_\Sigma(r) \mid r \in \mathcal{R}_A\} \subseteq \Sigma^*$.*

Although a restriction of not allowing runs to contain a substring from Q^* with more than one instance of any specific state, seems more natural to ensure that $\mathcal{R}_A(w)$ is finite, this does not correspond to how regex matchers handle ε-loops in NFAs (more on this later in Example 2).

For brevity, for a run $r = s_0\alpha_1 s_1 \cdots s_{n-1}\alpha_n s_n$, let $r_i = s_0\alpha_1 s_1 \cdots s_{i-1}\alpha_i s_i$, when $i \leq n$. The set $\mathcal{M}$ in an mNFA A plays no role in the definition of $\mathcal{L}(A)$, but influences ambiguity. We assume that all states p in an mNFA are *useful*, i.e. each $p \in Q$ is on an accepting run of some string w.

Definition 3. *For an mNFA $A = (\mathcal{M}, Q, \Sigma, \delta, q_0, F)$ and string w, we define the ambiguity of w in A as the maximum cardinality of a set $\overline{\mathcal{R}}_A(w) \subseteq \mathcal{R}_A(w)$, with the following property: If $r = s_0\alpha_1 s_1 \cdots s_{n-1}\alpha_n s_n$ and $r' = s_0'\alpha_1' s_1' \cdots s_{n'-1}'\alpha_{n'}' s_{n'}'$ are in $\mathcal{R}_A(w)$, then if $s_i = s_{i'}' \in \mathcal{M}$ and $\pi_\Sigma(r_i) = \pi_\Sigma(r_{i'}')$, we have $r_i = r_{i'}'$. We denote the ambiguity of w in A by $a_A'(w)$ and let $a_A(n) = \max_{|w| \leq n} a_A'(w)$.*

If $a_A(n) \leq 1$ for all $n \in \mathbb{N}$, A is unambiguous. *Let $d \in \mathbb{N}$ be minimal such that $a_A(n) \leq h(n)$ (if $a_A(n)$ is polynomial bounded), with h a polynomial of degree d. If such an exponent d exists, A has* ambiguity of degree d. *If $d = 0$, A has* finite ambiguity. *If $a_A(n)$ is not polynomial bounded, the ambiguity of A is* exponential.

In [6], terminology such as infinite degree of ambiguity and degree of growth of ambiguity is used. We will, in our more general setting, simply refer to these as infinite ambiguity and degree of ambiguity respectively. Note that memoizing more states will keep ambiguity the same or reduce it.

We let A^{all} be the mNFA obtained from the mNFA A by making all states in A accepting. We refer to $a_{A^{all}}(n)$ as the *prefix ambiguity* of A, and use terminology *prefix unambiguous, prefix ambiguity of degree d* and *exponential prefix ambiguity* for A, when A^{all} is unambiguous, has ambiguity of degree d, or has exponential ambiguity respectively. If A has a single final state that is also memoized, then A is unambiguous, but this does *not* imply that A^{all} is unambiguous, i.e. A may in fact have exponential prefix ambiguity. This is important in practice, as it implies that matching a string w with A using depth-first search may still explore a large number of non-accepting (prefixes of) runs before finding an accepting run, or ultimately rejecting, even though the ambiguity of A might be small.

For $q \in Q$, we denote by A^q the mNFA obtained by setting the final states of A equal to $\{q\}$. We refer to the ambiguity of A^q as the *ambiguity of A at state q*, and say A is unambiguous at q or has finite ambiguity at q, etc., when these statements hold true for A^q. In particular, it will be of interest when A is unambiguous at all states or has finite ambiguity at all states, i.e. these statements are true about A^q, for all $q \in Q$. Certainly, $a_A(n) \leq \sum_{q \in F} a_{A^q}(n)$ and $a_{A^{all}}(n) \leq \sum_{q \in Q} a_{A^q}(n)$, thus if A is unambiguous at all states, then $a_{A^{all}}(n) \leq |Q|$ for all n, and A has finite prefix ambiguity if and only if A^q has finite ambiguity for all $q \in Q$.

2.2 Memoized Regular Expressions

Next we add memoization to regexes, an extension not considered before as far as we know. A *memoized regular expression* (m-regex), over an alphabet Σ, where we assume $\Sigma \cap \{|, \cdot, *, \mapsto, \leftarrow\mapsto, \varepsilon, \varnothing\} = \varnothing$ to avoid confusion, is defined inductively as follows. Elements from $\Sigma \cup \{\varepsilon, \varnothing\}$ are m-regexes, and if E and F are m-regexes, then so are the expressions $(E \mid F), (E \cdot F), (E^*), (\mapsto E)$ or $(E \leftarrow\mapsto)$. Regular expressions (regexes) are those m-regexes without the memoization operators $\mapsto$ and $\leftarrow\mapsto$. Some parentheses may be dropped from m-regexes, using that operators are ordered according to precedence from high to low as follows: $\mapsto$ (left memoization), $\leftarrow\mapsto$ (right memoization), $*$ (Kleene closure or star), $\cdot$ (concatenation), and finally $|$ (union). Furthermore, outermost parentheses may be dropped, and $E \cdot E'$ written as EE'. We use E^+ as shorthand for $E \cdot E^*$, and $E\{m, n\}$, with $m \leq n$, $m, n \in \mathbb{N}$, as shorthand for $(E^m \mid E^{m+1} \mid \cdots \mid E^n)$, where E^i denotes the concatenation of i copies of E with itself, and E^0 denoting ε. We denote by $r(E)$ the regex obtained by removing all memoization operators from E. The language of an m-regex E, denoted $\mathcal{L}(E)$, is obtained by evaluating $r(E)$ as usual. When we say that E matches a string w, we mean that $w \in \mathcal{L}(E)$, as opposed to $vwv' \in \mathcal{L}(E)$, for $v, v' \in \Sigma^*$. We exclude m-regexes containing $\varnothing$ in the remainder of our discussion, i.e. for all m-regexes E we have $\mathcal{L}(E) \neq \varnothing$.

Now that we have defined regexes, we point out, via an example, the distinction between what is referred to as weak and strong ambiguity in [8], in particular since we generalize strong ambiguity, which we refer to simply as ambiguity. Let $E = (a^* \mid b^*)^*$, then E is weakly unambiguous (i.e. have no weak ambiguity), since no symbol from Σ is present in E more than once. Thus, each symbol in an input string matched by E can be uniquely identified with a symbol from Σ in E that was used during the match, in contrast to $F = (a \mid a)^*$. The regex E is, however, not strongly unambiguous, since the string aa can be matched in multiple ways using E, by using the outer Kleene closure a different number of times when matching an empty substring of aa either with the subexpression a^* or b^* in different places in aa.

We denote by $\mathbb{N}'$ the set $\mathbb{N} \cup \{\bar{i} \mid i \in \mathbb{N}\}$. Let E be an m-regex over Σ with $\Sigma \cap \mathbb{N}' = \varnothing$. For $F = r(E)$, we obtain F_0 from F inductively as follows. We replace ε by $0 \cdot \varepsilon \cdot 0$, $a \in \Sigma$ by $0 \cdot a \cdot 0$, and $(H \mid I), (H \cdot I), (H^*)$ by $0 \cdot (H_0 \mid I_0) \cdot 0$, $H_0 \cdot I_0$ and $0 \cdot (H_0)^* \cdot 0$ respectively. Next, relabel all symbols equal to 0 in F_0 uniquely using symbols in $\mathbb{N}$, starting from the left in F_0, in increasing order from 0, with each of the finitely many elements used from $\mathbb{N}$ regarded as a single symbol, to obtain a regex G over $\Sigma \cup \mathbb{N}$. We relabel $i \in \mathbb{N}$ as $\bar{i}$ in G if the corresponding subexpression in E, immediately following i in G, was left memoized in E, and similarly if the subexpression immediately preceding i in G was right memoized. Left memoizing a subexpression that is already left memoized has no effect, and similarly for right memoization. We denote the regex over $\Sigma \cup \mathbb{N}'$ obtained in this way from E by $\overline{E}$. Although $\mathcal{L}(\overline{E})$ depends on if we use left or right associativity for union in E, the choice we make in terms of associativity will not influence our further work. To avoid any confusion, we make the arbitrary choice of selecting left associativity.

Example 1. If $E = (a^*)^*$, then $\overline{E} = 0(1(2a3)^*4)^*5$, and $\overline{\mapsto(a|a)^*} = 0(\overline{1}(2a3|4a5)6)^*7$ (using that we assume that $\mapsto$ binds tighter than Kleene star).

Definition 4. *For an m-regex E and string w, we define an* accepting run *for w over E as a string r in $\mathcal{L}(\overline{E})$ with $\pi_\Sigma(r) = w$ and with r not having any substring $r' \in (\mathbb{N}')^*$, where r' contains a specific $nn' \in (\mathbb{N}')^2$ more than once. We denote the set of accepting runs for w over E by $\mathcal{R}_E(w)$ and let $\mathcal{R}_E = \cup_{w \in \Sigma^*} \mathcal{R}_E(w)$.*

Prefix runs of w of length k, denoted by $\mathcal{R}_E^{pre}(w, k)$, are defined to be prefixes r' of runs $r \in \mathcal{R}_E$, with $\pi_\Sigma(r')$ a prefix of w, $|\pi_\Sigma(r')| = k$ and with r' ending on an element from $\mathbb{N}'$. We let all prefix runs of w be $\cup_{0 \le k \le |w|} \mathcal{R}_E^{pre}(w, k)$ and denote this set by $\mathcal{R}_E^{pre}(w)$. Also, $\mathcal{R}_E^{pre}$ indicates the set of all prefix runs, i.e. $\cup_{w \in \Sigma^*} \mathcal{R}_E^{pre}(w)$.

Example 2. For $E = (a^*)^*$, $\mathcal{R}_E(\varepsilon) = \{05, 0145\}$ and $\mathcal{R}_E(a) = \{012a345, 012a34145\}$, since $\overline{E} = 0(1(2a3)^*4)^*5$. The sets $\mathcal{R}_E(\varepsilon)$ and $\mathcal{R}_E(a)$ are finite, because of the restriction that runs r should not have any substring $r' \in (\mathbb{N}')^*$, where r' contains a specific $nn' \in (\mathbb{N}')^2$ more than once. If we replace this restriction with the more natural seeming restriction of not allowing any specific $n \in \mathbb{N}'$ to be repeated, then $012a34145$ falls away from $\mathcal{R}_E(a)$, which will then disagree with for example the Java and Python regex matchers preferring the run $012a34145$ over $012a345$, and reporting an empty (last) capture/match with the subexpression a^* when matching a with $(a^*)^*$.

For the m-regex F given by $\mapsto(a|a)^*$, we have that $0\overline{1}2a3\overline{6}\overline{1}4a567$ is one of the four possible accepting runs of aa, since $\overline{F} = 0(\overline{1}(2a3|4a5)6)^*7$.

Definition 5. *For an m-regex E, let $A_E(w)$ be the maximum cardinality of a subset $\overline{\mathcal{R}}_E(w)$ of $\mathcal{R}_E(w)$ with the following property: If $v_1, v_2 \in \overline{\mathcal{R}}_E(w)$, where $r_1\overline{i}, r_2\overline{i}$, with $i \in \mathbb{N}$, are prefixes of v_1 and v_2 respectively with $\pi_\Sigma(r_1) = \pi_\Sigma(r_2)$, then $r_1 = r_2$. We let $a_E(n) = \max_{w \in \Sigma^*, |w| \le n} A_E(w) \in \mathbb{N}$. The function a_E is referred to as the* ambiguity *of E.*

We get a_E^{pre} by replacing $\mathcal{R}_E(w)$ with $\mathcal{R}_E^{pre}(w)$ to obtain a set $\overline{\mathcal{R}}_E^{pre}(w)$ of maximum cardinality $A^{pre}(w)$. Next let $a_E^{pre}(n) = \max_{w \in \Sigma^*, k \le n} A_E^{pre}(w, k)$, with $A_E^{pre}(w, k) = |\overline{\mathcal{R}}_E^{pre}(w) \cap \mathcal{R}_E^{pre}(w, k)|$. We refer to a_E^{pre} as the prefix ambiguity *of E.*

Similarly to how we used a_A in Definition 3 to define when A is unambiguous, has finite ambiguity, ambiguity of degree d or exponential ambiguity, we use a_E to define the same notions for E. We define E to be prefix unambiguous, *or has* prefix ambiguity of degree d, *or* exponential prefix ambiguity *analogously as in the case of mNFAs, but using a_E^{pre}.*

Example 3. For $E_1 = a^*a^*$, $\overline{E}_1 = 0(1a2)^*34(5a6)^*7$, and $\mathcal{R}_{E_1} = \{0(1a2)^{n_0}34(5a6)^{n_1}7 \mid n_0, n_1 \ge 0\}$. Note $\pi_\Sigma(0(1a2)^{n_0}34(5a6)^{n_1}7) = a^{n_0+n_1}$, which implies $a_{E_1}(n) = n + 1$ and therefore E_1 has ambiguity of degree 1. For $E_2 = a^*(\mapsto a^*)$, $\overline{E}_2 = 0(1a2)^*34(\overline{5}a6)^*7$, and $|\overline{\mathcal{R}}_{E_2}(a^n)| = 2$ for $n \ge 1$, and thus E_2 is finitely ambiguous but not unambiguous.

For an m-regex E, denote by $\mathcal{T}(E)$ the NFA constructed from $r(E)$ using the Thompson construction [9]. Since the Thompson construction mirrors our construction of how we obtain $\overline{E}$ from E, we identify the runs in $\mathcal{R}_E(w)$ with those on w in $\mathcal{T}(E)$. We turn $\mathcal{T}(E)$ into an mNFA, by memoizing the states in $\mathcal{T}(E)$ corresponding to how and which subexpressions are memoized in E, with $\mapsto$ memoizing an initial state corresponding to a subexpression and $\leftmapsto$ a final state. In the remainder of this paper, the notation $\mathcal{T}(E)$ is used to indicate the memoized version of the NFA constructed from the m-regex E. We thus regard the Thompson construction as a way of constructing mNFAs from m-regexes, and not simply a way of constructing NFAs from regexes. It should be noted that each memoization operator memoize precisely one state in $\mathcal{T}(E)$ (except for the case where we apply a left memoization operator more than once to the same subexpression, and similarly for right memoization). We denote by $\mathcal{T}^{all}(E)$ the mNFA obtained by making all states in $\mathcal{T}(E)$ accepting, similar to the notation A^{all} used for an mNFA A.

From the respective definitions it follows that (prefix) ambiguity agrees on E and $\mathcal{T}(E)$.

Proposition 1. *If E is an m-regex, $a_E(n) = a_{\mathcal{T}(E)}(n)$ and $a_E^{pre}(n) = a_{\mathcal{T}^{all}(E)}(n)$ for all $n \in \mathbb{N}$.*

Proof. This follows from the observation that accepting runs in E and $\mathcal{T}(E)$ can be uniquely identified with each other, and similarly for prefix runs in E and accepting runs in $\mathcal{T}^{all}(E)$. □

It can be seen that a_E (and a^{pre}) can be bounded by an exponential function by considering accepting runs in $\mathcal{T}(E)$ (or $\mathcal{T}^{all}(E)$), and using Proposition 1. Note that it is straightforward to reason that the number of (accepting) runs of w in $\mathcal{T}(E)$ (or $\mathcal{T}^{all}(E)$) is bounded by a function exponential in $|w|$.

Next, we discuss briefly why the product of the prefix ambiguity of an m-regex E and n, and equivalently, the product of the ambiguity of $\mathcal{T}^{all}(E)$ (i.e. the prefix ambiguity of $\mathcal{T}(E)$) and n, is an upper bound for the worst-case matching time of a backtracking matcher respecting memoization information, when matching strings up to length n using $\mathcal{T}(E)$. When given an input string w, with $|w| \leq n$, a backtracking matcher performs an input-directed depth-first search on $\mathcal{T}(E)$. For an input string w, we consider an ordered tree $btr_E(w)$, referred to as the backtracking tree of w, with a prefix traversal of $btr_E(w)$ producing the nodes in the order they are visited by the matcher. The nodes in the rightmost path in $btr(w)$ are the states in an accepting run of w, if $w \in \mathcal{L}(E)$, and thus once the matcher determines that a match is possible, the further exploration of prefix runs of w are terminated. The matcher uses the memoization information by not revisiting a memoized state after having read the same prefix of w as before, and having determined that no match is possible from this state using the remaining suffix of w. To improve the time complexity of our analysis in exchange for obtaining less precise matching time estimates, but always upper bound estimates, we bound the size of the backtracking tree $btr_E(w)$, by $c \cdot |w| \cdot \max_{0 \leq k \leq |w|} A_E^{pre}(w, k) \leq$

$c \cdot |w| \cdot a_E^{pre}(|w|)$, where c is a constant such that the longest prefix run of w goes through at most $c \cdot |w|$ states in $\mathcal{T}(E)$.

3   Generalization of Mohri's Ambiguity Results to mNFA

In this section we generalize results from [6] and [7] to be applicable to mNFAs. The next definition is taken from [7], but modified in a way to take memoization and ε-loops (by enforcing $v, v_i \in \Sigma^+$, and not simply $v, v_i \in \Sigma^*$) into account.

Definition 6. *The following are the three required properties for the characterization of ambiguity of an mNFA A.*

1. *(EDA) There exists a state p with at least two distinct cycles on $v \in \Sigma^+$ containing no memoized state.*
2. *(IDA) There exist two distinct states p and q with paths on $v \in \Sigma^+$ from p to p, p to q, and q to q. The loop on q should contain no memoized state.*
3. *(IDA$_d$) There exist $2d$ states $p_1, \ldots p_d, q_1, \ldots, q_d$ in A and $2d - 1$ strings $v_1, \ldots, v_d \in \Sigma^+$ and $u_1, \ldots, u_{d-1} \in \Sigma^*$, such that for all $1 \leq i \leq d$, $p_i \neq q_i$, we can read v_i on some path from p_i to p_i, p_i to q_i and q_i to q_i, while encountering no memoized state from q_i to q_i, and also read u_i on some path from q_i to p_{i+1}.*

Note that EDA implies IDA, since the two states required for IDA can be obtained from the two loops at p on v with no memoized states. Starting at p, there must be a first state q at which we obtain a split to states r and r' while reading v and looping back to p. These two states, in any order, can now be used as the two states required for IDA.

Theorem 1. *We can decide IDA for an mNFA $A = (\mathcal{M}, Q.\Sigma, \delta, q_0, F)$ in time $\mathcal{O}(|A|_\delta^3)$ if A is ε-loop free, and in time $\mathcal{O}(|A|_\delta^2|Q|^2)$ otherwise.*

Proof. First we provide the argument for when A has no ε-transitions, and then we point out how to add ε-transitions to our previous argument by using Mohri's filter transducer from [7], and finally, how to also allow ε-loops.

Let $P = Q \setminus \mathcal{M}$ and $R = Q \times Q \times P$. If $P = \varnothing$, then A does not have IDA, so we assume $P \neq \varnothing$. First assume A has no ε-transitions. We generalize the argument used in the proof of Lemma 3.4 in [6] on how to decide if an NFA, with no ε-transitions, has IDA. Let $G_3 = (R, E_3)$ and $G_4 = (R, E_4)$ be graphs with nodes given by R and edges E_3 and E_4 respectively, where we define E_3 and E_4 next. We let E_3 be all edges $((p_1, p_2, p_3), (q_1, q_2, q_3))$, with $q_i \in \delta(p_i, a)$ for some $a \in \Sigma$, $i = 1, 2, 3$. We let $E_4 = E_3 \cup E_3'$ with E_3' all edges $((p, q, q), (p, p, q))$ such that $p \in Q$, $q \in P$ and $p \neq q$. We can characterize IDA as (p, q, q) being reachable from (p, p, q) in G_3 for $p \neq q$, or as having a strongly connected component $\mathcal{C}$ in G_4 with $\mathcal{C}^2 \cap E_3' \neq \varnothing$. This establishes the result when we assume A has no ε-transitions.

Next assume we have ε-transitions, but no ε-loops. In this case when using $\delta(p_i, \varepsilon)$, for $i = 1, 2, 3$, to transition from one node to another in R, we are also allowed to simply stay at one or more of the p_i's without using δ. Just as is done in [7], where the result from [6] on deciding IDA is extended from NFAs without ε-transitions to NFAs with ε-transitions, by using what Mohri refers to as a filter transducer, we also apply the exact same filter transducer. This transducer ensures that the number of paths in a product NFA is counted correctly when ε-transitions are present, and also ensures that we do not only stay at p, or only at q, while taking only ε-transitions from p to q (on the 2nd component), when determining that we have a path from (p, p, q) to (p, q, q) in R.

Finally, we consider the case where ε-loops are also allowed. In this case, we remove all ε-transitions from the 3rd component P in R at the price of potentially increasing the number of transitions in P to $|Q|^2$, but without changing whether IDA is present or not. To achieve this, first note that ε self-loops at any given state can be removed, unless they are at a state that forms part of a loop while reading a non-empty word, in which case they cause EDA (and thus IDA). Otherwise, if $q \in \delta(p, a)$, and we have a path from q to q' while reading ε, we remove the ε-transitions and add q' as one of the destination states of $\delta(p, a)$, but if q' is already in this set, we end up with a parallel transition on a from p to q'. Again, parallel transitions do not influence IDA, unless they form part of a loop, in which case they also cause EDA (and thus IDA). Now we repeat the argument in the previous paragraph, since if we obtain the necessary paths for IDA, the fact that we changed P not to have ε-transitions, and the fact that the filter transducer will not allow paths from (p, p, q) to (p, q, q) to only stay at the same 3rd component q, will ensure that a path from (p, p, q) to (p, q, q) never involves reading only ε. $\square$

Next we generalize more results of Mohri, for the case where we allow ε-loops.

Lemma 1. *Let A be an NFA (i.e. no states are memoized). Then A has:*

  i) Exponential ambiguity if and only it has EDA;
 ii) Infinite ambiguity if and only if it has IDA; and
iii) Ambiguity of degree at least d, with $d \geq 1$, if and only if it has IDA_d.

Proof. In [7], it is shown that the three conditions EDA, IDA and IDA_d are necessary and sufficient if we do not have ε-loops. Consider the NFA $A = (Q, \Sigma, \delta, q_0, F)$, having ε-loops. We show how to extend Mohri's results to A. We construct an NFA $A_\varepsilon = (Q_\varepsilon, \Sigma, \delta_\varepsilon, (q_0, \varnothing), F_\varepsilon)$ from A, with no ε-loops, satisfying EDA, IDA or IDA_d if an only A does, and also having ambiguity equal to that of A. This will imply that the ambiguity results of Mohri are applicable even for NFA with ε-loops. We let $Q_\varepsilon = \{(p, S) \mid S \in \mathcal{P}(Q \times Q)\}$, $\delta_\varepsilon((p, S), a) = \{(q, \varnothing) \mid q \in \delta(p, a)\}$ if $a \in \Sigma$, and $\delta_\varepsilon((p, S), \varepsilon) = \{(q, S \cup \{(p, q)\}) \mid q \in \delta(p, \varepsilon), (p, q) \notin S\}$, and $F_\varepsilon = \{(p, S) \in Q_\varepsilon \mid p \in F\}$. Note that the definition of $\delta_\varepsilon((p, S), \varepsilon)$ implies A_ε has no ε-loops, and we can apply Mohri's results to A_ε and then obtained the desired ambiguity results for A. $\square$

Theorem 2. *Let A be an mNFA. Then A has:*

i) Exponential prefix ambiguity if and only A has EDA;
ii) Prefix ambiguity of degree d, with $d \geq 1$, if and only if A has IDA_d.

Proof. It is clear that EDA and IDA_d implies exponential prefix ambiguity and prefix ambiguity of degree d respectively.

Conversely, assume A has exponential (or polynomial of degree d) ambiguity and let $A = (\mathcal{M}, Q, \Sigma, \delta, q_0, F)$. Recall, A^p denotes the mNFA obtained by changing the set of final states of A to $\{p\}$. We make the simplifying assumption that no state in A has outgoing transitions both on ε and some symbols from Σ (although it is easy to extend our argument to the general case), which is for example the case for mNFAs of the form $\mathcal{T}(E)$. For $p \in Q$, let $I(p) = \{q \in Q \mid \delta(q, a) = p$ for some $a \in \Sigma\}$, and $I'(p) = \{q \in Q \mid \delta(q, \varepsilon) = p\}$. Note for $p \in Q$ we have $a_{A^p}(n) \leq \sum_{q \in I(p)} a_{A^q}(n-1) + \sum_{q \in I'(p)} a_{A^q}(n)$. Combining this inequality with Lemma 1 and the additional observations listed next, we obtain that a second loop at a state p reading the same word as the first, but containing a memoized state, will not cause exponential prefix ambiguity, and similar for IDA_d and loops at the q_i containing memoized states, and thus provide us with the desired result. Additional observations: (1) If $q \in \mathcal{M}$, then $a_{A^q}(n-1) = a_{A^q}(n) = 1$; (2) the mNFA A has exponential (polynomial of degree d) prefix ambiguity if and only if A^p has exponential (polynomial of degree d) ambiguity at some p (and not a higher degree of ambiguity at other states); (3) additional memoization can only decrease ambiguity; (4) memoizing a state in a loop at p for IDA or p_i for IDA_d (with p and p_i as in Definition 6), will not remove IDA or lower the degree of ambiguity. □

Example 4. Applying the previous theorem to the Thompson constructed mNFA for each m-regex given next, we obtain the following ambiguity. We have that $(a \mid a)^*$ is exponentially ambiguous, $\mapsto (a \mid a)^*$ is finitely prefix ambiguous (but not prefix unambiguous) and $(a \mid a)^* \hookleftarrow$ is unambiguous, but exponentially prefix ambiguous. Also, $(a^*)^*$ is exponentially ambiguous, $\mapsto (a^*)^*$ has ambiguity of degree 1 and $(\mapsto a^*)^*$ has finite ambiguity.

To wrap up this section, we consider relationships between ambiguity and prefix ambiguity, as well as relationships between (prefix) ambiguity of subexpressions of an m-regex and (prefix) ambiguity of the m-regex as a whole. Clearly, prefix ambiguity is an upper bound for ambiguity, and since all states are useful by assumption, Lemma 1 shows that for an NFA A, A has finite, polynomial of degree d or exponential prefix ambiguity, if and only if A has finite, polynomial of degree d or exponential ambiguity respectively. Also, Proposition 1 and Theorem 2 implies that we have the following prefix ambiguity relationships between an m-regex and its subexpressions. (1) If in the m-regex $G = (E \mid F)$, both E and F have (prefix) ambiguity of degree at most d and at least one of E or F has (prefix) ambiguity of degree d, then G has (prefix) ambiguity of degree d. A similar statement holds for exponential (prefix) ambiguity. (2) The m-regex E^* has exponential ambiguity if and only if E is ambiguous. (3) The m-regex $E \cdot F$

has exponential prefix ambiguity if at least one of E or F has exponential prefix ambiguity, but E and F could both be unambiguous while $E \cdot F$ has infinite ambiguity.

4 Hardness Results

In this section we prove that it is computationally difficult to find a minimal set of states to memoize in an NFA A to obtain an mNFA with finite prefix ambiguity.

Definition 7. *A directed graph $G = (V, E)$ and a natural number $k \in \mathbb{N}$ is an instance of the* FEEDBACK VERTEX SET *problem if and only if there exists some $V' \subseteq V$ such that $|V'| \leq k$ and every directed cycle in G contains at least one vertex from V'.*

That is, (G, k) is in FEEDBACK VERTEX SET if is possible to break all cycles by the removal at most k vertices.

Theorem 3 (see [10]). *Deciding* FEEDBACK VERTEX SET *is NP-complete.*

We now show by reduction from FEEDBACK VERTEX SET, that given an NFA $A = (Q, \Sigma, q_0, \delta, F)$, it is NP-hard to find some *smallest* $\mathcal{M} \subseteq Q$ such that $A_\mathcal{M} = (\mathcal{M}, Q, \Sigma, q_0, \delta, F)$ has finite prefix ambiguity, or equivalently, by Theorem 2, that $A_\mathcal{M}$ does not have IDA. Next we state this as a decision problem.

Definition 8. *For an NFA $A = (Q, \Sigma, q_0, \delta, F)$ and $k \in \mathbb{N}$, (A, k) is an instance of the* SMALL mNFA MEMOIZATION *problem if and only if there exists some $\mathcal{M} \subseteq Q$, with $|\mathcal{M}| \leq k$, such that the mNFA $A_\mathcal{M} = (\mathcal{M}, Q, \Sigma, q_0, \delta, F)$ has finite prefix ambiguity (or equivalently, $A_\mathcal{M}$ does not have IDA).*

Lemma 2. SMALL mNFA MEMOIZATION *is NP-hard.*

Proof. We show this by reduction from FEEDBACK VERTEX SET. Let $G = (V, E)$ be a directed graph and $k \in \mathbb{N}$. We construct an NFA $A^G_\mathcal{M}$, such that $(A^G_\mathcal{M}, |\mathcal{M}|)$, with $|\mathcal{M}| \leq k$, is an instance of SMALL mNFA MEMOIZATION if and only if (G, k) is an instance of the VERTEX FEEDBACK SET problem by the following procedure.

Let $A^G = (Q, \{a\}, q_0, \delta, \{q_f\})$, with $Q = V \cup \{q_0, q_f\}$) (q_0, q_f are new states not in V), and in δ we have the transitions: (1) $v' \in \delta(v, a)$ for $(v, v') \in E$; (2) $q_0, v \in \delta(q_0, a)$ for $v \in V$; (3) $q_f \in \delta(v, a)$ for $v \in V$. That is, we turn G into an NFA by making each edge a transition reading a single 'a', we add an initial state with a self-loop on 'a', from which every vertex in G is reachable on a single 'a', and a final state reachable from any vertex in G on an a-transition. That is, G gets turned into an NFA by having every edge read 'a', adding a new initial and final state, having every "state" in G reachable from the initial state on 'a', and having an a-transition from each "state" in G to the final state.

We leave the k the same in the reduction. Assume there is a $V' \subseteq V$, with $|V'| \le k$, such that G contains no cycles when all vertices in V' are removed. Choose $\mathcal{M} = V'$, and note that the mNFA $A_{\mathcal{M}}^G = (\mathcal{M}, Q, \{a\}, q_0, \delta, \{q_f\})$ cannot have IDA, as it contains only a single cycle without a state from $\mathcal{M}$ (the one on q_0).

Conversely, assume we have $\mathcal{M} \subseteq Q$, $|\mathcal{M}| = k$, that removes IDA from A, i.e. $A_{\mathcal{M}}^G$ does not have IDA. Given the definition of IDA, we may assume that both q_0 and q_f are not in $\mathcal{M}$. But then (G, k), with G being the subgraph

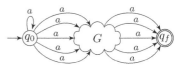

obtained from A^G by removing q_0 and q_f, is in FEEDBACK VERTEX SET, as any memoization-free cycle in that subautomaton in combination with the cycle on q_0 would cause IDA in A^G.   □

Finally, membership in NP is established by algorithm from Theorem 1.

Theorem 4. SMALL MNFA MEMOIZATION *is NP-complete.*

Proof. This combines Lemma 2 and Theorem 1. The latter establishes membership in NP since we can nondeterministically guess a certificate $\mathcal{M}$ and verify it in polynomial time by the algorithm presented in the proof of Theorem 1.   □

5   Memoization Schemes

The NP-hardness of finding minimal memoizations raises interest in both heuristics and focusing on NFAs of the form $\mathcal{T}(E)$, for selecting a small subset of states, to conserve space used by the matcher as much as possible. In [1], Davis proposed two such *selective memoization schemes.* The first memoizes all states with in-degree at least two, and the second memoizes all states which are "cycle ancestors", which on an m-regex E corresponds to memoizing every subexpression F^* as $(\mapsto F)^*$. We call this the *Closure Node* scheme, denoting the m-regex obtained by $CN(E)$, and observing that Theorem 2 implies $\mathcal{T}(CN(E))$ has finite prefix ambiguity.

On an m-regex E, the scheme of memoizing all states with in-degree at least two, denoted as $IN(E)$, memoizes each subexpression F^* as $\mapsto F^* \hookleftarrow$, and each subexpression $(F \mid G)$ as $(F \mid G) \hookleftarrow$, and thus (possibly) add additional memoization operators when compared to $CN(E)$. From the definition of ambiguity, it follows that $\mathcal{T}(IN(E))$ is unambiguous at all states.

We propose the *Infinite Ambiguity Removal* (IAR) memoization scheme, which for an m-regex E takes $CN(E)$ and removes precisely those memoization operators corresponding to memoizing states in $\mathcal{T}(E)$, that is not a state p for EDA, or a state q for IDA, with p and q as in Definition 6. This can be done with a modification to the algorithm outlined in the proof of Theorem 1 (with a formal discussion of the algorithm and its complexity left as future work). From Theorem 2, we have that $IAR(E)$ has finite prefix ambiguity. We leave it as future work to determine if this produces a memoization of minimal size, conjecturing this to be the case. Note that this would *not* contradict Theorem 4 as the hardness reduction relies on the construction of a general mNFA, where the Thompson automaton $\mathcal{T}(E)$ is of a restricted form.

To implement IAR, we extended the implementation to identify IDA and EDA in $\mathcal{T}(E)$, as discussed in [4]. This implementation was evaluated on implementation was evaluated on the RegExLib repository [11], and (ii) the Davis polyglot regex corpus [12], a dataset containing more than 500,000 regexes extracted from a large sample of software projects covering over eight different major programming languages. For both RegExLib and the polyglot corpus, more than 70% of regexes could be analysed based on regex features supported by our implementation, and for 12% of the RegExLib repository, the states to be memoized in order to determine IAR(E), took more than 1 second to compute, while for the polyglot corpus, only 3% of the regexes took in excess of 1 s.

Example 5. For $E = (a^* | a^*)^*$, we have that CN(E), IN(E) and IAR(E) are given by $\mapsto(\mapsto a^* | \mapsto a^*)^*$, $\mapsto((\mapsto a^* \hookleftarrow | \mapsto a^* \hookleftarrow) \hookleftarrow)^* \hookleftarrow$ and $\mapsto(a^* | a^*)^*$ respectively, but for $E' = a^* b^*$, CN(E') equals $(\mapsto a^*)(\mapsto b^*)$, whereas IAR($E'$) = E' (recall, $\mapsto$ has higher priority than Kleene star). For $F_k = (a|a)\{1,k\}$, with $k \in \mathbb{N}$, prefix ambiguity is 2^k for strings a^n, $n \geq k$, but IN(F_k) = $((a|a)\hookleftarrow)\{1,k\}$ has prefix ambiguity at most 2, and IN is the only memoization scheme introduced reducing ambiguity when applied to F_k.

6   Future Work

We are working on developing memoization schemes in which we combine the search for where IDA is present in $\mathcal{T}(E)$ (for a regex E), with the use of the atomic operator [5]. These schemes will be evaluated on repositories of regexes typically used by developers. It could be argued that the required subexpressions to be memoized or to which the atomic operator should be applied, could be computed offline, and then developers are allowed to specify memoization information in m-regexes (in addition to where to apply the atomic operator), but this will require matching engines to support m-regexes. Another option could be to let users specify which memoization scheme they would like to use, from a list of well-studied memoization schemes, based on memory and matching time requirements. An investigation should be done into the interplay between memoization and various regexes extensions, as was already started for lookaheads and backreferences in [1]. Formalizing the discussion on memoized prioritized NFAs, initiated near the end of Sect. 2, and confirming that the hardness result of Sect. 4 do not apply to NFAs of the form $\mathcal{T}(E)$, are natural next steps.

References

1. Davis, J.C., Servant, F., Lee, D.: Using selective memoization to defeat regular expression denial of service (ReDoS). In: 2021 IEEE Symposium on Security and Privacy (SP), Los Alamitos, CA, USA, May 2021, pp. 543–559. IEEE Computer Society (2021)

2. James, D.: On the impact and defeat of regular expression denial of service. Ph.D. thesis, Virginia Polytechnic Institute and State University (2020)

3. Spencer, H.: A Regular-Expression Matcher, pp. 35–71. Academic Press Professional Inc., USA (1994)

4. Weideman, N., van der Merwe, B., Berglund, M., Watson, B.: Analyzing matching time behavior of backtracking regular expression matchers by using ambiguity of NFA. In: Han, Y.-S., Salomaa, K. (eds.) CIAA 2016. LNCS, vol. 9705, pp. 322–334. Springer, Cham (2016). https://doi.org/10.1007/978-3-319-40946-7_27

5. Berglund, M., van der Merwe, B., Watson, B., Weideman, N.: On the semantics of atomic subgroups in practical regular expressions. In: Carayol, A., Nicaud, C. (eds.) CIAA 2017. LNCS, vol. 10329, pp. 14–26. Springer, Cham (2017). https://doi.org/10.1007/978-3-319-60134-2_2

6. Weber, A., Seidl, H.: On the degree of ambiguity of finite automata. Theoret. Comput. Sci. **88**(2), 325–349 (1991)

7. Allauzen, C., Mohri, M., Rastogi, A.: General algorithms for testing the ambiguity of finite automata. In: Ito, M., Toyama, M. (eds.) DLT 2008. LNCS, vol. 5257, pp. 108–120. Springer, Heidelberg (2008). https://doi.org/10.1007/978-3-540-85780-8_8

8. Brüggemann-Klein, A.: Regular expressions into finite automata. Theor. Comput. Sci. **120**(2), 197–213 (1993)

9. Thompson, K.: Programming techniques: regular expression search algorithm. Commun. ACM **11**(6), 419–422 (1968)

10. Karp, R.M.: Reducibility among combinatorial problems. In: Miller, R., Thatcher, J. (eds.) Complexity of Computer Computations, pp. 85–103. Plenum Press (1972)

11. Regular expression library. https://regexlib.com/. Accessed 05 Mar 2021

12. Davis, J.C., Michael IV, L.G., Coghlan, C.A., Servant, F., Lee, D.: Why aren't regular expressions a Lingua Franca? An empirical study on the re-use and portability of regular expressions. In: Proceedings of the 2019 27th ACM Joint Meeting on European Software Engineering Conference and Symposium on the Foundations of Software Engineering, ESEC/FSE 2019, pp. 443–454 (2019)

The Commutative Closure of Shuffle Languages over Group Languages is Regular

Stefan Hoffmann[✉]

Informatikwissenschaften, FB IV, Universität Trier, Universitätsring 15,
54296 Trier, Germany
hoffmanns@informatik.uni-trier.de

Abstract. We show that the commutative closure combined with the iterated shuffle is a regularity-preserving operation on group languages. In particular, for commutative group languages, the iterated shuffle is a regularity-preserving operation. We also give bounds for the size of minimal recognizing automata. Then, we use this result to deduce that the commutative closure of any shuffle language over group languages, i.e., a language given by a shuffle expression, i.e., expressions involving shuffle, iterated shuffle, concatenation, Kleene star and union in any order, starting with the group languages, always yields a regular language.

Keywords: Commutative closure · Group language · Permutation automaton · Shuffle expression · Shuffle · Iterated shuffle

1 Introduction

Having applications in regular model checking [1,7], or arising naturally in the theory of traces [8,35], one model for parallelism, the (partial) commutative closure has been extensively studied [12–14,16,18,20,28,30,34].

In [16], the somewhat informal notion of a *robust class* was introduced, meaning roughly a class[1] closed under some of the usual operations on languages, such as Boolean operations, product, star, shuffle, morphism, inverses of morphisms, residuals, etc. Motivated by two guiding problems formulated in [16], we formulate the following slightly altered, but related problems:

Problem 1. *When is the closure of a language under [partial] commutation regular?*

Problem 2. *Are there any robust classes for some common operations such that the commutative closure is (effectively) regular?*

---

[1] We relax the condition from [15] that it must be a class of regular languages. However, some mechanism to represent the languages from the class should be available.

© Springer Nature Switzerland AG 2021
S. Maneth (Ed.): CIAA 2021, LNCS 12803, pp. 53–64, 2021.
https://doi.org/10.1007/978-3-030-79121-6_5

By effectively regular, we mean the stipulation that an automaton of the result of the commutation operation is computable from a representational scheme for the language class at hand.

Here, we will investigate the commutation operation on the closure of the class (or variety thereof) of group languages under union, shuffle, iterated shuffle, concatenation and Kleene star. For the class of finite languages, this closure, called the class of *shuffle languages*, is definable by so called *shuffle expressions* [9, 23–26, 36]. This is also true in our case, but the atomic expressions are interpreted not as finite languages, but as group languages. In this sense, we use the term shuffle expressions, or shuffle language, in a wider sense, by allowing different atomic languages. It will turn out that the commutation operation yields a regular language on this class of languages, and it is indeed effectively regular. However, I do not know if the languages class itself consists only of regular languages.

The shuffle and iterated shuffle have been introduced and studied to understand the semantics of parallel programs. This was undertaken, as it appears to be, independently by Campbell and Habermann [4], by Mazurkiewicz [29] and by Shaw [36]. They introduced *flow expressions*, which allow for sequential operators (catenation and iterated catenation) as well as for parallel operators (shuffle and iterated shuffle). These operations have been studied extensively, see for example [9, 23–25].

The shuffle operation as a binary operation, but not the iterated shuffle, is regularity preserving on all regular languages. The size of recognizing automata was investigated in [2, 3, 5, 6, 17, 19].

2   Preliminaries and Definitions

By Σ we denote a finite set of symbols, i.e., an *alphabet*. By Σ^* we denote the set of all words with the concatenation operation. The *empty word*, i.e., the word of length zero, is denoted by ε. If $u \in \Sigma$, by $|u|$ we denote the length of u, and if $a \in \Sigma$, by $|u|_a$ we denote the number of times the letter a appears in u. A language is a subset $L \subseteq \Sigma^*$. For a language $L \subseteq \Sigma^*$, we set $L^+ = \{u_1 \cdots u_n \mid \{u_1, \ldots, u_n\} \subseteq L, n > 0\}$ and $L^* = L^+ \cup \{\varepsilon\}$. By $\mathbb{N}_0$, we denote the natural numbers with zero.

A finite (complete and deterministic[2]) *automaton* $\mathcal{A} = (\Sigma, Q, \delta, q_0, F)$ over Σ consists of a finite state set Q, a totally defined transition function $\delta : Q \times \Sigma \to Q$, start state $q_0 \in Q$ and final state set $F \subseteq Q$. The transition function could be extended to words in the usual way by setting, for $u \in \Sigma^*$, $a \in \Sigma$ and $q \in Q$, $\hat{\delta}(q, ua) = \delta(\hat{\delta}(q, u), a)$ and $\hat{\delta}(q, \varepsilon) = q$. In the following, we will drop the distinction with δ and will denote this extension also by $\delta : Q \times \Sigma^* \to Q$. The language *recognized*, or *accepted*, by $\mathcal{A}$ is $L(\mathcal{A}) = \{u \in \Sigma^* \mid \delta(q_0, u) \in F\}$.

A *permutation automaton* is an automaton such that for each letter $a \in \Sigma$, the function $\delta_a : Q \to Q$ given by $\delta_a(q) = \delta(q, a)$ for $q \in Q$ is bijective. We also

---

[2] Here, only complete and deterministic automata are used, hence just called automata for short.

say that the letter a permutes the state set. For a given permutation automaton $\mathcal{A} = (\Sigma, Q, \delta, q_0, F)$ and $a \in \Sigma$, the *order of the letter a in $\mathcal{A}$* is the smallest number $n > 0$ such that $\delta(q, a^n) = q$ for all $q \in Q$. This equals the order of the letter viewed as a permutation on Q. The maximal order of any permutation is given by Landau's function, which has growth rate $O(\exp(\sqrt{n \log n}))$ [11,27]. A language $L \subseteq \Sigma^*$ is a *group language*, if there exists a permutation automaton $\mathcal{A}$ such that $L = L(\mathcal{A})$. By $\mathcal{G}$ we denote the class of group languages. This class could be also seen as a variety [32,33].

We will also use *regular expressions* occasionally, for the definition of them, and also for a more detailed treatment of the above notions, we refer to any textbook on formal language theory or theoretical computer science, for example [21].

Let $\Sigma = \{a_1, \ldots, a_k\}$ be the alphabet. The map $\psi : \Sigma^* \to \mathbb{N}_0^k$ given by $\psi(w) = (|w|_{a_1}, \ldots, |w|_{a_k})$ is called the *Parikh morphism* [31]. If $L \subseteq \Sigma^*$, we set $\psi(L) = \{\psi(w) \mid w \in L\}$. For a given word $w \in \Sigma^*$, we define $\operatorname{perm}(w) := \{u \in \Sigma^* : \psi(u) = \psi(w)\}$. If $L \subseteq \Sigma^*$, then the *commutative* (or *permutational*) *closure* is $\operatorname{perm}(L) := \bigcup_{w \in L} \operatorname{perm}(w)$. A language is called *commutative*, if $\operatorname{perm}(L) = L$.

Definition 1. *The* shuffle operation, *denoted by* ⧢, *is defined by*

$$u \shuffle v = \{w \in \Sigma^* \mid w = x_1 y_1 x_2 y_2 \cdots x_n y_n \text{ for some words}$$

$$x_1, \ldots, x_n, y_1, \ldots, y_n \in \Sigma^* \text{ such that } u = x_1 x_2 \cdots x_n \text{ and } v = y_1 y_2 \cdots y_n\},$$

for $u, v \in \Sigma^*$ and $L_1 \shuffle L_2 := \bigcup_{x \in L_1, y \in L_2} (x \shuffle y)$ for $L_1, L_2 \subseteq \Sigma^*$.

In writing formulas without brackets, we suppose that the shuffle operation binds stronger than the set operations, and the concatenation operator has the strongest binding.

If $L_1, \ldots, L_n \subseteq \Sigma^*$, we set $\shuffle_{i=1}^n L_i = L_1 \shuffle \ldots \shuffle L_n$. The *iterated shuffle* of $L \subseteq \Sigma^*$ is $L^{\shuffle,*} = \bigcup_{n \geqslant 0} \shuffle_{i=1}^n L$.

Theorem 2 (Fernau et al. [9]). *Let $U, V, W \subseteq \Sigma^*$. Then,*

1. $U \shuffle V = V \shuffle U$ *(commutative law);*
2. $(U \shuffle V) \shuffle W = U \shuffle (V \shuffle W)$ *(associative law);*
3. $U \shuffle (V \cup W) = (U \shuffle V) \cup (U \shuffle W)$ *(distributive over union);*
4. $(U^{\shuffle,*})^{\shuffle,*} = U^{\shuffle,*}$;
5. $(U \cup V)^{\shuffle,*} = U^{\shuffle,*} \shuffle V^{\shuffle,*}$;
6. $(U \shuffle V^{\shuffle,*})^{\shuffle,*} = (U \shuffle (U \cup V)^{\shuffle,*}) \cup \{\varepsilon\}$.

The next result is taken from [9] and gives equations like $\operatorname{perm}(UV) = \operatorname{perm}(U) \shuffle \operatorname{perm}(V)$ or $\operatorname{perm}(U^*) = \operatorname{perm}(U)^{\shuffle,*}$ for $U, V \subseteq \Sigma^*$. A *semiring* is an algebraic structure $(S, +, \cdot, 0, 1)$ such that $(S, +, 0)$ forms a commutative monoid, $(S, \cdot, 1)$ is a monoid and we have $a \cdot (b+c) = a \cdot b + a \cdot c$, $(b+c) \cdot a = b \cdot a + c \cdot a$ and $0 \cdot a = a \cdot 0 = 0$.

Theorem 3 (Fernau et al. [9]). $\operatorname{perm} : \mathcal{P}(\Sigma^*) \to \mathcal{P}(\Sigma^*)$ *is a semiring morphism from the semiring $(\mathcal{P}(\Sigma^*), \cup, \cdot, \varnothing, \{\varepsilon\})$, that also respects the iterated catenation resp. iterated shuffle operation, to the semiring $(\mathcal{P}(\Sigma^*), \cup, \shuffle, \varnothing, \{\varepsilon\})$.*

As $\psi(U \shuffle V) = \psi(UV)$ and $\psi(U^*) = \psi(U^{\shuffle,*})$, we also find the next result.

Theorem 4. perm $: \mathcal{P}(\Sigma^*) \rightarrow \mathcal{P}(\Sigma^*)$ *is a semiring morphism from the semiring* $(\mathcal{P}(\Sigma^*), \cup, \shuffle, \varnothing, \{\varepsilon\})$ *to the semiring* $(\mathcal{P}(\Sigma^*), \cup, \shuffle, \varnothing, \{\varepsilon\})$ *that also respects the iterated shuffle operation.*

In [16] it was shown that the commutative closure is regularity-preserving on $\mathcal{G}$ using combinatorial arguments, and in [20] an automaton was constructed, yielding explicit bounds for the number of states needed in any recognizing automaton.

Theorem 5 ([20]])**.** *Let* $\Sigma = \{a_1, \ldots, a_k\}$ *and* $\mathcal{A} = (\Sigma, Q, \delta, q_0, F)$ *be a permutation automaton. Then* $\mathrm{perm}(L(\mathcal{A}))$ *is recognizable by an automaton with at most* $\left(|Q|^k \prod_{i=1}^k L_i\right)$ *many states, where* L_i *for* $i \in \{1, \ldots, k\}$ *denotes the order of* a_i. *Furthermore, the recognizing automaton is computable.*

3 Shuffle Languages over Arbitrary Language Classes

Here, we introduce shuffle languages over arbitrary language classes and proof a normal form result.

Definition 6. *Let* $\mathcal{L}$ *be a class of languages.*

1. $\mathcal{SE}(\mathcal{L})$ *is the closure of* $\mathcal{L}$ *under shuffle, iterated shuffle, union, concatenation and Kleene star.*
2. $Shuf(\mathcal{L})$ *is the closure of* $\mathcal{L}$ *under shuffle, iterated shuffle and union.*

For $\mathcal{L}_{Alp} = \{\varnothing, \{\varepsilon\}\} \cup \{\{a\} \mid a \in \Sigma$ for some alphabet $\Sigma\}$ and $\mathcal{L}_{Fin} = \{L \mid L \subseteq \Sigma^*$ for some alphabet and L is finite $\}$ the resulting closures were investigated in [9,23–25]. Note that $\mathcal{SE}(\mathcal{L}_{Alp}) = \mathcal{SE}(\mathcal{L}_{Fin})$. By Theorem 3, we can compute a shuffle expression over $\mathcal{L}_{Alp}$ for the commutative closure of any regular language by rewriting a regular expression and vice versa. Hence, the class $Shuf(\mathcal{L}_{Alp})$ equals the commutative closure of all regular languages. So, $Shuf(\mathcal{L}_{Alp}) \neq Shuf(\mathcal{L}_{Fin})$.

Proposition 7. *Let* $L \in Shuf(\mathcal{L})$. *Then,* L *is a finite union of languages of the form*

$$L_1 \shuffle \ldots \shuffle L_k \shuffle L_{k+1}^{\shuffle,*} \shuffle \ldots \shuffle L_n^{\shuffle,*}$$

with $1 \leq k \leq n$ *and* $L_i \in \mathcal{L}$ *for* $i \in \{1, \ldots, n\}$ *and this expression is computable.*

Proof. Theorem 2 provides an inductive proof of Proposition 7. Note that a similar statement has been shown in [23, Theorem 3.1] for $Shuf(\mathcal{L}_{Fin})$. However, as we do not assume that $\mathcal{L}$ is closed under shuffle or union, we only get the form as stated. □

Remark 1. By Theorem 2, we can write the languages in Proposition 7 also in the form $L_1 \shuffle \ldots \shuffle L_k \shuffle (L_{k+1} \cup \ldots \cup L_n)^{\shuffle,*}$. So, if $\mathcal{L}$ is closed under union, which is the case for languages from $\mathcal{G}$ over a common alphabet, we can write the languages in $Shuf(\mathcal{L})$ as a finite union of languages of the form $L_1 \shuffle \ldots \shuffle L_{n-1} \shuffle L_n^{\shuffle,*}$ with $L_1, \ldots, L_n \in \mathcal{L}$.

Lastly, with Theorem 3 and Theorem 4, we show that up to permutational equivalence $\mathcal{SE}(\mathcal{L})$ and $Shuf(\mathcal{L})$ give the same languages.

Proposition 8. *Let $\mathcal{L}$ be any class of languages. Suppose $L \in \mathcal{SE}(\mathcal{L})$. Then, we can compute $L' \in Shuf(L)$ such that* $\mathrm{perm}(L) = \mathrm{perm}(L')$.

Proof. By Theorem 3 and Theorem 4, we have, for $U, V \subseteq \Sigma^*$, $\mathrm{perm}(U \shuffle V) = \mathrm{perm}(U) \shuffle \mathrm{perm}(V) = \mathrm{perm}(U \cdot V)$ and $\mathrm{perm}(U^{\shuffle,*}) = \mathrm{perm}(U)^{\shuffle,*} = \mathrm{perm}(U^*)$. So, inductively, for $L \in \mathcal{SE}(\mathcal{G})$, by replacing every concatenation with the shuffle and every Kleene star with the iterated shuffle, we find $L' \in Shuf(\mathcal{G})$ such that $\mathrm{perm}(L) = \mathrm{perm}(L')$. □

4   The Commutative Closure on $\mathcal{SE}(\mathcal{G})$

By Proposition 8, the commutative closure on $\mathcal{SE}(\mathcal{L})$ for any language class $\mathcal{L}$ equals the commutative closure of $Shuf(\mathcal{L})$. Theorem 9 of this section, stating that the commutative closure combined with the iterated shuffle is regular, is the main ingredient in our proof that the commutative closure is regularity-preserving on $\mathcal{SE}(\mathcal{G})$ and the most demanding result in this work.

Note that, in general, this combined operation does not preserves regularity, as shown by $\mathrm{perm}(\{ab\})^{\shuffle,*} = \{w \in \{a,b\}^* \mid |w|_a = |w|_b\}$.

Theorem 9. *Let $\Sigma = \{a_1, \ldots, a_k\}$ and $\mathcal{A} = (\Sigma, Q, \delta, q_0, F)$ be a permutation automaton. Then*

$$\mathrm{perm}(L(\mathcal{A})^{\shuffle,*})$$

is recognizable by an automaton with at most $\left(|Q|^k \prod_{j=1}^{k} L_j \right) + 1$ many states, where L_j for $j \in \{1, \ldots, k\}$ denotes the order of a_j, and this automaton is effectively computable.

Proof (sketch). The method of proof, called *state label method*, is an extension of the one used in [20], which also includes a detailed motivation and intuition of this method.

In what follows, we will first give an intuitive outline of the method, geared toward our intended extension, of how to use it to recognize the commutative closure of a regular language. Then, we will show how to modify it to show our statement at hand. We will only sketch the method, and will leave out some details for the sake of the bigger picture.

The method consists in labeling the points of $\mathbb{N}_0^{|\Sigma|}$ with the states of a given automaton that are reachable from the start state by all words whose Parikh image equals the point under consideration.

As it turns out, a word is in the commutative closure if and only if it ends in a state labeled by a set which contains at least one final state.

Very roughly, the resulting labeling of $\mathbb{N}_0^{|\Sigma|}$ could be thought of as a more refined version of the Parikh map for regular languages, and in some sense as a blend between the well-known powerset construction, as we label with subsets of states, and the Parikh map, as we not only indicate for each point if there is a word in the language or not, but additionally store all states we could reach by words whose Parikh image equals the point in question.

More specifically, let $\mathcal{A} = (\Sigma, Q, \delta, q_0, F)$ be an automaton. In [20], the point $p \in \mathbb{N}_0^{|\Sigma|}$ was labeled by the set

$$S_p = \{\delta(q_0, u) \mid \psi(u) = p\}$$

and the following holds true: $v \in \mathrm{perm}(L(\mathcal{A})) \Leftrightarrow S_{\psi(v)} \cap F \neq \emptyset$.

Then, along any line parallel to the axis, which corresponds to reading in a single fixed letter, by finiteness, the state labels are ultimately periodic. However, for each such line, the onset of the period and the period itself may change. For example, take the automaton with state set $Q = \{q_0, q_1, q_2\}$ over $\Sigma = \{a, b\}$ and transition function, for $q \in Q$ and $x \in \Sigma$,

$$\delta(q, x) = \begin{cases} q_1 \text{ if } q = q_0, x = a; \\ q_0 \text{ if } q = q_1, x = b; \\ q_2 \text{ otherwise.} \end{cases}$$

Then, $L(\mathcal{A}) = (ab)^*$ and, for $p = (p_a, p_b) \in \mathbb{N}_0^2$,

$$S_p = \begin{cases} \{q_0, q_2\} \text{ if } p_a = p_b; \\ \{q_1, q_2\} \text{ if } p_a = p_b + 1; \\ \{q_2\} \quad \text{otherwise.} \end{cases}$$

Let $c \in \mathbb{N}_0$. Then, along the lines $\{(p_a, p_b) \in \mathbb{N}_0^2 \mid p_a = c\}$, we have $S_{(c, c+2)} = S_{(c, c+1)}$ and the point $(c, c+1)$ is the earliest onset after which the state labeling S_p gets periodic on this line.

However, if, for any line parallel to the axis, we can bound the onset of the period and the period itself *uniformly*, i.e., independently of the line we are considering, then the commutative closure is regular, and moreover we can construct a recognizing automaton with these uniform bounds.

This was shown in [20] and it was shown that for group languages, we have such uniform bounds.

Note that in our example, we do not have such a uniform bound, as the onset, for example, for the lines going in the direction $(0, 1)$ starting at $(c, 0)$ (i.e. reading in the letter b) was $c + 1$, i.e., it grows and is not uniformly bounded. In fact, $\mathrm{perm}((ab)^*) = \{u \in \{a, b\}^* : |u|_a = |u|_b\}$ is not regular.

Up to now, the method only works for the commutative closure. So, let us now describe how to modify it such that we get an automaton for the iterated shuffle of the commutative closure of a given automaton.

First, recall that, by Theorem 3, we have

$$\mathrm{perm}(L(\mathcal{A}))^{\sqcup\!\sqcup,*} = \mathrm{perm}(L(\mathcal{A})^*).$$

The usual construction for the Kleene star associates a final state with the start state, and this is in some sense what we are doing now. More formally, in the state labeling, we add the start state each time we read a final state, i.e., we have another labeling which we describe next.

Let $\Sigma = \{a_1, \ldots, a_k\}$ and $e_i = \psi(a_i) = (0, \ldots, 0, 1, 0, \ldots, 0) \in \mathbb{N}_0^k$ be the vector with 1 precisely at the i-th position and zero everywhere else. If $\mathcal{A} = (\Sigma, Q, \delta, q_0, F)$ is an automaton, set

$$T_{(0,\ldots,0)} = \{q_0\} \quad \text{and} \quad T_p = \bigcup_{\exists i \in \{1, \ldots k\}: p = q + e_i} \delta(S_q^+, a_i) \text{ for } p \neq (0, \ldots, 0),$$

where

$$S_p^+ = \begin{cases} T_p \cup \{q_0\} & \text{if } T_p \cap F \neq \emptyset; \\ T_p & \text{if } T_p \cap F = \emptyset. \end{cases}$$

Then, $v \in \mathrm{perm}(L(\mathcal{A})^*) \Leftrightarrow S_p^+ \cap F \neq \emptyset$ or $v = \varepsilon$.

Note the extra condition that checks for the empty word. This is a technicality, that surely could be omitted if $q_0 \in F$, but not in the general case. Please see Fig. 1 for a visual explanation in the case of a binary alphabet.

$$\begin{array}{ccc}
\vdots & \vdots & \\
b\uparrow & b\uparrow & \\
S_{(p_a-1,p_b+1)}^+ \xrightarrow{a} S_{(p_a,p_b+1)}^+ \xrightarrow{a} \cdots \\
b\uparrow & b\uparrow & \\
S_{(p_a-1,p_b)}^+ \xrightarrow{a} S_{(p_a,p_b)}^+ \xrightarrow{a} \cdots
\end{array}$$

$$T_{(p_a,p_b+1)} = \delta(S_{(p_a-1,p_b+1)}^+, a) \cup \delta(S_{(p_a,p_b)}^+, b) \tag{1}$$

$$S_{(p_a,p_b+1)}^+ = \begin{cases} T_{(p_a,p_b+1)} \cup \{s_0\} & \text{if } T_{(p_a,p_b+1)} \cap F \neq \emptyset; \\ T_{(p_a,p_b+1)} & \text{otherwise,} \end{cases} \tag{2}$$

Fig. 1. Illustration of how state labels are updated for the iterated shuffle if new input symbols are read with $\Sigma = \{a, b\}$. For the state label $S_{(p_a,p_b)}$, after reading the letter b, we will end up at $S_{(p_a,p_b+1)}$ and the state label is updated according to Equation (1) and Equation (2). Seen from the state label $S_{(p_a-1,p_b)}$, we account for both paths given by the words ab and ba when ending at $(p_a, p_b + 1)$, hence the union in the definition of $T_{(p_a,p_b+1)}$.

Finally, the same sufficient condition of regularity in terms of the new state labels S_p^+ could be derived as in the previous case, namely if they are uniformly bounded in the axis-parallel directions, then the commutative closure is regular.

Now, the sets T_p are defined by the actions of the letters a_i on previous state labels S_q^+. In a similar way to which it is done in [20], for a permutation automaton, we can show that we can find such uniform bounds.

Intuitively, the reason is that if we always permute the state labels, they cannot get smaller as we read in more letters. Hence, they have to grow and eventually get periodic. Also, we can show, as we only have cycles, that after a certain number of letters have been read, we have exploited all ways that these sets could grow, i.e., we know that after we have read a certain numbers of letters we must end up in a period, and this period could also be bounded uniformly (but of course, depending on $\mathcal{A}$).

To be a little more quantitative here, if L_i denotes the order of a_i, then, for each line going in the direction e_i, we can show that after at most $(|Q| - 1)L_j$ many steps we must enter the period, and the smallest period has to divide L_j. This in turn could be used to derive that an automaton with at most

$$\prod_{i=1}^{k}((|Q| - 1)L_j + L_j) = |Q|^k \prod_{i=1}^{k} L_j$$

many states could recognize $\mathrm{perm}(L(\mathcal{A})^+)$. Note that this statement is only valid for the state labeling S_p^+, and hence only applies to $\mathrm{perm}(L(\mathcal{A})^+)$. So, to recognize $\mathrm{perm}(L(\mathcal{A})^*)$, and incorporate the additional test for the empty word, we have to add one more state.

Actually, a full formal treatment, especially the steps mentioned in the previous paragraphs, is quite involved and incorporates a detailed construction of the recognizing automaton out of the state label method and a detailed analysis of the action of the permutational letters on the state set. I refer to [20] and to the extended version of this paper, which will appear in a special issue [18], for a treatment of these issues in the context of the mere commutative closure.

Lastly, note that the constructions are effective, as we only have to label a bounded number of grid points of $\mathbb{N}_0^k$, and the state labels are computable from the transition function of $\mathcal{A}$.   □

So, with Theorem 9, we can derive our next result.

Theorem 10. *Let $L \in \mathcal{S}huf(\mathcal{G})$. Then $\mathrm{perm}(L)$ is effectively regular.*

Proof. By Proposition 7, we only need to consider languages of the form $L_1 \shuffle \ldots \shuffle L_k \shuffle L_{k+1}^{\shuffle,*} \shuffle \ldots \shuffle L_n^{\shuffle,*}$ with $L_i \in \mathcal{G}$. By Theorem 4, $\mathrm{perm}(L_1 \shuffle \ldots \shuffle L_k \shuffle L_{k+1}^{\shuffle,*} \shuffle \ldots \shuffle L_n^{\shuffle,*})$ equals

$$\mathrm{perm}(L_1) \shuffle \ldots \shuffle \mathrm{perm}(L_k) \shuffle \mathrm{perm}(L_{k+1}^{\shuffle,*}) \shuffle \ldots \shuffle \mathrm{perm}(L_n^{\shuffle,*}).$$

The shuffle is regularity-preserving [3,5,22], where an automaton for it is computable. So, by Theorem 5 and Theorem 9 the above language is effectively regular, where again for the commutative closure of a group language an automaton is computable similarly as outlined at the end of the proof sketch for Theorem 5. Hence, $\mathrm{perm}(L)$ is effectively regular.   □

So, with Proposition 8 our next result follows.

Theorem 11. *Let $L \in \mathcal{SE}(\mathcal{G})$. Then $\mathrm{perm}(L)$ is effectively regular.*

5   Commutative Group Languages

By Theorem 9, we can deduce that for commutative group languages $L \subseteq \Sigma^*$, the iterated shuffle is a regularity-preserving operation. Also, for a commutative regular language in general, it is easy to see that for a minimal automaton $\mathcal{A} = (\Sigma, Q, \delta, q_0, F)$ we must have $\delta(q, ab) = \delta(q, ba)$ for any $q \in Q$ and $a, b \in \Sigma$ [10]. Furthermore, if $\mathcal{A} = (\Sigma, Q, \delta, q_0, F)$ is a minimal permutation automaton for a commutative language, then the order of each letter $a \in \Sigma$ equals the minimal $n > 0$ such that $\delta(q_0, a^n) = q_0$. For if $q \in Q$, then, by minimality, there exists $u \in \Sigma^*$ such that $\delta(q_0, u) = q$, which yields $\delta(q, a^n) = \delta(\delta(q_0, u), a^n) = \delta(q_0, a^n u) = \delta(\delta(q_0, a^n), u) = \delta(q_0, u) = q$. So, combining our observations, we get the next result.

Proposition 12. *Let $\Sigma = \{a_1, \ldots, a_k\}$ and $L \subseteq \Sigma^*$ be a commutative group language with minimal permutation automaton $\mathcal{A} = (\Sigma, Q, \delta, q_0, F)$ such that $L = L(\mathcal{A})$. Then, the iterated shuffle $L^{\sqcup,*}$ is regular and recognizable by an automaton with at most $(|Q|^k \prod_{i=1}^{k} p_i) + 1$ many states, where $p_i > 0$ is minimal such that $\delta(q_0, a_i^{p_i}) = q_0$ for $i \in \{1, \ldots, k\}$.*

6   The n-times Shuffle

We just note in passing that the method of proof of Theorem 9 could also be adapted to yield a bound for the size of a recognizing automaton of the n-times shuffle combined with the commutative closure on group languages that is better than applying the bounds from [3,5,20] individually.

Proposition 13. *Let $\mathcal{A}_i = (\Sigma, Q_i, \delta_i, q_i, F_i)$ for $i \in \{1, \ldots, n\}$ be n permutation automata. Then*

$$
sc(perm(L(\mathcal{A}_1)) \sqcup \ldots \sqcup perm(L(\mathcal{A}_n))) \leq \left(\sum_{i=1}^{n} Q_i \right)^k \prod_{j=1}^{k} lcm(L_j^{(1)}, \ldots, L_j^{(n)})
$$

where $L_j^{(i)}$ for $i \in \{1, \ldots, n\}$ and $j \in \{1, \ldots, k\}$ denotes the order of the letter a_j as a permutation on Q_i.

7   Conclusion

We have shown that the commutative closure of any shuffle language over group languages is regular. However, it is unknown if any shuffle language over the group languages is a regular languages itself. As a first step, the question if the iterated shuffle of a group language is regular might be investigated. I conjecture this to be true, but do not know how to prove it for general group languages. Observe that merely by noting that the commutative closure is regular, we cannot conclude that the original language is regular. For example, consider the non-regular context-free language given by the grammar G over $\{a, b\}$ with rules

$$
S \rightarrow aTaS \mid \varepsilon, \quad T \rightarrow bSbT \mid \varepsilon.
$$

and start symbol S.

Proposition 14. *The language $L \subseteq \{a, b\}^*$ generated by the above grammar G is not regular, but its commutative closure is regular.*

Proof. 1. $L \cap (ab)^*(ba)^* = \{(ab)^n(ba)^n \mid n \geqslant 0\}$.
It is easy to see that $\{(ab)^n(ba)^n \mid n \geqslant 0\} \subseteq L \cap (ab)^*(ba)^*$. For the other inclusion, we will first show that if

$$S \to u$$

with $u \in (ab)^*(ba)^*$, then $u = \varepsilon$ or $S \to abSba \to u$ with $u = abvba$, which implies $v \in (ab)^*(ba)^*$. So assume $S \to u$ with $u \neq \varepsilon$. Then, we must have

$$S \to aTaS \to u,$$

As, by assumption $u \notin \Sigma^* aa\Sigma^*$, we must apply $S \to \varepsilon$ and could not apply $T \to \varepsilon$. So, the following steps are necessary

$$S \to aTaS \to aTa \to abSbTa \to u. \tag{3}$$

Assume we expand T into a non-empty word, then

$$abSbTa \to abSbbSbTa.$$

As the factor bb occurs at most once in any word from $(ab)^*(ba)^*$, the above must expand to $abSbbSba$. This, in turn, implies that the first S must expand into a word from $(ab)^*a$. However, such a word always contains either an odd number of a's or an odd number of b's, and by the production rules, as these letters are always introduced in pairs, this is not possible. Hence, we cannot expand T in Equation (3) into a non-empty word and we must have $T \to \varepsilon$. Then,

$$S \to aTaS \to aTa \to abSba \to u.$$

So, we can write $u = abvba$ with $v \in (ab)^*(ba)^*$.
Finally, we reason inductively. If $u = \varepsilon$, then $u \in \{(ab)^n(ba)^n \mid n \geqslant 0\}$. Otherwise, by the previously shown statement, we have $u = abvba$ with $S \to v$ and $v \in (ab)^*(ba)^*$. Hence, inductively, we can assume $v = (ab)^n(ba)^n$ for some $n \geqslant 0$, which implies $u = (ab)^{n+1}(ba)^{n+1}$.
2. The generated language is not regular.
Assume L is regular. Then, with the above result, also $\{(ab)^n(ba)^n \mid n \geqslant 0\}$ would be regular. However, for the homomorphism $\varphi : \{c, d\}^* \to \{a, b\}^*$ given by $\varphi(c) = ab$, $\varphi(d) = ba$ we have $\{c^n d^n \mid n \geqslant 0\} = \varphi^{-1}(\{(ab)^n(ba)^n \mid n \geqslant 0\})$. As the last language is well-known to be not regular, and as regular languages are closed under inverse homomorphic mappings, the language $\{(ab)^n(ba)^n \mid n \geqslant 0\}$ could not be regular.
3. The commutative closure of L is $\{u \in \{a, b\}^* : |w|_a \equiv 0 \pmod 2, |w|_b \equiv 0 \pmod 2, |w|_a \geqslant \min\{1, |w|_b\}\}$, which is a regular language.
We have, for any $n \geqslant 0$ and $m \geqslant 0$, that $a(bb)^m a(aa)^n \in L$ and $\varepsilon \in L$. Also, as each rule introduces the letters a or b in pairs, any word in L has an even

number of a and b's and as we can only introduce the letter b with the non-terminal T, which we only can apply after producing at least one a, we see that if we have at least one b, then we need to have at least one a. Combining these observations yields that the commutative closure equals the language written above and the defining conditions of this language could be realized by automata.

So, we have shown the claims made in the proposition. □

Acknowledgement. I thank the anonymous reviewers who took their time reading through this work.

References

1. Bouajjani, A., Muscholl, A., Touili, T.: Permutation rewriting and algorithmic verification. Inf. Comput. **205**(2), 199–224 (2007)
2. Broda, S., Machiavelo, A., Moreira, N., Reis, R.: Automata for regular expressions with shuffle. Inf. Comput. **259**(2), 162–173 (2018)
3. Brzozowski, J., Jirásková, G., Liu, B., Rajasekaran, A., Szykuła, M.: On the state complexity of the shuffle of regular languages. In: Câmpeanu, C., Manea, F., Shallit, J. (eds.) DCFS 2016. LNCS, vol. 9777, pp. 73–86. Springer, Cham (2016). https://doi.org/10.1007/978-3-319-41114-9_6
4. Campbell, R.H., Habermann, A.N.: The specification of process synchronization by path expressions. In: Gelenbe, E., Kaiser, C. (eds.) OS 1974. LNCS, vol. 16, pp. 89–102. Springer, Heidelberg (1974). https://doi.org/10.1007/BFb0029355
5. Câmpeanu, C., Salomaa, K., Yu, S.: Tight lower bound for the state complexity of shuffle of regular languages. J. Autom. Lang. Comb. **7**(3), 303–310 (2002)
6. Caron, P., Luque, J., Patrou, B.: A combinatorial approach for the state complexity of the shuffle product. J. Autom. Lang. Comb. **25**(4), 291–320 (2020)
7. Cécé, G., Héam, P., Mainier, Y.: Efficiency of automata in semi-commutation verification techniques. RAIRO Theor. Inf. Appl. **42**(2), 197–215 (2008)
8. Diekert, V., Rozenberg, G. (eds.): The Book of Traces. World Scientific (1995)
9. Fernau, H., Paramasivan, M., Schmid, M.L., Vorel, V.: Characterization and complexity results on jumping finite automata. Theo. Comp. Sci. **679**, 31–52 (2017)
10. Fernau, H., Hoffmann, S.: Extensions to minimal synchronizing words. J. Autom. Lang. Comb. 24(2–4), 287–307 (2019). https://doi.org/10.25596/jalc-2019-287
11. Gao, Y., Moreira, N., Reis, R., Yu, S.: A survey on operational state complexity. J. Automata, Lang. Comb. **21**(4), 251–310 (2017)
12. Ginsburg, S., Spanier, E.H.: Bounded regular sets. Proc. Am. Math. Soc. **17**, 1043–1049 (1966)
13. Ginsburg, S., Spanier, E.H.: Semigroups, Presburger formulas, and languages. Pac. J. Math. **16**(2), 285–296 (1966)
14. Gohon, P.: An algorithm to decide whether a rational subset of n^k is recognizable. Theor. Comput. Sci. **41**, 51–59 (1985)
15. Cano Gómez, A., Álvarez, G.I.: Learning commutative regular languages. In: Clark, A., Coste, F., Miclet, L. (eds.) ICGI 2008. LNCS (LNAI), vol. 5278, pp. 71–83. Springer, Heidelberg (2008). https://doi.org/10.1007/978-3-540-88009-7_6
16. Gómez, A.C., Guaiana, G., Pin, J.: Regular languages and partial commutations. Inf. Comput. **230**, 76–96 (2013)

17. Hoffmann, S.: State complexity, properties and generalizations of commutative regular languages. Inf. Comput. (submitted)
18. Hoffmann, S.: State complexity bounds for the commutative closure of group languages. J. Automata, Lang. Comb. (submitted)
19. Hoffmann, S.: Commutative regular languages – properties and state complexity. In: Ćirić, M., Droste, M., Pin, J.-É. (eds.) CAI 2019. LNCS, vol. 11545, pp. 151–163. Springer, Cham (2019). https://doi.org/10.1007/978-3-030-21363-3_13
20. Hoffmann, S.: State complexity bounds for the commutative closure of group languages. In: Jirásková, G., Pighizzini, G. (eds.) DCFS 2020. LNCS, vol. 12442, pp. 64–77. Springer, Cham (2020). https://doi.org/10.1007/978-3-030-62536-8_6
21. Hopcroft, J.E., Ullman, J.D.: Introduction to Automata Theory, Languages, and Computation. Addison-Wesley Publishing Company (1979)
22. Ito, M.: Algebraic Theory of Automata and Languages. World Scientific (2004)
23. Jantzen, M.: The power of synchronizing operations on strings. Theor. Comput. Sci. **14**, 127–154 (1981)
24. Jantzen, M.: Extending regular expressions with iterated shuffle. Theor. Comput. Sci. **38**, 223–247 (1985)
25. Jedrzejowicz, J., Szepietowski, A.: Shuffle languages are in P. Theor. Comput. Sci. **250**(1—-2), 31–53 (2001)
26. Kimura, T.: An algebraic system for process structuring and interprocess communication. In: Chandra, A.K., Wotschke, D., Friedman, E.P., Harrison, M.A. (eds.) Proceedings of the 8th Annual ACM Symposium on Theory of Computing, May 3–5 1976, Hershey, Pennsylvania, USA, pp. 92–100. ACM (1976)
27. Landau, E.G.H.: Über die maximalordnung der permutationen gegebenen grades. Archiv der Mathematik und Physik **5**(3), 92–103 (1903)
28. L'vov, M.K. (Kiev): Commutative closures of regular semigroup languages, **2**, 54–58 (1973). https://doi.org/10.1007/BF01069078
29. Mazurkiewicz, A.: Parallel recursive program schemes. In: Bečvář, J. (ed.) MFCS 1975. LNCS, vol. 32, pp. 75–87. Springer, Heidelberg (1975). https://doi.org/10.1007/3-540-07389-2_183
30. Muscholl, A., Petersen, H.: A note on the commutative closure of star-free languages. Inf. Process. Lett. **57**(2), 71–74 (1996)
31. Parikh, R.: On context-free languages. J. ACM **13**(4), 570–581 (1966)
32. Pin, J.: Varieties Of Formal Languages. Plenum Publishing Co. (1986)
33. Pin, Jean-Eric: Syntactic semigroups. In: Rozenberg, Grzegorz, Salomaa, Arto (eds.) Handbook of Formal Languages, pp. 679–746. Springer, Heidelberg (1997). https://doi.org/10.1007/978-3-642-59136-5_10
34. Redko, V.: On the commutative closure of events. Dopovidi Akad. Nauk Urkain. RSR, pp. 1156–1159 (1963)
35. Sakarovitch, J.: The "last" decision problem for rational trace languages. In: Simon, I. (ed.) LATIN 1992, 1st Latin American Symposium on Theoretical Informatics, São Paulo, Brazil, April 6–10, 1992, Proceedings. Lecture Notes in Computer Science, vol. 583, pp. 460–473. Springer (1992). https://doi.org/10.1007/BFb0023848
36. Shaw, A.C.: Software descriptions with flow expressions. IEEE Trans. Softw. Eng. **4**, 242–254 (1978)

Efficient Enumeration of Regular Expressions for Faster Regular Expression Synthesis

Su-Hyeon Kim, Hyeonseung Im, and Sang-Ki Ko[(✉)]

Department of Computer Science and Engineering, Kangwon National University,
1, Gangwondaehak-gil, Chuncheon-si, Gangwon-do, South Korea
{tngus98207,hsim,sangkiko}@kangwon.ac.kr

Abstract. We study the problem of synthesizing regular expressions from a set of positive and negative strings. The previous synthesis algorithm proposed by Lee *et al.* [12] relies on the best-first enumeration of regular expressions. To improve the performance of the enumeration process, we define a new normal form of regular expressions called the *concise normal form* which allows us to significantly reduce the search space by pruning those not in the normal form while still capturing the whole class of regular languages. We conduct experiments with two benchmark datasets and demonstrate that our synthesis algorithm based on the proposed normal form outperforms the previous algorithm in terms of runtime complexity and scalability.

Keywords: Regular expression · Program synthesis · Normal form · Enumerative search

1 Introduction

Regular expressions (REs) are widely used for the pattern matching problem to effectively and efficiently describe strings of interest. Due to their compact representations and various advantages, REs are supported in many practical applications such as search engines, text processing, programming languages, and compilers. However, writing a minimal and correct RE for a given set of strings is error-prone and sometimes difficult even for experts. With recent advances in the program synthesis technology [8], to help novice users, many researchers have investigated various methods that automatically generate REs from a set of positive and negative examples [12,17], natural language descriptions [10,14], or both [3,19].

In order to synthesize a RE satisfying the provided examples, it is often inevitable to enumerate REs in some order and check if each RE satisfies the synthesis constraints. Lee *et al.* [12] proposed a best-first enumeration algorithm called AlphaRegex which synthesizes a RE from a set of positive and negative strings. They also suggested various pruning algorithms that identify

© Springer Nature Switzerland AG 2021
S. Maneth (Ed.): CIAA 2021, LNCS 12803, pp. 65–76, 2021.
https://doi.org/10.1007/978-3-030-79121-6_6

semantically equivalent (language-equivalent) expressions and prune out hopeless intermediate expressions determined by given positive and negative examples to reduce the search space. Indeed, their pruning algorithms drastically improved the naïve enumerative search algorithm, yet still far from being scalable for more complex examples.

Meanwhile, there has been much interest in the descriptional complexity of REs including several heuristics for simplifying them [2,5–7]. Brüggemann-Klein introduced the *star normal form* (snf) to improve the time complexity of constructing the position automata from REs from cubic to quadratic time. While Brüggemann-Klein considered REs recursively defined with union, concatenation, and Kleene-star, Gruber and Gulan [7] extended the definition of the snf with the question operator $R_1^?$ defined as $L(R_1^?) = \{\epsilon\} \cup L(R_1)$ and called their extension the *strong star normal form* (ssnf). A RE R is in ssnf if for any subexpression of the form R_1^* or $R_1^?$, the language represented by R_1 does not include the empty string ϵ. They also showed that the ssnf is more concise than the previous snf and still computable in linear time as snf is. Lee and Shallit [11] discussed enumeration of REs and corresponding regular languages using unambiguous grammars generating REs and their commutative images. They also provided exact numbers of regular languages representable by REs of given length. Broda *et al.* [1] studied the average behavior of REs in ssnf by computing the asymptotic estimates for the number of REs in ssnf and conducted several experiments for corroborating the estimates.

In this paper, we revisit the problem of synthesizing a RE from a given set of positive and negative examples. In particular, we aim to improve the performance of previous studies by introducing a new normal form called the *concise normal form* (cnf) of REs for an efficient enumeration during the best-first search. We introduce several rules where the equivalence of REs is identifiable in polynomial time and incorporate the rules to define the cnf. We show that the cnf is considerably more concise than the ssnf by actually enumerating all expressions in each normal form up to a given length. Finally, we demonstrate that our RE synthesis algorithm based on the cnf improves the previous state-of-the-art algorithm AlphaRegex.

The rest of the paper is organized as follows. Section 2 gives some definitions and notations. We introduce our normal form definition in Sect. 3 and the synthesis algorithm in Sect. 4. Finally, the experimental results are provided in Sect. 5.

2 Preliminaries

This section briefly recalls the basic definitions used throughout the paper. For complete background knowledge in automata theory, the reader may refer to textbooks [9,18].

Let Σ be a finite alphabet and Σ^* be the set of all strings over the alphabet Σ. A *regular expression* (RE) over Σ is $a \in \Sigma$, or is obtained by applying the following rules finitely many times. For REs R_1 and R_2, the union $R_1 + R_2$, the concatenation $R_1 \cdot R_2$, the star R_1^*, and the question $R_1^?$ are also REs. Note that $L(R_1^?)$ is defined as $L(R_1) \cup \{\epsilon\}$. Two REs R_1 and R_2 are *equivalent* if $L(R_1) = L(R_2)$. When R_1 and R_2 are equivalent, we write $R_1 \equiv R_2$ instead of $L(R_1) = L(R_2)$ for notational convenience.

The *reverse Polish notation* (RPN) length of R is denoted by $\mathrm{rpn}(R)$ and defined as $\mathrm{rpn}(R) = |R|_\Sigma + |R|_+ + |R|_\cdot + |R|_* + |R|_?$. For instance, $\mathrm{rpn}(ab^?)$ is 4 since we also count the question operator and the (hidden) concatenation operator between a and $b^?$. In other words, $\mathrm{rpn}(R)$ is the number of nodes in the corresponding syntax tree of R. As we deal with REs in the form of parse trees internally, $\mathrm{rpn}(R)$ can be considered as more accurate measure for representing the complexity of the REs.

Let S be a set of REs and $c_k \in \mathbb{N}$ for $1 \leq k \leq 5$ be a natural number implying the cost of a regular operator or a symbol. We define the *cost* of REs using the cost function $C : S \to \mathbb{N}$ which associates a cost with each expression as follows:

$$C(a) = c_1$$
$$C(R_1 + R_2) = C(R_1) + C(R_2) + c_2$$
$$C(R_1 \cdot R_2) = C(R_1) + C(R_2) + c_3$$
$$C(R^*) = C(R) + c_4$$
$$C(R^?) = C(R) + c_5$$

Let $\preceq$ be a relation on S, and $\preceq^*$ a transitive closure of $\preceq$. A rewriting system $(S, \preceq)$ is said to be *terminating* if there is no infinite descending chain $R_0 \preceq R_1 \preceq R_2 \preceq \cdots$, where $R_k \in S$ for $k \in \mathbb{N}$. In a terminating rewriting system $(S, \preceq)$, every element in S has at least one normal form.

Here we introduce the concept of 'similar' REs which is a weaker notion of the equivalence between two regular languages represented by REs. Owens *et al.* [13] formally define the concept of being 'similar' to approximate the least equivalence relation on REs as follows:

Definition 1. *Let $\approx$ denote the equivalence relation on REs including the following equations:*

$$R + R \approx R \qquad\qquad (R^*)^* \approx R^*$$
$$R_1 + R_2 \approx R_2 + R_1 \qquad\qquad (R^?)^? \approx R^?$$
$$(R_1 + R_2) + R_3 \approx R_1 + (R_2 + R_3) \qquad (R^*)^? \approx R^*$$
$$(R_1 \cdot R_2) \cdot R_3 \approx R_1 \cdot (R_2 \cdot R_3) \qquad (R^?)^* \approx R^*$$

Two REs R_1 and R_2 are similar if $R_1 \approx R_2$ and dissimilar otherwise.

It is trivial that the following statement holds from simple algebraic consequences of the inductive definition of REs.

Corollary 1. *If $R_1 \approx R_2$, then $R_1 \equiv R_2$.*

Given a set of positive and negative strings, we consider the problem of synthesizing a concise RE that is consistent with the given strings. The examples are given by a pair (P, N) of two sets of strings, where $P \subseteq \Sigma^*$ is a set of *positive strings* and $N \subseteq \Sigma^*$ is a set of *negative strings*.

Then, our goal is to find a RE R that accepts all positive strings in P while rejecting all negative strings in N. Formally, R satisfies the following condition:

$$P \subseteq L(R) \text{ and } L(R) \cap N = \emptyset.$$

Since there are infinitely many REs satisfying the condition, we aim at finding the most concise RE among all such expressions. We utilize the cost function C to quantify the conciseness of REs.

3   Concise Normal Form for REs

Now we define the relation $\preceq$ of REs to define a terminating RE rewriting system $(S, \preceq)$ that produces a more concise RE in terms of RPN (or at least a RE with the same RPN). Let R and R_k be REs for any natural number k. First, we consider the case when a RE has a subexpression that is formed by the concatenation of similar REs.

Lemma 1 (Redundant Concatenation (RC) Rule 1). *For a RE R, the following equivalences hold:*

(i) $R^? R \preceq RR^?$
(ii) $R^* R \preceq RR^*$
(iii) $R^* R^? \preceq R^? R^* \preceq R^*$

Using the lemma above, we consider all REs with subexpressions in the form of $R^? R$, $R^* R$, $R^* R^?$, or $R^? R^*$ as redundant, as we can always rewrite those subexpressions as $RR^?$, RR^*, or R^* without changing the language represented by the resulting RE. We can further consider the following type of redundant concatenation even when two concatenated subexpressions do not share exactly the same expression.

Lemma 2 (RC Rule 2). *If $\epsilon \in L(R_1)$ and $L(R_1) \subseteq L(R_2^*)$, then $R_1 R_2^* \preceq R_2^*$ and $R_2^* R_1 \preceq R_2^*$.*

Lemma 3 (Kleene-Concatenation-Kleene (KCK) Rule).
   If $L(R_1) \cup L(R_3) \subseteq L(R_2^*)$, then $(R_1 R_2^* R_3)^* \preceq (R_1 R_2^* R_3)^?$.

Lemma 4 (Kleene-Concatenation-Question (KCQ) Rule).
   If $L(R_1) \cup L(R_3) \subseteq L(R_2^*)$ and $\epsilon \in L(R_1) \cap L(R_3)$, then $(R_1 R_2 R_3)^* \preceq R_2^*$.

When the question operator is used for the concatenation of two REs, we find the following rule.

Lemma 5 (Question-Concatenation (QC) Rule).
   $(RR^*)^? \preceq R^*$ and $(RR^?)^? \preceq R^? R^?$ hold.

When the union operator is used for multiple subexpressions, we find the following four equivalence cases.

Lemma 6 (Union-Question (UQ) rule). $R_1 + R_2^? \preceq (R_1 + R_2)^?$ *holds.*

Lemma 7 (Inclusive Union (IU) Rule). *If* $L(R_1) \subseteq L(R_2)$, *then* $R_1 + R_2 \preceq R_2$.

We also use a rule named the *factoring rule*, which trivially holds by a simple algebraic law (distributive law), to factor the common prefix or suffix of REs within a union operator until there is no such subexpression.

Corollary 2 (Factoring Rule).
$R_1 R_2 + R_1 R_3 \preceq R_1(R_2 + R_3)$ *and* $R_2 R_1 + R_3 R_1 \preceq (R_2 + R_3)R_1$ *hold.*

Finally, we use the following observation when a Kleene-star operator is used for an expression that represents each symbol in the alphabet, as the resulting expression is equivalent to Σ^* (Sigma-star), which represents all possible strings over the alphabet Σ.

Corollary 3 (Sigma-star Rule). *If* $\Sigma \subseteq L(R)$, *then* $R^* \preceq \Sigma^*$.

Corollary 4. *If* $R_1 \preceq R_2$, *then* $\mathrm{rpn}(R_1) \geq \mathrm{rpn}(R_2)$ *and* $R_1 \equiv R_2$ *hold.*

Now we are ready to introduce our new normal form for REs called the *concise normal form* (cnf). Simply speaking, a RE is in cnf if its every subexpression does not fall into a case introduced thus far. We formally define the cnf as follows:

Definition 2. *We define a RE R to be in* cnf *if R does not contain a subexpression in any of the following forms:*

1. R^* *or* $R^?$ *where* $\epsilon \in L(R)$ *(ssnf)*
2. $R^? R$, $R^* R$, $R^* R^?$ *or* $R^? R^*$ *(RC Rule 1)*
3. $R_1 R_2^*$ *or* $R_2^* R_1$ *where* $\epsilon \in L(R_1)$ *and* $L(R_1) \subseteq L(R_2^*)$ *(RC Rule 2)*
4. $(R_1 R_2^* R_3)^*$ *where* $L(R_1) \cup L(R_3) \subseteq L(R_2^*)$ *(KCK Rule)*
5. $(R_1 R_2 R_3)^*$ *where* $L(R_1) \cup L(R_3) \subseteq L(R_2^*)$, $\epsilon \in L(R_1) \cap L(R_3)$ *(KCQ Rule)*
6. $(RR^*)^?$ *or* $(RR^?)^?$ *(QC Rule)*
7. $R_1 + R_2^?$ *(UQ Rule)*
8. $R_1 + R_2$ *where* $L(R_1) \subseteq L(R_2)$ *(IU Rule)*
9. $R_1 R_2 + R_1 R_3$ *or* $R_2 R_1 + R_3 R_1$ *(Factoring Rule)*
10. R^* *where* $R \neq a_1 + a_2 + \cdots + a_n$ *and* $\Sigma \subseteq L(R)$ *(Sigma-star Rule)*

In order to prove that there always exists a RE in cnf for any given RE, we prove the following result:

Lemma 8. *The rewriting system* $(S, \preceq)$ *is terminating.*

Proof. For the sake of contradiction, suppose that $(S, \preceq)$ is not terminating and there is an infinite chain $R_0 \preceq R_1 \preceq R_2 \preceq \cdots$. Since Corollary 4 guarantees that the RPN length of REs does not increase by $(S, \preceq)$, it is easy to verify that there exists a RE R which is repeated infinitely many times in the chain.

Therefore, it suffices to consider the following cases where the rewriting system results in the same RPN length:

(i) $R^?R \preceq RR^?$ (By Lemma 1)
(ii) $(R_1 R_2^* R_3)^* \preceq (R_1 R_2^* R_3)^?$ (By Lemma 3)
(iii) $(RR^?)^? \preceq R^?R^?$ (By Lemma 5)
(iv) $R_1 + R_2^? \preceq (R_1 + R_2)^?$ (By Lemma 6)

In the following, we demonstrate that no rule can initiate an infinite chain of REs with proof by cases.

Case (i): Assume that the infinite chain is formed by the first rewriting relation $R^?R \preceq RR^?$. This implies that there exists a derivation in the form of $R_1 RR^? R_2 \preceq^* R_1 R^? RR_2$ for any $R_1, R_2 \in S$. Since there is no relation that rewrites the concatenation of two expressions other than $R^?R \preceq RR^?$, we should consider derivations of the following form:

$$R_1 RR^? R_2 \preceq R_1' R_1'' RR^? R_2' R_2'' \preceq^* R_1 RR^? R_2,$$

where $R_1 = R_1' R_1''$ and $R_2 = R_2' R_2''$.

In this case, $R_1'' R$ should be converted into $R_1''' R^?$ where $(R_1''')^? = R_1''$ by the case (i) since there is no other possibility to convert $R^?$ into R. Hence, we have the intermediate expression $R_1' R_1''' R^? R^? R_2' R_2''$. Now, we can see that $\mathrm{rpn}(R_1' R_1''') < \mathrm{rpn}(R_1)$ and therefore there is no possibility to reach $R_1 RR^? R_2$ by the rewriting system.

Case (ii): Let us consider the second case $(R_1 R_2^* R_3)^* \preceq (R_1 R_2^* R_3)^?$. It is easy to see that the rule cannot be used to form the infinite chain of REs as the rule replaces a Kleene-star operator with a question operator. Since there is no relation that places the removed question operator back, it is simply impossible to use the rule in the infinite chain.

Case (iii): The third case $(RR^?)^? \preceq R^?R^?$ can be applied when concatenation is used inside the question operator. In order to move back to the form before the rule is applied, we need a relation that places a question operator enclosing an expression which is a concatenation of two expressions. However, there is no such rule in the rewriting system.

Case (iv): The fourth case $R_1 + R_2^? \preceq (R_1 + R_2)^?$ can be applied when union is used inside the question operator. In order to move back to the form before the rule is applied, we need a relation that places a question operator enclosing an expression which is a union of two expressions. However, there is no such rule in the rewriting system.

Since we have shown that an infinite chain of REs by the rewriting system $(S, \preceq)$ cannot exist, the proof is completed.   □

As a corollary of Lemma 8, we observe the following result:

Corollary 5. *Given a RE R, there always exists a RE R' in* cnf *such that $R \equiv R'$.*

Unfortunately, it is well-known that the problem of testing inclusion between two REs is PSPACE-complete [16]. Hence, we can easily deduce that the problem of testing whether a given RE is in cnf is also PSPACE-complete as follows:

Lemma 9. *Given a RE R, the problem of determining whether or not R is in* cnf *is PSPACE-complete.*

Proof. Without loss of generality, we assume that two REs R_1 and R_2 do not share the common prefix or suffix as we can easily factor out them. We also assume that R_1 and R_2 do not contain a question operator.

Note that testing $L(R_1) \subseteq L(R_2)$ is PSPACE-complete. Now a RE $R_1 + R_2$ can be converted into a cnf expression R_2 if and only if $L(R_1) \subseteq L(R_2)$. Therefore, it is easily seen that the problem of determining whether a given RE is in cnf is also PSPACE-complete.   □

Since the cnf testing is PSPACE-complete, we instead introduce a relaxed concept of the cnf called the *soft concise normal form* (scnf) by relaxing the language inclusion restrictions in the cnf such as $L(R_1) \subseteq L(R_2)$.

We first introduce a weaker notion of the language inclusion relation as follows which can be determined in linear time:

Definition 3. *Given two REs R_1 and R_2 over $\Sigma = \{a_1, a_2, \ldots, a_n\}$, we define $R_1 \sqsubseteq R_2$ if R_1 and R_2 satisfy one of the following conditions:*

(i) $R_1 \approx R_2$
(ii) $R_2 = R^*$ *for any $R \in S$ such that $\Sigma \subseteq L(R)$*
(iii) $R_2 = R_1^*$
(iv) $R_2 = R_1^?$
(v) $R_2 = R^*$ *and $R_1 = R^?$ for any $R \in S$*
(vi) $R_2 = (R_1 + R)^*$ *for any $R \in S$*

Note that the following relation trivially holds:

Corollary 6. *If $R_1 \sqsubseteq R_2$, then $L(R_1) \subseteq L(R_2)$.*

Now we formally define the scnf as follows:

Definition 4. *We define a RE r to be in* scnf *if r does not contain a subexpression in Definition 2 where every restriction in the form of $L(R_1) \subseteq L(R_2)$ is replaced by $R_1 \sqsubseteq R_2$.*

Actually, it turns out that it is possible to determine whether or not a given RE is in scnf in polynomial time.

Lemma 10. *Given a RE R, we can determine whether or not R is in* scnf *in polynomial time.*

4   RE Synthesis Algorithm

We synthesize REs by relying on the best-first search while only considering REs in scnf as REs not in scnf have more concise expressions representing the same regular languages. Hence, we can prune out numerous REs by simply checking if the expressions are in the scnf regardless of the given examples.

4.1   Best-First Search Algorithm

As in the AlphaRegex [12], we utilize the best-first search to find the most concise RE consistent with the given examples. Starting from the simplest form of REs, we examine more complicated expressions until finding the solution.

We introduce a *hole* ($\square$) that is to be replaced with some concrete RE. We call REs with holes the *templates*. In order to perform the best-first search, we rely on a priority queue to determine the next candidate. After pushing the initial template $\square$ into the priority queue, we retrieve each template with the minimal cost determined by the cost function C from the priority queue. For each retrieved template, we generate more complicated templates or concrete expressions by replacing holes with each symbol in Σ, ϵ, $\emptyset$, $\square+\square$, $\square\cdot\square$, $\square^*$, and $\square^?$ and push them into the priority queue to continue the best-first search. The search algorithm terminates when we find a solution which is consistent with the given examples and not redundant.

We also use the additional pruning rule considered in AlphaRegex. Given a template R, we define $\widehat{R}$ ($\widetilde{R}$, resp.) to be a concrete RE obtained by replacing every hole in R with Σ^* ($\emptyset$, resp.). Informally, $\widehat{R}$ is an over-approximation of R as Σ^* is the most general RE and $\widetilde{R}$ is an under-approximation of R as $\emptyset$ is an expression for the smallest set of strings among all REs. During the search, we prune a template R if either $P \nsubseteq L(\widehat{R})$ or $L(\widetilde{R}) \cap N \neq \emptyset$ holds as it is already impossible for R to reach any concrete expression consistent with (P, N).

4.2   Finding Redundancy Using Positive Examples

Meanwhile, we can further prune out the search space by relying on the set of positive strings that the resulting RE should accept. In AlphaRegex [12], the authors define a RE to be *redundant* if the RE contains an operator that can be omitted while still accepting the positive strings.

We first explain the functions introduced in the AlphaRegex here to be self-contained as follows:

$$\begin{aligned}
\mathsf{un}(a) &= a \ (a \in \Sigma) & \mathsf{sp}(a) &= \{a\} \ (a \in \Sigma) \\
\mathsf{un}(R_1+R_2) &= \mathsf{un}(R_1)+\mathsf{un}(R_2) & \mathsf{sp}(R_1 + R_2) &= \mathsf{sp}(R_1) \cup \mathsf{sp}(R_2) \\
\mathsf{un}(R_1 \cdot R_2) &= \mathsf{un}(R_1) \cdot \mathsf{un}(R_2) & \mathsf{sp}(R_1 \cdot R_2) &= \{R_1' \cdot R_2, R_1 \cdot R_2' \mid R_i' \in \mathsf{sp}(R_i)\} \\
\mathsf{un}(R^*) &= R \cdot R \cdot R^* & \mathsf{sp}(R^*) &= \{R^*\} \\
\mathsf{un}(\square) &= \square & \mathsf{sp}(\square) &= \{\square\}
\end{aligned}$$

Lee *et al.* introduced the un and sp functions to check the redundancy of star and union operators used in REs, respectively. Given a RE R (possibly with holes) and a set P of positive examples, they define R to be *redundant* if there exists a regular expression $R' \in \mathsf{sp}(\mathsf{un}(R))$ such that $L(\widehat{R'}) \cap P = \emptyset$. For instance, consider a set $P = \{0, 01, 011, 0111\}$ and two templates: $1^* \cdot \square$ and $0^* \cdot \square$. Then, $1^* \cdot \square$ is redundant since $\mathsf{sp}(\mathsf{un}(1^* \cdot \square)) = \{111^* \cdot \square\}$ and apparently $L(111^* \cdot \Sigma^*)$ does not contain any string in P. Analogously, $0^* \cdot \square$ is also redundant.

Algorithm 1: Our Synthesis Algorithm

Input : Positive and negative strings (P, N)
Output: A RE R consistent with (P, N)
Initialize a priority queue Q;
Push the initial template $\square$ into Q;
repeat
    Pop a minimal cost template R from Q;
    if R *is a complete RE* **then**
        if R *is consistent with* (P, N) **then**
          | **return** R
    else
        foreach $R' \in \mathsf{next}(R)$ **do**
          if $P \subseteq L(\widehat{R'})$ *or* $L(\widetilde{R'}) \cap N = \emptyset$ **then**
            if R' *is in* scnf **then**
              if R' *not redundant for* P **then**
                | Push R' into Q;
until $Q \neq \emptyset$;

4.3 Our Synthesis Algorithm

Algorithm 1 shows the final synthesis algorithm. We first initialize a priority queue Q that internally sorts templates according to their costs calculated by the cost function C in increasing order. We first push the simplest template $\square$ into Q and repeat the following procedure.

1. We retrieve a minimal cost template R from Q and check whether or not R is a complete RE and consistent with the given examples (P, N). If so, we return R as a synthesized RE. Otherwise, we proceed to the next step.
2. If R is a template with holes, then we generate templates by replacing a hole with one of Σ, ϵ, $\emptyset$, $\square + \square$, $\square \cdot \square$, $\square^*$, or $\square^?$ (defined as the set $\mathsf{next}(R)$). For each generated template R', we test whether or not R' has a possibility of evolving into a RE satisfying the given examples. If so, we also test whether R' is in scnf and not redundant for positive examples P. If R' qualifies the tests, then we push R' into Q.

5 Experimental Results

We conduct several experiments to verify that the proposed normal form of REs significantly reduces the number of REs when enumerating all possible regular languages. By doing so, we first show that the new normal form is more efficient to enumerate distinct regular languages that are given in the form of REs by pruning out numerous REs not in the new normal form. Second, we demonstrate that the proposed normal form is useful when synthesizing a RE from a set of positive and negative strings by enumerating all possible candidates by pruning a vast amount of the search space during the enumeration process.

Table 1. The number of REs in a given RPN length.

rpn(R)	Exact Enum. [11]	Base	ssnf [7]	scnf	Pruning Ratio
1	2	2	2	2	0.00
2	4	4	4	4	0.00
3	7	7	7	5	28.57
4	13	38	38	24	36.84
5	32	106	90	42	60.38
6	90	364	312	146	59.89
7	189	1,444	1,236	481	66.69
8	580	5,170	3,650	1,278	75.28
9	1,347	19,741	14,849	4,636	76.52
10	3,978	77,838	52,388	14,675	81.15
11	-	302,908	188,820	46,978	84.49
12	-	1,206,042	741,108	165,818	86.25
13	-	4,853,655	2,690,537	537,446	88.93

5.1   Exact Enumeration of REs in Normal Form

First, we count the number of REs in a given RPN length and compare it with the number of REs in scnf in Table 1. Recall that Lee *et al.* [11] attempted to obtain the asymptotic estimates on the number of regular languages specified by REs of given size n by the aid of the Chomsky-Schützenberger theorem [4] and singularity analysis of the algebraic formal power series. Note that the upper bound and lower bound obtained in [11] are $O(3.9870^n)$ and $\Omega(2.2140^n)$.

In order to estimate the expected growth rate of the numbers given in Table 1, we fit exponential curves to enumeration results using SciPy's scipy.optimize.curve_fit function which implements a non-linear least-square fit. As a result, we obtain the following estimates for the number of all valid REs and the number of all REs in the proposed normal form of a given RPN length as follows:

$$0.067 \times 4.022^n + 882.444 \text{ and } 0.108 \times 3.275^n - 303.477.$$

As the numbers are growing exponentially, our synthesis algorithm is expected to run exponentially faster than simple enumeration-based algorithm and scale much better for more complicated examples.

5.2   Performance of RE Synthesis

For experiments of RE synthesis, we utilize two benchmark datasets: the AlphaRegex dataset and random dataset. The AlphaRegex dataset consists of 25 REs from famous textbooks [9,15] on automata and formal language theory. The authors of AlphaRegex created a set of positive and negative examples for

Table 2. Comparisons of performance of AlphaRegex and our synthesis algorithm.

Benchmark	Method	Avg. Count	Avg. Time	Success Ratio
Random	AlphaRegex	7,445	9.36 s	83.3%
	AlphaRegex + Redundancy Check	4,432	6.84 s	87.4%
	Ours	3,478	4.39 s	87.9%
	Ours + Redundancy Check	**1,813**	**2.68 s**	**91.9%**
AlphaRegex	AlphaRegex	7,038	8.71 s	76.0%
	AlphaRegex + Redundancy Check	5,190	7.38 s	88.0%
	Ours	3,814	4.66 s	88.0%
	Ours + Redundancy Check	**2,202**	**3.11 s**	**96.0%**

each RE in the dataset[1]. Note that both datasets only consist of REs over binary alphabet $\{0, 1\}$.

The random dataset contains 1,000 distinct randomly generated REs. We first start from an initial template '□' and randomly replace a hole in the template by one of $a \in \Sigma$, ϵ, $\emptyset$, $\square + \square$, $\square \cdot \square$, $\square^*$, or $\square^?$. We repeat the process 10 times and complete the template by randomly replacing every hole with one of the symbols in Σ. If it is impossible to generate 10 positive examples from the random RE as it can only describe a finite number of strings or its length is shorter than 7, we re-generate a RE. We generate a set of 10 positive examples and 10 negative examples for each random RE. In order to generate positive examples, we utilize a Python library called the Xeger[2]. For generating negative examples, we first randomly choose a number n between 1 and 15 and generate a random string of length n. We repeat the process until we have 10 distinct strings that cannot be described by the RE.

The experimental results are shown in Table 2. We compare our algorithm implemented in Python 3 with our implementation of AlphaRegex on the two benchmark datasets with or without the redundancy checking algorithm introduced in AlphaRegex. Note that we use our implementation of AlphaRegex instead of the original OCaml implementation of AlphaRegex for a fair comparison. We set the limit on the number of visited templates to be 100,000 and consider the examples synthesized before reaching the successful limit. The average numbers (e.g., count and time) are calculated only for the successful examples. The experimental results show that our synthesis algorithm is faster than AlphaRegex in terms of both the average number of visited templates (including complete REs) to find the solution and the actual runtime of our Python implementation.

---

[1] The OCaml implementation of AlphaRegex and dataset are publicly available at https://github.com/kupl/AlphaRegexPublic.

[2] https://pypi.org/project/xeger/.

Acknowledgements. This work was supported by the National Research Foundation of Korea (NRF) grant funded by the Korean government (MIST) (No. 2020R1A4A3079947).

References

1. Broda, S., Machiavelo, A., Moreira, N., Reis, R.: On average behaviour of regular expressions in strong star normal form. Int. J. Found. Comput. Sci. **30**(6–7), 899–920 (2019)
2. Brüggemann-Klein, A.: Regular expressions into finite automata. Theoret. Comput. Sci. **120**(2), 197–213 (1993)
3. Chen, Q., Wang, X., Ye, X., Durrett, G., Dillig, I.: Multi-modal synthesis of regular expressions. In: PLDI 2020, pp. 487–502 (2020)
4. Chomsky, N., Schützenberger, M.: The algebraic theory of context-free languages. In: Computer Programming and Formal Systems. Studies in Logic and the Foundations of Mathematics, vol. 35, pp. 118–161. Elsevier (1963)
5. Ellul, K., Krawetz, B., Shallit, J.O., Wang, M.: Regular expressions: new results and open problems. J. Autom. Lang. Comb. **10**(4), 407–437 (2005)
6. Frishert, M., Watson, B.W.: Combining regular expressions with (near-)optimal Brzozowski automata. In: Domaratzki, M., Okhotin, A., Salomaa, K., Yu, S. (eds.) CIAA 2004. LNCS, vol. 3317, pp. 319–320. Springer, Heidelberg (2005). https://doi.org/10.1007/978-3-540-30500-2_34
7. Gruber, H., Gulan, S.: Simplifying regular expressions. In: Dediu, A.-H., Fernau, H., Martín-Vide, C. (eds.) LATA 2010. LNCS, vol. 6031, pp. 285–296. Springer, Heidelberg (2010). https://doi.org/10.1007/978-3-642-13089-2_24
8. Gulwani, S.: Dimensions in program synthesis. In: PPDP 2010, pp. 13–24 (2010)
9. Hopcroft, J., Ullman, J.: Introduction to Automata Theory, Languages, and Computation, 2nd edn. Addison-Wesley, Reading (1979)
10. Kushman, N., Barzilay, R.: Using semantic unification to generate regular expressions from natural language. In: NAACL-HLT 2013, pp. 826–836 (2013)
11. Lee, J., Shallit, J.: Enumerating regular expressions and their languages. In: Domaratzki, M., Okhotin, A., Salomaa, K., Yu, S. (eds.) CIAA 2004. LNCS, vol. 3317, pp. 2–22. Springer, Heidelberg (2005). https://doi.org/10.1007/978-3-540-30500-2_2
12. Lee, M., So, S., Oh, H.: Synthesizing regular expressions from examples for introductory automata assignments. In: GPCE 2016, pp. 70–80 (2016)
13. Owens, S., Reppy, J.H., Turon, A.: Regular-expression derivatives re-examined. J. Funct. Program. **19**(2), 173–190 (2009)
14. Park, J., Ko, S., Cognetta, M., Han, Y.: Softregex: Generating regex from natural language descriptions using softened regex equivalence. In: EMNLP-IJCNLP 2019, pp. 6424–6430 (2019)
15. Sipser, M.: Introduction to the Theory of Computation. Cengage Learning (2012)
16. Stockmeyer, L.J., Meyer, A.R.: Word problems requiring exponential time: preliminary report. In: STOC 1973, pp. 1–9 (1973)
17. Wang, X., Gulwani, S., Singh, R.: FIDEX: filtering spreadsheet data using examples. In: OOPSLA 2016, pp. 195–213 (2016)
18. Wood, D.: Theory of Computation. Harper & Row (1987)
19. Ye, X., Chen, Q., Wang, X., Dillig, I., Durrett, G.: Sketch-driven regular expression generation from natural language and examples. Trans. Assoc. Comput. Linguist. **8**, 679–694 (2020)

Degrees of Restriction
for Two-Dimensional Automata

Taylor J. Smith[(✉)] and Kai Salomaa

School of Computing, Queen's University, Kingston, ON K7L 2N8, Canada
{tsmith,ksalomaa}@cs.queensu.ca

Abstract. A three-way (resp., two-way) two-dimensional automaton has a read-only input head that moves in three (resp., two) directions on a finite array of cells labelled by symbols of the input alphabet. Restricting the input head movement of a two-dimensional automaton results in a model that is weaker in terms of recognition power.

In this paper, we introduce the notion of "degrees of restriction" for two-dimensional automata, and we develop sets of extended two-dimensional automaton models that allow for some bounded number of restricted moves. We establish recognition hierarchies for both deterministic and nondeterministic extended three-way two-dimensional automata, and we find similar hierarchies for both deterministic and nondeterministic extended two-way two-dimensional automata. We also prove incomparability results between nondeterministic and deterministic extended three-way two-dimensional automata. Lastly, we consider closure properties for some operations on languages recognized by extended three-way two-dimensional automata.

Keywords: Closure properties · Degrees of restriction · Extended two-dimensional automata · Recognition properties

1 Introduction

The two-dimensional automaton model is a generalization of the one-dimensional (or string) automaton model that takes as input an array or matrix of symbols from some alphabet Σ. The input head of such an automaton can move either upward, downward, leftward, or rightward within its input word. The two-dimensional automaton model was introduced by Blum and Hewitt [2].

If we restrict the input head movement of a two-dimensional automaton so that it cannot move in certain directions, then we obtain variants of the model that are weaker in terms of recognition power. If we forbid only upward moves, then we obtain what is known as a three-way two-dimensional automaton. Similarly, if we forbid both upward and leftward moves, then we obtain

---

T. J. Smith and K. Salomaa—Supported by Natural Sciences and Engineering Research Council of Canada Grant OGP0147224.

© Springer Nature Switzerland AG 2021
S. Maneth (Ed.): CIAA 2021, LNCS 12803, pp. 77–89, 2021.
https://doi.org/10.1007/978-3-030-79121-6_7

what is known as a two-way two-dimensional automaton. The three-way two-dimensional automaton model was introduced by Rosenfeld [9], while the two-way two-dimensional automaton model was introduced by Anselmo et al. [1] and formalized by Dong and Jin [3].

Motivated by the question of how the accepting power of two-dimensional computational models is affected by the number of input head reversals, Morita et al. [8] studied "input head reversal-bounded" two-dimensional Turing machines. In their paper, Morita et al. considered two-dimensional Turing machines operating on square tapes whose input heads may switch their vertical direction of movement some bounded number of times. The authors investigated a relationship between deterministic and nondeterministic input head reversal-bounded two-dimensional Turing machines, proposed a reversal hierarchy of space-bounded two-dimensional Turing machines, and established necessary and sufficient conditions for three-way two-dimensional Turing machines to simulate reversal-bounded four-way two-dimensional automata.

In the present paper, we consider a similar idea, which we term "degrees of restriction" for two-dimensional automata. We introduce an i-extended three-way two-dimensional automaton model, $i \in \mathbb{N}$, where the computation on any input word may move downward, leftward, and rightward, and is additionally permitted to make at most i upward moves. Similarly, we introduce an (i, j)-extended two-way two-dimensional automaton, $i, j \in \mathbb{N}$, which is permitted to make at most i upward moves and at most j leftward moves in a computation. The i and j bounds can be viewed as being maintained by a counter stored on an auxiliary tape that the automaton can only read from and decrement; this is to prevent the automaton from using the tape as general storage. Equivalently, the counter can be viewed as a stack containing some predefined number of unary symbols that can only be popped.

Automata with reversal-bounded counters have been studied in the past; for example, see Ibarra's survey [4]. However, the models defined in past work differ from our present model in that the counters of the former models may be either decremented or incremented. For simplicity, in our model, we assume that counters may only be decremented. Our model also differs from those considered by Morita et al. in that we do not restrict the number of input head reversals (e.g., down-to-up or up-to-down), but rather the number of restricted moves made by the input head (e.g., upward moves only). Thus, in our model, an automaton can make any number of normal input head moves, but only a limited number of restricted moves.

2   Preliminaries

A two-dimensional word consists of a finite array, or rectangle, of cells each labelled by a symbol from a finite alphabet Σ. When a two-dimensional word is written on the input tape of a two-dimensional automaton, the cells around the word are labelled by a special boundary marker $\# \notin \Sigma$. A two-dimensional automaton has a finite state control that is capable of moving its input head in four directions within its input word: up, down, left, and right (denoted by U, D, L, and R, respectively).

Definition 1 (Two-dimensional automaton). *A two-dimensional automaton is a tuple* $(Q, \Sigma, \delta, q_0, q_{\text{accept}})$, *where* Q *is a finite set of states,* Σ *is the input alphabet (with* $\# \notin \Sigma$ *acting as a boundary symbol),* $\delta : (Q \setminus \{q_{\text{accept}}\}) \times (\Sigma \cup \{\#\}) \to Q \times \{U, D, L, R\}$ *is the partial transition function, and* $q_0, q_{\text{accept}} \in Q$ *are the initial and accepting states, respectively.*

We can modify the deterministic model given in Definition 1 to be nondeterministic by changing the transition function to map to $2^{Q \times \{U,D,L,R\}}$. We denote the deterministic and nondeterministic two-dimensional automaton models by 2DFA-4W and 2NFA-4W, respectively.

By restricting the movement of the input head, we obtain the aforementioned restricted variants of the two-dimensional automaton model. By prohibiting upward movements, we obtain the three-way two-dimensional automaton model. Similarly, by prohibiting both upward and leftward movements, we obtain the two-way two-dimensional automaton model.

Definition 2 (Three-way/two-way two-dimensional automaton). *A three-way (resp., two-way) two-dimensional automaton is a tuple* $(Q, \Sigma, \delta, q_0,$ $q_{\text{accept}})$ *as in Definition 1, where the transition function* δ *is restricted to use only the directions* $\{D, L, R\}$ *(resp., the directions* $\{D, R\}$*).*

We denote deterministic and nondeterministic three-way two-dimensional automata by 2DFA-3W and 2NFA-3W, respectively, while the two-way model is denoted by the suffix -2W.

Additional details about the two-dimensional automaton model and its restrictions can be found in surveys by Inoue and Takanami [6], Kari and Salo [7], and the first author [11].

We now move on to defining the main models of the paper, which we call "extended" two-dimensional automata. We denote a (deterministic) i-extended three-way two-dimensional automaton by 2DFA-3W[i], where i is the number of upward moves the input head is permitted to make. Similarly, we denote a (deterministic) (i, j)-extended two-way two-dimensional automaton by 2DFA-2W[i, j], where i (resp., j) is the number of upward (resp., leftward) moves the input head is permitted to make.

Clearly, 2DFA-2W[∞, ∞] = 2DFA-3W[∞] = 2DFA-4W. Similarly, 2DFA-2W $[0, \infty]$ = 2DFA-3W, and 2DFA-2W[$\infty, 0$] is equivalent to 2DFA-3W$^{\circlearrowleft}$, or the class of deterministic three-way two-dimensional automata where the transition function is restricted to use only the directions $\{U, D, R\}$. Lastly, 2DFA-3W[0] = 2DFA-3W and 2DFA-2W[0, 0] = 2DFA-2W. All of the previous definitions and results apply also to nondeterministic models.

Remark 1. One could alternatively define the extended two-dimensional automaton model in terms of a four-way two-dimensional automaton that is only permitted to use at most i upward moves and at most j leftward moves. In this

```
# # # # # # # # # # # #
# *  ···  * 1 *  ···  * 1 *  ···  * #
# *  ···  * 1 *  ···  * 1 *  ···  * #
# # # # # # # # # # # #
```

Fig. 1. An example of a word in the language L_1 from the proof of Theorem 1, where the symbol $*$ denotes either 0 or 1

paper, however, we formulate the model in terms of three-way/two-way two-dimensional automata, as we feel this formulation better demonstrates how our model fits into the landscape of more well-known models from the literature.

3 Recognition Properties

3.1 Three-Way Recognition

We begin by examining relationships between three-way and four-way two-dimensional automata and the i-extended three-way variant.

Theorem 1. *2NFA-3W[0] $\subset$ 2NFA-3W[1].*

Proof. Let $\Sigma = \{0, 1\}$. We define the language L_1 to be the language of all two-dimensional words w with two rows such that w contains at least two occurrences of "stacked 1s"; that is, at least two columns j where $w[1, j] = w[2, j] = 1$. An example of a word in the language L_1 is illustrated in Fig. 1.

An automaton $\mathcal{A} \in$ 2NFA-3W[1] recognizes words in L_1 via the following procedure:

1. The input head of $\mathcal{A}$ moves rightward and scans the first row of the input word until it nondeterministically selects an occurrence of 1.
2. The input head moves downward to verify that the symbol in the second row is a 1.
3. The input head moves rightward and scans the second row of the input word until it nondeterministically selects another occurrence of 1.
4. The input head moves upward to verify that the symbol in the first row is a 1.

Clearly, this procedure requires only one upward move, which is performed in Step 4.

Recall that any automaton $\mathcal{A}' \in$ 2NFA-3W[0] is in fact a three-way two-dimensional automaton. For the sake of contradiction, suppose such an automaton $\mathcal{A}'$, with m states, recognizes the language L_1.

Let $u(i, j, z)$ denote the single-row (i.e., one-dimensional) word of length z where cells at positions i and j contain the symbol 1, $1 \leq i < j \leq z$, and all other positions contain the symbol 0. Furthermore, let $w(i, j, z)$ denote the two-row word where both rows are exactly the word $u(i, j, z)$. This two-dimensional word contains exactly two occurrences of "stacked 1s", while all other cells contain 0s.

Choose a length z such that $(z-1)/2 > m$. The automaton $\mathcal{A}'$ must accept all words $w(i,j,z)$, where $1 \leq i < j \leq z$. For each such word, let $C(i,j,z)$ denote an accepting computation of $\mathcal{A}'$ on that word. Since $z(z-1)/2 > m \cdot z$, there exist two different computations $C(i,j,z)$ and $C(r,s,z)$, with $i \neq r$ or $j \neq s$, such that in both computations $C(i,j,z)$ and $C(r,s,z)$ the automaton $\mathcal{A}'$ makes a downward move to the second row in the same column and same state. Without loss of generality, all accepting computations of $\mathcal{A}'$ must make a downward move, since otherwise all symbols on the second row of the input word could be 0.

However, as a consequence of this observation, $\mathcal{A}'$ will also accept the two-dimensional word w_0 where the first row is the word $u(i,j,z)$ and the second row is $u(r,s,z)$. Since $i \neq r$ or $j \neq s$, the word w_0 contains at most one occurrence of "stacked 1s" and, therefore, is not in the language L_1. $\square$

We can use a similar argument to generalize the previous theorem to work for any number of upward moves i.

Theorem 2. *2NFA-3W$[i] \subset$ 2NFA-3W$[i+1]$.*

Proof. Recall the language L_1 from the proof of Theorem 1. We create a family of languages L_i, $i \geq 2$, by taking i copies of L_1 and concatenating row-wise to form a new language. In this way, we create a language of two-dimensional words each consisting of $2i$ rows where rows $2j$ and $2j+1$, $0 \leq j < i$, contain at least two occurrences of "stacked 1s" as defined earlier.

An automaton $\mathcal{B} \in$ 2NFA-3W$[i+1]$ recognizes words in L_{i+1} via the following procedure:

1. The input head of $\mathcal{B}$ follows the process presented in the proof of Theorem 1 to verify that the first two rows of the input word contain at least two occurrences of "stacked 1s".
2. After verifying that the first two rows satisfy this condition, the input head moves back to the left border of the input word and then makes two downward moves.
3. The automaton repeats these two steps until all consecutive pairs of rows are checked.

The first two steps of this procedure require one upward move, and since there are a total of $2i+2$ rows in the input word, the procedure must be repeated $i+1$ times. Therefore, in order for $\mathcal{B}$ to accept an input word, it must make a total of $i+1$ upward moves.

For the sake of contradiction, suppose an automaton $\mathcal{B}' \in$ 2NFA-3W$[i]$ with m states also recognizes words in L_{i+1}. Each word in L_{i+1} consists of $2i+2$ rows where, for each odd c, the cth and $(c+1)$st rows form a word in L_1. Choose the number of columns z such that

$$(z-1)/2 > m \cdot (i+1). \tag{1}$$

Let $v(j,k,z)$ denote a two-dimensional word with z columns each of length $2i+2$, where the jth and kth columns, $1 \leq j < k \leq z$, consist entirely of 1s and all other symbols are 0. Let $C(j, k, z)$ denote an accepting computation of $\mathcal{B}'$ on the word $v(j, k, z)$.

Since $C(j, k, z)$ can make at most i upward moves, by the choice of z in Eq. 1, there exist $C(j, k, z)$ and $C(r, s, z)$, with $(j, k) \neq (r, s)$, such that for some even row value x, both $C(j, k, z)$ and $C(r, s, z)$ do not make an upward move from row x to row $x - 1$ and both $C(j, k, z)$ and $C(r, s, z)$ make a downward move from row $x - 1$ to row x in the same column and same state.

However, as a consequence of this observation, $\mathcal{B}'$ must accept a word where the first $x - 1$ rows are from $v(j, k, z)$ and the last $2i + 3 - x$ rows are from $v(r, s, z)$. Since $j \neq r$ and $k \neq s$, the $(x - 1)$st and xth rows do not form a word in L_1.   □

Combining Theorems 1 and 2 together with the fact that, for all $i \geq 1$, 2NFA-3W$[i] \subset$ 2NFA-3W$[\infty] =$ 2NFA-4W, we obtain a recognition hierarchy amongst nondeterministic extended three-way two-dimensional automata. A similar hierarchy exists for deterministic models.

Theorem 3. *For all $i \geq 1$,*

$$2DFA\text{-}3W \subset \cdots \subset 2DFA\text{-}3W[i] \subset 2DFA\text{-}3W[i + 1] \subset \cdots \subset 2DFA\text{-}4W.$$

The proof of Theorem 3 goes through in a similar way to other proofs in this section, but it uses a different language M_i to separate different classes in the hierarchy. We define the language M_1 to be the language of all two-dimensional words with two rows where each word contains exactly two occurrences of "stacked 1s" as defined earlier,[1] and where all other symbols of the word are 0s. We can then create a family of languages M_i, $i \geq 2$, by taking i copies of M_1 and concatenating row-wise.

3.2   Deterministic vs Nondeterministic Three-Way Recognition

Thus far, we have established that separate hierarchies exist for deterministic and nondeterministic i-extended three-way two-dimensional automata. When we compare deterministic and nondeterministic models to each other, however, it turns out that the models are incomparable. This stands in contrast to the usual relationship between deterministic and nondeterministic three-way two-dimensional automata, where 2DFA-3W $\subset$ 2NFA-3W [9]. In what follows, we present a series of lemmas building up to the main result of this section.

Lemma 1. *There exists a language M_1 that is recognized by an automaton in 2DFA-3W$[1]$ and not recognized by any automaton in 2NFA-3W$[0]$.*

Proof. Let $\Sigma = \{0, 1\}$. Recall the definition of the language M_1 from the discussion following Theorem 3. We shall use this language again in the present proof.

---

[1] Note that the language M_1 differs from the language L_1 in that words in M_1 contain *exactly* two occurrences of "stacked 1s", while words in L_1 contain *at least* two occurrences of "stacked 1s".

An automaton $\mathcal{M} \in$ 2DFA-3W[1] recognizes M_1 via the following procedure:

1. The input head of $\mathcal{M}$ scans the first row of its input word and verifies that the row contains exactly two occurrences of 1.
2. The input head returns to the leftmost occurrence of 1 in the first row and makes one downward move to verify that the symbol in the corresponding column of the second row is also 1.
3. The input head scans the second row of its input word and verifies that the row contains exactly two occurrences of 1.
4. The input head returns to the rightmost occurrence of 1 in the second row and makes one upward move to verify that the symbol in the corresponding column of the first row is also 1.

Clearly, this procedure requires only one upward move.

However, an automaton $\mathcal{N} \in$ 2NFA-3W[0] cannot recognize any words in the language M_1 by an argument analogous to that given in the proof of Theorem 1 showing that no automaton $\mathcal{B} \in$ 2NFA-3W[0] can recognize words in the language L_1.   □

We may generalize the previous argument to apply to i-extended three-way two-dimensional automata for any value of $i \geq 1$.

Lemma 2. *There exists a language M_{i+1} that is recognized by an automaton in 2DFA-3W[$i + 1$] and not recognized by any automaton in 2NFA-3W[i].*

Next, we consider the opposite direction.

Lemma 3. *There exists a language N_2 that is recognized by an automaton in 2NFA-3W[0] and not recognized by any automaton in 2DFA-3W[1].*

Proof. Let $\Sigma = \{0, 1\}$. We define the language N_1 to be the language of all two-dimensional words consisting of two rows that contain at least one occurrence of "stacked 1s". We then define N_2 to be the language created by concatenating two copies of N_1 row-wise; that is, N_2 is the language of all two-dimensional words consisting of four rows, where the first two rows and the last two rows each contain at least one occurrence of "stacked 1s".

An automaton $\mathcal{P} \in$ 2NFA-3W[0] recognizes words in N_2 via the following procedure:

1. The input head of $\mathcal{P}$ moves rightward and scans the first row of the input word until it nondeterministically selects an occurrence of 1.
2. The input head moves downward to verify that the symbol in the second row is a 1.
3. The input head moves to the leftmost symbol, makes a downward move to the third row of the input word, and scans the third row until it nondeterministically selects another occurrence of 1.
4. The input head moves downward to verify that the symbol in the fourth row is a 1.

Moreover, this procedure does not require any upward moves.

To show that no automaton $\mathcal{Q} \in$ 2DFA-3W[1] is capable of recognizing words in N_2, we first require an intermediate claim.

Claim. No automaton $\mathcal{Q}' \in$ 2DFA-3W[0] is capable of recognizing words in N_1.

Suppose that an automaton $\mathcal{Q} \in$ 2DFA-3W[1] recognizes words in N_2. As a consequence of the preceding claim, $\mathcal{Q}$ cannot correctly verify that the first two rows of its input word form a word from N_1 without making an upward move. If, for all input words, $\mathcal{Q}$ reads the first two rows without making an upward move, then it will enter the third row of an input word whose first two rows do not form a word from N_1. If we suppose the third and fourth rows of this input word consist entirely of 1s, then this forces $\mathcal{Q}$ to accept an illegal input word.

Thus, for some input words, $\mathcal{Q}$ must make an upward move in the first two rows, thereby exhausting its single upward move before it reaches the third row. Again, as a consequence of the preceding claim, it follows that $\mathcal{Q}$ cannot correctly verify that the third and fourth rows of its input word form a word from N_1. Therefore, if $\mathcal{Q}$ accepts all words in N_2, it must also accept some words not in N_2. □

As a consequence of Lemmas 1 and 3, we obtain the aforementioned result.

Theorem 4. *The classes 2NFA-3W[0] and 2DFA-3W[1] are incomparable.*

Remark 2. As we did with Lemmas 1 and 2, it seems reasonable to extend Lemma 3 to show that there exists a language recognized by an automaton in 2NFA-3W[i] and not recognized by any automaton in 2DFA-3W[$i+1$] for all $i \geq 1$. However, we would require a language different from that used in Lemma 3 to do so, as all languages N_i, $i \geq 1$, are recognized by an automaton in 2NFA-3W[0].

3.3   Two-Way Recognition

In this section, we turn to examining relationships between two-way and three-way two-dimensional automata and the (i, j)-extended two-way variant.

We prove our first result relating to extended two-way two-dimensional automata in a manner similar to the three-way case presented in Theorem 1.

Theorem 5. *2NFA-2W[0, 0] ⊂ 2NFA-2W[1, 0].*

Proof. Let $\Sigma = \{0, 1\}$. Recall the language L_1 from the proof of Theorem 1.

An automaton $\mathcal{C} \in$ 2NFA-2W[1, 0] recognizes words in L_1 in exactly the same way as the automaton $\mathcal{A} \in$ 2NFA-3W[1] from the proof of Theorem 1. Again, this process requires only one upward move, and no leftward moves are needed.

Recall that any automaton $\mathcal{C}' \in$ 2NFA-2W[0, 0] is in fact a two-way two-dimensional automaton. For the sake of contradiction, suppose such an automaton $\mathcal{C}'$ recognizes the language L_1. Then $\mathcal{C}'$ must necessarily accept the word

$$\begin{matrix} 1 & 1 \\ 1 & 1 \end{matrix}.$$

Moreover, the accepting computation of C' on this word cannot visit all cells of the word. Thus, if we change the one unvisited cell to contain a 0 instead of a 1, then C' must also accept this word not in L_1. $\qquad\square$

We now move on to proving the generalized form of the previous theorem. The idea of the proof is similar to that used in Theorem 2, but due to the fact that the model under consideration cannot move leftward, we must consider a simplified version of the language L_{i+1} that does not require an automaton to make leftward moves in order to accept words from the language.

Theorem 6. *2NFA-2W$[i, 0] \subset$ 2NFA-2W$[i + 1, 0]$.*

Proof. Let $\Sigma = \{0, 1\}$. We define the language K_{i+1}, $i \geq 1$, to be the language of all two-dimensional words u with two rows such that u contains at least $2i + 2$ occurrences of "stacked 1s".

An automaton $\mathcal{D} \in$ 2NFA-2W$[i + 1, 0]$ recognizes words in K_{i+1} via the following procedure:

1. The input head of $\mathcal{D}$ moves rightward and scans the first row of the input word until it nondeterministically selects the first occurrence of "stacked 1s". The input head then moves downward to verify the other occurrence of 1.
2. The input head moves rightward and scans the second row of the input word until it nondeterministically selects the second occurrence of "stacked 1s". The input head then moves upward to verify the other occurrence of 1.
3. The input head repeats the previous two steps a total of $i + 1$ times to verify that a total of $2i + 2$ columns of the input word contain "stacked 1s".

Altogether, this procedure requires a total of $i+1$ upward moves, and no leftward moves.

For the sake of contradiction, suppose an automaton $\mathcal{D}' \in$ 2NFA-2W$[i, 0]$ recognizes the language K_{i+1}. Then $\mathcal{D}'$ must accept the two-dimensional word u_0 consisting of two rows, where each row consists of the string 1^{2i+2}. However, an accepting computation of $\mathcal{D}'$ cannot visit all cells of u_0, since it can only make i upward moves. Moreover, an accepting computation of $\mathcal{D}'$ cannot backtrack through the word, as it cannot make any leftward moves. Thus, if we change one unvisited cell in u_0 to contain a 0 instead of a 1, then $\mathcal{D}'$ must also accept this word not in K_{i+1}. $\qquad\square$

Combining Theorems 5 and 6 together with the fact that, for all $i \geq 1$, 2NFA-2W$[i, 0] \subset$ 2NFA-2W$[\infty, 0] =$ 2NFA-3W$^{\circlearrowleft}$, we obtain another recognition hierarchy for the two-way case. Naturally, we get a similar hierarchy as before for deterministic models.

Theorem 7. *For all $i \geq 1$,*

$$\text{2DFA-2W} \subset \cdots \subset \text{2DFA-2W}[i, 0] \subset \text{2DFA-2W}[i + 1, 0] \subset \cdots \subset \text{2DFA-3W}^{\circlearrowleft}.$$

To prove Theorem 7, we use the singleton language S_i over the alphabet $\Sigma = \{0, 1\}$ consisting of one word of dimension $2 \times i$, $i \geq 1$, where all symbols are 1. Then, in a manner similar to the proof of Theorem 6, we can show that a deterministic two-way two-dimensional automaton making $(i+1)$ upward moves can recognize the word in S_{2i+2}, while no deterministic two-way two-dimensional automaton making i upward moves can visit all cells in such a word.

Since the classes 2DFA-3W/2NFA-3W and 2DFA-3W$^\circlearrowleft$/2NFA-3W$^\circlearrowleft$ are equivalent up to rotation,[2] both of the two-way hierarchies are upper-bounded by the class of languages recognized by traditional three-way two-dimensional automata.

Moreover, if a two-way two-dimensional automaton can recognize a language using at most i upward moves and no leftward moves, then the "transpose" of that language (i.e., each word in that language reflected about its diagonal) can be recognized by a two-way two-dimensional automaton using no upward moves and at most i leftward moves. Therefore, there exist analogous hierarchies for the $(0, i)$-extended models 2NFA-2W$[0, i]$ and 2DFA-2W$[0, i]$, where $i \geq 1$.

4   Closure Properties

In this section, we take a brief diversion to investigate some closure properties for extended two-dimensional automata. From past work [5,10], we know that the classes of languages recognized by nondeterministic three-way and nondeterministic four-way two-dimensional automata are closed under the operations of union and reversal (or "row reflection"). On the other hand, the deterministic counterparts of these language classes are closed only under language complement [12]. Thus, it is worthwhile to determine whether closure holds for the "in-between" models of 2DFA-3W$[i]$ and 2NFA-3W$[i]$.

It seems clear that the class 2NFA-3W$[i]$ is closed under union, since we can simply take the set of automata recognizing each language in the union and nondeterministically choose which automaton to use on a given input word.

Proposition 1. *For all $i \geq 1$, the class 2NFA-3W$[i]$ is closed under union.*

Using an approach based on that used to prove closure for the traditional three-way two-dimensional automaton model, we can show that deterministic i-extended three-way two-dimensional automata are closed under complement.

Theorem 8. *For all $i \geq 1$, the class 2DFA-3W$[i]$ is closed under complement.*

Proof. Let $\mathcal{A} \in$ 2DFA-3W$[i]$. We show that there exists an automaton $\mathcal{A}' \in$ 2DFA-3W$[i]$ such that, if $\mathcal{A}$ accepts some input word, $\mathcal{A}'$ does not, and vice versa.

---

[2] By "up to rotation", we mean that a language L recognized by an automaton $\mathcal{A} \in$ 2NFA-3W$^\circlearrowleft$ can also be recognized by an automaton $\mathcal{A}' \in$ 2NFA-3W if each word in L is rotated clockwise by 90 degrees. The same applies to deterministic models.

If $\mathcal{A}$ halts on every input word, then we simply swap the accepting and non-accepting states of $\mathcal{A}$ to obtain the automaton $\mathcal{A}'$. Otherwise, $\mathcal{A}$ loops infinitely on some input word, and we must show that $\mathcal{A}'$ can simulate the computation of $\mathcal{A}$ while ensuring that, in each row of its input word, the input head of $\mathcal{A}'$ either moves upward or downward, or the computation halts in that row.

To do so, $\mathcal{A}'$ simulates the computation of $\mathcal{A}$ in the style of Theorem 1 of Szepietowski [12]. The details of the construction are largely similar, with the exception of how right crossing sequences are computed. In our simulation, right crossing sequences may now account for a new outcome, $\{\uparrow\}$, corresponding to the case where the input head of $\mathcal{A}$ leaves the current row by making an upward move. This outcome is in addition to the existing outcomes given by Szepietowski, $\{\ell, \downarrow, \leftarrow\}$, which correspond to looping within the current row, leaving the current row by moving downward, and moving leftward beyond the leftmost boundary of the crossing sequence, respectively. We make an analogous change to the method of computing left crossing sequences. Since $\mathcal{A}$ can only make a limited number of upward moves, $\mathcal{A}'$ will never enter a "vertical loop" (i.e., a loop where the input head of $\mathcal{A}$ returns infinitely often to an earlier row via upward moves). Thus, we need only to detect and handle loops within a single row, which is done by our modified form of Szepietowski's construction. Lastly, $\mathcal{A}'$ accepts if and only if $\mathcal{A}$ does not accept, and vice versa.   □

Going further, an interesting set of language operations to study would be operations that are closed for either three- or four-way two-dimensional automata, but not both. For instance, union, intersection, reversal, and rotation are closed for 2DFA-4W, but not for 2DFA-3W. Similarly, intersection and rotation are closed for 2NFA-4W but not for 2NFA-3W, while row concatenation and row closure are closed for 2NFA-3W but not for 2NFA-4W. (Full details may be found in the surveys on two-dimensional automata [6, 7, 11].) Using our model, we could determine whether an operation becomes closed at some intermediate stage, or whether any modification to input head movement results in loss of closure.

5   Conclusion

Restricting the input head movement of a two-dimensional automaton results in a model that is weaker in terms of recognition power. However, based on past related work, it is reasonable to assume that this recognition power is affected by permitting some bounded number of input head reversals. In this paper, we considered the notion of degrees of restriction, and we developed extended two-dimensional automaton models in both three-way and two-way variants. We established that separate strict recognition hierarchies exist for both deterministic and nondeterministic i-extended three-way two-dimensional automata, and similar hierarchies exist for the two-way model. When we consider deterministic and nondeterministic extended three-way two-dimensional automata together, however, we find that the two models are incomparable. This is in contrast to the usual strict containment relationship between deterministic and nondeterministic three-way two-dimensional automata. We also investigated closure properties of extended three-way two-dimensional automata, finding that the nondeterministic model is closed under union and the deterministic model is closed under complement.

There remain some natural avenues for further study on this model. For the extended two-way two-dimensional automaton model, it would be worthwhile to investigate what kind of "sub-hierarchy" might result when modifying the numbers of permitted upward and leftward moves simultaneously, rather than separately. There also remains the problem of establishing a relationship between 2DFA-2W$[i, j]$ and 2NFA-2W$[i, j]$, similar to the result of Theorem 4. Moreover, the question of closure status persists for some operations such as reversal for 2NFA-3W$[i]$.

Lastly, in the introduction, we mentioned related work of Morita et al. on input-head reversal-bounded two-dimensional Turing machines, and we contrasted our model with theirs. We may alternatively consider a three-way two-dimensional automaton model more closely related to the model of Morita et al., where the automaton has two modes of operation (specifically, where its vertical direction of movement is either downward or upward) and it may switch between these two modes some constant k number of times. We may also consider extended two-dimensional automaton models with non-constant bounds on the number of upward or leftward moves. Investigating such models may prove to be interesting and could lead to results similar to those presented in this paper.

References

1. Anselmo, M., Giammarresi, D., Madonia, M.: New operations and regular expressions for two-dimensional languages over one-letter alphabet. Theor. Comput. Sci. **340**(2), 408–431 (2005)
2. Blum, M., Hewitt, C.: Automata on a 2-dimensional tape. In: Miller, R.E. (ed.) SWAT 1967, pp. 155–160 (1967)
3. Dong, J., Jin, W.: Comparison of two-way two-dimensional finite automata and three-way two-dimensional finite automata. In: Yang, X. (ed.) CSSS 2012, pp. 1904–1906 (2012)
4. Ibarra, O.H.: Automata with reversal-bounded counters: a survey. In: Jürgensen, H., Karhumäki, J., Okhotin, A. (eds.) DCFS 2014. LNCS, vol. 8614, pp. 5–22. Springer, Cham (2014). https://doi.org/10.1007/978-3-319-09704-6_2
5. Inoue, K., Takanami, I.: Three-way tape-bounded two-dimensional Turing machines. Inf. Sci. **17**, 195–220 (1979)
6. Inoue, K., Takanami, I.: A survey of two-dimensional automata theory. Inf. Sci. **55**(1–3), 99–121 (1991)
7. Kari, J., Salo, V.: A survey on picture-walking automata. In: Kuich, W., Rahonis, G. (eds.) Algebraic Foundations in Computer Science. LNCS, vol. 7020, pp. 183–213. Springer, Heidelberg (2011). https://doi.org/10.1007/978-3-642-24897-9_9
8. Morita, M., Inoue, K., Ito, A., Wang, Y.: Some properties on input head reversal-bounded two-dimensional Turing machines. IEICE Trans. Inf. Syst. **E86-D**(2), 201–212 (2003)

9. Rosenfeld, A.: Picture Languages: Formal Models for Picture Recognition, Computer Science and Applied Mathematics. Academic Press, New York (1979)
10. Sipser, M.: Halting space-bounded computations. Theor. Comput. Sci. **10**(3), 335–338 (1980)
11. Smith, T.J.: Two-dimensional automata. Technical report 2019–637, Queen's University, Kingston (2019)
12. Szepietowski, A.: Some remarks on two-dimensional finite automata. Inf. Sci. **63**(1–2), 183–189 (1992)

The Range of State Complexities of Languages Resulting from the Cascade Product—The Unary Case (Extended Abstract)

Markus Holzer[(⊠)] and Christian Rauch

Institut für Informatik, Universität Giessen, Arndtstr. 2, 35392 Giessen, Germany
{holzer,christian.rauch}@informatik.uni-giessen.de

Abstract. We investigate the state complexity of languages resulting from the cascade product of two minimal deterministic finite automata with n and m states, respectively. More precisely we study the magic number problem of the cascade product operation and show what range of complexities can be produced in case the left automaton is unary, that is, has only a singleton letter alphabet. Here we distinguish the cases when the involved automata are reset automata, permutation automata, permutation-reset automata, or do not have any restriction on their structure. It turns out that the picture on the obtained state complexities of the cascade product is diverse, and for all cases, except where the left automaton is a unary permutation(-reset) or a deterministic finite automaton without structural restrictions, and the right one is a reset automaton or a deterministic finite automaton without structural restrictions, we are able to identify state sizes that *cannot* be reached—these numbers are called "magic."

1 Introduction

Originally, the magic number problem for finite automata [8] asks whether there exists a minimal n-state nondeterministic finite automaton whose equivalent minimal deterministic finite automaton (DFA) has α states for all n and α with $n \leq \alpha \leq 2^n$. A number α not satisfying this condition is called a *magic number* for n. The problem was solved in [9], showing that for ternary languages *no* magic numbers exist contrary to the unary case [3]. It is worth noting that for binary languages the original problem from [8] is still open.

Observe that the idea behind the magic number problem is not limited to the determinization of nondeterministic finite automata. In fact, shortly after the introduction of the magic number problem several papers studied regularity preserving operations from a magic number perspective. In [7] it was shown that for the intersection of DFAs *no* number in the interval $[1, nm]$ is magic— this already holds for binary automata. Besides intersection also other formal language operations such as, e.g., union [7], concatenation [9], square [2], star [1],

© Springer Nature Switzerland AG 2021
S. Maneth (Ed.): CIAA 2021, LNCS 12803, pp. 90–101, 2021.
https://doi.org/10.1007/978-3-030-79121-6_8

reversal, and the cut operation [6] were investigated on the quest for magic numbers. It turned out that magic numbers are quite rare. For instance, for the star of unary languages there are linearly many magic numbers [1]. On the other hand, star of binary languages has no magic numbers. For the cut operation on unary automata the interval $2m$ up to $n - 1$ turns out to be magic. Thus, these complexities cannot be reached by the cut operation on m- and n-state DFAs, if $2m \leq n - 1$.

We contribute to the list of magic number problems for operations on automata by studying the cascade product, which is the main ingredient to the celebrated Krohn-Rhodes Theorem [10] that states that any finite automaton can be decomposed into (several) simple "automata prime factors." Here we are not interested in the classification of regular languages by automata prime factors. Instead, we investigate the descriptional complexity of the cascade operation on two finite automata A and B, only. We further limit our study to the case where the left automaton A is unary. For a better fine grain investigation of the subject in question we use minimal DFAs only from the following automata classes as operands to the cascade product operation: reset automata (RFA), permutation automata (PFA), permutation-reset automata (PRFA), and automata with no structural restrictions (DFA)—for unary automata every permutation-reset automaton is in fact either a reset or a permutation automaton. We list our findings in Table 1. A careful inspection of the table reveals that the right automaton B in the cascade product is more important for the number of reachable states in the product than the left one. Moreover, the picture turns out to be quite diverse. For instance, in case the left automaton is a unary RFA all combinations for the cascade product lead to magic numbers, which is not the case for the remaining products where a RFA is the right automaton in the product. The most complex situation appears whenever PFAs or PRFAs are involved. In these cases the set structure of the reachable number of states is mostly determined by the size n of the left automaton and the non-trivial divisors t of n. These cases lead to a significant amount of magic numbers. In fact, for all cases where magic numbers exist, except for the case where both devices are RFAs, the number $nm - 1$ turns out to be always magic. For the cascade product of an n-state unary PFA or a DFA with an m-state finite automaton in general the whole range $\{1, 2, \ldots, nm\}$ can be obtained, and thus no magic numbers exist in these cases. This is not too surprising since the cascade product can simulate the intersection of two automata—compare with [7]. The obtained results are in sharp contrast to the general case, when we do not restrict to unary automata as left operands in the cascade product. In [5] it was shown that for the general case, magic numbers only exist for the cascade product of two permutation automata. In all other cases the cascade products do not have magic numbers at all.

2   Preliminaries

We recall some definitions on finite automata as contained in [4]. A *deterministic finite automaton* (DFA) is a quintuple $A = (Q, \Sigma, \cdot, q_0, F)$, where Q is the finite

Table 1. The range of state complexities for the cascade product of a minimal unary n-state automaton A and a minimal m-state finite state device B of the mentioned types. The parameter t used in the set descriptions is a non-trivial divisor of n or k, depending on the case we are in. Moreover, the operation $\oplus$ on sets of numbers S_1 and S_2 is defined as $S_1 \oplus S_2 = \{\, x + y \mid x \in S_1 \text{ and } y \in S_2 \,\}$. In all cases where magic numbers exist, except for the cascade product of two RFAs, the number $nm - 1$ turns out to be magic.

Automata		State complexities of minimal DFAs for $L(A \circ B)$	Magic number(s)	
A	B			
RFA	RFA	$\{1, 2, 3\}$	Yes	Theorem 5
	PFA	$\{1, 2, \ldots, m + 1\}$	Yes	Theorem 6
	PRFA			
	DFA			
PFA	RFA	$\{1, 2, \ldots, 2n\}$	No	Theorem 7
	PFA	$\{1\} \cup \{\, nx \mid 1 \le x \le m \,\} \cup \{\, tx \mid 1 \le x < m \,\}$	Yes	Theorem 9
	PRFA	$\{1, 2, \ldots, 2n\} \cup \{\, nx \mid 1 \le x \le m \,\} \cup \{\, tx \mid 1 \le x < m \,\}$	Yes	Theorem 17
	DFA	$\{1, 2, \ldots, nm\}$	No	Theorem 18
DFA	RFA	$\{1, 2, \ldots, 2n\}$	No	Theorem 7
	PFA	$\bigcup_{k=1}^{n} (M_k \oplus [0, n - k])$, where	Yes	Theorems 19 and 20
	PRFA	$M_k = \{1\} \cup \{\, kx \mid 1 \le x \le m \,\} \cup \{\, tx \mid 1 \le x < m \,\}$		
	DFA	$\{1, 2, \ldots, nm\}$	No	Theorem 18

set of *states*, Σ is the finite set of *input symbols*, $q_0 \in Q$ is the *initial state*, $F \subseteq Q$ is the set of *accepting states*, and the *transition function* $\cdot$ maps $Q \times \Sigma$ to Q. The *language accepted* by the DFA A is defined as

$$L(A) = \{\, w \in \Sigma^* \mid q_0 \cdot w \in F \,\},$$

where the transition function is recursively extended to a mapping $Q \times \Sigma^* \to Q$ in the usual way. Obviously, every letter $a \in \Sigma$ induces a mapping on the state set Q to Q by $q \mapsto \delta(q, a)$, for every $q \in Q$. A DFA is *unary*, if the input alphabet Σ is a singleton set, that is, $\Sigma = \{a\}$, for some input symbol a. Moreover, a DFA is said to be a *permutation-reset* automaton (PRFA), if every input letter induces either a permutation or a constant mapping on the state set. If every letter of the automaton induces only permutations on the state set, then we simply speak of a *permutation* automaton (PFA). Finally, a DFA is said to be a *reset* automaton (RFA), if every letter induces either the identity or a constant mapping on the state set. The class of reset, permutation, permutation-reset, and deterministic automata in general are referred to as RFA, PFA, PRFA, and FA, respectively. It is obvious that the following chain of inclusions $X\mathsf{FA} \subseteq \mathsf{PRFA} \subseteq \mathsf{FA}$, where $X \in \{\mathsf{P}, \mathsf{R}\}$, holds. Moreover, it is not hard to see that the classes RFA and PFA are incomparable.

In [10] the *cascade product* of two DFAs $A = (Q_A, \Sigma, \cdot_A, q_{0,A}, F_A)$ and $B = (Q_B, Q_A \times \Sigma, \cdot_B, q_{0,B}, F_B)$, denoted by $A \circ B$, is defined as the automaton

$$A \circ B = (Q_A \times Q_B, \Sigma, \cdot, (q_{0,A}, q_{0,B}), F_A \times F_B),$$

where the transition function is given by

$$(p, q) \cdot a = (p \cdot_A a, q \cdot_B (p, a)),$$

for $p \in Q_A$, $q \in Q_B$, and $a \in \Sigma$. We say that A is the *left automaton* and B the *right automaton* in the cascade product $A \circ B$. It is obvious that the cascade product of two DFAs contains their direct product. In order to explain our notation we give a small example.

Example 1. Consider the PFA $A = (\{q_0, q_1, q_2, q_3\}, \{a\}, \cdot_A, q_0, \{q_0, q_1, q_2\})$, where the transitions are given by $q_i \cdot_A a = q_{i+1 \bmod 4}$, for $0 \leq i \leq 3$. Moreover, let

$$B = (\{p_0, p_1\}, \{q_0, q_1, q_2, q_3\} \times \{a\}, \cdot_B, p_0, \{p_0\})$$

be the PFA, where for all states and letters the transition function $\cdot_B$ acts like the identity, except for the letters (q_0, a) and (q_1, a). In this case, let $p_0 \cdot_B (q_0, a) = p_1$ and $p_1 \cdot_B (q_0, a) = p_0$. Moreover, let $p_0 \cdot_B (q_1, a) = p_1$ and $p_1 \cdot_B (q_1, a) = p_0$. The automata A and B are depicted in Fig. 1 on the top and lower right, respectively. It is easy to see that both automata are minimal.

By construction the cascade product of A and B is given by

$$A \circ B = (\{q_0, q_1, q_2, q_3\} \times \{p_0, p_1\}, \Sigma, \cdot, (q_0, p_0), \{q_0, q_1, q_2\} \times \{p_0\}),$$

where the transition function can be deduced from Fig. 1 on the lower left. Observe, that $A \circ B$ is also a PFA and that not all states are initially reachable. From the initially reachable part of $A \circ B$ the states (q_0, p_0) and (q_2, p_0) (states (q_1, p_1) and (q_3, p_0), respectively) are equivalent. Because these states are the only initially reachable ones and only two of the four are accepting, the minimal DFA which accepts the language $L(A \circ B)$ has exactly two states.

The following result is immediate by the lower bound results on the operational complexity of the intersection operation on finite automata [7].

Theorem 2. *Let A be an n-state and B an m-state DFA. Then nm states are sufficient and necessary in the worst case for any DFA accepting $L(A \circ B)$. The lower bound even holds for automata with binary input alphabet.*

When considering the descriptional complexity of the cascade product, we limit ourselves to the case where the involved automata are non-trivial, i.e., they have more than one state. This is due to the fact that if the right automaton in the operation under consideration is a singleton device, then the cascade product accepts either the empty set or the same language as the involved other device. If the left automaton is a singleton device, then the cascade product accepts either the empty language or the language L that is the image of the language that the right automaton accepts under the bijective mapping $(q, a) \mapsto a$ for the letters a of the left automaton, where q is the state of the left automaton. Therefore, only 1- or m-state automata, for $m \geq 1$, appear as results of a cascade product with a trivial automaton. Thus, in the forthcoming we only consider non-trivial automata.

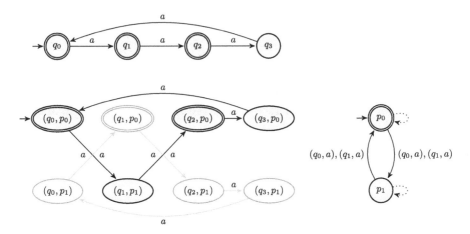

Fig. 1. The example automata A and B on the top and lower right, respectively. For a better visibility not all transitions of an automaton are shown. In particular, this is the case for automaton B, where self-loops are only depicted by dotted loops without letters. The cascade product $A \circ B$ is depicted on the lower left.

3   Results on the Cascade Product

This section is fourfold. In the first subsection we investigate the magic number problem for the cascade product, where at least one automaton is a reset device, while in the second subsection we study the magic number problem when both automata are PFAs. Afterwards we study the case, where the left automaton is a PFA and the right automaton is a PRFA. Finally we investigate the magic number problem for the cascade product, where at least one automaton is an arbitrary DFA. Before we start our studies we present a lemma on the minimality of PFAs that is used very often in the subsections to come without further notice. It is helpful and provides important information about the properties of PFAs.

Lemma 3. *Let A be a PFA with a sole accepting state with all states reachable from the initial state. Then A is minimal. Minimality is preserved even if the initial state is changed to any other state.*

Now we are ready for the first subsection considering the cascade product, where at least one automaton is a reset device.

3.1   At Least One Automaton is a Reset Automaton

Before we start our investigation on the cascade product where at least one automaton is a RFA, we take a closer look on minimal reset devices. It is easy to see that one cannot distinguish more than two non-accepting states, because the word that proves both of these states distinguishable must contain at least one letter that acts as a reset and therefore after reading this letter both states are mapped to the same state and thus cannot be shown inequivalent anymore.

A similar reasoning applies to accepting states. Hence, every minimal RFA has at most one accepting and one non-accepting state. Thus, we have shown the following result, where the single state case is trivial.

Lemma 4. *Every minimal reset automaton has at most two states.* $\qquad\square$

Although minimal RFAs form a very restricted class of automata their cascade product is worth to be considered in detail. We find the following situation—recall, that we only deal with non-trivial automata:

Theorem 5. *Let A and B be two minimal non-trivial RFAs, that is, both devices are 2-state automata. (i) If A is a unary automaton, then the minimal DFA accepting the language $L(A \circ B)$ has α states with $1 \leq \alpha \leq 3$ and (ii) if A has an input alphabet of at least two letters, then the minimal DFA accepting the language $L(A \circ B)$ has α states with $1 \leq \alpha \leq 4$.*

One can try to generalize the results of the previous theorem to other automata classes such as permutation automata for the right automaton in the product. In fact, one can show that for a non-trivial minimal unary RFA A and a minimal m-state PFA B, any DFA accepting the language $A \circ B$ has at most $m + 1$ states. Next we show that the whole interval $[1, m + 1]$ can be reached, if the left automaton is a minimal non-trivial unary RFA.

Theorem 6. *Let $m \geq 1$. Then for every α with $1 \leq \alpha \leq m + 1$, there exists a minimal non-trivial unary RFA A and a minimal m-state PFA B such that the minimal DFA for the language $L(A \circ B)$ has α states.*

This completes the case where the right automaton of the cascade product is a PFA. Now the question arises what happens if the PFA appears as the left automaton in the cascade product with a RFA. Compared to the previous case already for minimal unary PFAs and non-trivial RFAs the whole interval $[1, 2n]$, where n is the number of states of the PFA, can be reached. Observe that in the unary case the next theorem is in stark contrast to Theorem 6.

Theorem 7. *Let $n \geq 1$. Then for every α with $1 \leq \alpha \leq 2n$, there exists a minimal unary n-state PFA A and a minimal non-trivial RFA B such that the minimal DFA accepting the language $L(A \circ B)$ has exactly α states. The result holds true even in the case if A is has an input alphabet of arbitrary size.* $\qquad\square$

Since PFA $\subseteq$ PRFA $\subseteq$ FA holds the results from this subsection, where PFAs are involved, immediately generalize to permutation-reset and finite automata in general.

3.2   Two Permutation Automata

Before we start with the descriptional complexity analysis of the cascade product of two permutation automata we prove a useful result that is helpful to determine which deterministic state complexities are reachable and which ones are not.

Lemma 8. *The cascade product $A \circ B$ of two permutation automata A and B is a permutation automaton, too.*

Now we are ready to give an overview of all possible deterministic state complexities that can arise. We call a divisor t of a number n *non-trivial* if t is neither equal to 1 or n.

Theorem 9. *Let $n, m \geq 2$ and t be a non-trivial divisor of n. Then for every α in $\{1\} \cup \{ nx \mid 1 \leq x \leq m \} \cup \{ tx \mid 1 \leq x < m \}$, and only for those, there exists a minimal unary n-state PFA A and a minimal m-state PFA B such that the minimal DFA for the language $L(A \circ B)$ has α states.*

In a series of lemmata we first show how to reach each of the above specified values. Afterwards we show that only these values can be obtained. We start with the values of the form nx, for $1 \leq x \leq m$.

Lemma 10. *Let $n, m \geq 2$ and x with $1 \leq x \leq m$. Then for every α that is equal to nx, there exists a minimal unary n-state PFA A and a minimal m-state PFA B such that the minimal DFA for the language $L(A \circ B)$ has α states.*

With additional effort we can also show that every divisor of n is also reachable. This obviously includes the cases 1 and t of Theorem 9.

Lemma 11. *Let $n, m \geq 2$. Then for every α that is equal to one or to a non-trivial divisor of n, there exists a minimal unary n-state PFA A and a minimal m-state PFA B such that the minimal DFA for the language $L(A \circ B)$ has α states.*

We can extend the statement from the above lemma to the multiples of the divisors of n with some side conditions.

Lemma 12. *Let $n, m \geq 2$. Moreover, assume that x satisfies $2 \leq x \leq m-1$ and that t is a non-trivial divisor of n. Then for every α that is equal to tx, there exists a minimal unary n-state PFA A and a minimal m-state PFA B such that the minimal DFA for the language $L(A \circ B)$ has α states.*

The Lemmata 10, 11, and 12 thus show the reachability of the number of states in the cascade product of a unary PFA with a PFA as claimed in Theorem 9. Hence, it remains to prove that these are the only numbers that can be obtained. To this end we first prove two structural properties of cascade products of PFAs.

Lemma 13. *Let A and B be minimal n- and m-state PFAs, respectively. Then there is an x with $1 \leq x \leq m$ such that for every state q in A the number of initially reachable states in $A \circ B$ that have q as their first component is exactly x. As a direct consequence the initially reachable part of $A \circ B$ has exactly nx states.*

The next lemma provides information about the equivalence classes of the cascade product of permutation automata.

Lemma 14. *Let $A \circ B$ be the cascade product of two minimal PFAs A and B. Then the minimal deterministic finite automata that accepts $L(A \circ B)$ has α states, where α is a divisor of the quantity of initially reachable states of $A \circ B$. Furthermore, every state of $A \circ B$ has the same number of equivalent states, if $A \circ B$ is strongly connected.*

The last two lemmata obviously imply that only the numbers in

$$\{\, tx \mid t \text{ is a divisor of } n \text{ and } 1 \leq x \leq m \,\}$$

can be reached in the cascade product of two PFAs. This set differently written is equal to

$$\{1, 2, \ldots, m\} \cup \{\, nx \mid 1 \leq x \leq m \,\}$$
$$\cup \{\, tx \mid t \text{ is a non-trivial divisor of } n \text{ and } 1 \leq x < m\}$$
$$\cup \{\, tm \mid t \text{ is a non-trivial divisor of } n \,\},$$

where the unions are eventually *not* disjoint. In order to prove Theorem 9 it remains to exclude those numbers α that do not have a representation as given there. Because we showed already that $\alpha = 1$ is reachable we assume that $\alpha \geq 2$. Due to the Lemma 13 we know that the number of initially reachable states in $A \circ B$ is nx, for an integer $1 \leq x \leq m$. Moreover, by Lemma 14 we know that α is a divisor of nx. Now we distinguish two cases depending on the greatest common divisor t of n and α.

1. Case $t = 1$. Recall that α is the number of states of the minimal automaton accepting $L(A \circ B)$. First observe that the word a^α is the shortest word that only permutes equivalent states of $A \circ B$ and on the other hand the word a^n is the shortest word which induces the identity mapping on the states of A. Because α and n are coprime the smallest word which fulfills both conditions is $a^{n\alpha}$. This in turn implies that every mapping $a^{j\alpha}$, for $1 \leq j \leq n$, has a different image in A for a given state. Because $\alpha \geq 2$, there is at least one accepting and one non-accepting state that is initially reachable in $A \circ B$. We pick an arbitrary initially reachable accepting state (q, p) in $A \circ B$. Then by applying the mappings $a^{j\alpha}$, for $1 \leq j \leq n$, to (q, p) one observes that every of the obtained images has a different first component. Because (q, p) is accepting we obtain that n different states of A have to be accepting, which is a contradiction to the minimality of A.

2. Case $t > 1$. Then we distinguish two subcases:
   (a) Assume $\alpha/t \neq m$. Trivially, α equals $t \cdot \alpha/t$, where t is a divisor of n and α/t is a divisor of x. Because $t > 1$ we obtain the reachability of α by the Lemmata 10 and 12.
   (b) In this case we observe that $\alpha = t\alpha/t = tm$ and because there is no other common divisor of n and α it follows that n/t and m are coprime. We will show in the following theorem that α is not reachable in this case.

Theorem 15. *Let $n, m \geq 2$ and t be a non-trivial divisor of n. Then for every α that is equal to tm, there does* not *exist a minimal unary n-state PFA A and a minimal m-state PFA B such that the minimal DFA for the language $L(A \circ B)$ has α states, if the numbers m and $\frac{n}{t}$ are relatively prime.*

This completes our investigation on the cascade product of two permutation automata and eventually proves Theorem 9. Finally we want to point out that for example the numbers $nm - 1$ are magic numbers for every non-trivial minimal n-state PFA A and minimal m-state PFA B. This can be easily seen because for $n, m \geq 2$ we have (i) $1 < 3 \leq nm - 1$, (ii) $n(m - 1) < nm - 1 < nm$, and (iii) $tx \leq t(m-1) < nm-1$, for every non-trivial divisor t of n and $1 \leq x \leq m-1$. Therefore the reachability of $nm - 1$ is excluded by Theorem 9.

3.3 Permutation Automata with Permutation-Reset Automata

The next case that we consider for the cascade product is that of a unary permutation automaton with a permutation-reset device. We will see that a few further numbers on the state complexity are added to the case considered in the previous subsection. We start with the following lemma.

Lemma 16. *Let $n, m \geq 2$. Then for every α with $1 \leq \alpha \leq 2n$, there exists a minimal unary n-state PFA A and a minimal non-trivial PRFA B such that the minimal DFA accepting the language $L(A \circ B)$ has exactly α states.*

Since permutation-reset automata subsume permutation and reset automata we may safely conclude that at least all state sizes that appear in the cascade product $A \circ B$ of a permutation automaton A with an automaton B of the above types can be reached. Thus, by Theorems 7, 9, and Lemma 16 this results in the set $\{1, 2, \ldots, 2n\} \cup \{ nx \mid 1 \leq x \leq m \} \cup \{ tx \mid 1 \leq x < m \}$ of reachable state numbers. In the following theorem we show that these are indeed the only cases that can be reached for the cascade product of a unary PFA with a PRFA.

Theorem 17. *Let $n, m \geq 2$ and t be a non-trivial divisor of n. Then for every α in $\{1, 2, \ldots, 2n\} \cup \{ nx \mid 1 \leq x \leq m \} \cup \{ tx \mid 1 \leq x < m \}$, and only for those, there exists a minimal unary n-state PFA A and a minimal m-state PRFA B such that the minimal DFA for the language $L(A \circ B)$ has α states.*

Clearly for $m = 2$ there are no magic numbers for the cascade product of a minimal n-state PFA and a minimal m-state PRFA. But for $m > 2$ we have that $2n < nm - 1$, and therefore $nm - 1$ is a magic number for every pair n, m with $n \geq 2$ and $m \geq 3$.

3.4 Deterministic Finite Automata Without Restrictions

In order to complete our study on the cascade product for unary automata it remains to consider the cases, where in particular the right automaton is allowed to be a DFA in general. We will show that in this case there do not exist magic numbers, i.e., we obtain the whole interval $[1, nm]$.

Theorem 18. *Let $n, m \geq 2$. Then for every α in the interval $[1, nm]$ there exists a minimal unary n-state PFA A and a minimal m-state DFA B such that the minimal DFA for the language $L(A \circ B)$ has α states.*

By Theorem 18 we know that there are no magic numbers in the integer interval $[1, nm]$, if we allow the right automaton to be an arbitrary DFA. Because PFA $\subset$ PRFA $\subset$ FA we can transfer this result one-to-one to the case where both automata are DFAs.

It remains to consider the case where the left automaton is a DFA and the right one is a PFA or a PRFA. We need some notation for the next theorem: for two sets S_1 and S_2 of numbers let $S_1 \oplus S_2 := \{x + y \mid x \in S_1 \text{ and } y \in S_2\}$. Now we are ready for the statement, where the right automaton is a PFA.

Theorem 19. *Let $n, m \geq 2$. For k with $1 \leq k \leq n$ we define*

$$M_k = \{1\} \cup \{kx \mid 1 \leq x \leq m\}$$
$$\cup \{tx \mid t \text{ is a non-trivial divisor of } k \text{ and } 1 \leq x < m\}.$$

Observe that $M_1 = \{x \mid 1 \leq x \leq m\}$, because 1 does not have any non-trivial divisors. Then for every α in $\bigcup_{k=1}^{n}(M_k \oplus [0, n-k])$, and only for those, there exists a minimal unary n-state DFA A and a minimal m-state PFA B such that the minimal DFA for the language $L(A \circ B)$ has α states.

Finally, we show that there is no improvement on the reachable numbers if we use a PRFA B instead of a PFA as right operand in the cascade product with a DFA as left operand.

Theorem 20. *Let $n, m \geq 2$. Let M_k, for $1 \leq k \leq n$, be defined as in the previous theorem. Then for every α in $\bigcup_{k=1}^{n}(M_k \oplus [0, n-k])$, and only for those, there exists a minimal unary n-state DFA A and a minimal m-state PRFA B such that the minimal DFA for the language $L(A \circ B)$ has α states.*

One may ask whether all numbers in the integer interval $[1, nm]$ are reachable by Theorems 19 and 20. This is in fact not the case. For instance, if $n = 3$ and $m = 4$ then the reader may verify that we can only reach the values $\{1, 2, 3, 4, 5, 6, 7, 8, 9, 12\}$, because

$$M_1 \oplus [0, n-1] = (\{1, 2, 3, 4\} \oplus [0, 2]) = \{1, 2, 3, 4, 5, 6\},$$
$$M_2 \oplus [0, n-2] = (\{1, 2, 4, 6, 8\} \oplus [0, 1]) = \{1, 2, 3, 4, 5, 6, 7, 8, 9\},$$

and

$$M_3 \oplus [0, n-3] = (\{1, 3, 6, 9, 12\} \oplus [0]) = \{1, 3, 6, 9, 12\}.$$

A list of all magic numbers, for n and m with $2 \leq n, m \leq 6$ is given in Table 2. The interested reader may have noticed that the number $nm - 1$ appears in all non-empty sets in the presented table. This holds in general and can be seen as follows: (i) the largest number describable by an addition of $n - k$ to the elements of M_k, for $k < n - 1$, is less or equal to $(n-1)m + 1$, (ii) the largest number in M_{n-1} is $(n-1)m$, which gives the number $(n-1)m+1$, that for $m > 2$, is strictly less than $(n-1)m+m-1 = nm-1$, (iii) the second largest number in the set M_n is $n(m-1)$, which is strictly less than $nm-1$, and (iv) the largest number in M_n is nm, which is strictly greater than $nm-1$. This shows that $nm-1$ is not a member of $\bigcup_{k=1}^{n}(M_k \oplus [0, n-k])$ and thus is a magic number.

Table 2. The sets of magic numbers for the cascade product of a minimal unary n-state DFA A and a minimal m-state PFA B, for $2 \leq n, m \leq 6$, w.r.t. the interval $[1, nm]$.

DFA A	PFA or PRFA B with m states				
n-states	2	3	4	5	6
2	$\emptyset$	$\{5\}$	$\{7\}$	$\{7, 9\}$	$\{9, 11\}$
3	$\emptyset$	$\{8\}$	$\{10, 11\}$	$\{13, 14\}$	$\{14, 16, 17\}$
4	$\emptyset$	$\{11\}$	$\{11, 14, 15\}$	$\{14, 17, 18, 19\}$	$\{17, 21, 22, 23\}$
5	$\emptyset$	$\{14\}$	$\{18, 19\}$	$\{18, 19, 22, 23, 24\}$	$\{22, 23, 26, 27, 28, 29\}$
6	$\emptyset$	$\{17\}$	$\{19, 22, 23\}$	$\{19, 23, 27, 28, 29\}$	$\{23, 27, 28, 29, 32, 33, 34, 35\}$

4   Conclusions

The Krohn-Rhodes Theorem [10] states that for every DFA A there exists a cascade product of PRFAs that is equivalent to A. The descriptional complexity version of this statement [11,12] gives exponential upper and lower bounds on the size of the cascade product of A. To our knowledge the descriptional complexity of the cascade product for two automata was not investigated so far. We close this gap in this paper, by studying the problem in question for unary automata as left operands in the cascade product. In this way we are able to draw a complete picture for the studied cases and identify magic numbers, that is, size values that cannot be obtained by a cascade product of two minimal automata. See Table 1 for the obtained results in detail. The general problem, i.e., the descriptional complexity of the cascade product for non-unary left operands is studied in [5].

References

1. Čevorová, K.: Kleene star on unary regular languages. In: Jurgensen, H., Reis, R. (eds.) DCFS 2013. LNCS, vol. 8031, pp. 277–288. Springer, Heidelberg (2013). https://doi.org/10.1007/978-3-642-39310-5_26
2. Čevorová, K., Jirásková, G., Krajňáková, I.: On the square of regular languages. In: Holzer, M., Kutrib, M. (eds.) CIAA 2014. LNCS, vol. 8587, pp. 136–147. Springer, Cham (2014). https://doi.org/10.1007/978-3-319-08846-4_10
3. Geffert, V.: Magic numbers in the state hierarchy of finite automata. Inf. Comput. **205**(11), 1652–1670 (2007)
4. Harrison, M.A.: Introduction to Formal Language Theory. Addison-Wesley (1978)

5. Holzer, M., Rauch, C.: The range of state complexities of languages resulting from the cascade product-the general case (2021). Proc. DLT, to appear
6. Holzer, M., Hospodár, M.: The range of state complexities of languages resulting from the cut operation. In: Martín-Vide, C., Okhotin, A., Shapira, D. (eds.) LATA 2019. LNCS, vol. 11417, pp. 190–202. Springer, Cham (2019). https://doi.org/10.1007/978-3-030-13435-8_14
7. Hricko, M., Jirásková, G., Szabari, A.: Union and intersection of regular languages and descriptional complexity. In: Mereghetti, C., Palano, B., Pighizzini, G., Wotschke, D. (eds.) Proceedings of the 7th Workshop on Descriptional Complexity of Formal Systems, pp. 170–181. Universita degli Studi di Milano, Como, Italy (2005)
8. Iwama, K., Kambayashi, Y., Takaki, K.: Tight bounds on the number of states of DFAs that are equivalent to n-state NFAs. Theor. Comput. Sci. **237**(1–2), 485–494 (2000)
9. Jirásková, G.: Magic numbers and ternary alphabet. Int. J. Found. Comput. Sci. **22**(2), 331–344 (2011)
10. Krohn, K., Rhodes, J.: Algebraic theory of machines. Int. Trans. AMS **116**, 450–464 (1965)
11. Maler, O.: On the Krohn-Rhodes cascaded decomposition theorem. In: Manna, Z., Peled, D.A. (eds.) Time for Verification. LNCS, vol. 6200, pp. 260–278. Springer, Heidelberg (2010). https://doi.org/10.1007/978-3-642-13754-9_12
12. Maler, O., Pnueli, A.: Tight bounds on the complexity of cascaded decomposition of automata. In: Proceedings of the 31st Annual Symposium on Foundations of Computer Science, pp. 672–682. IEEE Computer Society Press, St. Louis, Missouri, USA (1990)

Guessing the Buffer Bound
for k-Synchronizability

Cinzia Di Giusto📶, Laetitia Laversa$^{(\boxtimes)}$📶, and Etienne Lozes📶

Université Côte d'Azur, CNRS, I3S, Sophia Antipolis, France
`laetitia.laversa@univ-cotedazur.fr`

Abstract. A communicating system is k-synchronizable if all of the message sequence charts representing the executions can be divided into slices of k sends followed by k receptions. It was previously shown that, for a fixed given k, one could decide whether a communicating system is k-synchronizable. This result is interesting because the reachability problem can be solved for k-synchronizable systems. However, the decision procedure assumes that the bound k is fixed. In this paper we improve this result and show that it is possible to decide if such a bound k exists.

Keywords: Communicating automata · MSC · Synchronizability

1 Introduction

Communicating finite state machines [4] model distributed systems where participants exchange messages via FIFO buffers. Due to the unboundedness of the buffers, the model is Turing powerful as soon as there are two participants and two queues. In order to recover decidability, several works introduced restrictions on the model, for instance: lossiness of the channels [1], specific topologies, or bounded context switching [13]. Another line of research focused on analyzing the system under the assumption that the semantics is synchronous [2,5,6,8,9,11,12,14] or that buffers are bounded. This assumption is not as restrictive as it may seem at first, because several systems enjoy the property that their execution, although not necessarily bounded, can be simulated by a causally equivalent bounded execution. Existentially k-bounded communicating systems [10] are precisely the systems whose message sequence charts can be generated by k-bounded executions. In particular, the reachability problem is decidable for existentially k-bounded communicating systems. A limitation of this framework is that the bound k on the buffer size must be fixed. A natural question is whether the existence of such a bound can be decided. Genest, Kuske and Muscholl answered this question negatively [10]. Bouajjani et al. [3][1] introduced a variant of existentially k-bounded communicating systems they called k-synchronizable systems. A system is k-synchronizable if each of its execution is causally equivalent to a sequence of communication rounds composed of at most

---

[1] The results in [3] have then been refined in [7].

© Springer Nature Switzerland AG 2021
S. Maneth (Ed.): CIAA 2021, LNCS 12803, pp. 102–114, 2021.
https://doi.org/10.1007/978-3-030-79121-6_9

k sends followed by at most k receptions. In particular, each execution of a k-synchronizable system is causally equivalent to a k-bounded execution (provided all messages are eventually received). Like for existentially bounded systems, the reachability problem becomes decidable for k-synchronizable systems, and the membership problem - whether a given system is k-synchronizable for a fixed given k is decidable as well. Bouajjani et al. conjectured that the existence of a bound k on the size of the communication rounds was undecidable.

Instead, in this paper, we show that this problem is decidable. This result contrasts with the negative result about the same question for existentially bounded communicating systems. There is an important difference between existentially bounded and k-synchronizable ones that explains this situation. Existentially bounded systems deal with peer-to-peer communications, with one buffer per pair of machines, whereas k-synchronizable systems deal with mailbox communications where one buffer per machine merges all incoming messages.

The paper is organized as follows: in the next section, we introduce preliminary definitions on communicating automata and k-synchronizable systems. In Sect. 3 we explain the general strategy for computing the bound k, which is to compute the automata of two regular languages: the language of reachable exchanges, and the language of prime exchanges. In Sect. 4 we focus on reachable exchanges, and in Sect. 5 on prime exchanges. Section 6 lastly computes the bound k. Finally Sect. 7 concludes with some final remarks. Additional material and proofs can be found here: https://arxiv.org/abs/2104.14408.

2   Preliminaries

Let $\mathbb{V}$ be a finite set of messages and $\mathbb{P}$ a finite set of processes exchanging messages. A send action, denoted $send(p, q, v)$, designates the sending of message v from process p to process q, storing it in the queue of q. Similarly, a receive action $rec(q, v)$ expresses that process q pops message v from its queue of incoming messages. We write a to denote a send or receive action. Let $S = \{send(p, q, v) \mid p, q \in \mathbb{P}, v \in \mathbb{V}\}$ be the set of send actions and $R = \{rec(q, v) \mid q \in \mathbb{P}, v \in \mathbb{V}\}$ the set of receive actions. S_p and R_p stand for the set of sends and receives of process p respectively.

A *system* is a tuple $\mathfrak{S} = ((L_p, \delta_p, l_p^0) \mid p \in \mathbb{P})$ where, for each process p, L_p is a finite set of local control states, $\delta_p \subseteq (L_p \times (S_p \cup R_p) \times L_p)$ is the transition relation and l_p^0 is the initial state. In the rest of the paper, when talking about a system $\mathfrak{S}$, we may also identify it with the global automaton obtained as the product of the process automata and denoted $(L_\mathfrak{S}, \delta_\mathfrak{S}, \mathbf{l_0})$ where $L_\mathfrak{S} = \Pi_{p \in \mathbb{P}} L_p$ is the set of global control states, $\mathbf{l_0} = (l_p^0)_{p \in \mathbb{P}}$ is the initial global control state and $((l_1, \cdots, l_q, \cdots, l_n), a, (l_1, \cdots, l_q', \cdots, l_n)) \in \delta_\mathfrak{S}$ iff $(l_q, a, l_q') \in \delta_q$ for $q \in \mathbb{P}$. We write $\mathbf{l}$ in bold to denote the tuple of control states $(l_p)_{p \in \mathbb{P}}$, and we sometimes write $l_q \xrightarrow{a}_q l_q'$ (resp. $\mathbf{1} \xrightarrow{a} \mathbf{1'}$) for $(l_q, a, l_q') \in \delta_q$ (resp. $(\mathbf{1}, a, \mathbf{1'}) \in \delta_\mathfrak{S}$). We write $\xRightarrow{a_1 \cdots a_n}$ for $\xrightarrow{a_1} \cdots \xrightarrow{a_n}$.

A *configuration* is a pair $(\mathbf{1}, \mathtt{Buf})$ where $\mathbf{1} = (l_p)_{p \in \mathbb{P}} \in L_\mathfrak{S}$ is a global control state of $\mathfrak{S}$, and $\mathtt{Buf} = (b_p)_{p \in \mathbb{P}} \in (\mathbb{V}^*)^{\mathbb{P}}$ is a vector of buffers, each b_p being a word over $\mathbb{V}$. $\mathtt{Buf_0}$ stands for the vector of empty buffers. The mailbox semantics of a system is defined by the two rules below.

$$[\text{SEND}] \qquad\qquad\qquad [\text{RECEIVE}]$$

$$\frac{1 \xrightarrow{send(p,q,v)} 1' \quad b'_q = b_q \cdot v}{(1, \mathtt{Buf}) \xmapsto{send(p,q,v)} (1', \mathtt{Buf}[b'_q/b_q])} \qquad \frac{1 \xrightarrow{rec(q,v)} 1' \quad b_q = v \cdot b'_q}{(1, \mathtt{Buf}) \xmapsto{rec(q,v)} (1', \mathtt{Buf}[b'_q/b_q])}$$

In this paper, we focus on **mailbox** semantics. An execution $e = a_1 \cdots a_n$ is a sequence of actions in $S \cup R$ such that $(1_0, \mathtt{Buf_0}) \xmapsto{a_1} \cdots \xmapsto{a_n} (1, \mathtt{Buf})$ for some 1 and $\mathtt{Buf}$. As usual, $\overset{e}{\Longmapsto}$ stands for $\xmapsto{a_1} \cdots \xmapsto{a_n}$. We write $asEx(\mathfrak{S})$ to denote the set of executions of a system $\mathfrak{S}$. Executions impose a total order over the actions. To stress the causal dependencies between messages we use message sequence charts (MSCs) that only impose an order between matched pairs of actions and between the actions of a same process.

Definition 1. *A message sequence chart μ is a tuple $(Ev, \lambda, \prec_{po}, \prec_{src})$ such that (1) Ev is a finite set of events partially ordered under $(\prec_{po} \cup \prec_{src})^*$, (2) $\lambda : Ev \to S \cup R$ tags each event with an action, (3) for each process p, $\prec_{po}$ induces a total order on the events of p, i.e. on $\lambda^{-1}(S_p \cup R_p)$, (4) $(Ev, \prec_{src})$ is the graph of a bijection between a subset of $\lambda^{-1}(S)$ and the whole of $\lambda^{-1}(R)$ (5) for all $s \prec_{src} r$, there are p, q, v such that $\lambda(s) = send(p, q, v)$ and $\lambda(r) = rec(q, v)$.*

We say that $s \in \lambda^{-1}(S)$ is a matched send if there exists r such that $s \prec_{src} r$. Otherwise, we say that s is unmatched. When v is either an unmatched $send(p, q, v)$ or a pair of matched actions $\{send(p, q, v), rec(q, v)\}$, we write $\mathsf{proc}_S(v)$ for p and $\mathsf{proc}_R(v)$ for q. Note that $\mathsf{proc}_R(v)$ is defined even if v is unmatched. An MSC is depicted with vertical timelines (one for each process) where time goes from top to bottom. Points on the lines represent events of this process. We draw an arc between two matched events and a dashed arc to depict an unmatched send. The concatenation $\mu_1 \cdot \mu_2$ of two MSCs is the union of the two MSCs where, for each p, all p-events of μ_1 are considered $\prec_{po}$ smaller than all p-events of μ_2. We write $msc(e)$ for the MSC associated with the execution e, and we say that a sequence of actions e is a linearization of a given MSC if it is the sequence of actions induced by a total order extending $(\prec_{po} \cup \prec_{src})^*$. We write $asTr(\mathfrak{S})$ for the set $\{msc(e) \mid e \in asEx(\mathfrak{S})\}$. We write $1 \overset{\mu}{\rightsquigarrow} 1'$ to denote that $1 \overset{e}{\Longrightarrow} 1'$ for any linearization e of μ. Finally, we recall from [7] the definition of causal delivery that allows to consider only MSCs that correspond to executions in the mailbox semantics.

Definition 2 (Causal delivery). *Let $\mu = (Ev, \lambda, \prec_{po}, \prec_{src})$ be an MSC. We say that μ satisfies causal delivery if it admits a linearization with the total order $<$ such that for any two events $s_1, s_2 \in Ev$, if $s_1 < s_2$, $\lambda(s_1) = send(p, q, v)$ and $\lambda(s_2) = send(p', q, v')$ for a same destination process q, then either s_2 is unmatched, or there are r_1, r_2 such that $s_1 \prec_{src} r_1$, $s_2 \prec_{src} r_2$, and $r_1 < r_2$.*

A k-exchange (with $k \geq 1$) is an MSC that admits a linearization $e \in S^{\leq k} R^{\leq k}$ starting with at most k sends and followed by at most k receives. An MSC is k-synchronous if it can be chopped into a sequence of k-exchanges.

Definition 3 (k-synchronous). *An MSC μ is k-synchronous if $\mu = \mu_1 \cdot$*
$\mu_2 \cdots \mu_n$ where, for all $i \in [1..n]$, μ_i is a $k - exchange$.

For instance, the MSC μ_1 depicted on Fig. 1 is 2-
synchronous, as it can be split in two 2-exchanges.

An execution e is k-synchronizable if $msc(e)$ is k-
synchronous. A system $\mathfrak{S}$ is *k-synchronizable* if all its executions are k-synchronizable.

Fig. 1. MSC μ_1

Theorem 1 ([3,7]). *It is decidable whether a system $\mathfrak{S}$ is k-synchronizable for*
a given k. Moreover, it is decidable to know whether a control state is reachable
under the assumption that $\mathfrak{S}$ is k-synchronizable.

This result is interesting but somehow incomplete as it assumes that a fixed
value of the parameter k has been found. We aim at answering this limitation
by computing the *synchronizability degree* of a given system.

Definition 4 (Synchronizability degree). *The synchronizability degree*
$\mathsf{sd}(\mathfrak{S})$ *of a system $\mathfrak{S}$ is the smallest k such that $\mathfrak{S}$ is k-synchronizable. In par-*
ticular, $\mathsf{sd}(\mathfrak{S}) = \infty$ if $\mathfrak{S}$ is not k-synchronizable for any k.

3   Largest Prime Reachable Exchange

In this section, we relate the synchronizability degree of a system to the size of
a "maximal, prime, reachable exchange". We start with defining these notions.

An *exchange* is a k-exchange for some arbitrary k, and we call k the size of
the exchange. An exchange μ is *reachable* if there exist exchanges $\mu_1, \cdots, \mu_n$ for
some $n \geq 0$ and such that $\mu_1 \cdots \mu_n \cdot \mu \in asTr(\mathfrak{S})$. An exchange μ is *prime* if
there does not exist a decomposition $\mu = \mu_1 \cdot \mu_2$ in two non-empty exchanges.
For instance, the 2-exchange (depicted by the MSC μ_2, Fig. 2) with linearization:

$$send(p,q,v_1) \cdot send(r,q,v_2) \cdot rec(q,v_1) \cdot rec(q,v_2)$$

is not prime, as it can be factored in two 1-exchanges
as follows

$$send(p,q,v_1) \cdot rec(q,v_1) \quad \cdot \quad send(r,q,v_2) \cdot rec(q,v_2).$$

Fig. 2. MSC μ_2

The size of the biggest prime reachable exchange is related to the synchronizability degree $\mathsf{sd}(\mathfrak{S})$ by the following property.

Lemma 1. *Let $k \in \mathbb{N} \cup \{\infty\}$ be the supremum of the sizes of all prime reachable*
exchanges. (1) If $k = \infty$, then $\mathsf{sd}(\mathfrak{S}) = \infty$ (2) if $k < \infty$, then either $\mathfrak{S}$ is
k-synchronizable and $\mathsf{sd}(\mathfrak{S}) = k$, or $\mathfrak{S}$ is not k-synchronizable and $\mathsf{sd}(\mathfrak{S}) = \infty$.

Since by Theorem 1 it is decidable whether $\mathfrak{G}$ is k-synchronizable, it is enough to know k in order to compute $\mathsf{sd}(\mathfrak{G})$. In order to compute k, we have to address two problems: the number of exchanges is possibly infinite, and one should examine sequences of arbitrarily many exchanges. To solve these issues, we are going to reduce to a problem on regular languages. Let $\Sigma = \{!?, !\} \times \mathbb{V} \times \mathbb{P}^2$; for better readability, we write $!?v^{p \to q}$ (resp. $!v^{p \to q}$) for a Σ-symbol. To every Σ-word w we associate an MSC $msc(w)$ as follows. Consider the substitutions $\sigma_1 : \Sigma \to S$ and $\sigma_2 : \Sigma \to R \cup \{\epsilon\}$ such that $\sigma_1(!?v^{p \to q}) = \sigma_1(!v^{p \to q}) = send(p, q, v)$, $\sigma_2(!?v^{p \to q}) = rec(q, v)$ and $\sigma_2(!v^{p \to q}) = \epsilon$. Then $msc(w)$ is defined as $msc(\sigma_1(w)\sigma_2(w))$. Clearly, it is an exchange (by construction, it admits a linearization in $S^* R^*$), but more remarkably any reachable exchange can be represented by such a word.

Lemma 2. *For all reachable exchanges μ, there exists $w \in \Sigma^*$ s.t. $\mu = msc(w)$.*

The proof follows from the fact that it is always possible to receive messages in the same global order as they have been sent. Such a property would not hold for peer-to-peer communications (see a counter-example in the long version).

We can now define two languages over Σ:

$$\mathcal{L}_r = \{w \in \Sigma^* \mid msc(w) \text{ is reachable}\} \text{ and } \mathcal{L}_p = \{w \in \Sigma^* \mid msc(w) \text{ is prime}\}$$

Then the bound k we are looking for is the length of the longest word in $\mathcal{L}_r \cap \mathcal{L}_p$. It suffices to show that both $\mathcal{L}_r$ and $\mathcal{L}_p$ are effective regular languages to get an algorithm for computing k. This is the content of Sects. 4 and 5.

4   Regularity of Reachable Exchanges

In this section, we aim at defining a finite state automaton that accepts a word $w \in \Sigma^*$ iff $msc(w)$ is reachable, that is, iff there exists $\mu_1, \mu_2, \ldots, \mu_n$ such that $\mu_1 \cdot \mu_2 \cdots \mu_n \cdot msc(w) \in asTr(\mathfrak{G})$. Now, observe that the prefix $\mu_1 \cdot \mu_2 \cdots \mu_n$ brings the system in a certain global control state that conditions what can be done by $msc(w)$. Moreover, the presence of unmatched messages in a buffer imposes that none of the subsequent messages sent to the same buffer can be read.

The construction of the automaton accepting $\mathcal{L}_r$ proceeds in three separate steps. First, we build an automaton that accepts the language of all words that code an exchange, starting in a certain global control state **in**, and ending in another global control state **fin**, and possibly not satisfying causal delivery. Secondly, we consider the set of MSCs that satisfy causal delivery. We define automata that recognize the words coding MSCs starting from a certain "buffer state" and ending in another "buffer state", the "buffer state" characterizing whether or not the MSC satisfies causal delivery. Finally, we show that $\mathcal{L}_r$ is a boolean combination of the languages of some of these automata.

4.1 Automata of the Control States

We consider triples of global states $(\mathbf{in}, \mathbf{mid}, \mathbf{fin})$, representing the exchanges such that $\mathbf{mid}$ can be reached only with sends from $\mathbf{in}$ and $\mathbf{fin}$ can be reached only with receptions from $\mathbf{mid}$. We want to define an automaton $\mathrm{SR}(\mathbf{in}, \mathbf{mid}, \mathbf{fin})$ that recognizes the words coding such exchanges. Intuitively, $\mathrm{SR}(\mathbf{in}, \mathbf{mid}, \mathbf{fin})$ is a product of on the one hand the global automaton $\mathfrak{S}$ restricted to send transitions and on the other hand $\mathfrak{S}$ restricted to receive transitions. For each send action, either the reception is available and a matched message possible, or there is no corresponding reception and so we obtain an unmatched message.

Definition 5 (Automaton of control states). *Let $\mathfrak{S}$ be a system and* $\mathbf{in}, \mathbf{mid}, \mathbf{fin}$ *global states.* $\mathrm{SR}(\mathbf{in}, \mathbf{mid}, \mathbf{fin}) = (L_{\mathrm{SR}}, \delta_{\mathrm{SR}}, 1^0_{\mathrm{SR}}, F_{\mathrm{SR}})$ *is the automaton where:*

- $L_{\mathrm{SR}} = \{(1,1') \mid 1,1' \in L_{\mathfrak{S}}\}$; $1^0_{\mathrm{SR}} = (\mathbf{in}, \mathbf{mid})$; $F_{\mathrm{SR}} = \{(\mathbf{mid}, \mathbf{fin})\}$;
- *for each* $(1_\mathbf{s}, send(p,q,v), 1'_\mathbf{s}) \in \delta_{\mathfrak{S}}$:
  - $((1_\mathbf{s}, 1), !v^{p \to q}, (1'_\mathbf{s}, 1)) \in \delta_{\mathrm{SR}}$ *for* $1 \in L_{\mathfrak{S}}$;
  - *if* $(1_\mathbf{r}, rec(q,v), 1'_\mathbf{r}) \in \delta_{\mathfrak{S}}$ *then* $((1_\mathbf{s}, 1_\mathbf{r}), !?v^{p \to q}, (1'_\mathbf{s}, 1'_\mathbf{r})) \in \delta_{\mathrm{SR}}$

We denote $\mathcal{L}(\mathrm{SR}(\mathbf{in}, \mathbf{mid}, \mathbf{fin}))$ the language of a such automaton. This is an example of the construction.

Example 1. Let $\mathfrak{S}_1$ be the system whose process automata p, q and r are depicted in Fig. 3. For the triple $(\mathbf{in}, \mathbf{mid}, \mathbf{fin})$ where $\mathbf{in} = (0,0,0), \mathbf{mid} = (2,0,1)$ and $\mathbf{fin} = (2,1,2)$, automaton $\mathrm{SR}(\mathbf{in}, \mathbf{mid}, \mathbf{fin})$ recognizes the following language:

$$\mathcal{L}(\mathrm{SR}(\mathbf{in}, \mathbf{mid}, \mathbf{fin})) = \; !?a^{p \to r}(!c^{p \to q}!?b^{r \to q} + !?b^{r \to q}!c^{p \to q})$$
$$+ \; !?b^{r \to q}!?a^{p \to r}!c^{p \to q}$$

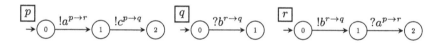

Fig. 3. System $\mathfrak{S}_1$

Lemma 3. $w \in \mathcal{L}(\mathrm{SR}(\mathbf{in}, \mathbf{mid}, \mathbf{fin}))$ *for some* $\mathbf{mid}$ *iff* $\mathbf{in} \overset{msc(w)}{\rightsquigarrow} \mathbf{fin}$.

4.2   Automata of Causal Delivery Exchanges

Let us now move to the trickier part, namely the recognition of words coding MSCs that satisfy causal delivery. Let $\mu = (Ev, \lambda, \prec_{po}, \prec_{src})$ be an MSC, and $v \in \lambda^{-1}(S)$ a send event, we write $ev_S(v)$ for the event v and, when it exists, $ev_R(v)$ for the event $v' \in \lambda^{-1}(R)$ such that $v \prec_{src} v'$. We say that v is unmatched if $ev_R(v)$ is undefined. We recall from [3] the notion of conflict graph. Intuitively, it captures some (but not all) causal dependencies between events. The figure on the right represents an MSC and its associated conflict graph (Fig. 4).

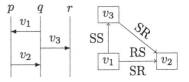

Fig. 4. MSC μ_3 and its conflict graph

Definition 6 (Conflict Graph). *The conflict graph* $\mathsf{CG}(\mu)$ *of an MSC* $\mu = (Ev, \lambda, \prec_{po}, \prec_{src})$ *is the labeled graph* $(V, \{\xrightarrow{XY}\}_{X,Y \in \{R,S\}})$ *where* $V = \lambda^{-1}(S)$, *and for all* $v, v' \in V$, *there is a XY dependency edge* $v \xrightarrow{XY} v'$ *between* v *and* v' *($X, Y \in \{S, R\}$), if* $ev_X(v)$ *and* $ev_Y(v')$ *are defined and* $ev_X(v) \prec_{po} ev_Y(v')$.

The *extended conflict graph* [7] $\mathsf{ECG}(\mu)$ is obtained by adding all dashed edges $v \overset{XY}{\dashrightarrow} v'$ satisfying the relation $\overset{XY}{\dashrightarrow}$ in Fig. 5. Intuitively, $v \overset{XY}{\dashrightarrow} v'$ expresses that the event X of v must happen before the event Y of v' due to: their order on the same machine (Rule 1), or the fact that a send happens before its matching receive (Rule 2), or to the mailbox semantics (Rules 3 and 4), or because of a chain of such dependencies (Rule 5). This captures all constraints induced by the mailbox communication, and it has been shown that an MSC satisfies causal delivery if and only if its extended conflict graph is acyclic (Theorem 2 in [7]).

We build an automaton that recognizes the words w such that $msc(w)$ satisfies causal delivery. To this aim, we associate to each MSC a "buffer state" that contains enough information to determine whether its extended conflict graph is acyclic. We write $\mathbb{B}$ for the set $(2^{\mathbb{P}} \times 2^{\mathbb{P}})^{\mathbb{P}}$. The *buffer state* $\mathcal{B}(\mu) \in \mathbb{B}$ of the MSC μ is the tuple $\mathcal{B}(\mu) = (\mathcal{C}^{\mu}_{S,p}, \mathcal{C}^{\mu}_{R,p})_{p \in \mathbb{P}}$ such that for all $p \in \mathbb{P}$:

$$\mathcal{C}^{\mu}_{S,p} = \{\mathsf{proc}_S(v) \mid v' \overset{SS}{\dashrightarrow} v \ \& \ v' \text{ is unmatched} \ \& \ \mathsf{proc}_R(v') = p\} \cup$$
$$\{\mathsf{proc}_S(v) \mid v \text{ is unmatched} \ \& \ \mathsf{proc}_R(v) = p\}$$
$$\mathcal{C}^{\mu}_{R,p} = \{\mathsf{proc}_R(v) \mid v' \overset{SS}{\dashrightarrow} v \ \& \ v' \text{ is unmatched} \ \& \ \mathsf{proc}_R(v') = p \ \& \ v \text{ is matched}\}$$

We can show that the $\mathsf{ECG}(\mu)$ is acyclic if for all $p \in \mathbb{P}$, $p \notin \mathcal{C}^{\mu}_{R,p}$ (immediate consequence of Theorem 2 in [7]). Moreover, we write $\mathbb{B}_{good}$ for the subset of $\mathbb{B}$ formed by the tuples $(C_{S,p}, C_{R,p})_{p \in \mathbb{P}}$ such that $p \notin C_{R,p}$ for all p.

Proposition 1 ([7]). *For* $w \in \Sigma^*$, $msc(w)$ *satisfies causal delivery if and only if* $\mathcal{B}(\mu(w)) \in \mathbb{B}_{good}$.

Noticing that $\mathbb{B}$ is finite, we build an automaton $\mathcal{A}(B_0, B_1)$ with $B_0, B_1 \in \mathbb{B}$. The intuition behind these two buffer states is that B_0 summarises the conflict graph derived from previous exchanges and B_1 summarises the conflict graph obtained when a new exchange is added.

$$(\text{Rule 1}) \ \frac{v_1 \xrightarrow{XY} v_2}{v_1 \xdashrightarrow{XY} v_2} \qquad (\text{Rule 2}) \ \frac{v \text{ is matched}}{v \xdashrightarrow{SR} v} \qquad (\text{Rule 3}) \ \frac{v_1 \xrightarrow{RR} v_2}{v_1 \xdashrightarrow{SS} v_2}$$

$$(\text{Rule 4}) \ \frac{\begin{array}{c} v_1 \text{ is matched} \quad v_2 \text{ is unmatched} \\ \mathsf{proc}_R(v_1) = \mathsf{proc}_R(v_2) \end{array}}{v_1 \xdashrightarrow{SS} v_2} \qquad (\text{Rule 5}) \ \frac{v_1 \xdashrightarrow{XY\ YZ} v_2}{v_1 \xdashrightarrow{XZ} v_2}$$

Fig. 5. Deduction rules for extended dependency edges of the conflict graph

Definition 7 (Automaton of causal exchanges). *The automaton $\mathcal{A}(B_0, B_1)$ is defined as follows:*

- $\mathbb{B}$ *is the set of states,*
- B_0 *is the initial state (hereafter, we assume that $B_0 = (C_{S,p}^{(0)}, C_{R,p}^{(0)})_{p\in\mathbb{P}}$).*
- $\{B_1\}$ *is the set of final states*
- *the transition relation $(\xrightarrow{a})_{a\in\Sigma}$ is defined as follows:*

  • $(C_{S,p}, C_{R,p})_{p\in\mathbb{P}} \xrightarrow{!?v^{p\to q}} (C'_{S,p}, C'_{R,p})_{p\in\mathbb{P}}$ *holds if for all $r \in \mathbb{P}$: let the intermediate set $C''_{S,r}$ be defined by*

$$C''_{S,r} = \begin{cases} C_{S,r} \cup \{p\} & \text{if } p \in C_{R,r}^{(0)} \text{ or } q \in C_{R,r} \\ C_{S,r} & \text{otherwise} \end{cases}$$

  Then

$$C'_{S,r} = \begin{cases} C''_{S,r} \cup C_{S,q} & \text{if } p \in C''_{S,r} \\ C_{S,r} & \text{otherwise} \end{cases} \quad \text{and} \quad C'_{R,r} = \begin{cases} C_{R,r} \cup \{q\} \cup C_{R,q} & \text{if } p \in C''_{S,r} \\ C_{R,r} & \text{otherwise} \end{cases}$$

  • $(C_{S,p}, C_{R,p})_{p\in\mathbb{P}} \xrightarrow{!v^{p\to q}} (C'_{S,p}, C'_{R,p})_{p\in\mathbb{P}}$ *holds if for all $r \in \mathbb{P}$,*

$$C'_{S,r} = \begin{cases} C_{S,r} \cup \{p\} & \text{if } q = r \text{ or } q \in C_{R,r} \\ C_{S,r} & \text{otherwise} \end{cases} \quad \text{and} \quad C'_{R,r} = C_{R,r}$$

Let $\mathcal{L}(B_0, B_1)$ denote the language recognized by $\mathcal{A}(B_0, B_1)$.

Example 2. Consider $\mu_4 = msc(w)$ with $w = !v_3^{p_1 \to p_2} !? v_4^{p_3 \to p_2} !? v_5^{p_4 \to p_6} !? v_6^{p_6 \to p_7}$ and assume we start with B_0 such that $C_{S,p_5} = \{p_4\}$ and $C_{R,p_5} = \{p_3\}$. Then the update of B (or, more precisely, of C_{S,p_5}, C_{R,p_5}, and C_{S,p_2}) after reading each message is shown below. Note how v_6 has no effect, despite the fact that $p_6 \in C_{R,p_5}$ at the time the message is read (Fig. 6).

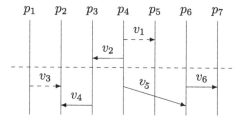

Fig. 6. MSC μ_4

$$
\begin{array}{c|ccccc}
C_{S,p_5} & \{p_4\} & \{p_4\} & \{p_1,p_3,p_4\} & \{p_1,p_3,p_4\} & \{p_1,p_3,p_4\} \\
C_{R,p_5} & \{p_3\} \xrightarrow{!v_3} \{p_3\} \xrightarrow{!?v_4} \{p_2,p_3\} \xrightarrow{!?v_5} \{p_2,p_3,p_6\} \xrightarrow{!?v_6} \{p_2,p_3,p_6\} \\
C_{S,p_2} & \emptyset & \{p_1\} & \{p_1\} & \{p_1\} & \{p_1\}
\end{array}
$$

Next lemma states that $\mathcal{A}(B, B')$ recognizes the words w such that $msc(w)$, starting with an initial buffer state B, ends in final buffer state B'.

Lemma 4. *Let $B, B' \in \mathbb{B}$ and $w \in \Sigma^*$. Then $w \in \mathcal{L}(B, B')$ if and only if for all MSC μ such that $B = \mathcal{B}(\mu)$, $B' = \mathcal{B}(\mu \cdot msc(w))$.*

4.3   Language of Reachable Exchanges

The only thing that remains to do is to combine the previous automata to define one that recognizes the (codings of) reachable exchanges. The language $\mathcal{L}(\mathrm{SR}(\mathbf{in}, \mathbf{mid}, \mathbf{fin}))$ contains arbitrary exchanges which do not necessarily satisfy causal delivery. Here comes into play the $\mathcal{A}(B, B')$ automata, where we take B and $B' \in \mathbb{B}_{good}$ in order to ensure causal delivery.

Let

$$
\mathcal{L}_{\mathrm{C}}(\mathbf{in}, \mathbf{fin}, B, B') \stackrel{\text{def}}{=} \bigcup_{\mathbf{mid} \in L_{\mathfrak{S}}} \mathcal{L}(\mathrm{SR}(\mathbf{in}, \mathbf{mid}, \mathbf{fin})) \cap \mathcal{L}(B, B').
$$

Intuitively, $\mathcal{L}_{\mathrm{C}}(\mathbf{in}, \mathbf{fin}, B, B')$ is the language of (codings of) exchanges between global states $\mathbf{in}$ and $\mathbf{fin}$ starting with an initial buffer state B and ending in final buffer state B'; when moreover $B, B' \in \mathbb{B}_{good}$, these exchanges satisfy causal delivery.

The last step is to combine causal delivery exchanges so that they can be performed by the system one after the other from the initial state $\mathbf{l_0}$. This motivates the definition of the following set $\mathcal{R}$ of *reachable languages*. Let $B_\emptyset = (\emptyset, \emptyset)_{p \in \mathbb{P}}$.

Definition 8 (Reachable languages). *Given a system $\mathfrak{S} = (L_{\mathfrak{S}}, \delta_{\mathfrak{S}}, \mathbf{l_0})$, the set $\mathcal{R}$ of reachable languages is the least set of languages of the form $\mathcal{L}_C(\mathbf{in}, \mathbf{fin}, B_i, B_f)$ defined as follows.*

1. *for any $\mathbf{l} \in L_{\mathfrak{S}}$ and $B \in \mathbb{B}_{good}$, $\mathcal{L}_C(\mathbf{l_0}, \mathbf{l}, B_\emptyset, B)$ is in $\mathcal{R}$*
2. *for any $\mathbf{l_1}, \mathbf{l_2}, \mathbf{l_3} \in L_{\mathfrak{S}}$ and any $B_1, B_2, B_3 \in \mathbb{B}_{good}$, if $\mathcal{L}_C(\mathbf{l_1}, \mathbf{l_2}, B_1, B_2) \in \mathcal{R}$ and $\mathcal{L}_C(\mathbf{l_1}, \mathbf{l_2}, B_1, B_2) \neq \emptyset$ then $\mathcal{L}_C(\mathbf{l_2}, \mathbf{l_3}, B_2, B_3) \in \mathcal{R}$.*

Then the union $\bigcup \mathcal{R}$ of all reachable languages is equal to the language $\mathcal{L}_{\mathrm{r}} = \{w \in \Sigma^* \mid msc(w) \text{ is reachable}\}$. As a consequence, we get the following result.

Theorem 2. *$\mathcal{L}_r$ is a regular language and is accepted by an effective finite state automaton.*

5   Prime Exchanges

We reformulate the primality of an exchange in terms of its conflict graph. We say that the conflict graph $\mathsf{CG}(\mu)$ associated with the MSC μ is strongly connected if for all $v, v' \in V$ it holds that $v \to^* v'$, where $\to^*$ is the reflexive transitive closure of $\to = \bigcup_{X,Y \in \{S,R\}} \xrightarrow{XY}$.

Lemma 5. *An exchange μ is prime iff $\mathsf{CG}(\mu)$ is strongly connected.*

Next we discuss the construction of the automaton that recognizes $\{w \in \Sigma^* \mid msc(w)$ is prime$\}$. Since there are infinitely many $\mathsf{CG}(msc(w))$, in order to have a finite state automaton, we compute a finite abstractions of $\mathsf{CG}(msc(w))$ that is sound in the sense that $\mathsf{CG}(msc(w))$ is strongly connected if and only if its abstraction is of a certain shape. Let us now define this abstraction.

We need to define some graph transformations. The graphs we are going to manipulate are oriented graphs labeled with a pair of set of processes on each vertex. We call such objects P-graphs. Formally, a P-graph is a tuple $(V, E, \lambda_S, \lambda_R)$ with $E \subseteq V \times V$ and $\lambda_X : V \to 2^{\mathbb{P}}$ for $X \in \{S, R\}$. The P-graph $\mathsf{pgr}(\mu)$ associated with the conflict graph $\mathsf{CG}(\mu) = (V, \{\xrightarrow{XY}\}_{X,Y \in \{S,R\}})$ is $(V, E, \lambda_S, \lambda_R)$ where (1) $(v, v') \in E$ if $v \xrightarrow{XY} v'$ for some X, Y, (2) $\lambda_S(v) = \{\mathsf{proc}_S(v)\}$, and (3) if v is matched, then $\lambda_R(v) = \{\mathsf{proc}_R(v)\}$, and if v is unmatched $\lambda_R(v) = \emptyset$.

The first graph transformation we consider consists in merging the vertices that belong to a same strongly connected component (SCC). Formally, let $G = (V, E, \lambda_S, \lambda_R)$ be a P-graph, and let $\mathsf{merge}(G) = (V', E', \lambda_S, \lambda_R)$ be defined by (1) V' is the set of maximal SCCs of G, (2) for two distinct maximal SCCs U, U', $(U, U') \in E'$ if there are $v \in U$ and $v' \in U'$ such that $(v, v') \in E^+$ (the transitive closure of E), (3) for $X = S, R$, $\lambda_X(U) = \bigcup_{v \in U} \lambda_X(v)$.

The second graph transformation we consider consists in erasing some of the processes that appear in the labels. Let $G = (V, E, \lambda_S, \lambda_R)$ be a fixed P-graph, and let $v \in V$, $X \in \{S, R\}$, and $p \in \lambda_X(v)$ be fixed. We say that p is X-redundant in v if there are v_1, v_2 such that (1) $(v_1, v) \in E^+$ and $(v, v_2) \in E^+$, and (2) $p \in \lambda_X(v_1) \cap \lambda_X(v_2)$. Intuitively, p is redundant in v if it also appears in the label of an ancestor and a descendant of v. We define the P-graph $\mathsf{erase}(G)$ as $(V, E, \lambda'_S, \lambda'_R)$ where for all $X \in \{S, R\}$, for all $v \in V$, $\lambda'_X(v)$ is the set of processes $p \in \lambda_X(v)$ such that p is not X-redundant at v.

The last graph transformation we consider consists in sweeping out the vertices labeled with empty sets of processes. Formally, for $G = (V, E, \lambda_S, \lambda_R)$, the P-graph $\mathsf{sweep}(G)$ is $(V', E', \lambda_S, \lambda_R)$ where $V' = \{v \in V \mid \lambda_S(v) \cup \lambda_R(v) \neq \emptyset\}$ and $E' = E \cap V' \times V'$. The abstraction $\alpha(G)$ of a P-graph G is defined as $\mathsf{sweep}(\mathsf{erase}(\mathsf{merge}(G)))$. An example of the construction is in Fig. 7.

Lemma 6. $\mathsf{CG}(\mu)$ *is strongly connected iff* $\alpha(\mathsf{pgr}(\mu))$ *is a single vertex graph.*

By construction, for any process p, and for any $X \in \{S, R\}$, there are at most two vertices v of $\alpha(\mathsf{pgr}(\mu))$ such that $p \in \lambda_X(v)$. From this, we deduce that $\alpha(\mathsf{pgr}(\mu))$ has at most $2|\mathbb{P}|$ vertices, and as a consequence:

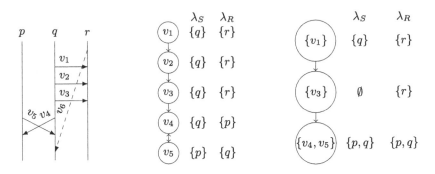

Fig. 7. MSC μ_5, its associated P-graph $\mathsf{pgr}(\mu_5)$, and the abstraction $\alpha(\mathsf{pgr}(\mu_5))$.

Lemma 7. $\sharp\{\alpha(\mathsf{pgr}(\mu)) \mid \mu \text{ is an exchange}\} \leq 2^{6|\mathbb{P}|^2}$.

There are therefore finitely many $\alpha(\mathsf{pgr}(\mu))$. This allows us to define the automaton that computes $\alpha(\mathsf{pgr}(msc(w)))$ for any $w \in \Sigma^*$ and accepts w in the language of this new automaton when this P-graph is a single vertex graph. Let $G = (V, E, \lambda_S, \lambda_R)$ and a letter $\dagger v^{p \to q} \in \Sigma$ be fixed. We want to define the transition function δ_g of our automaton, or in other words, the P-graph $\delta_g(G, \dagger v^{p \to q})$ reached after adding the message $\dagger v^{p \to q}$ to the MSC. We let $\delta_g(G, \dagger v_0^{p \to q}) = \alpha(G')$. $G' = (V', E', \lambda'_S, \lambda'_R)$ is defined as follows: (1) $V' = V \uplus \{v_0\}$, (2) $\lambda'_S(v_0) = \{p\}$, (3) if $\dagger =!?$, then $\lambda'_R(v_0) = \{q\}$, and if $\dagger =!$, then $\lambda'_R(v_0) = \emptyset$, (4) for all $v \in V$, for all $X \in \{S, R\}$, $\lambda'_X(v) = \lambda_X(v)$, and (5) the set of edges E' is defined as

$$E' = E \cup \{(v, v_0) \mid p \in \lambda_S(v)\} \cup \{(v_0, v) \mid p \in \lambda_R(v)\}$$
$$\cup \begin{cases} \{(v, v_0) \mid q \in \lambda_S(v) \cup \lambda_R(v)\} & \text{if } \dagger =!? \\ \emptyset & \text{if } \dagger =! \end{cases}$$

For example, consider the MSC μ of Fig. 7 and let $G = \alpha(\mathsf{pgr}(\mu))$ be its associated abstracted P-graph. Let G' be defined as above while reading $!?v_6^{r \to q}$. Then G' is the graph on the right, and $\delta_g(G, v_6^{r \to q})$ is a single vertex graph (Fig. 8).

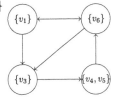

Fig. 8. Graph G'

Lemma 8. $\delta_g(\alpha(\mathsf{pgr}(msc(w))), \dagger v^{p \to q}) = \alpha(\mathsf{pgr}(msc(w \cdot \dagger v^{p \to q})))$.

Theorem 3. *There is an effective deterministic finite state automaton $\mathcal{A}$ with less than $2^{6|\mathbb{P}|^2}$ states such that $\mathcal{L}(\mathcal{A}) = \{w \in \Sigma^* \mid msc(w) \text{ is prime}\}$.*

6 Computation of k

So far we have shown: in Lemma 1, we established that a way to compute $\mathsf{sd}(\mathfrak{S})$ was to compute the length k of the largest prime reachable exchange. To every word $w \in \Sigma^*$, we associated an MSC $msc(w)$, and we showed that for every reachable MSC μ, there exists a word $w \in \Sigma^*$ such that $\mu = msc(w)$ (Lemma 2). We deduced that k corresponds to the length of the longest word of $\mathcal{L}_\mathrm{r} \cap \mathcal{L}_\mathrm{p}$, if

$\mathcal{L}_r \cap \mathcal{L}_p$ is finite, otherwise $k = \infty$. In Sect. 4, we showed that $\mathcal{L}_r$ is an effective regular language, and, in Sect. 5, we showed that $\mathcal{L}_p$ is also an effective regular language. We deduce that $\mathcal{L}_r \cap \mathcal{L}_p$ is therefore an effective regular language, and that k is computable (since the finiteness and the length of the longest word of a regular language are computable). With a careful analysis of the automata that come into play, we can give an upper bound on k.

Theorem 4. $\mathsf{sd}(\mathfrak{S})$ *is computable, and if* $\mathsf{sd}(\mathfrak{S}) < \infty$ *then* $\mathsf{sd}(\mathfrak{S}) < |\mathfrak{S}|^2 2^{8|\mathbb{P}|^2}$, *where* $|\mathfrak{S}|$ *is the number of global control states and* $|\mathbb{P}|$ *the number of processes.*

As an immediate consequence of Theorems 1 and 4, we get the following.

Theorem 5. *The following problem is decidable : given a system* $\mathfrak{S}$, *does there exists a* k *such that* $\mathfrak{S}$ *is* k-*synchronizable.*

7   Conclusion

We established that it is possible to determine whether there exists a bound k such that a given communicating system is k-synchronizable. For this, we showed how the set of sequences of actions that compose an exchange of arbitrary size can be represented as a regular language, which was possible thanks to the mailbox semantics of communications. We leave for future work to decide whether it would be possible to extend our result to peer-to-peer semantics.

References

1. Abdulla, P.A., Jonsson, B.: Verifying programs with unreliable channels. Inf. Comput. **127**(2), 91–101 (1996)
2. Basu, S., Bultan, T.: On deciding synchronizability for asynchronously communicating systems. Theor. Comput. Sci. **656**, 60–75 (2016)
3. Bouajjani, A., Enea, C., Ji, K., Qadeer, S.: On the completeness of verifying message passing programs under bounded asynchrony. In: Chockler, H., Weissenbacher, G. (eds.) CAV 2018. LNCS, vol. 10982, pp. 372–391. Springer, Cham (2018). https://doi.org/10.1007/978-3-319-96142-2_23
4. Brand, D., Zafiropulo, P.: On communicating finite-state machines. J. ACM **30**(2), 323–342 (1983)
5. Chaouch-Saad, M., Charron-Bost, B., Merz, S.: A reduction theorem for the verification of round-based distributed algorithms. In: Bournez, O., Potapov, I. (eds.) RP 2009. LNCS, vol. 5797, pp. 93–106. Springer, Heidelberg (2009). https://doi.org/10.1007/978-3-642-04420-5_10
6. Chou, C., Gafni, E.: Understanding and verifying distributed algorithms using stratified decomposition. In: 1988 Proceedings of the Seventh Annual ACM Symposium on Principles of Distributed Computing, pp. 44–65. ACM (1988)
7. Di Giusto, C., Laversa, L., Lozes, E.: On the k-synchronizability of systems. In: Goubault-Larrecq, J., König, B. (eds.) FoSSaCS 2020. LNCS, vol. 12077, pp. 157–176. Springer, Cham (2020). https://doi.org/10.1007/978-3-030-45231-5_9
8. Elrad, T., Francez, N.: Decomposition of distributed programs into communication-closed layers. Sci. Comput. Program. **2**(3), 155–173 (1982)

9. Finkel, A., Lozes, É.: Synchronizability of communicating finite state machines is not decidable. In: ICALP 2017, pp. 122:1–122:14 (2017)
10. Genest, B., Kuske, D., Muscholl, A.: On communicating automata with bounded channels. Fundam. Inform. **80**(1–3), 147–167 (2007)
11. von Gleissenthall, K., Kici, R.G., Bakst, A., Stefan, D., Jhala, R.: Pretend synchrony: synchronous verification of asynchronous distributed programs. PACMPL **3**(POPL), 59:1–59:30 (2019)
12. Kragl, B., Qadeer, S., Henzinger, T.A.: Synchronizing the asynchronous. In: CONCUR 2018, vol. 118, pp. 21:1–21:17 (2018)
13. La Torre, S., Madhusudan, P., Parlato, G.: Context-bounded analysis of concurrent queue systems. In: Ramakrishnan, C.R., Rehof, J. (eds.) TACAS 2008. LNCS, vol. 4963, pp. 299–314. Springer, Heidelberg (2008). https://doi.org/10.1007/978-3-540-78800-3_21
14. Lipton, R.J.: Reduction: a method of proving properties of parallel programs. Commun. ACM **18**(12), 717–721 (1975)

State Complexity of Permutation and Related Decision Problems on Alphabetical Pattern Constraints

Stefan Hoffmann$^{(\boxtimes)}$ (iD)

Informatikwissenschaften, FB IV, Universität Trier,
Universitätsring 15, 54296 Trier, Germany
`hoffmanns@informatik.uni-trier.de`

Abstract. We investigate the state complexity of the permutation operation, or the commutative closure, on Alphabetical Pattern Constraints (APC). This class corresponds to level 3/2 of the Straubing-Thérien hierarchy and includes the finite, the piecewise-testable, or $\mathcal{J}$-trivial, and the $\mathcal{R}$-trivial and $\mathcal{L}$-trivial languages. We give a sharp state complexity bound expressed in terms of the longest strings in the unary projection languages of an associated finite language. This bound is already sharp for the subclass of finite languages. Additionally, for two subclasses, we give sharp bounds expressed in terms of the size of a recognizing input automaton and the size of the alphabet. Lastly, we investigate the inclusion and universality problem on APCs up to permutational equivalence. These two problems are known to be PSPACE-complete on APCs in general, even for fixed alphabets. However, we show them to be decidable in polynomial time for fixed alphabets if we only want to solve them up to permutational equivalence.

Keywords: State complexity · Finite automata · Alphabetic pattern constraint language · Commutative closure · Inclusion problem

1 Introduction

In *regular model checking* [1], a set of initial configurations is modelled as a regular language and the actions of the system are modeled as a rewriting relation. For example, suppose we have an arbitrary number of processes that are connected linearly and need access to a common resource, but only one at a time and in order, starting from the first processor. Then, the state of a given processor could be modeled by $\Sigma = \{0, 1\}$, where 1 means the processor has access to the resource, and 0 otherwise. The set of initial configurations is then the regular languages 10^*, where a specific initial configuration is determined by the number of processors involved. The transition relation is given by the rule $10 \mapsto 01$ and the set of reachable configurations is the the language 0^*10^*. The bad configurations are given by the language $(0 + 1)^*1(0 + 1)^*1(0 + 1)^*$, and we see that intersection of this set with the reachable configurations is empty.

© Springer Nature Switzerland AG 2021
S. Maneth (Ed.): CIAA 2021, LNCS 12803, pp. 115–126, 2021.
https://doi.org/10.1007/978-3-030-79121-6_10

The computation of the set of reachable configurations is the closure of the set of initial configurations under the rewriting relation. However, in this generality, the framework is Turing-complete and hence restrictions have to be imposed. In [2] the class of *Alphabetical Pattern Constraints* (APC) was introduced as a class to describe initial and bad configurations, given by forbidden patterns, that is closed under semi-commutations. The constructions in [2] rely on an inductive transformation of an APC expression into another APC expression for the closure. Here, our constructions will give a more direct and efficient procedure for the full commutative closure and will also yield deterministic automata, which we then use to devise polynomial time decision procedures for the inclusion and universality problem up to permutational equivalence.

The state complexity of a regular language L is the minimal number of states needed in a deterministic automaton recognizing L. Investigating the state complexity of the result of a regularity-preserving operation on regular languages, depending on the state complexity of the regular input languages, was first initiated in [15] and systematically started in [31]. As the number of states of a recognizing automaton could be interpreted as the memory required to describe the recognized language and is directly related to the runtime of algorithms employing regular languages, obtaining state complexity bounds is a natural question with applications in verification, natural language processing or software engineering [8].

In general, the permutation operation is not regularity-preserving. But it is regularity-preserving on finite languages, APCs and on group languages [2,9, 11]. The state complexity on group languages was studied in [11], but it is not known if the derived bounds are tight. The state complexity of the permutation operation on finite languages was first investigated in [5,18]. However, sharp bounds were only obtained for subclasses and it is unknown if the general bound stated in [5,18] is sharp. Surely, every finite language is an APC.

The *dot-depth hierarchy* [6] is an infinitely increasing hierarchy whose union is the class of star-free languages. This hierarchy was motivated by alternately increasing the combinatorial and sequential complexity of languages and corresponding recognizing devices [4,20]. Later, the more fundamental *Straubing-Thérien hierarchy* was introduced [21,27,28]. Here, we start with $\{\varnothing, \Sigma^*\}$ at level zero and, alternately, build (1) the half-levels: finite unions of *marked products* of the form $L_0 a_1 L_1 a_1 \cdots a_k L_k$ with $k \geqslant 0$, $a_1, \ldots, a_k \in \Sigma$ and $L_1, \ldots, L_k$ from the previous full-level or, (2) the full levels: the *Boolean closure* of the previous half-level. More formally, set $\mathcal{L}(0) = \{\varnothing, \Sigma^*\}$ and for $n \geqslant 0$, level $\mathcal{L}(n + \frac{1}{2})$ consists of all finite unions of languages $L_0 a_1 L_1 a_2 \cdots a_k L_k$ with $k \geqslant 0$, $L_0, \ldots, L_k \in \mathcal{L}(n)$ and $a_1, \ldots, a_k \in \Sigma$, and level $\mathcal{L}(n + 1)$ consists of all finite Boolean combinations of languages from level $\mathcal{L}(n + \frac{1}{2})$. Every star-free language is contained in some level of this hierarchy, which is also infinitely increasing. The different levels could also be characterized logically by the quantifier alternation of first order sentences [29].

The membership problem and related decision and separation problems with respect to the levels of both hierachies, and their connection to logic, have sparked much interest [14,21,29]. The APCs precisely correspond to the languages of level $3/2$ in the Straubing-Thérien hierarchy [2,14].

Green's relations are five equivalence relations, named $\mathcal{H}$, $\mathcal{R}$, $\mathcal{L}$, $\mathcal{J}$ and $\mathcal{D}$, that characterize the elements of a semigroup in terms of the principal ideals they generate [10]. By the notion of the syntactic monoid [17,23], these relations entered into formal language theory and proved to be useful in the classification of formal languages [7,13,19]. For example, it turned out that the $\mathcal{J}$-trivial, or piecewise-testable languages, are precisely the languages of level one in the Straubing-Thérien hierarchy [19,26]. The $\mathcal{H}$-trivial languages are precisely the star-free languages [24]. Also, the $\mathcal{R}$-trivial and the $\mathcal{L}$-trivial languages are properly contained in level $3/2$ of the Straubing-Thérien hierarchy, i.e., are APCs [2,3,14].

2   Preliminaries and Definitions

We assume the reader to have some basic knowledge of automata and complexity theory. For all unexplained notions, as, for example, regular expressions, the Nerode equivalence relation and more formal definitions of PSPACE, the class of problems solvable with polynomially bounded space, and P, the class of problems solvable in polynomial time, we refer the reader to [12].

For an alphabet (finite nonempty set) Σ, denote by Σ^* the set of all finite words over the alphabet Σ including the *empty word* ε. If $u \in \Sigma^*$ and $a \in \Sigma$, by $|u|$ we denote the *length* of u and by $|u|_a$ the number of occurrences of the symbol a in u. A *language* over Σ is any subset of Σ^*. Let $L \subseteq \Sigma^*$. We set $\mathrm{Pref}(L) = \{u \in \Sigma^* \mid \exists v \in \Sigma^* : uv \in L\}$. A word $u \in \Sigma^*$ is a *prefix* of a word $v \in \Sigma^*$, if $u \in \mathrm{Pref}(\{v\})$. For $a \in \Sigma$, the *one-letter projection language* is $\pi_a(L) = \{a^{|u|_a} : u \in L\}$ and, for $u \in \Sigma^*$, we set $\pi_a(u) = a^{|u|_a}$.

For a natural number $n \geqslant 0$, we set $[n] = \{0, \ldots, n-1\}$. For a finite subset A of natural numbers, by $\max A$ and $\min A$ we denote the maximal and minimal element in A with respect to the usual order, where we set $\max \varnothing = \min \varnothing = 0$.

A *nondeterministic finite automaton (NFA)* is given by $\mathcal{A} = (\Sigma, Q, \delta, q_0, F)$, where Σ is an *input alphabet*, Q a finite set of *states*, $\delta : Q \times \Sigma \to 2^Q$ the *transition function*, having a set of states as image, q_0 the *initial state* and $F \subseteq Q$ the set of *final states*. If, for any $q \in Q$ and $a \in \Sigma$, we have $|\delta(q,a)| \leqslant 1$, then $\mathcal{A}$ is called a *partial deterministic finite automaton (PDFA)*. If $\mathcal{A}$ is a PDFA, then the transition function is often written as a partial function $Q \times \Sigma \to Q$. In the usual way, the transition function δ can be extended to the domain $Q \times \Sigma^*$. The *language recognized* by $\mathcal{A}$ is $L(\mathcal{A}) = \{u \in \Sigma^* \mid \delta(q_0, u) \cap F \neq \varnothing\}$. We will also need the finite *simple language* $L^{\mathrm{simple}}(\mathcal{A}) = \{w \in L(\mathcal{A}) \mid \delta(q_0, w) \setminus \left(\bigcup_{u \in \mathrm{Pref}(w) \setminus \{w\}} \delta(q_0, u)\right) \neq \varnothing\}$ associated with $\mathcal{A}$. This is the set of all words that label paths with no loops[1].

---

[1] The length of the longest word in $L^{\mathrm{simple}}(\mathcal{A})$ is called the *depth* in [16].

Lemma 1. *Let $a \in \Sigma$ and $n = \max\{|u|_a \mid u \in L^{\text{simple}}(\mathcal{A})\} + 1$. Then, for any $w \in \Sigma^*$ with[2] $|w|_a \geqslant n$, we have: $w \in \text{perm}(L) \Leftrightarrow wa \in \text{perm}(L)$.*

The *state complexity* of a regular language is the smallest number of states in any PDFA recognizing the language.

Let $\mathcal{A} = (\Sigma, Q, \delta, q_0, F)$. A state $q \in Q$ is said to be *reachable* from a state $p \in Q$, if there exists $u \in \Sigma^*$ such that $q \in \delta(p, u)$.

An automaton is called *partially ordered*, if the reachability relation is a partial order. Equivalently, if the only loops are self-loops. Partially ordered automata are also known as *weakly acyclic* automata [22].

The *shuffle operation* of two languages $U, V \subseteq \Sigma^*$ is defined by

$$U \amalg V = \{w \in \Sigma^* \mid w = x_1 y_1 x_2 y_2 \cdots x_n y_n \text{ for some words}$$

$$x_1, \ldots, x_n, y_1, \ldots, y_n \in \Sigma^* \text{ such that } x_1 x_2 \cdots x_n \in U \text{ and } y_1 y_2 \cdots y_n \in V\}.$$

and $u \amalg v = \{u\} \amalg \{v\}$ for $u, v \in \Sigma^*$. For languages $L_1, \ldots, L_n \subseteq \Sigma^*$, we set $\amalg_{i=1}^{n} L_i = L_1 \amalg \ldots \amalg L_n$. Let $L \subseteq \Sigma^*$. If $L = \amalg_{a \in \Sigma}\{a^{|u|_a} \mid u \in L\}$, then we call it a *strict shuffle language*.

Example 1. Let $\Sigma = \{a, b\}$.

1. If $u \in \Sigma^*$, then $\text{perm}(u)$ is a strict shuffle language.
2. The language $\{u \in \{a, b\}^* \mid |u|_a = 1 \text{ and } 2 \leqslant |u| \leqslant n\} = \{a\} \amalg \{b, b^2, \ldots, b^{n-1}\}$ is a strict shuffle language.
3. $\text{perm}(\{aabb, ab\})$ is not a strict shuffle language.
4. $\text{perm}(\{aaabbb, abbb, aaab, ab\})$ is a strict shuffle language.

The *permutation operation*, or *commutative closure*, on a language is the set of words that we get when permuting the letters of the words from the language. Formally, for $L \subseteq \Sigma^*$, we set $\text{perm}(L) = \{u \in \Sigma^* \mid \exists v \in L \ \forall a \in \Sigma : |u|_a = |v|_a\}$. For example, $\text{perm}(\{abb\}) = \{abb, bab, bba\}$. For $u \in \Sigma^*$, we also write $\text{perm}(u)$ for $\text{perm}(\{u\})$. A language $L \subseteq \Sigma^*$ is called *commutative*, if $\text{perm}(L) = L$. Note that for strict shuffle languages $L \subseteq \Sigma^*$ we have $\text{perm}(L) = L$.

An *Alphabetical Pattern Constraint* (APC) is an expression[3] $p_1 + \ldots + p_n$, where each p_i is of the form $\Sigma_0^* a_1 \Sigma_1^* \cdots a_n \Sigma_n^*$ with $\Sigma_0, \ldots, \Sigma_n \subseteq \Sigma$ and $a_1, \ldots, a_n \in \Sigma$. In the following, we will *not distinguish between the expression and the language* it denotes, and taking the liberty to denote "+" by the union symbol as well. Hence, an APC is a finite union of languages of the form $\Sigma_0^* a_1 \Sigma_1^* \cdots a_n \Sigma_n^*$ as above. Equivalently, as concatenation distributes over union, it is the closure of the subsets $\Gamma^*, \Gamma \subseteq \Sigma$, and $\{a\}$ for $a \in \Sigma$ under concatenation and finite union[4]. The APCs are precisely the languages recognized by partially ordered NFAs [14,25].

---

[2] The assumption $|w|_a \geqslant n$ is needed. For example, consider $L = a^{n-1}b^*$.

[3] With the shorthand $\Gamma^* = (a_1 + \ldots + a_n)^*$ for $\Gamma = \{a_1, \ldots, a_n\} \subseteq \Sigma$.

[4] Note that, for $\Sigma_0, \Sigma_1 \subseteq \Sigma$ nonempty, we have $\Sigma_0^* \Sigma_1^* = \Sigma_0^* \cup \bigcup_{a \in \Sigma_1} \Sigma_0^* a \Sigma_1^*$.

3   State Complexity Bound of Permutation on APCs

The APCs are closed under the permutation operation. However, they are not closed under complementation. For example, the complement of $\Sigma^* aa\Sigma^* \cup \Sigma^* bb\Sigma^* \cup b\Sigma^* \cup \Sigma^* a$ over $\Sigma = \{a, b\}$ is $(ab)^*$. As $\text{perm}((ab)^*) = \{u \in \Sigma^* \mid |u|_a = |u|_b\}$ is not regular, it is not an APC. This also shows that level 3/2 of the Straubing-Thérien hierarchy is the lowest level in which the permuation of any language is regular.

Remark 1. Let $L = \bigcup_{i=1}^m \Sigma_0^{(i)} a_1^{(i)} \Sigma_1^{(i)} \cdots a_{n_i}^{(i)} \Sigma_{n_i}^{(i)}$. Set $\Gamma^{(i)} = \Sigma_0^{(i)} \cup \ldots \cup \Sigma_{n_i}^{(i)}$. Then, $\text{perm}(L) = \bigcup_{i=1}^m \text{perm}(a_1^{(i)} \cdots a_{n_i}^{(i)} \Gamma^{(i)}) = \bigcup_{i=1}^m \text{perm}(a_1^{(i)} \cdots a_{n_i}^{(i)}) \sqcup\!\sqcup \Gamma^{(i)}$. Hence, the permutational closure, as a finite union of languages of the form $\Gamma^* a_1 \Gamma^* \ldots a_n \Gamma^*$, is itself an APC.

Theorem 2. *Let L be an APC recognized by a partially ordered NFA $\mathcal{A}$. Then, $\text{perm}(L)$ is recognizable by a PDFA that uses at most (where we set $\max \varnothing = 0$)*

$$\prod_{a \in \Sigma} (\max\{|u|_a : u \in L^{\text{simple}}(\mathcal{A})\} + 1)$$

many states and this bound is sharp even for finite languages.

Proof. Suppose we have k symbols and $\Sigma = \{a_1, \ldots, a_k\}$. Set $n_j = \max\{|u|_{a_j} \mid u \in L^{\text{simple}}(\mathcal{A})\} + 1$ for $j \in \{1, \ldots, k\}$. Construct $\mathcal{B} = (\Sigma, Q, \delta, q_0, F)$ with $Q = [n_1 + 1] \times \ldots \times [n_k + 1]$ and

$\delta((s_1, \ldots, s_k), a_j) =$
$$\begin{cases} (s_1, \ldots, s_{j-1}, s_j + 1, s_{j+1}, \ldots, s_k) & \text{if } s_j < n_j; \\ (s_1, \ldots, s_k) & \text{if } s_j = n_j \text{ and } a_1^{s_1} \cdots a_k^{s_k} a_j \in \text{perm}(\text{Pref}(L)). \end{cases}$$

Also $q_0 = (0, \ldots, 0)$ and $F = \{\delta(q_0, w) \mid w \in L \text{ and } \forall j \in \{1, \ldots, k\} : |w|_{a_j} \leqslant n_j\}$.

<u>Claim:</u> We have $L(\mathcal{B}) = \text{perm}(L)$.

Proof of the Claim: By Lemma 1, for any $w \in \Sigma^*$ with $|w|_{a_j} \geqslant n_j$, we have

$$w \in \text{perm}(L) \Leftrightarrow wa_j \in \text{perm}(L).$$

Let $w \in \text{perm}(L)$. Then $a_1^{\min\{n_1, |w|_{a_1}\}} \cdots a_k^{\min\{n_k, |w|_{a_k}\}} \in \text{perm}(L)$. Hence,

$$\delta(q_0, a_1^{\min\{n_1, |w|_{a_1}\}} \cdots a_k^{\min\{n_k, |w|_{a_k}\}}) \in F.$$

Furthermore, if $|w|_{a_j} \geqslant n_j$, then, for

$$q = (\min\{n_1, |w|_{a_1}\}, \ldots, \min\{n_k, |w|_{a_k}\}),$$

we have $\delta(q, a_j) = q$ for any $j \in \{1, \ldots, k\}$ such that $|w|_{a_j} \geqslant n_j$. So,

$$\delta(q_0, w) = \delta(q_0, a_1^{\min\{n_1, |w|_{a_1}\}} \cdots a_k^{\min\{n_k, |w|_{a_k}\}}) \in F.$$

Conversely, suppose $\delta(q_0, w) \in F$. If $|w|_{a_j} > n_j$ with $j \in \{1, \ldots, k\}$, then, for the state $q = (\min\{n_1, |w|_{a_1}\}, \ldots, \min\{n_k, |w|_{a_k}\})$, we have $\delta(q, a_j) = q$ and so $\mathrm{perm}(a_1^{\min\{n_1, |w|_{a_1}\}} \cdots a_k^{\min\{n_k, |w|_{a_k}\}} a_j) \subseteq \mathrm{perm}(L)$ by the above definition of the transition function δ. Hence, the letter a_j could be appended $n_j - |w|_{a_j}$ many times and $\mathcal{B}$ stays in the same state, for every such letter with $|w|_{a_j} > n_j$. So, we find $\mathrm{perm}(a_1^{|w|_{a_1}} \cdots a_k^{|w|_{a_k}}) \subseteq \mathrm{perm}(L)$, which is equivalent to $w \in \mathrm{perm}(L)$. [*End, Proof of the Claim*]

That the bound is sharp is shown in Remark 2.   □

Lemma 3. *Let $\mathcal{A} = (\Sigma, Q, \delta, q_0, F)$ be a partially ordered NFA. If any NFA for $L^{\mathrm{simple}}(\mathcal{A})$ needs at least n states, then $|Q| \geqslant n$. A similar statement holds true for PDFAs.*

Let $\mathcal{A} = (\Sigma, Q, \delta, q_0, F)$ be a partially ordered NFA. As $L^{\mathrm{simple}}(\mathcal{A})$ is finite, every path from the start state to a final state in any recognizing automaton has no loops. Hence, the length of a longest string in $L^{\mathrm{simple}}(\mathcal{A})$ is a lower bound for the number of states of any NFA recognizing $L^{\mathrm{simple}}(\mathcal{A})$. Surely, for $a \in \Sigma$ and $u \in L^{\mathrm{simple}}(\mathcal{A})$, the number $|u|_a$ is a lower bound for the length of the longest string in $L^{\mathrm{simple}}(\mathcal{A})$. So, combining with Lemma 3, we have $\max\{|u|_a : u \in L^{\mathrm{simple}}(\mathcal{A})\} \leqslant |Q|$ for $a \in \Sigma$. This yields the next corollary to Theorem 2.

Corollary 4. *Let L be an APC recognized by a partially ordered NFA with n states. Then, $\mathrm{perm}(L)$ is recognizable by a PDFA with at most $n^{|\Sigma|}$ many states.*

We have formulated Theorem 2 and the above corollary in terms of partially ordered NFAs recognizing a given APC. However, APC expressions and partially ordered NFAs are closely connected, for example, see Lemma 9 in Sect. 6. Hence a corresponding statement could be made for APC expressions, where $L^{\mathrm{simple}}(\mathcal{A})$ corresponds to the set of words resulting if we delete all subexpressions Σ_i^* in the parts of the unions.

4   When $\mathrm{perm}(L^{\mathrm{simple}}(\mathcal{A}))$ Is a Strict Shuffle Language

Here, we investigate a class of languages for which we can devise a sharp bound expressed in the size of the input NFA. The bound is formulated with the number of states and the size of the alphabet of the input automaton. As the bound is sharp for a subclass of languages, it also yields a lower bound for the general case.

For finite strict shuffle languages, we can derive the following lower bound for the size of recognizing NFAs, which we will need in the proof of Theorem 6.

Lemma 5. *Let $L \subseteq \Sigma^*$ be finite. If $\mathrm{perm}(L)$ is a strict shuffle language, then any NFA recognizing L needs at least $(\sum_{a \in \Sigma} \max\{|u| : u \in \pi_a(L)\}) + 1$ many states.*

Next, we state the main result of this section.

Theorem 6. *Let L be an APC language recognized by a partially ordered NFA $\mathcal{A}$ with n states such that* $\mathrm{perm}(L^{\mathrm{simple}}(\mathcal{A}))$ *is a strict shuffle language. Then,* $\mathrm{perm}(L)$ *is recognizable by a PDFA with at most*

$$\left\lceil \frac{n-1}{|\Sigma|} + 1 \right\rceil^{|\Sigma|}$$

many states and this bound is sharp even for finite languages.

Proof. By Lemma 5, any automaton for $L^{\mathrm{simple}}(\mathcal{A})$ needs at least $(\Sigma_{a\in\Sigma} \max\{|u|_a : u \in \pi_a(L)\}) + 1$ many states. So, by Lemma 3 we have $0 \leqslant (\Sigma_{a\in\Sigma} \max\{|u|_a : u \in \pi_a(L)\}) + 1 \leqslant n$. The value $\prod_{a\in\Sigma}(\max\{|u|_a : u \in L^{\mathrm{simple}}(\mathcal{A})\} + 1)$ from Theorem 2 with the constraint $0 \leqslant (\Sigma_{a\in\Sigma} \max\{|u|_a : u \in \pi_a(L)\}) + 1 \leqslant n$ is maximized[5] if $\max\{|u|_a : u \in L^{\mathrm{simple}}(\mathcal{A})\}$ equals $(n-1)/|\Sigma|$ for every $a \in \Sigma$, which gives the claim. That the bound is sharp is shown in Remark 2. □

Note that for a single word $u \in \Sigma^*$, we have $\mathrm{perm}(u) = \bigsqcup_{a\in\Sigma} \pi_a(u)$, i.e., the commutative closure is a strict shuffle language. Hence, we get the next corollary from Theorem 6, which is also sharp, as shown by Remark 2.

Corollary 7. *Let $L = \Sigma_0^* a_1 \Sigma_1^* a_2 \cdots a_m \Sigma_m^*$. Then,* $\mathrm{perm}(L)$ *is recognizable by a PDFA with at most* $\lceil m/|\Sigma| + 1 \rceil^{|\Sigma|}$ *many states. In particular, the commutative closure of a single word u could be recognized by a PDFA with at most* $\lceil |u|/|\Sigma| + 1 \rceil^{|\Sigma|}$ *many states and this bound is sharp.*

Proof. The NFA $\mathcal{A}$ with state set $Q = \{q_0, q_1, \ldots, q_m\}$, transition function $\delta(q_i, a) = \{q_i : a \in \Sigma_i\} \cup \{q_{i+1} : i < m \text{ and } a = a_{i+1}\}$ for $i \in \{0, \ldots, m\}$ and $a \in \Sigma$, start state q_0 and final state set $\{q_m\}$ recognizes L. We have $L^{\mathrm{simple}}(\mathcal{A}) = \{a_1 a_2 \cdots a_m\}$ and $\mathrm{perm}(L^{\mathrm{simple}}(\mathcal{A}))$ is a strict shuffle language. Note that, by Lemma 3 and Lemma 5, $\mathcal{A}$ has the least possible number of states. Then, Theorem 6 gives the claim and the bound is sharp by Remark 2. □

Remark 2. Suppose $\Sigma = \{a_1, \ldots, a_k\}$. Let $m > 0$ and $u = a_1^m \cdots a_k^m$. Then, any PDFA recognizing $\mathrm{perm}(u)$ needs at least $(m+1)^k$ many states. For let $0 \leqslant m_i, n_i \leqslant m$, $i \in \{1, \ldots, k\}$, such that there exists $j \in \{1, \ldots, k\}$ with $m_j < n_j$. Then, choose r_i for each $i \in \{1, \ldots, k\}$ such that $n_i + r_i = m$. Set $w = a_1^{n_1} \cdots a_k^{n_k} a_1^{r_1} \cdots a_k^{r_k}$. As $|w|_{a_i} = m$ for any $i \in \{1, \ldots, k\}$, we find $w \in \mathrm{perm}(u)$. However, for $w' = a_1^{m_1} \cdots a_k^{m_k} a_1^{r_1} \cdots a_k^{r_k}$ we have $|w'|_{a_j} < m$, so that $w' \notin \mathrm{perm}(u)$. So, w and w' represent different Nerode right-congruence classes [12] for the language $\mathrm{perm}(u)$, which yields the lower bound for the number of states of any recognizing automaton.

As u is recognizable by a minimal NFA $\mathcal{A}$ with $k\cdot m+1$ many states, $|u|_{a_i} = m$ for any $i \in \{1, \ldots, k\}$ and $L^{\mathrm{simple}}(\mathcal{A}) = L(\mathcal{A})$, as $L(\mathcal{A})$ is finite, the bounds of Theorem 2, Theorem 6 and of Corollary 7 are all meet by this example.

---

[5] More precisely, if $\Sigma = \{a_1, \ldots, a_k\}$, we seek to maximize the function $f(x_1, \ldots, x_n) = \prod_{i=1}^{k}(x_i + 1)$ due to the constraint $0 \leqslant \sum_{i=1}^{k} x_i \leqslant n - 1$, which happens for $x_1 = \ldots = x_k = \frac{n-1}{k}$ with maximum value $\left(\frac{n-1}{k} + 1\right)^k$.

5   State Complexity on General Chain Automata

A *general chain automaton* $\mathcal{A} = (\Sigma, Q, \delta, q_0, F)$ is a NFA such that the state set is totally ordered, i.e., we can assume $Q = \{0, \ldots, n-1\}$ with the usual order and $q_0 = 0$ and $F = \{n-1\}$ and, for any $q \in Q \setminus \{n-1\}$ and $a \in \Sigma$, we have $\delta(q, a) \subseteq \{q, q+1\}$. If $\mathcal{A}$ is a general chain automaton, then $L^{\text{simple}}(\mathcal{A}) \subseteq \Sigma^{n-1}$.

These automata, with no self-loops allowed[6], were introduced in [5] under the name chain automata. The sharp bound we will give is essentially an adaption of the bound derived in [5]. Note that we only have a result for binary alphabets.

Proposition 8. *Let $\Sigma = \{a, b\}$ and $\mathcal{A}$ be a general chain automaton with n states. Then, $\text{perm}(L(\mathcal{A}))$ is recognizable by a PDFA with at most $\frac{n^2+n+1}{3}$ many states and this bound is sharp even on finite languages.*

Proof (sketch). Let the set of states of $\mathcal{A}$ be $\{0, \ldots, n-1\}$, where 0 is the start state and $n-1$ is the only final state. Set $\Gamma = \{x \in \Sigma \mid \exists q \in Q : q \in \delta(q, x)\}$, the symbols which label self-loops. Note that $L(\mathcal{A})$ is finite if and only if $\Gamma = \emptyset$. For $0 \leqslant h \leqslant n-2$, the transitions only go from h to $h+1$ or we have a self-loop from h to h. We have three possibilities for outgoing transitions from a state $0 \leqslant h \leqslant n-2$ that are not self-loops:

1. $\{h+1\} \subseteq \delta(h, a)$ and $\delta(h, b) \cap \{h+1\} = \emptyset$ (a-transition);
2. $\{h+1\} \subseteq \delta(h, b)$ and $\delta(h, a) \cap \{h+1\} = \emptyset$ (b-transition);
3. $\{h+1\} \subseteq \delta(h, a) \cap \delta(h, b)$ ($a\&b$-transition).

The order of the different types of transitions (a, b, or $a\&b$) of $\mathcal{A}$ does not affect the language $\text{perm}(L(\mathcal{A}))$. A similar reasoning applies to the self-loops. Hence, without loss of generality, we can assume that $\mathcal{A}$ has first a (possibly empty) sequence of a-transitions, followed by a (possibly empty) sequence of b-transitions, followed by a (possibly empty) sequence of $a\&b$-transitions and only self-loops with labels from the (possibly empty) subset $\Gamma \subseteq \Sigma$ at the final state. Thus, we can assume that $L(\mathcal{A}) = a^i b^j (a+b)^k \Gamma^*$ for some non-negative integers i, j, k such that $i + j + k = n - 1$. By modifiying a construction from [5], we can construct a PDFA for $\text{perm}(L(\mathcal{A})$ with $f(i, j, k) = (i+1) \cdot (j+1) + k \cdot j + k \cdot i + k$ many states. In order to get an upper bound for the state complexity of $\text{perm}(L(\mathcal{A}))$ as a function of the size of $\mathcal{A}$, we determine for which values of i, j, k, where $i + j + k = n - 1$, the function $f(i, j, k)$ has a maximal value. The function f is maximized if $ij + kj + ki$ is maximal, thus if $i = j = k = \frac{n-1}{3}$. More generally,

$$\max_{i+j+k=n-1} f(i, j, k) = \begin{cases} \frac{n^2+n+1}{3} & \text{if } n \equiv 1 \pmod 3; \\ \frac{n^2+n}{3} & \text{otherwise.} \end{cases}$$

In [5, Lemma 4.2], as every chain automaton is a general chain automaton recognizing a finite language, it was shown that for $n \equiv 1 \pmod 3$ there exists a language recognized by a chain automaton with n states such that any automaton for the commutative closure needs at least $\frac{n^2+n+1}{3}$ many states.   □

---

[6] This is no restriction when we have no self-loops.

6 Complexity Results

Here, we consider the alphabet to be fixed in advance and not part of the input.

In model checking, when the specification and the implementation could be represented by finite automata, the inclusion problem arises naturally [1,30]. In this problem, we are given two automata and ask if the recognized language of the first is contained in the recognized language of the second automaton. In [2] it was shown that the universality problem, i.e., deciding if a given APC[7] denotes Σ^*, is PSPACE-complete, *even for fixed binary alphabets*. This implies PSPACE-completeness of the inclusion problem.

Here, we show the somewhat surprising result that the above decision problems are polynomial time solvable modulo permutational equivalence, i.e., if we ask the same questions for the commutative closure of the input languages, see Theorem 11 and Corollary 12.

This result is not as artificial as it might seem. For example, consider the introductory example from regular model checking in Sect. 1. Here, the set of reachable configurations 0^*10^* is closed under the commutative closure, as well as the set of bad configurations $(0 + 1)^*1(0 + 1)^*1(0 + 1)^*$ and its complement. More specifically, these sets are commutative languages and the original decision problem is equivalent to the same decision problem modulo permutational equivalence.

At the heart of this result lies the fact that the PDFA constructed in the proof of Theorem 2 could be constructed, for a fixed alphabet, in polynomial time. This will be shown in Proposition 10. But before this result, let us first state that, with respect to polynomial time, it makes no difference if the input is given as an APC expression or a partially ordered NFA.

Lemma 9. *For a given partially ordered NFA $\mathcal{A}$ an APC expression of $L(\mathcal{A})$ could be computed in P and for every APC expression a partially ordered NFA is computable in P. This result also holds for variable input alphabets.*

So, we are ready to derive that from a given partially ordered NFA, a PDFA recognizing the commutative closure could be computed in P.

Proposition 10. *Given a partially ordered NFA $\mathcal{A}$ with n states, the recognizing PDFA for $\mathrm{perm}(L(\mathcal{A}))$ from Theorem 2 could be constructed in polynomial time for a fixed alphabet. More precisely in time $O(n^{|\Sigma|+2})$.*

Proof (sketch). This is only a rough and intuitive outline of the procedure.

Let $\Sigma = \{a_1, \ldots, a_k\}$ and $\mathcal{A} = (\Sigma, S, \mu, s_0, E)$ be a partially ordered NFA. We outline a polynomial time algorithm to compute $\mathcal{B} = (\Sigma, Q, \delta, q_0, F)$ as defined in the proof of Theorem 2. We can assume that s_0 is minimal for the partial order of $\mathcal{A}$ and every maximal state is final. Set $n_a = \max\{|u|_a : u \in L^{\mathrm{simple}}(\mathcal{A})\}$ for $a \in \Sigma$

---

[7] Or a partially ordered NFA, which follows by Lemma 9.

The state set, and hence the numbers n_a, could be computed by a dynamic programming scheme starting at the maximal final states and ending at the start state. For each letter $a \in \Sigma$, we store at every state q the number $\max\{|u|_a \mid \delta(q, u) \in F$ and no loops are entered by u in $\mathcal{A}\}$, i.e., the longest unary projection string for that letter when starting at this state, ending at a final state and traversing no self-loops[8]. For a final maximal state, those numbers are initialized to zero and for every other state, they are computable from the predecessor states. For the start state, the last state in this procedure, these are precisely the numbers n_a, from which Q is easily constructible.

The computation of the transition function and the final state set is more involved. Note that for states $(s_1, \ldots, s_k) \in Q$ with $s_i < n_{a_i}$ for $i \in \{1, \ldots, k\}$ the transition function is easily computable. The only difficulty is to determine which "boundary" states should be labeled by self-loops. We do this by constructing an auxiliary automaton $\mathcal{A}'$ out of $\mathcal{A}$ by "unfolding" the self-loops into paths of length $|S| + 1$. The automaton $\mathcal{A}'$ then has no loops anymore. Now, we label the states of this auxiliary automaton with those states from Q that are reachable in $\mathcal{B}$ by words that go from the start state to the state under consideration of $\mathcal{A}'$. If such a word passes an unfolded path completely, then, as they are sufficiently long, we know that it must traverse a self-loop in $\mathcal{A}$ labeled by the same letter a as the unfolded path. In this case, for every "boundary" state of Q in the labeling of the target state of the word in $\mathcal{A}'$ we add a self-loop for the letter a to that state from Q in $\mathcal{B}$.

Finally, a state from Q is declared to be final if and only if it appears in a label of a final state of $\mathcal{A}'$.

This procedure indeed computes $\mathcal{B}$ and could be made to run in the stated time bound.   □

With Proposition 10, we derive that, given two APCs, the inclusion problem modulo permutational equivalence is solvable in polynomial time.

Theorem 11. *Fix an alphabet Σ. Then, the following problem is in P:*
Input: *Two APC expressions L_1, L_2 over Σ^*.*
Question: *Is $\mathrm{perm}(L_1) \subseteq \mathrm{perm}(L_2)$?*

Given an APC, the universality problem modulo permutational equivalence is solvable in polynomial time, as it is reducible to the corresponding inclusion problem up to permutational equivalence.

Corollary 12. *Fix an alphabet Σ. Then, the following problem is in P:*
Input: *An APC expression L over Σ^*.*
Question: *Is $\mathrm{perm}(L) = \Sigma^*$?*

As for commutative languages $L \subseteq \Sigma^*$ we have $\mathrm{perm}(L) = L$, we get the next corollary. This generalizes a corresponding reduction of complexity for unary alphabets [14].

---

[8] So, essentially we are working in the automaton that results if we delete all self-loops, which gives a recognizing automaton for $L^{\mathrm{simple}}(\mathcal{A})$ for partially ordered NFAs $\mathcal{A}$.

Corollary 13. *Fix an alphabet Σ. Given an APC describing a commutative language, the universality problem is in P. Also, given two APCs describing commutative languages, the inclusion problem is solvable in polynomial time.*

7 Conclusion

We have given a sharp upper bound for the number of states needed in a deterministic recognizing automata for the commutative closure of APCs. Additionally, we have shown that the recognizing automaton could be computed in polynomial time for fixed alphabets. Using this result, we have shown that the inclusion and universality problem modulo permutational equivalence are solvable in polynomial time for a fixed input alphabet. This contrasts with the general inclusion and universality problem for APCs. Both are PSPACE-complete even for binary alphabets [14]. For two subclasses of the APC languages, we have given sharp bounds for the commutative closure expressed in the size of the input automata. In the case that the language is given by a general chain automaton, the result was only established for binary alphabets. The case for larger alphabets is still open.

Acknowledgement. I thank the anonymous reviewers for careful reading, noticing a reoccurring typo in the proof of Theorem 1 that was luckily spotted and fixed and helping me identifying some unclear formulations throughout the text.

References

1. Abdulla, P.A., Jonsson, B., Nilsson, M., Saksena, M.: A survey of regular model checking. In: Gardner, P., Yoshida, N. (eds.) CONCUR 2004. LNCS, vol. 3170, pp. 35–48. Springer, Heidelberg (2004). https://doi.org/10.1007/978-3-540-28644-8_3
2. Bouajjani, A., Muscholl, A., Touili, T.: Permutation rewriting and algorithmic verification. Inf. Comput. **205**(2), 199–224 (2007)
3. Brzozowski, J.A., Fitch, F.E.: Languages of $\mathcal{R}$-trivial monoids. J. Comput. Syst. Sci. **20**(1), 32–49 (1980)
4. Brzozowski, J.A.: Hierarchies of aperiodic languages. RAIRO Theor. Inform. Appl. **10**(2), 33–49 (1976)
5. Cho, D., Goc, D., Han, Y., Ko, S., Palioudakis, A., Salomaa, K.: State complexity of permutation on finite languages over a binary alphabet. Theor. Comput. Sci. **682**, 67–78 (2017)
6. Cohen, R.S., Brzozowski, J.A.: Dot-depth of star-free events. J. Comput. Syst. Sci. **5**(1), 1–16 (1971)
7. Colcombet, T.: Green's relations and their use in automata theory. In: Dediu, A.-H., Inenaga, S., Martín-Vide, C. (eds.) LATA 2011. LNCS, vol. 6638, pp. 1–21. Springer, Heidelberg (2011). https://doi.org/10.1007/978-3-642-21254-3_1
8. Gao, Y., Moreira, N., Reis, R., Yu, S.: A survey on operational state complexity. J. Autom. Lang. Comb. **21**(4), 251–310 (2017)
9. Gómez, A.C., Guaiana, G., Pin, J.: Regular languages and partial commutations. Inf. Comput. **230**, 76–96 (2013)
10. Green, J.A.: On the structure of semigroups. Ann. Math. (Second Ser.) **54**, 163–172 (1951)

11. Hoffmann, S.: State complexity bounds for the commutative closure of group languages. In: Jirásková, G., Pighizzini, G. (eds.) DCFS 2020. LNCS, vol. 12442, pp. 64–77. Springer, Cham (2020). https://doi.org/10.1007/978-3-030-62536-8_6

12. Hopcroft, J.E., Ullman, J.D.: Introduction to Automata Theory, Languages, and Computation. Addison-Wesley Publishing Company, Boston (1979)

13. Pin, J.E.: Varieties Of Formal Languages. Plenum Publishing Co., New York (1986)

14. Krötzsch, M., Masopust, T., Thomazo, M.: Complexity of universality and related problems for partially ordered nfas. Inf. Comput. **255**, 177–192 (2017)

15. Maslov, A.N.: Estimates of the number of states of finite automata. Dokl. Akad. Nauk SSSR **194**(6), 1266–1268 (1970)

16. Masopust, T., Krötzsch, M.: Partially ordered automata and piecewise testability. CoRR abs/1907.13115 (2019). http://arxiv.org/abs/1907.13115

17. McNaughton, R., Papert, S.A.: Counter-Free Automata (M.I.T. Research Monograph No. 65). The MIT Press, Cambridge (1971)

18. Palioudakis, A., Cho, D.-J., Goč, D., Han, Y.-S., Ko, S.-K., Salomaa, K.: The state complexity of permutations on finite languages over binary alphabets. In: Shallit, J., Okhotin, A. (eds.) DCFS 2015. LNCS, vol. 9118, pp. 220–230. Springer, Cham (2015). https://doi.org/10.1007/978-3-319-19225-3_19

19. Pin, J.: Syntactic semigroups. In: Rozenberg, G., Salomaa, A. (eds.) Handbook of Formal Languages, vol. 1, pp. 679–746. Springer, Heidelberg (1997). https://doi.org/10.1007/978-3-642-59136-5_10

20. Pin, J.: The dot-depth hierarchy, 45 years later. In: Konstantinidis, S., Moreira, N., Reis, R., Shallit, J.O. (eds.) The Role of Theory in Computer Science - Essays Dedicated to Janusz Brzozowski, pp. 177–202. World Scientific (2017)

21. Place, T., Zeitoun, M.: Generic results for concatenation hierarchies. Theor. Comput. Syst. **63**(4), 849–901 (2019)

22. Ryzhikov, A.: Synchronization problems in automata without non-trivial cycles. Theor. Comput. Sci. **787**, 77–88 (2019)

23. Schützenberger, M.P.: On an application of semi groups methods to some problems in coding. IRE Trans. Inf. Theory **2**(3), 47–60 (1956)

24. Schützenberger, M.P.: On finite monoids having only trivial subgroups. Inf. Control **8**(2), 190–194 (1965)

25. Schwentick, T., Thérien, D., Vollmer, H.: Partially-ordered two-way automata: a new characterization of da. In: Kuich, W., Rozenberg, G., Salomaa, A. (eds.) DLT 2001. LNCS, vol. 2295, pp. 239–250. Springer, Heidelberg (2002). https://doi.org/10.1007/3-540-46011-X_20

26. Simon, I.: Piecewise testable events. In: Brakhage, H. (ed.) GI-Fachtagung 1975. LNCS, vol. 33, pp. 214–222. Springer, Heidelberg (1975). https://doi.org/10.1007/3-540-07407-4_23

27. Straubing, H.: A generalization of the schützenberger product of finite monoids. Theor. Comput. Sci. **13**, 137–150 (1981)

28. Thérien, D.: Classification of finite monoids: the language approach. Theor. Comput. Sci. **14**, 195–208 (1981)

29. Thomas, W.: Classifying regular events in symbolic logic. J. Comput. Syst. Sci. **25**(3), 360–376 (1982)

30. Vardi, M.Y.: An automata-theoretic approach to linear temporal logic. In: Moller, F., Birtwistle, G. (eds.) Logics for Concurrency. LNCS, vol. 1043, pp. 238–266. Springer, Heidelberg (1996). https://doi.org/10.1007/3-540-60915-6_6

31. Yu, S., Zhuang, Q., Salomaa, K.: The state complexities of some basic operations on regular languages. Theoret. Comput. Sci. **125**(2), 315–328 (1994)

Algorithms for Probabilistic and Stochastic Subsequential Failure Transducers

Diana Geneva, Georgi Shopov, and Stoyan Mihov$^{(\boxtimes)}$

Institute of Information and Communication Technologies,
Bulgarian Academy of Sciences, 2, Acad. G. Bonchev Str., 1113 Sofia, Bulgaria
{dageneva,gshopov,stoyan}@lml.bas.bg

Abstract. This paper introduces a framework for building probabilistic models with subsequential failure transducers. We first show how various types of subsequential transducers commonly used in natural language processing are represented by probabilistic and conditional probabilistic subsequential failure transducers. Afterwards we introduce efficient algorithms for composition of conditional probabilistic subsequential transducers with probabilistic subsequential failure transducers and weight pushing (canonization) of probabilistic subsequential failure transducers. Those algorithms are applicable to many tasks for representing probabilistic models with subsequential failure transducers. One such task is the construction of the $HCLG$ weighted transducer used in speech recognition which we describe in detail. At the end, empirical results and comparison between the presented $HCLG$ failure weighted transducer and the standard $HCLG$ weighted transducer constructions are shown.

Keywords: Weighted transducers · Failure transducers · Probabilistic models

1 Introduction

Weighted finite-state transducers (WFST) are widely used for representing probability distributions over words such as language models, pronunciation lexicons, and hidden Markov models in automatic speech recognition (ASR) [8], and translation transformations in statistical machine translation [5]. In [1] it is shown that a back-off n-gram language model can be efficiently represented as a subsequential failure transducer. In practice however the failure transitions are often

Supported by the Bulgarian Ministry of Education and Science via grant DO1-200/2018 "Electronic healthcare in Bulgaria". We acknowledge the provided access to the e-infrastructure of the Centre for Advanced Computing and Data Processing, with the financial support by the Grant BG05M2OP001-1.001-0003, financed by the Science and Education for Smart Growth Operational Program and co-financed by the EU through the European structural and Investment funds.

© Springer Nature Switzerland AG 2021
S. Maneth (Ed.): CIAA 2021, LNCS 12803, pp. 127–139, 2021.
https://doi.org/10.1007/978-3-030-79121-6_11

substituted with ε-transitions [1,8]. The benefit is that general constructions for finite-state transducers can be applied. The drawback is twofold. First, since new non-valid paths are introduced, the output of the transducer is not equivalent to the original one. Second, the transducer is not deterministic anymore and there are many paths for one input. In [1] a procedure for eliminating some of the non-valid paths is presented. This procedure has the property that the maximal output probability for a given input in the resulting transducer will be equal to the output probability of this input in the original failure transducer. However, the resulting transducer might still contain more than one successful path for a given input and its size typically becomes 2 to 3 times the size of the input transducer.

In this paper we explore another approach. We introduce a framework for building probabilistic models with failure transducer constructions. Particularly, we show how to efficiently construct the $HCLG$ transducer [7] used in many modern ASR systems. We perform all constructions on failure transducers but we maintain the determinism on the input and thus obtain subsequential failure transducers as a result. The main advantages of our approach are:

– we directly construct deterministic devices – subsequential failure transducers, thus, avoiding additional determinizations,
– the resulting transducers represent correct probabilistic models.

Related work is conducted in [3] where specialized algorithms including intersection, failure transition removal and shortest distance for weighted failure automata are presented. As opposed to [3] here we focus our attention on subsequential failure transducers only. We present efficient, direct constructions which preserve the sequentiality of the failure transducers.

The formal definitions and detailed proofs of the constructions presented in this paper are provided separately in [4].

2   Preliminaries

We will use the standard notions of alphabet, word, language etc. from formal language theory. We will call a language L over the alphabet Σ *prefix-free* if $(\forall \alpha, \beta \in L)((\exists \gamma \in \Sigma^*)(\alpha\gamma = \beta) \implies \alpha = \beta)$. Throughout the paper we will distinguish between words as elements of the free monoid and *lexicon words* which occur in natural language. With $\mathcal{R}$ we will denote the monoid $\langle \mathbb{R}_+, \times, 1 \rangle$ of non-negative real numbers with multiplication as the monoid operation. In this paper we consider only subsequential transduction devices introduced by Schützenberger [12]. For reasons of brevity, we will deliberately omit the word "subsequential".

A *transducer* is a tuple $\mathcal{T} := \langle \Sigma, \langle M, \otimes, \bar{1} \rangle, Q, s, F, \delta, \lambda, \iota, \rho \rangle$, where Σ is an alphabet, $\langle M, \otimes, \bar{1} \rangle$ is a monoid, Q is a finite set of states, $s \in Q$ is an initial state, $F \subseteq Q$ is a set of final states, $\delta: Q \times \Sigma \to Q$ is a partial transition function, $\lambda: Q \times \Sigma \to M$ is a partial output function, $\iota \in M$ is an initial output, $\rho: F \to M$ is a total final output function, and $\text{Dom}(\delta) = \text{Dom}(\lambda)$.

The *generalized transition function* $\delta^* : Q \times \Sigma^* \to Q$ and the *generalized output function* $\lambda^* : Q \times \Sigma^* \to M$ are the natural extensions of δ and λ over $Q \times \Sigma^*$.

For each $q \in Q$ the function $\mathcal{O}_T^q : \Sigma^* \to M$ is defined for $\alpha \in \Sigma^*$ as $\mathcal{O}_T^q(\alpha) := \lambda^*(q, \alpha) \otimes \rho(\delta^*(q, \alpha))$ if $\delta^*(q, \alpha) \in F$ and is undefined otherwise. The function $\mathcal{O}_T : \Sigma^* \to M$, defined for $\alpha \in \Sigma^*$ as $\mathcal{O}_T(\alpha) := \iota \otimes \mathcal{O}_T^s(\alpha)$, is *the function represented by the transducer* T. A state $q \in Q$ is called *co-accessible* in T if $\mathrm{Dom}(\mathcal{O}_T^q) \neq \varnothing$.

A *failure transducer* is a tuple $\mathcal{F} := \langle \Sigma, \langle M, \otimes, \bar{1} \rangle, Q, s, F, \delta, \lambda, \iota, \rho, f, \varphi \rangle$ where $\langle \Sigma, \langle M, \otimes, \bar{1} \rangle, Q, s, F, \delta, \lambda, \iota, \rho \rangle$ is a transducer, $f : Q \to Q$ is a partial failure transition function, $\varphi : Q \to M$ is a partial failure output function, and $\mathrm{Dom}(f) = \mathrm{Dom}(\varphi)$. We define the *completed transition function* $\delta_f : Q \times \Sigma \to Q$ and the *completed output function* $\lambda_f : Q \times \Sigma \to M$ inductively:

$$\delta_f(q, \sigma) := \begin{cases} \delta(q, \sigma) & \text{if } ! \delta(q, \sigma) \\ \delta_f(f(q), \sigma) & \text{otherwise} \end{cases} \quad \lambda_f(q, \sigma) := \begin{cases} \lambda(q, \sigma) & \text{if } ! \lambda(q, \sigma) \\ \varphi(q) \otimes \lambda_f(f(q), \sigma) & \text{otherwise} \end{cases}$$

where with $! \delta(q, \sigma)$ (resp. $! \lambda(q, \sigma)$) we denote that $(q, \sigma) \in \mathrm{Dom}(\delta)$ (resp. $(q, \sigma) \in \mathrm{Dom}(\lambda)$).

The *expanded transducer* of the failure transducer $\mathcal{F}$ is the transducer $T := \langle \Sigma, M, Q, s, F, \delta_f, \lambda_f, \iota, \rho \rangle$. For each $q \in Q$ we define $\mathcal{O}_{\mathcal{F}}^q := \mathcal{O}_T^q$. The function $\mathcal{O}_{\mathcal{F}} := \mathcal{O}_T$ is called *the function represented by the failure transducer* $\mathcal{F}$. A state $q \in Q$ is *co-accessible* in $\mathcal{F}$ if it is co-accessible in T.

Definition 1. *A failure transducer is* monotonic *if for every* $q \in \mathrm{Dom}(f)$ *and every* $a \in \Sigma$ *it holds that* $q \in F \implies f(q) \in F$ *and* $! \delta(q, a) \implies ! \delta(f(q), a)$.

The *signature* of a (failure) transducer state q is the set of labels for which q has an outgoing transition, i.e. $\mathrm{Sig}(q) := \{\sigma \in \Sigma \mid ! \delta(q, \sigma)\}$. If the failure transducer is monotonic then $\mathrm{Sig}(q) \subseteq \mathrm{Sig}(f(q))$. Therefore the signatures of the states in every failure cycle are identical and thus the failure transitions in the cycle are redundant. In what follows, we will assume that every monotonic failure transducer that we consider has no failure cycles since they can be efficiently removed.

3   Probabilistic Transducers

In speech recognition a widely used approach is to construct the so-called *HCLG* transducer [7,8]. This transducer is constructed by composing (from right to left) the language model transducer G with the lexicon transducer L, the context-dependency transducer C, and the HMM transducer H. We will show that the transducer G can be represented by a probabilistic failure transducer.

Definition 2. *A transducer* T *over the monoid* $\mathcal{R}$ *is* probabilistic *if* $\mathcal{O}_T$ *is a probability distribution over* Σ^*, *i.e.* $(\forall \alpha \in \mathrm{Dom}(\mathcal{O}_T))(\mathcal{O}_T(\alpha) \in [0, 1])$ *and* $\sum_{\alpha \in \mathrm{Dom}(\mathcal{O}_T)} \mathcal{O}_T(\alpha) = 1$. *In order to emphasize that* T *represents a probability*

distribution, in what follows with $P_T(\alpha)$ we shall denote $\mathcal{O}_T(\alpha)$. We will use the expression $e(q)$ to mean $\rho(q)$ if $q \in F$ and 0 otherwise. We call T stochastic if
$$(\forall q \in Q) \left(e(q) + \sum_{a \in \Sigma:\ !\delta(q,a)} \lambda(q,a) = 1 \right).$$

We call a failure transducer *probabilistic (stochastic)* if its corresponding expanded transducer is probabilistic (stochastic). Note that stochastic failure transducers may have failure outputs greater than 1.

Allauzen et al. have shown [1] that a smoothed n-gram language model can be represented by a failure transducer G. The transducer G maps a given sequence of lexicon words $w_1 w_2 \ldots w_n$ to the smoothed n-gram probability for the sequence $P(w_1 w_2 \ldots w_n)$. A typical back-off formulation of a smoothed n-gram language model is represented by the probability of a lexicon word w given a history h as follows: $P(w|h) := \hat{P}(w|h)$ if hw occurs, $P(w|h) := \alpha_h P(w|h')$ otherwise, where $\hat{P}$ is an empirical estimate of the probability that reserves probabilities for unseen n-grams, α_h is a normalizing back-off weight and h' is obtained by removing the earliest lexicon word from the history h. A failure transducer that represents the n-gram language model has states corresponding to the observed sequences of length $< n$. Its proper transitions (δ transitions) represent the case in which hw occurs and have weights equal to $\hat{P}(w|h)$. The failure transitions represent the other case and have weights α_h. It is assumed that every sentence in the corpus ends with the special lexicon word \$. A state h is final if $\hat{P}(\$|h) > 0$ and $\rho(h) = \hat{P}(\$|h)$. Figure 1a depicts a failure transducer that represents a small bigram language model.

We can note that the failure transducer G is monotonic because the failure transitions enter states corresponding to shorter history. Also, the normalization constants α_h ensure that $\sum_w P(w|h) = 1$, which implies that $e(h) + \sum_w \lambda_f(h,w) = 1$. Therefore, G is monotonic and stochastic.

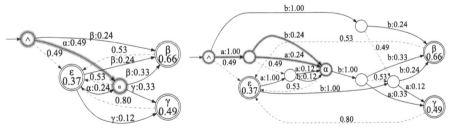

(a) Monotonic stochastic failure transducer for the smoothed bigram language model estimated from the corpus $\{\alpha\beta, \alpha\gamma, \beta\}$.

(b) Composition of the transducer for the phonetization lexicon $\alpha \mapsto \{\langle ab, 0.5\rangle, \langle aa, 0.5\rangle\}$, $\beta \mapsto \{\langle bb, 1\rangle\}$, and $\gamma \mapsto \{\langle ba, 1\rangle\}$ with the transducer from Figure 1a.

Fig. 1. The transducer G (left) and the composition $L \circ G$ (right).

4   Conditional Probabilistic Transducers

We next show that the transducers L, C, and H used to construct the $HCLG$ transducer can be represented by conditional probabilistic transducers.

Definition 3. *A conditional probabilistic transducer is a transducer* $\mathcal{T} := \langle \Sigma,$ $\Omega^* \times \mathcal{R}, Q, s, F, \delta, \lambda, \iota, \rho \rangle$ *such that for every* $\beta \in \text{Proj}_1(\text{Range}(\mathcal{O}_\mathcal{T}))$ *it holds that* $\sum_{\alpha \in \text{Dom}(\mathcal{O}_\mathcal{T}(\bullet|\beta))} \mathcal{O}_\mathcal{T}(\alpha \mid \beta) = 1$, *where the function* $\mathcal{O}_\mathcal{T}(\bullet \mid \beta) \colon \Sigma^* \to \mathbb{R}_+$ *for* $\alpha \in \Sigma^*$ *is defined as* $\mathcal{O}_\mathcal{T}(\alpha \mid \beta) := r$ *if* $\mathcal{O}_\mathcal{T}(\alpha) = \langle \beta, r \rangle$ *and is undefined otherwise. Again, in order to emphasize that* $\mathcal{T}$ *represents a conditional probability distribution, in what follows with* $P_\mathcal{T}(\alpha \mid \beta)$ *we shall denote* $\mathcal{O}_\mathcal{T}(\alpha \mid \beta)$.

The conditional probabilistic transducer L. The transducer L represents the pronunciation probabilities for the lexicon words. Here we assume that the set of lexicon words coincides with Ω. Given a sequence of lexicon words the transducer L represents the probability distribution over all phonetizations of the given sequence. In what follows the set of phones will be denoted with Σ. If the conditional probabilistic transducer $\mathcal{V} := \langle \Sigma, \Omega^* \times \mathcal{R}, Q_1, s_1, F_1, \delta_1, \lambda_1, \iota_1, \rho_1 \rangle$ represents the phonetizations of single lexicon words then the transducer L is equal to the iteration (Kleene-Star) of $\mathcal{V}$. We have that $\text{Proj}_1(\text{Range}(\mathcal{O}_\mathcal{V})) = \Omega$ because $\mathcal{V}$ provides phonetizations for all lexicon words. Without loss of generality we can assume that $\text{Dom}(\mathcal{O}_\mathcal{V})$ is prefix-free (this condition can easily be satisfied by adding new end word symbols to Σ), there are no transitions that enter s_1, $\text{Range}(\rho_1) = \{\langle \varepsilon, 1 \rangle\}$ and $\iota_1 = \langle \varepsilon, 1 \rangle$.

Under these assumptions we construct the conditional probabilistic transducer L equal to the iteration (Kleene-Star) of $\mathcal{V}$ as

$$L = \mathcal{V}^* := \langle \Sigma, \Omega^* \times \mathcal{R}, Q_1 \setminus F_1, s_1, \{s_1\}, \delta_3, \lambda_1, \langle \varepsilon, 1 \rangle, \{\langle s_1, \langle \varepsilon, 1 \rangle \rangle\} \rangle,$$

where $\delta_3 := \delta_1 \restriction_{(Q_1 \setminus F_1) \times \Sigma \times (Q_1 \setminus F_1)} \cup \{\langle p_1, a, s_1 \rangle \mid \langle p_1, a, q_1 \rangle \in \delta_1, q_1 \in F_1\}$. It follows that $\text{Dom}(\mathcal{O}_{\mathcal{V}^*}) = \text{Dom}(\mathcal{O}_\mathcal{V})^*$ and for every sequence of phonetizations $\bar{\alpha}_1, \bar{\alpha}_2, \ldots, \bar{\alpha}_n \in \Sigma^*$ of lexicon words $\beta_1, \beta_2, \ldots, \beta_n \in \Omega$ it follows that $\mathcal{O}_{\mathcal{V}^*}(\bar{\alpha}_1 \bar{\alpha}_2 \ldots \bar{\alpha}_n | \beta_1 \beta_2 \ldots \beta_n) = \prod_{i=1}^n P_\mathcal{V}(\bar{\alpha}_i | \beta_i)$. Since $\mathcal{V}$ is conditional probabilistic, summing in the above equation over all phonetizations of $\beta_1, \beta_2, \ldots, \beta_n$ we can observe that $L = \mathcal{V}^*$ is conditional probabilistic.

The conditional probabilistic transducer C. The context-dependency transducer C maps from context-dependent phones to context-independent phones. The context-dependent phones consist of l phones to the left (left context), central phone, and r phones to the right (right context). The states of the conditional probabilistic transducer C represent the last $l + r$ read context-independent phones. The transitions have context-dependent phones as labels and are of the form $p_1 p_2 \ldots p_{l+r} \xrightarrow{p_1 p_2 \ldots p_{l+r} q} p_2 p_3 \ldots p_{l+r} q$. The corresponding output of the transition is $\langle q, 1 \rangle$. Insufficient contexts are padded with a special empty phone symbol. C is conditional probabilistic since for every sequence of context-independent phones β there exists a unique sequence of context-dependent phones α, such that $\mathcal{O}_C(\alpha) = \langle \beta, 1 \rangle$.

The conditional probabilistic transducer H. The transducer H represents the HMM set, i.e. the Kleene-Star of the union of the HMMs for individual context-dependent phones. Each of the HMMs is a stochastic and conditional probabilistic transducer. The input symbols on the transitions are unique identifiers of the transitions in the HMM corresponding to the given context-dependent phone. Therefore, the union of the HMMs is prefix-free. Thus its Kleene-Star is conditional probabilistic and can be obtained using the same construction as the $\mathcal{V}^*$ transducer.

5   Composition of Conditional Probabilistic Transducers with Probabilistic Failure Transducers

In the previous section we showed how to construct efficiently the probabilistic failure transducer G and the conditional probabilistic transducers L, C and H. Here we introduce a general construction method for composing a conditional probabilistic transducer with a probabilistic failure transducer and obtaining a probabilistic failure transducer as a result. Using this general method we can construct the $HCLG$ transducer by the composition $H \circ (C \circ (L \circ G))$. In addition, we also introduce a more efficient construction for composition, applicable when certain conditions are satisfied by the conditional probabilistic transducer.

5.1   Generic Composition

In this subsection let $\mathcal{T} := \langle \Sigma, \Omega^* \times \mathcal{R}, Q_1, s_1, F_1, \delta_1, \lambda_1, \iota_1, \rho_1 \rangle$ be a conditional probabilistic transducer and $\mathcal{F} := \langle \Omega, \mathcal{R}, Q_2, s_2, F_2, \delta_2, \lambda_2, \iota_2, \rho_2, f_2, \varphi_2 \rangle$ be a probabilistic failure transducer. As a natural extension of the composition of transducers [8] and the intersection of weighted finite automata with failure transitions [3] we obtain a construction for the composition of $\mathcal{T}$ and $\mathcal{F}$.

Definition 4. *The* composition *of* $\mathcal{T}$ *and* $\mathcal{F}$ *is the failure transducer* $\mathcal{T} \circ \mathcal{F} := \langle \Sigma, \mathcal{R}, Q_1 \times Q_2, s, F, \delta, \lambda, \iota, \rho, f, \varphi \rangle$, *where*

$s := \langle s_1, \delta_{2 f_2}^*(s_2, \mathrm{Proj}_1(\iota_1)) \rangle$,

$F := \{\langle p_1, p_2 \rangle \mid p_1 \in F_1, \langle p_2, \mathrm{Proj}_1(\rho_1(p_1)), q_2 \rangle \in \delta_{2 f_2}^*, q_2 \in F_2\}$,

$\delta := \{\langle \langle p_1, p_2 \rangle, a, \langle q_1, p_2 \rangle \rangle \mid \langle p_1, a, q_1 \rangle \in \delta_1, \langle p_1, a, \langle \varepsilon, o_1 \rangle \rangle \in \lambda_1, p_2 \in Q_2\} \cup$
$\quad\quad \{\langle \langle p_1, p_2 \rangle, a, \langle q_1, q_2 \rangle \rangle \mid \langle p_1, a, q_1 \rangle \in \delta_1, \langle p_1, a, \langle \omega\alpha, o_1 \rangle \rangle \in \lambda_1, \langle p_2, \omega, r_2 \rangle \in \delta_2,$
$\quad\quad\quad\quad\quad\quad \langle p_2, \omega\alpha, q_2 \rangle \in \delta_{2 f_2}^*\}$,

$\lambda := \{\langle \langle p_1, p_2 \rangle, a, o_1 \rangle \mid \langle p_1, a, \langle \varepsilon, o_1 \rangle \rangle \in \lambda_1, p_2 \in Q_2\} \cup$
$\quad\quad \{\langle \langle p_1, p_2 \rangle, a, o_1 o_2 \rangle \mid \langle p_1, a, \langle \omega\alpha, o_1 \rangle \rangle \in \lambda_1, \langle p_2, \omega, r_2 \rangle \in \delta_2,$
$\quad\quad\quad\quad\quad\quad \langle p_2, \omega\alpha, o_2 \rangle \in \lambda_{2 f_2}^*\}$,

$\iota := \mathrm{Proj}_2(\iota_1)\iota_2\lambda_{2 f_2}^*(s_2, \mathrm{Proj}_1(\iota_1))$,

$\rho := \{\langle \langle p_1, p_2 \rangle, o_1 o_2 o_3 \rangle \mid \langle p_1, p_2 \rangle \in F, \langle p_1, \langle \alpha, o_1 \rangle \rangle \in \rho_1, \langle p_2, \alpha, o_2 \rangle \in \lambda_{2 f_2}^*,$

$$\langle \delta_2{}^*_{f_2}(p_2, \alpha), o_3 \rangle \in \rho_2 \},$$

$$f := \{ \langle \langle p_1, p_2 \rangle, \langle p_1, q_2 \rangle \rangle \mid p_1 \in Q_1, \langle p_2, q_2 \rangle \in f_2 \},$$

$$\varphi := \{ \langle \langle p_1, p_2 \rangle, o_2 \rangle \mid p_1 \in Q_1, \langle p_2, o_2 \rangle \in \varphi_2 \}.$$

The above composition reflects the chain rule $P(\alpha, \beta) = P(\alpha \mid \beta) P(\beta)$. In our case β is uniquely identified by α, therefore $P_{\mathcal{T} \circ \mathcal{F}}(\alpha) = P_{\mathcal{T}}(\alpha \mid \beta) P_{\mathcal{F}}(\beta)$. The following proposition formalizes this idea. The proof can be found in [4].

Proposition 1. *Let* $\mathrm{Proj}_1(\mathrm{Range}(\mathcal{O}_{\mathcal{T}})) \supseteq \mathrm{Dom}(\mathcal{O}_{\mathcal{F}})$. *Then*

1. $(\forall \alpha \in \mathrm{Dom}(\mathcal{O}_{\mathcal{T} \circ \mathcal{F}}))(P_{\mathcal{T} \circ \mathcal{F}}(\alpha) = P_{\mathcal{T}}(\alpha \mid \beta) P_{\mathcal{F}}(\beta))$, *where* $\beta = \mathrm{Proj}_1(\mathcal{O}_{\mathcal{T}}(\alpha))$;
2. $\mathcal{T} \circ \mathcal{F}$ *is probabilistic;*
3. *if* $\mathcal{F}$ *is monotonic and for every* $p \in \mathrm{Dom}(f_2)$, $\alpha \in \mathrm{Proj}_1(\mathrm{Range}(\lambda_1))$ *and* $\beta \in \mathrm{Proj}_1(\mathrm{Range}(\rho_1))$ *we have that* $! \delta_2{}^*_{f_2}(p, \alpha) \implies ! \delta_2{}^*_{f_2}(f_2(p), \alpha)$ *and* $\delta_2{}^*_{f_2}(p, \beta) \in F_2 \implies \delta_2{}^*_{f_2}(f_2(p), \beta) \in F_2$, *then* $\mathcal{T} \circ \mathcal{F}$ *is monotonic.*

In particular, when $\mathcal{T} = L$ and $\mathcal{F} = G$, the third statement of Proposition 1 follows from the monotonicity of G and $\mathrm{Proj}_1(\mathrm{Range}(\lambda_1 \cup \rho_1)) \subseteq \Omega \cup \{\varepsilon\}$. Also, since $\mathrm{Proj}_1(\mathrm{Range}(\mathcal{O}_L)) = \Omega^*$, we obtain that $L \circ G$ is monotonic and probabilistic. Figure 1a depicts a monotonic stochastic failure transducer for a simple language model. Therefore, its composition with a lexicon transducer will be monotonic and probabilistic (see Fig. 1b). Similarly the compositions $C \circ LG$ and $H \circ CLG$ yield monotonic and probabilistic failure transducers.

In practice the construction from Definition 4 might produce many states that are redundant. This particularly applies when composing L with G. We present a more efficient construction for this special case in Subsect. 5.2. This construction is also applicable for composing H with CLG more efficiently.

5.2 Special Case Composition

Let $\mathcal{V} := \langle \Sigma, \Omega^* \times \mathcal{R}, Q_1, s_1, F_1, \delta_1, \lambda_1, \iota_1, \rho_1 \rangle$ be a trim (i.e. $(\forall q \in Q_1)(\exists \alpha, \beta \in \Sigma^*)(\delta_1^*(s_1, \alpha) = q \wedge \delta_1^*(q, \beta) \in F_1)$) conditional probabilistic transducer, which satisfies the conditions: $\mathrm{Proj}_1(\mathrm{Range}(\mathcal{O}_{\mathcal{V}})) = \Omega$ and $\mathrm{Dom}(\mathcal{O}_{\mathcal{V}})$ is prefix-free. Let $\mathcal{F} := \langle \Omega, \mathcal{R}, Q_2, s_2, F_2, \delta_2, \lambda_2, \iota_2, \rho_2, f_2, \varphi_2 \rangle$ be a monotonic probabilistic failure transducer in which every state is co-accessible. Let us consider Definition 4 for the special case where $\mathcal{T} = \mathcal{V}^*$. We obtain $\mathcal{V}^*$ by redirecting the transitions ending in final states to the initial state. To express this we introduce the function $E : Q_1 \rightarrow Q_1$, such that $E(p) := s_1$ if $p \in F_1$ and $E(p) := p$ otherwise. Every successful path in $\mathcal{V}$ is of the form

$$p_1^0 \xrightarrow{a_1 : \varepsilon / o_1} \dots \xrightarrow{a_{i-1} : \varepsilon / o_{i-1}} p_1^{i-1} \xrightarrow{a_i : \omega / o_i} p_1^i \xrightarrow{a_{i+1} : \varepsilon / o_{i+1}} \dots \xrightarrow{a_n : \varepsilon / o_n} p_1^n,$$

where $p_1^0 = s_1$ and $p_1^n \in F_1$. If we have a transition in $\mathcal{F}$ of the form $p_2 \xrightarrow{\omega : o'} q_2$, then we obtain the following path in the composition:

$$\langle p_1^0, p_2 \rangle \xrightarrow{a_1 : o_1} \dots \xrightarrow{a_{i-1} : o_{i-1}} \langle p_1^{i-1}, p_2 \rangle \xrightarrow{a_i : o_i o'} \langle p_1^i, q_2 \rangle \xrightarrow{a_{i+1} : o_{i+1}} \dots \xrightarrow{a_n : o_n} \langle E(p_1^n), q_2 \rangle.$$

If $\omega \notin \mathrm{Sig}(p_2)$, then according to Definition 4 the states $\langle p_1^1, p_2 \rangle, \ldots, \langle p_1^{i-1}, p_2 \rangle$ are constructed but are redundant in $\mathcal{V}^* \circ \mathcal{F}$. In order to avoid constructing those states, we will restrict the states of $\mathcal{V}$, which we consider, to those on a successful path with label from the signature of the corresponding state in $\mathcal{F}$. Formally, we define the states to the left (Q_ω^l) and to the right (Q_ω^r) of transitions with output ω.

Definition 5. *Let $\omega \in \Omega$. We define*

$$\Delta_\omega := \{\langle p_1, a, q_1 \rangle \in \delta_1 \mid \mathrm{Proj}_1(\lambda_1(p_1, a)) = \omega\},$$

$$Q_\omega^l := \bigcup_{\langle p_1, a, q_1 \rangle \in \Delta_\omega} \{l_1 \mid (\exists \alpha \in \Sigma^*)(\langle l_1, \alpha, p_1 \rangle \in \delta_1^*)\},$$

$$Q_\omega^r := \bigcup_{\langle p_1, a, q_1 \rangle \in \Delta_\omega} \{r_1 \mid (\exists \alpha \in \Sigma^*)(\langle q_1, \alpha, r_1 \rangle \in \delta_1^*)\}.$$

For the example path in $\mathcal{V}$, the states $p_1^0, p_1^1, \ldots, p_1^{i-1}$ are from Q_ω^l and $p_1^i, p_1^{i+1}, \ldots, p_1^n$ are from Q_ω^r. Clearly the sets Q_ω^l and Q_ω^r are disjoint and any transition between two states in Q_ω^l or two states in Q_ω^r outputs ε and some probability. If for every $\omega \in \Omega$ we have Δ_ω (the transitions with output ω), the sets Q_ω^l and Q_ω^r can be computed in linear time with respect to their size with a simple traversal from respectively the source states of the transitions towards the initial state (having explicit backward transitions) and from the target states of the transitions towards the final states. We also observe that the failure transitions of the states with first coordinate in Q_ω^r are useless.

Proposition 2. *Let $\mathcal{W} := \langle \Sigma, \mathcal{R}, Q, \langle s_1, s_2 \rangle, \{s_1\} \times F_2, \delta, \lambda, \iota_2, \rho, f, \varphi \rangle$, where*

$$Q := \bigcup_{\langle p_2, \omega, q_2 \rangle \in \delta_2} Q_\omega^l \times \{p_2\} \cup E(Q_\omega^r) \times \{q_2\},$$

$$\delta := \bigcup_{\langle p_2, \omega, q_2 \rangle \in \delta_2} \begin{aligned} &\{\langle \langle p_1, p_2 \rangle, a, \langle q_1, p_2 \rangle \rangle \mid p_1, q_1 \in Q_\omega^l, \langle p_1, a, q_1 \rangle \in \delta_1\} \cup \\ &\{\langle \langle p_1, p_2 \rangle, a, \langle E(q_1), q_2 \rangle \rangle \mid \langle p_1, a, q_1 \rangle \in \Delta_\omega\} \cup \\ &\{\langle \langle p_1, q_2 \rangle, a, \langle E(q_1), q_2 \rangle \rangle \mid p_1, q_1 \in Q_\omega^r, \langle p_1, a, q_1 \rangle \in \delta_1\}, \end{aligned}$$

$$\lambda := \bigcup_{\langle p_2, \omega, q_2 \rangle \in \delta_2} \begin{aligned} &\{\langle \langle p_1, p_2 \rangle, a, o_1 \rangle \mid p_1 \in Q_\omega^l, \langle p_1, a, \langle \varepsilon, o_1 \rangle \rangle \in \lambda_1\} \cup \\ &\{\langle \langle p_1, p_2 \rangle, a, o_1 o_2 \rangle \mid \langle p_1, a, \langle \omega, o_1 \rangle \rangle \in \lambda_1, \langle p_2, \omega, o_2 \rangle \in \lambda_2\} \cup \\ &\{\langle \langle p_1, q_2 \rangle, a, o_1 \rangle \mid p_1 \in Q_\omega^r, \langle p_1, a, \langle \varepsilon, o_1 \rangle \rangle \in \lambda_1\}, \end{aligned}$$

$$\rho := \{\langle \langle s_1, p_2 \rangle, o_2 \rangle \mid \langle p_2, o_2 \rangle \in \rho_2\},$$

$$f := \bigcup_{\langle p_2, \omega, q_2 \rangle \in \delta_2} \{\langle \langle p_1, p_2 \rangle, \langle p_1, r_2 \rangle \rangle \mid p_1 \in Q_\omega^l, \langle p_2, r_2 \rangle \in f_2\},$$

$$\varphi := \bigcup_{\langle p_2, \omega, q_2 \rangle \in \delta_2} \{\langle \langle p_1, p_2 \rangle, o_2 \rangle \mid p_1 \in Q_\omega^l, \langle p_2, o_2 \rangle \in \varphi_2\}.$$

Then $\mathcal{W}$ is trim and $\mathcal{O}_\mathcal{W} = \mathcal{O}_{\mathcal{V}^* \circ \mathcal{F}}$.

The construction from Proposition 2 can be implemented in linear time with respect to the transitions of the resulting transducer. The proof of the proposition can be found in [4].

6   Canonization

It has been shown that stochastic transducers are more effective than non-stochastic ones for speech recognition decoding [9]. As discussed the transducer G is stochastic. If LG is stochastic, then $C \circ LG$ is also stochastic because all weights in C are equal to 1. It can be easily observed that in this case $H \circ CLG$ will also be stochastic, since H is constructed from stochastic HMMs. However, the presented constructions for composition do not ensure that LG is stochastic.

It is easily shown that the stochasticity in the monoid $\mathcal{R}$ is equivalent to canonicity with respect to the semiring $\mathcal{R}^+ := \langle \mathbb{R}_+, +, \times, 0, 1 \rangle$.

Definition 6. *The transducer* $\mathcal{T} := \langle \Sigma, \langle K, \otimes, \bar{1} \rangle, Q, s, F, \delta, \lambda, \iota, \rho \rangle$ *is canonical with respect to the semiring* $\mathcal{K} := \langle K, \oplus, \otimes, \bar{0}, \bar{1} \rangle$ *if for every* $q \in Q$ *it holds that* $\bigoplus_{\alpha \in \text{Dom}(\mathcal{O}_\mathcal{T}^q)} \mathcal{O}_\mathcal{T}^q(\alpha) = \bar{1}$.

We call a failure transducer *canonical* if its expanded transducer is canonical. The standard canonization algorithm is based on modification of the weights of a given transducer so that the transition weights of every given state sum to $\bar{1}$. For a probabilistic (failure) transducer $\mathcal{T}$ and a state p with $S_\mathcal{T}(q)$ we denote the sum $\sum_{\alpha \in \text{Dom}(\mathcal{O}_\mathcal{T}^q)} \mathcal{O}_\mathcal{T}^q(\alpha)$. The weight-pushing is defined as updating the probability r of a given transition from the state p to the state q to $\frac{rS_\mathcal{T}(q)}{S_\mathcal{T}(p)}$. Next we extend the standard canonization algorithm for the case of probabilistic failure transducers.

Proposition 3. *Let* $\mathcal{W} := \langle \Sigma, \mathcal{R}, Q, s, F, \delta, \lambda, \iota, \rho, f, \varphi \rangle$ *be a probabilistic failure transducer and* $\mathcal{W}_\mathcal{C} := \langle \Sigma, \mathcal{R}, Q, s, F, \delta, \lambda_\mathcal{C}, \iota_\mathcal{C}, \rho_\mathcal{C}, f, \varphi_\mathcal{C} \rangle$, *where*

- $\lambda_\mathcal{C} := \{ \langle p, a, \frac{rS_\mathcal{W}(\delta(p,a))}{S_\mathcal{W}(p)} \rangle \mid \langle p, a, r \rangle \in \lambda \}$;
- $\iota_\mathcal{C} := \iota S_\mathcal{W}(s)$;
- $\rho_\mathcal{C} := \{ \langle p, \frac{r}{S_\mathcal{W}(p)} \rangle \mid \langle p, r \rangle \in \rho \}$;
- $\varphi_\mathcal{C} := \{ \langle p, \frac{rS_\mathcal{W}(f(p))}{S_\mathcal{W}(p)} \rangle \mid \langle p, r \rangle \in \varphi \}$.

Then $\mathcal{O}_{\mathcal{W}_\mathcal{C}} = \mathcal{O}_\mathcal{W}$ *and* $\mathcal{W}_\mathcal{C}$ *is stochastic and canonical with respect to* $\mathcal{R}^+$.

The construction in Proposition 3 requires the computation of the sums $S_\mathcal{W}(q)$, which is computationally expensive. In this section we show how this can be achieved more efficiently in case $\mathcal{W}$ is obtained by composing a conditional probabilistic transducer $\mathcal{V}^*$ with a monotonic and stochastic failure transducer $\mathcal{F}$, where $\mathcal{V}$ is acyclic. This is the case for LG. The main idea of the specialized construction is to avoid the expansion of failure transitions by constructing an acyclic graph with nodes corresponding to transducer states with restricted signatures.

Let V and $\mathcal{F}$ be as in Subsect. 5.2. Also, let $\mathcal{F}$ be stochastic and $W := \langle \Sigma, \mathcal{R}, Q, s, F, \delta, \lambda, \iota, \rho, f, \varphi \rangle$ be the failure transducer from Proposition 2, equivalent to the composition of V^* and $\mathcal{F}$. Since W is probabilistic, the sums $S_W(q)$ exist for every $q \in Q$ and Proposition 3 can be used to obtain the canonical form of W. Since $\mathcal{F}$ is stochastic, it is also canonical with respect to $\mathcal{R}^+$, i.e. for every state q of $\mathcal{F}$, $S_{\mathcal{F}}(q) = 1$. We show that the states of W with s_1 as first coordinate also satisfy this property.

Let $\omega \in \Omega$ and Γ_ω^V be the set of all words from Σ^* for which V produces ω as output. i.e. $\Gamma_\omega^V := \{\alpha \in \Sigma^* \mid \mathrm{Proj}_1(\mathcal{O}_V(\alpha)) = \omega\}$. For example, in the case of the lexicon transducer L, Γ_ω^L represents the set of all phonetizations of ω. Then for every transition $\langle p, \omega, q \rangle \in \delta_2$ in $\mathcal{F}$ and every $\alpha \in \Gamma_\omega^V$, there will be a path in W from $\langle s_1, p \rangle$ to $\langle s_1, q \rangle$ with input label α. Therefore, the sum of the outputs of the paths from $\langle s_1, p \rangle$ to $\langle s_1, q \rangle$ in W with input labels in Γ_ω^V will be equal to the output of the transition $\langle p, \omega, q \rangle$ in $\mathcal{F}$. This is illustrated in Fig. 1. The highlighted transition in Fig. 1a with input α and output 0.49 is transformed into the two highlighted paths in Fig. 1b with inputs aa and ab (the phonetizations of α) and outputs 0.245. Using this observation and the fact that $\mathcal{F}$ is stochastic, the following proposition can be proved.

Proposition 4. $(\forall p \in Q_2)\,(S_W(\langle s_1, p \rangle) = 1)$.

Therefore, it is sufficient to compute $S_W(q)$ only for the states $q \in Q$ such that $\mathrm{Proj}_1(q) \neq s_1$. Thus, we consider the failure transducer $\widetilde{W}$ in which the transitions from W that begin in such states are omitted and those states are made final with final output 1. Let $\widetilde{W} := \langle \Sigma, \mathcal{R}, Q, s, Q_{s_1}, \widetilde{\delta}, \widetilde{\lambda}, \iota, Q_{s_1} \times \{1\}, \widetilde{f}, \widetilde{\varphi} \rangle$, where $Q_{s_1} = \{\langle p, q \rangle \in Q \mid p = s_1\}$, $\overline{Q}_{s_1}$ is $Q \setminus Q_{s_1}$, $\widetilde{\delta} := \delta \upharpoonright_{\overline{Q}_{s_1} \times \Sigma}$, $\widetilde{\lambda} := \lambda \upharpoonright_{\overline{Q}_{s_1} \times \Sigma}$, $\widetilde{f} := f \upharpoonright_{\overline{Q}_{s_1} \times \Sigma}$, and $\widetilde{\varphi} := \varphi \upharpoonright_{\overline{Q}_{s_1} \times \Sigma}$. From Proposition 4 it follows that $(\forall q \in Q)(S_{\widetilde{W}}(q) = S_W(q))$.

We reduce the problem of finding $S_{\widetilde{W}}(q)$ to the single-source shortest distance problem with respect to the semiring $\mathcal{R}^+$ [6] in a special graph corresponding to $\widetilde{W}$. The graph contains a node for each state in the transducer and an edge for each δ and failure transition. If there is a δ transition from p with label a then all δ_f transitions from p with a that begin with a failure transition are invalid. In order to avoid such paths in the graph we clone the target states of the failure transitions and allow from each cloned state only edges that correspond to δ-transitions that are not defined in the source of the failure transition (see Fig. 2).

We construct a labeled weighted acyclic graph, which in addition to the states from $\widetilde{W}$ contains the cloned states, such that only the valid paths in $\widetilde{W}$ are represented. Let $\mathcal{G} := (V, E)$, where

$$V := Q \cup \{\langle q, \widetilde{f}(q) \rangle \mid q \in \mathrm{Dom}(\widetilde{f})\},$$

$$E := \{\langle p, \langle a, \widetilde{\lambda}(p, a) \rangle, q \rangle \mid \langle p, a, q \rangle \in \widetilde{\delta}\} \cup \{\langle p, \langle \varepsilon, \widetilde{\varphi}(p) \rangle, \langle p, q \rangle \rangle \mid \langle p, q \rangle \in \widetilde{f}\} \cup$$

$$\{\langle \langle p, q \rangle, \langle a, \widetilde{\lambda}(q, a) \rangle, r \rangle \mid \langle p, q \rangle \in \widetilde{f}, \langle q, a, r \rangle \in \widetilde{\delta}, \neg!\,\widetilde{\delta}(p, a)\} \cup$$

$$\{\langle \langle p, q \rangle, \langle \varepsilon, \widetilde{\varphi}(q) \rangle, \langle q, r \rangle \rangle \mid \langle p, q \rangle \in \widetilde{f}, \langle q, r \rangle \in \widetilde{f}\}.$$

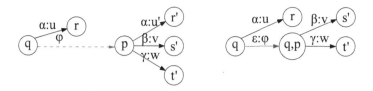

Fig. 2. $\langle q, p \rangle$ in the graph (right) is a clone of p in the failure transducer (left).

It then follows that $S_{\widetilde{\mathcal{W}}}(q)$ is the shortest distance from the new vertex x to the vertex q in the graph $\widetilde{\mathcal{G}} := (V \cup \{x\}, E^{rev} \cup \{x\} \times \{1\} \times Q_{s_1})$, which represents the reverse of the graph $\mathcal{G}$ extended with the initial vertex x. An important property of $\widetilde{\mathcal{G}}$ is that it is acyclic, since V is acyclic, there are no δ cycles because the transtions are restricted to those from $\overline{Q}_{s_1}$, and there are no failure cycles. This allows the sums $S_{\widetilde{\mathcal{W}}}(q)$ for $q \in \overline{Q}_{s_1}$ to be computed in linear time with respect to the size of $\widetilde{\mathcal{G}}^1$.

Thus, the procedure to construct the canonical form of $\mathcal{W}$ consists of first building the graph $\widetilde{\mathcal{G}}$, using $\widetilde{\mathcal{G}}$ to compute the values $S_{\mathcal{W}}(q)$, and applying Proposition 3 to push the weights of $\mathcal{W}$. Formal proofs of the above propositions are presented in [4].

7   Experimental Results and Conclusion

In our experiments we applied the presented constructions for building the $HCLG$ transducer for the LibriSpeech ASR language model [10] and compared them with the corresponding Kaldi [11] implementation which uses OpenFst [2]. All experiments are performed on a dual Intel Xeon Silver 4210 CPU at 2.20 GHz machine with 384 GB RAM running Debian Linux. The source code for the experiments can be requested from the authors by e-mail. For obtaining the $HCLG$ transducer we applied the following steps:

1. The stochastic failure transducer G is constructed using the construction from [1];
2. From the lexicon we construct $L \circ G$ using Subsect. 5.2, thus obtaining a probabilistic failure transducer;
3. Using the procedure from Sect. 6, we construct a stochastic failure transducer equivalent to $L \circ G$ which we additionally quasi minimize[2];
4. We construct the context-dependecy transducer C and compose it with the stochastic failure transducer LG, using Definition 4; The resulting failure transducer CLG is trim and stochastic;

---

[1] In comparison with the corresponding algorithm for ϕ-WFA presented in [3] we empirically observed that our algorithm introduces significantly less states and transitions.

[2] We use the standard automata minimization procedure considering failure transitions as proper transitions with special label.

5. From the definition of the HMMs using Proposition 2 we construct the failure transducer $HCLG$ which is stochastic, and which we additionally quasi minimize.

For constructing the standard WFST we used the standard Kaldi recipe . The main differences are that in the Kaldi recipe two intermediate deteminizations and additional optimization tricks are applied. The table below presents size and time comparison between the Kaldi construction of the HCLG WFST and our construction of the HCLG failure WFST.

Transducer	WFST			Failure WFST		
	States	Transitions	Time	States	Transitions	Time
G	7.6M	93.5M	4 m 24 s	7.6M	93.5M	1 m 47 s
LG	85.1M	230.5M	17 m 40 s	288.0M	717.9M	2 m 45 s
$min\&push(LG)$	72.7M	211.3M	1 h 10 m 30 s	254.7M	646.2M	20 m 34 s
CLG	73.6M	219.3M	1 h 20 m 14 s	255.1M	649.5M	27 m 13s
$min(HCLG)$	89.4M	316.7M	2 h 29 m 14 s	536.9M	1 213.1M	1h 22 m 34 s

The experiments show that the size of the failure WFST gets approximately 3-4 times bigger than the corresponding WFST but the construction time is around two times shorter. The main benefit of the presented approach is that the resulting failure WFST is deterministic, has no invalid paths, and represents a correct probability distribution.

References

1. Allauzen, C., Mohri, M., Roark, B.: Generalized algorithms for constructing statistical language models. In: ACL (2003)
2. Allauzen, C., Riley, M., Schalkwyk, J., Skut, W., Mohri, M.: OpenFst: a general and efficient weighted finite-state transducer library. In: Holub, J., Žd'árek, J. (eds.) CIAA 2007. LNCS, vol. 4783, pp. 11–23. Springer, Heidelberg (2007). https://doi.org/10.1007/978-3-540-76336-9_3
3. Allauzen, C., Riley, M.D.: Algorithms for weighted finite automata with failure transitions. In: Câmpeanu, C. (ed.) Implementation and Application of Automata, pp. 46–58. Springer International Publishing, Cham (2018)
4. Geneva, D., Shopov, G., Mihov, S.: Composition and Weight Pushing of Monotonic Subsequential Failure Transducers Representing Probabilistic Models. arXiv e-prints arXiv:2003.09364 (March 2020)
5. Kumar, S., Deng, Y., Byrne, W.: A weighted finite state transducer translation template model for statistical machine translation. Nat. Lang. Eng. **12**(1), 35–76 (2006)
6. Mohri, M.: Semiring frameworks and algorithms for shortest-distance problems. J. Automata Lang. Comb. **7**(3), 321–350 (2002)
7. Mohri, M., Pereira, F., Riley, M.: Weighted finite-state transducers in speech recognition. Comput. Speech Lang. **16**(1), 69–88 (2002)

8. Mohri, M., Pereira, F., Riley, M.: Speech recognition with weighted finite-state transducers. In: Benesty, J., Sondhi, M.M., Huang, Y.A. (eds.) Springer Handbook of Speech Processing. SH, pp. 559–584. Springer, Heidelberg (2008). https://doi.org/10.1007/978-3-540-49127-9_28

9. Mohri, M., Riley, M.: A weight pushing algorithm for large vocabulary speech recognition. In: Seventh European Conference on Speech Communication and Technology (2001)

10. Panayotov, V., Chen, G., Povey, D., Khudanpur, S.: LibriSpeech: an asr corpus based on public domain audio books. In: 2015 IEEE International Conference on Acoustics, Speech and Signal Processing (ICASSP), pp. 5206–5210, April 2015

11. Povey, D., et al.: The Kaldi speech recognition toolkit. In: IEEE 2011 workshop (2011)

12. Schützenberger, M.: Sur une variante des fonctions sequentielles. Theor. Comput. Sci. **4**(1), 47–57 (1977)

Ambiguity Hierarchies for Weighted Tree Automata

Andreas Maletti, Teodora Nasz, Kevin Stier[(✉)], and Markus Ulbricht

Institute of Computer Science, Universität Leipzig,
PO box 100 920, 04009 Leipzig, Germany
{maletti,nasz,stier,mulbricht}@informatik.uni-leipzig.de

Abstract. Weighted tree automata (WTA) extend classical weighted automata (WA) to the non-linear structure of trees. The expressive power of WA with varying degrees of ambiguity has been extensively studied. Unambiguous, finitely ambiguous, and polynomially ambiguous WA over the tropical (as well as the arctic) semiring strictly increase in expressive power. The recently developed pumping results of MAZOWIECKI and RIVEROS (STACS 2018) are lifted to trees in order to achieve the same strict hierarchy for WTA over the tropical (as well as the arctic) semiring.

1 Introduction

Trees are a fundamental data structure in computer science and are used in many application areas like natural language processing, database theory, and compiler construction. All the mentioned applications require effective representations of sets of trees. These requirements triggered detailed investigations of various classes of such sets since the 1960s [11,12] and yielded an abundance of representations [6]. The most robust class is the class of regular tree languages [7,27]. It is generated by finite-state tree automata, which are a natural generalization of finite-state automata, which generate the regular languages [28]. Finite-state tree automata are a very effective representation and most standard decision problems remain decidable and the problem complexity is often similar to that of the corresponding problem for finite-state automata [6].

Quantitative extensions of finite-state automata, called weighted automata (WA) [25], as well as finite-state tree automata, called weighted tree automata (WTA) [8], have been proposed and thoroughly investigated. The weights are usually taken from a semiring like the nonnegative integers $\mathbb{N}$, the tropical semiring $\mathbb{T}$ [26] or the arctic semiring $\mathbb{A}$.

It is well-known that the computational properties improve dramatically for deterministic devices. While deterministic finite-state automata are as expressive as general finite-state automata, this equivalence breaks down for weighted automata over relevant semirings [2]. Thus, less restricted devices have been investigated as well. While general finite-state automata might allow exponentially many successful runs (in the length of the input) on a given input,

K. Stier—Financially supported by DFG Research Training Group 1763 (QuantLA).

S. Maneth (Ed.): CIAA 2021, LNCS 12803, pp. 140–151, 2021.
https://doi.org/10.1007/978-3-030-79121-6_12

deterministic finite-state automata naturally permit at most one successful run for each input that is additionally locally determined. We obtain polynomially ambiguous, finitely ambiguous, and unambiguous automata by requiring that for each input the number of successful runs is restricted by a polynomial, by a uniform bound, and by 1, respectively. The expressive power of weighted automata and weighted tree automata of limited ambiguity is actively investigated [17,18,21,22], but essential questions remain open.

Recently, it was established that unambiguous, finitely ambiguous, and polynomially ambiguous WA over the tropical semiring $\mathbb{T}$ strictly increase in expressive power [19]. This result was achieved with the help of pumping lemmas, which were also used to derive the same result [5] for the arctic semiring $\mathbb{A}$. The inclusion is obvious, but for the strictness results, pumping lemmas for the smaller classes are developed [19, Theorems 7, 14, and 18] and [5, Theorems 6.1 and 6.5]. These together with specific examples from the larger class that do not obey the pumping conditions establish the strictness.

Our goal is the development of a similar hierarchy for WTA. To this end, we utilize the same approach and develop the corresponding pumping results for WTA over $\mathbb{T}$ (Theorems 3, 7, and 11) and over $\mathbb{A}$ (Theorems 9 and 13). The main ingredient is a matrix representation of the behavior of a WTA along a tree decomposition into contexts (see Section 3) since it allows us to consider WTA as special weighted automata and apply the theorems of [5,19]. Along the way we prove that unambiguous WTA over $\mathbb{T}$ and $\mathbb{A}$ can be expressed as WTA over $\mathbb{N}_\infty$ (Lemma 1). In the end, we achieve the desired results and thus prove that finitely ambiguous WTA over $\mathbb{T}$ and $\mathbb{A}$ are strictly more expressive than unambiguous WTA (Theorems 4 and 5) and strictly less expressive than polynomially ambiguous WTA (Theorems 8 and 10). Finally, Theorems 12 and 14 illustrate that polynomially ambiguous WTA over those semirings are strictly less expressive than general WTA.

2   Preliminaries

Basic Notation. We denote the set of nonnegative integers (including 0) by $\mathbb{N}$. For every $k \in \mathbb{N}$ we use the subset $[k] = \{i \in \mathbb{N} \mid 1 \le i \le k\}$. For any set S the set of all finite words over S is $S^* = \bigcup_{k \in \mathbb{N}} S^k$, where $S^k = S \times \cdots \times S$ containing k factors S and $S^0 = \{\varepsilon\}$ contains just the *empty word* ε. The *length* $|w|$ of a word $w = s_1 \cdots s_k \in S^*$ with $s_1, \ldots, s_k \in S$ is $|w| = k$; i.e., the number of occurrences of symbols in w. Given words $v, w \in S^*$, their concatenation is written $v.w$ or simply vw.

Trees. A *ranked alphabet* (Σ, rk) is a pair consisting of a finite set Σ and a mapping $\mathrm{rk} \colon \Sigma \to \mathbb{N}$ that assigns a rank to each symbol of Σ. If there is no risk of confusion, we denote a ranked alphabet (Σ, rk) by just Σ. We also write $\sigma^{(k)}$ to indicate that $\mathrm{rk}(\sigma) = k$. Moreover, for every $k \in \mathbb{N}$ we let $\Sigma^{(k)} = \{\sigma \in \Sigma \mid \mathrm{rk}(\sigma) = k\}$. Given a ranked alphabet Σ and a set Z, the set $\mathrm{T}_\Sigma(Z)$ of Σ" trees indexed by Z is the smallest set T such that $Z \subseteq T$ and $\sigma(t_1, \ldots, t_k) \in T$ for every $k \in \mathbb{N}$, $\sigma \in \Sigma^{(k)}$, and $t_1, \ldots, t_k \in T$. We abbreviate $\mathrm{T}_\Sigma(\emptyset)$ simply to T_Σ, and any subset $L \subseteq \mathrm{T}_\Sigma$ is called a *tree language*.

Next, we recall some notions for trees. Let $t \in T_\Sigma(Z)$ be a tree for a ranked alphabet Σ and a set Z. The set $\mathrm{pos}(t)$ of *positions* of t is inductively defined for all $z \in Z$ by $\mathrm{pos}(z) = \{\varepsilon\}$ and for all $k \in \mathbb{N}$, $\sigma \in \Sigma^{(k)}$, and $t_1, \ldots, t_k \in T_\Sigma(Z)$ by $\mathrm{pos}(\sigma(t_1, \ldots, t_k)) = \{\varepsilon\} \cup \{ip \mid i \in [k], p \in \mathrm{pos}(t_i)\}$. The *height* of t is $\mathrm{height}(t) = \max_{p \in \mathrm{pos}(t)} |p|$, and the *size* of t is $\mathrm{size}(t) = |\mathrm{pos}(t)|$. A *leaf* of t is a position $p \in \mathrm{pos}(t)$ such that $p1 \notin \mathrm{pos}(t)$. We denote the set of all leaves of t by $\mathrm{leaf}(t)$. Given a position $p \in \mathrm{pos}(t)$, the label $t(p)$ of t at p and the subtree $t|_p$ of t at p are given by $z(\varepsilon) = z|_\varepsilon = z$ for all $z \in Z$ and

$$\big(\sigma(t_1, \ldots, t_k)\big)(p) = \begin{cases} \sigma & \text{if } p = \varepsilon \\ t_i(p') & \text{if } p = ip' \text{ with } i \in \mathbb{N} \text{ and } p' \in \mathrm{pos}(t_i) \end{cases}$$

$$\sigma(t_1, \ldots, t_k)|_p = \begin{cases} \sigma(t_1, \ldots, t_k) & \text{if } p = \varepsilon \\ t_i|_{p'} & \text{if } p = ip' \text{ with } i \in \mathbb{N} \text{ and } p' \in \mathrm{pos}(t_i) \end{cases}$$

for all $k \in \mathbb{N}$, $\sigma \in \Sigma^{(k)}$, and $t_1, \ldots, t_k \in T_\Sigma(Z)$. Finally, the *replacement* $t[t']_p$ of the subtree at position $p \in \mathrm{pos}(t)$ by a tree $t' \in T_\Sigma(Z)$ is given by $z[t']_\varepsilon = t'$ for all $z \in Z$ and

$$\sigma(t_1, \ldots, t_k)[t']_\varepsilon = t'$$
$$\sigma(t_1, \ldots, t_k)[t']_{ip'} = \sigma(t_1, \ldots, t_{i-1}, t_i[t']_{p'}, t_{i+1}, \ldots, t_k)$$

for every $k \in \mathbb{N}$, $\sigma \in \Sigma^{(k)}$, $t_1, \ldots, t_k \in T_\Sigma(Z)$, $i \in [k]$, and $p' \in \mathrm{pos}(t_i)$.

We reserve the use of the special symbol $\square$. A tree $t \in T_\Sigma(\{\square\})$ is a *context*, if there exists exactly one $p \in \mathrm{pos}(t)$ with $t(p) = \square$; i.e., there is exactly one occurrence of $\square$ in t. The set of all such contexts is denoted by C_Σ. Given a context $C \in C_\Sigma$ and a tree $t \in T_\Sigma(\{\square\})$, the substitution $C[t]$ of t into C yields the tree $C[t]_p$, where p is the unique position $p \in \mathrm{pos}(C)$ with $C(p) = \square$. Note that $C[C'] \in C_\Sigma$ for $C, C' \in C_\Sigma$. Similarly, we write C^k for $C[\cdots C[C] \cdots]$ containing k times the context C. The set of *decompositions* of $\xi \in T_\Sigma \cup C_\Sigma$ is

$$D(\xi) = \bigcup_{\substack{k \geq 1 \\ C_1, \ldots, C_{k-1} \in C_\Sigma \\ \xi' \in C_\Sigma \cup T_\Sigma}} \{(C_1, \ldots, C_{k-1}, \xi') \mid \xi = C_1[\cdots C_{k-1}[\xi'] \cdots]\}.$$

Note that $\xi \in T_\Sigma$ iff $\xi' \in T_\Sigma$ for every $(C_1, \ldots, C_{k-1}, \xi') \in D(\xi)$. The *depth* $\mathrm{depth}(C)$ of a context $C \in C_\Sigma$ is $\mathrm{depth}(C) = |p|$, where $p \in \mathrm{pos}(C)$ is the unique position with $C(p) = \square$. A context $c \in C_\Sigma$ of depth 1 is *elementary*, and the set of all such elementary contexts is denoted by E_Σ. A decomposition $(E_1, \ldots, E_k) \in D(C)$ of a context $C \in C_\Sigma$ is *elementary* if $E_1, \ldots, E_k \in E_\Sigma$. In fact, the monoid $(C_\Sigma, \cdot[\cdot], \square)$ is freely generated by E_Σ [4], which proves the existence of an elementary decomposition for each context. Finally, let $t \in T_\Sigma$, $\mathcal{C} = (D_n, C_n, \ldots, D_1, C_1, s) \in D(t)$ and $\mathcal{D} = (D'_n, C'_n, \ldots, D'_1, C'_1, s') \in D(t)$ be decompositions of the tree t. We call $\mathcal{D}$ a *refinement* of $\mathcal{C}$ (refining the occurrences of C_i) if for every $i \in [n]$ there exist $L_i, R_i \in C_\Sigma$ such that $D'_i = R_{i+1}[D_i[L_i]]$, $s' = R_1[s]$, and $C_i = L_i[C'_i[R_i]]$, where $R_{n+1} = \square$.

Weighted Automata. A *commutative semiring* [13,15] is a tuple $(S, +, \cdot, 0, 1)$ such that both $(S, +, 1)$ and $(S, \cdot, 1)$ are commutative monoids, $\cdot$ distributes over $+$, and $0 \cdot s = 0$ for all $s \in S$. More specifically we consider

- the Boolean semiring $\mathbb{B} = (\{0, 1\}, \vee, \wedge, 0, 1)$,
- the extended Boolean semiring $\mathbb{B}_\infty = (\{0, 1, \infty\}, \vee, \wedge, 0, 1)$ with $\infty \vee n = \infty$ for all $n \in \{0, 1, \infty\}$ and $\infty \wedge 0 = 0$ and $\infty \wedge 1 = \infty \wedge \infty = \infty$,
- the tropical semiring $\mathbb{T} = (\mathbb{N} \cup \{\infty\}, \min, +, \infty, 0)$,
- the arctic semiring $\mathbb{A} = (\mathbb{N} \cup \{-\infty\}, \max, +, -\infty, 0)$, and
- the extended semiring $\mathbb{N}_\infty = (\mathbb{N} \cup \{\infty\}, +, \cdot, 0, 1)$ of nonnegative integers.

We will refer to a semiring $(S, +, \cdot, 0, 1)$ by its carrier set S.

A *weighted automaton* (WA) [24] over S is a tuple $\mathcal{A} = (Q, A, I, (M_a)_{a \in A}, F)$, where Q is a finite set of *states*, A is a finite set of *symbols*, $M_a \in S^{Q \times Q}$ is a *transition weight* matrix for every $a \in A$, and $I, F \in S^Q$ are *initial* and *final weight* vectors, respectively. Given a word $w = a_1 \cdots a_n$ with $a_1, \ldots, a_n \in A$, we let $M_w = M_{a_1} \cdot \ldots \cdot M_{a_n}$ with standard matrix multiplication using the semiring operations.

Finally, the weighted language $\llbracket \mathcal{A} \rrbracket \colon A^* \to S$ recognized by $\mathcal{A}$ is defined for every $w \in A^*$ by $\llbracket \mathcal{A} \rrbracket(w) = I^T \cdot M_w \cdot F$. A weighted language $f \colon A^* \to S$ is *recognizable* if there exists a WA recognizing it.

A *weighted tree automaton* (WTA) [10] over S is a tuple $\mathcal{T} = (Q, \Sigma, \Delta, \mathrm{wt}, F)$, where Q is a finite set of *states*, Σ is a ranked alphabet, $\Delta \subseteq \bigcup_{k \in \mathbb{N}} Q^k \times \Sigma^{(k)} \times Q$ is a set of *transitions*, $\mathrm{wt} \colon \Delta \to S$ is a *transition weight* function, and $F \in S^Q$ is a *root weight* vector. We generally assume that $\mathrm{wt}(\tau) \neq 0$ for all $\tau \in \Delta$, and we write $\sigma(q_1, \ldots, q_k) \xrightarrow{s} q$ for a transition $\tau = (q_1, \ldots, q_k, \sigma, q) \in \Delta$ with $\mathrm{wt}(\tau) = s$. Weighted tree automata over the Boolean semiring (i.e., for $S = \mathbb{B}$) are also called *tree automata* (TA) and their weight function 'wt' is superfluous. Given $t \in T_\Sigma$, a mapping $r \colon \mathrm{pos}(t) \to Q$ is called *run* of $\mathcal{A}$ on t, if $(r(p1), \ldots, r(pk), t(p), r(p)) \in \Delta$ for all $p \in \mathrm{pos}(t)$, where $k = \mathrm{rk}(t(p))$. The run is *accepting* if $F_{r(\varepsilon)} \neq 0$. We denote the set of all accepting runs of $\mathcal{T}$ on t by $\mathrm{Run}_\mathcal{T}(t)$. Moreover, for every $q \in Q$ let $\mathrm{Run}_\mathcal{T}^q(t) = \{r \in \mathrm{Run}_\mathcal{T}(t) \mid r(\varepsilon) = q\}$ be the set of runs with root label q. The *weight* of a run $r \in \mathrm{Run}_\mathcal{T}(t)$ is

$$\mathrm{wt}_\mathcal{T}(r) = \prod_{\substack{p \in \mathrm{pos}(t) \\ k = \mathrm{rk}(t(p))}} \mathrm{wt}\big(r(p1), \ldots, r(pk), t(p), r(p)\big).$$

The weighted tree language $\llbracket \mathcal{T} \rrbracket \colon T_\Sigma \to S$ *recognized* by $\mathcal{T}$ is defined for every tree $t \in T_\Sigma$ by $\llbracket \mathcal{T} \rrbracket(t) = \sum_{r \in \mathrm{Run}_\mathcal{T}(t)} \mathrm{wt}_\mathcal{T}(r) \cdot F_{r(\varepsilon)}$. A weighted tree language $f \colon T_\Sigma \to S$ is *recognizable* if there exists a WTA recognizing it. The class of recognizable weighted tree languages over S is denoted by $\mathrm{RTL}(S)$.

3   Matrix Representation and Ambiguity

For our pumping arguments we first need a matrix-like representation for the weighted tree language recognized by a WTA $\mathcal{T} = (Q, \Sigma, \Delta, \text{wt}, F)$ that is similar to that of weighted automata. Since processing a symbol σ of rank k requires k vectors from the subtrees, we can directly utilize KRONECKER products [9] or tensor products [23], but a simpler approach [3] using contexts, whose processing again will only require a single vector for the subtree replacing $\square$, actually suffices for our purposes. Our run semantics is rather unsuitable for this purpose, so let us recall the equivalent initial algebra semantics [1]. We immediately present the extended variant that can handle contexts as well. For every $\xi \in T_\Sigma(\{\square\})$ we inductively define the weight matrix $\text{wt}_\mathcal{T}(\xi) \in S^{Q \times Q}$ by

- $\text{wt}_\mathcal{T}(\square)_{q,q} = 1$ and $\text{wt}_\mathcal{T}(\square)_{q,q'} = 0$ for all $q, q' \in Q$ with $q \neq q'$, and
- for all $k \in \mathbb{N}$, $\sigma \in \Sigma^{(k)}$, $t_1, \ldots, t_k \in T_\Sigma(\{\square\})$, and $q, q' \in Q$

$$\text{wt}_\mathcal{T}\big(\sigma(t_1, \ldots, t_k)\big)_{q,q'} = \sum_{(q_1, \ldots, q_k, \sigma, q') \in \Delta} \text{wt}(q_1, \ldots, q_k, \sigma, q') \cdot \prod_{i=1}^{k} \text{wt}_\mathcal{T}(t_i)_{q,q_i}.$$

Note that $\text{wt}_\mathcal{T}(t)_{q_1,q'} = \text{wt}_\mathcal{T}(t)_{q_2,q'}$ for all $q_1, q_2, q' \in Q$ and $t \in T_\Sigma$. Hence we identify $\text{wt}_\mathcal{T}(t)$ with a vector of S^Q and obtain $[\![\mathcal{T}]\!](t) = \text{wt}_\mathcal{T}(t)^T \cdot F$ for all $t \in T_\Sigma$ by [3, Lemma 4.1.13] as well as

$$\text{wt}_\mathcal{T}(c[\xi]) = \text{wt}_\mathcal{T}(\xi) \cdot \text{wt}_\mathcal{T}(c) \tag{1}$$

for all contexts $c \in C_\Sigma$ and $\xi \in T_\Sigma \cup C_\Sigma$ by [3, Lemma 4.1.8].

Next we recall the relevant notions of *ambiguity*. Let $\mathcal{T} = (Q, \Sigma, \Delta, \text{wt}, F)$ be a WTA. For a given $\ell \in \mathbb{N}$, the WTA $\mathcal{T}$ is ℓ-*ambiguous* if every tree $t \in T_\Sigma$ has at most ℓ accepting runs; i.e., $|\text{Run}_\mathcal{T}(t)| \leq \ell$. It is *unambiguous* (or a UA-WTA) if it is 1-ambiguous, and it is *finitely ambiguous* (or an FA-WTA) if there exists $\ell \in \mathbb{N}$ such that $\mathcal{T}$ is ℓ-ambiguous. For the notions of '*polynomially ambiguous*' and '*exponentially ambiguous*' we distinguish two variants: one based on the size and another based on the height of the input tree. More precisely, $\mathcal{T}$ is *polynomially ambiguous* in $f \colon T_\Sigma \to \mathbb{N}$ if there exists a polynomial P such that $|\text{Run}_\mathcal{T}(t)| \leq P(f(t))$ for all $t \in T_\Sigma$. We say that $\mathcal{T}$ is a PA-WTA (respectively, a PAH" WTA) if it is polynomially ambiguous in 'size' (respectively, in 'height'). Similarly, $\mathcal{T}$ is *exponentially ambiguous* in $f \colon T_\Sigma \to \mathbb{N}$ if there exists an exponential e such that $|\text{Run}_\mathcal{T}(t)| \leq e(f(t))$. We say that $\mathcal{T}$ is an EA-WTA (respectively, an EAH-WTA) if it is exponentially ambiguous in 'size' (respectively, in 'height'). Note that every WTA $(Q, \Sigma, \Delta, \text{wt}, F)$ is an EA-WTA because there are naturally at most $|Q|^{\text{size}(t)}$ runs for every input tree t. We use the same prefixes π in front of RTL(S) for the class of weighted tree languages over S that are recognizable by π-WTA. For example, PA-RTL(S) is the class of those weighted tree languages over S that are recognizable by WTA that are polynomially ambiguous in size.

4 Unambiguous vs. Finitely Ambiguous

In this section we present a weighted tree language over the tropical semiring $\mathbb{T}$ that is recognized by a FA-WTA but cannot be recognized by any UA-WTA, which proves that UA-RTL($\mathbb{T}$) $\subsetneq$ FA-RTL($\mathbb{T}$). The main component of this result is a pumping result for recognizable weighted tree languages over $\mathbb{N}_\infty$, which is applicable due to the folklore result UA-RTL($\mathbb{T}$) $\subseteq$ RTL($\mathbb{N}_\infty$), which we recall first. The inclusion follows from the well-known construction that is used to show that size $\in$ RTL($\mathbb{N}_\infty$).

Lemma 1. UA-RTL($\mathbb{T}$) $\subseteq$ RTL($\mathbb{N}_\infty$).

The matrix representation allows us to apply a well-known result of idempotent elements, which we recall next. Given a monoid $(M, \cdot, 1)$ an element $m \in M$ is *idempotent* if $m \cdot m = m$. The following well-known result for finite monoids, which states that any sequence of sufficiently many factors contains a nonempty subsequence of factors whose product is idempotent, is the main tool for our first pumping result.

Lemma 2 (e.g. [14, Theorem 3.1]). *Let M be a finite monoid. There exists a constant $N > 0$ such that for all $n \geq N$ and $x_1, \ldots, x_n \in M$ there exist $\ell, u \in \mathbb{N}$ with $\ell < u \leq n$ such that $\prod_{i=\ell+1}^{u} x_i$ is idempotent.*

Theorem 3 (Pumping Lemma for RTL($\mathbb{N}_\infty$)). *Let $f \in$ RTL($\mathbb{N}_\infty$). There exists $N \in \mathbb{N}$ such that for each tree $t \in T_\Sigma$ and decomposition $\mathcal{C} = (D, C, s) \in D(t)$ with $\mathrm{depth}(C) \geq N$ there is a refinement $(D', B, s') \in D(t)$ of $\mathcal{C}$ with $B \neq \square$ such that*

- $f\big(D'[B^h[s']]\big) = f\big(D'[B^{h+1}[s']]\big)$ *for all $h \geq N$ or*
- $f\big(D'[B^h[s']]\big) < f\big(D'[B^{h+1}[s']]\big)$ *for all $h \geq N$.*

Next we present a weighted tree language $f \in$ FA-RTL($\mathbb{T}$) \ UA-RTL($\mathbb{T}$) inspired by [19, Examples 2 and 8]. We explicitly show $f \in$ FA-RTL($\mathbb{T}$) as well as $f \notin$ RTL($\mathbb{N}_\infty$) using Theorem 3. The latter result yields $f \notin$ UA-RTL($\mathbb{T}$) by Lemma 1. For those particular weighted tree languages in the differences we use a ranked alphabet with a single binary symbol and a single nullary symbol. By various encodings (e.g., first-child-next-sibling [6, Proposition 8.3.2]) these results apply to essentially any ranked alphabet. This correspondence extends to weighted tree languages (see [16, Lemma 4.2]).

Theorem 4. UA-RTL($\mathbb{T}$) $\subsetneq$ FA-RTL($\mathbb{T}$).

Proof. Let $\Sigma = \{\sigma^{(2)}\alpha^{(0)}\}$ be a ranked alphabet and $\mathcal{T} = (Q, \Sigma, \Delta, \mathrm{wt}, F)$ a WTA over $\mathbb{T}$ with $Q = \{q_\ell, q_r, q_\alpha\}$, $F(q) = 0$ for each $q \in Q$, and the following transitions and weights

$$\{\alpha \xrightarrow{0} q_\alpha \quad \sigma(q_\alpha, q_\ell) \xrightarrow{1} q_\ell \quad \sigma(q_\ell, q_\alpha) \xrightarrow{0} q_\ell \quad \sigma(q_\ell, q_\ell) \xrightarrow{0} q_\ell \quad \sigma(q_\alpha, q_\alpha) \xrightarrow{1} q_\ell$$

$$\sigma(q_r, q_\alpha) \xrightarrow{1} q_r \quad \sigma(q_\alpha, q_r) \xrightarrow{0} q_r \quad \sigma(q_r, q_r) \xrightarrow{0} q_r \quad \sigma(q_\alpha, q_\alpha) \xrightarrow{1} q_r\}.$$

Clearly, T has two runs for each input tree t, in which we mark all leaves by q_α and then proceed to count either occurrences of $L = \sigma(\alpha, \square)$ using q_ℓ or occurrences of $R = \sigma(\square, \alpha)$ using q_r. We thus calculate the minimum of occurrences of L and R, and $f = [\![T]\!] \in$ FA-RTL(T).

Now let us apply our pumping lemma in order to prove that no WTA over $\mathbb{N}_\infty$ can recognize f. We observe that $f(R^n[L^m[\alpha]]) = \min(m, n)$ for all $m, n \in \mathbb{N}$. Assume that $f \in$ RTL($\mathbb{N}_\infty$). Let N be the constant of Theorem 3 applied to f, and let $t = R^{(N+1)^2}[L^N[\alpha]]$ and $\mathcal{C} = (D, C, \alpha) \in D(t)$ be a decomposition, where $D = R^{(N+1)^2}$ and $C = L^N$. Theorem 3 yields a refinement $(D', B, s') \in D(t)$ of $\mathcal{C}$; i.e., $B = L^n$ for some $0 < n < N$. However,

$$f(D'[B^N[s']]) = (n+1)N - n \; < \; (n+1)N = f(D'[B^{N+1}[s']])$$
$$f(D'[B^{(N+1)^2}[s']]) = (N+1)^2 \qquad = (N+1)^2 = f(D'[B^{2(N+1)^2}[s']]),$$

contradicting Theorem 3. Hence $f \notin$ RTL($\mathbb{N}_\infty$). Since UA-RTL(T) $\subseteq$ RTL($\mathbb{N}_\infty$) by Lemma 1 we obtain $f \notin$ UA-RTL(T) as desired.   □

Since clearly UA-RTL(T) $=$ UA-RTL($\mathbb{A}$), we may replace the minimum in the proof of Theorem 4 with a maximum and similar calculations show that this language is not in RTL($\mathbb{N}_\infty$), either.

Theorem 5. UA-RTL($\mathbb{A}$) $\subsetneq$ FA-RTL($\mathbb{A}$).

5 Finitely Vs. Polynomially Ambiguous

The second pumping lemma will allow us to give a weighted tree language over T, which can be recognized by a PA-WTA, but cannot be recognized by any FA-WTA. The theorem itself works on point-wise minima of recognizable weighted tree languages over $\mathbb{N}_\infty$. We call $f \colon T_\Sigma \to \mathbb{N}_\infty$ a *point-wise recognizable minimum* if there exist $k \in \mathbb{N}$ and recognizable weighted tree languages $f_1, \ldots, f_k \in$ RTL($\mathbb{N}_\infty$) of type $f_1, \ldots, f_k \colon T_\Sigma \to \mathbb{N}_\infty$ such that for all $t \in T_\Sigma$ it holds that $f(t) = \min\{f_1(t), \ldots, f_k(t)\}$. To relate this notion to finitely ambiguous weighted tree languages over T, we recall the following result.

Theorem 6 ([20, Theorem 2]). *Let $\ell \in \mathbb{N}$ and $T = (Q, \Sigma, \Delta, \mathrm{wt}, F)$ be an ℓ-ambiguous WTA over the commutative semiring S. Then there exist ℓ unambiguous WTA $\mathcal{U}_1, \ldots, \mathcal{U}_\ell$ over S such that $[\![T]\!] = \sum_{i=1}^{\ell} [\![\mathcal{U}_i]\!]$.*

Let us now move on to the pumping lemma. To this end, let $t \in T_\Sigma$ be a tree and $\mathcal{D} = (D_n, C_n, \ldots, D_1, C_1, s) \in D(t)$ be a decomposition of t. Additionally, let $h \in \mathbb{N}$ and $\varphi = (\varphi_1, \ldots, \varphi_n) \in \mathbb{B}^n$ be a selector. Then we let

$$\mathcal{D}_\varphi^h = D_n[C_n^{\varphi_n \cdot h}[\cdots D_1[C_1^{\varphi_1 \cdot h}[s]] \cdots]]. \qquad (2)$$

Theorem 7 (Pumping Lemma for Point-wise Minima). *Let $f\colon T_\Sigma \to \mathbb{N}_\infty$ be a point-wise recognizable minimum. Then there exists $N \in \mathbb{N}$ such that for each tree $t \in T_\Sigma$ and decomposition $C = (D_n, C_n, \ldots, D_1, C_1, s) \in D(t)$ of t with $n \geq N$ and $\mathrm{depth}(C_j) \geq N$ for all $j \in [n]$ the following holds. There is a refinement $\mathcal{D} = (D'_n, B_n, \ldots, D'_1, B_1, s') \in D(t)$ of C with $B_1, \ldots, B_n \neq \square$ such that for every subset $\Phi \subseteq \mathbb{B}^n$ with $|\Phi| \geq N$*

- *there exists $\varphi \in \Phi$ such that $f(\mathcal{D}^h_\varphi) < f(\mathcal{D}^{h+1}_\varphi)$ for all h sufficiently large or*
- *there are $\varphi, \psi \in \Phi$ with $\varphi \neq \psi$ such that $f(\mathcal{D}^h_{\varphi \vee \psi}) = f(\mathcal{D}^{h+1}_{\varphi \vee \psi})$ for all h sufficiently large.*

Finally, we give a weighted tree language $f \in \text{PA-RTL}(\mathbb{T}) \setminus \text{FA-RTL}(\mathbb{T})$ inspired by [19, Examples 3 and 15]. To this end, we show that $f \in \text{PA-RTL}(\mathbb{T})$ and that f is not a point-wise recognizable minimum over $\mathbb{T}$ using Theorem 7. By Theorem 6 we can then conclude that $f \notin \text{FA-RTL}(\mathbb{T})$.

Theorem 8. $\text{FA-RTL}(\mathbb{T}) \subsetneq \text{PA-RTL}(\mathbb{T})$.

Proof. We consider the ranked alphabet $\Sigma = \{\sigma^{(2)}, \alpha^{(0)}\}$ and the two elementary contexts $R = \sigma(\square, \alpha)$ and $L = \sigma(\alpha, \square)$. Additionally, we consider the WTA $\mathcal{T} = (Q, \Sigma, \Delta, \mathrm{wt}, F)$ over $\mathbb{T}$ with $Q = \{q_\ell, q_r, q_\alpha\}$, $F(q_\ell) = F(q_\alpha) = \infty$ and $F(q_r) = 0$, and the following transitions and weights

$$\{\alpha \xrightarrow{0} q_\alpha \quad \sigma(q_\alpha, q_\ell) \xrightarrow{1} q_\ell \quad \sigma(q_\ell, q_\alpha) \xrightarrow{0} q_\ell \quad \sigma(q_\alpha, q_\alpha) \xrightarrow{0} q_\ell \quad \text{(counting } L)$$

$$\sigma(q_r, q_\alpha) \xrightarrow{1} q_r \quad \sigma(q_\alpha, q_r) \xrightarrow{0} q_r \quad \sigma(q_\alpha, q_\alpha) \xrightarrow{0} q_r \quad \text{(counting } R)$$

$$\sigma(q_\ell, q_\alpha) \xrightarrow{0} q_r \quad \sigma(q_\alpha, q_\ell) \xrightarrow{1} q_r\}. \quad \text{(switch)}$$

In each run, reading the input tree bottom-up the WTA $\mathcal{T}$ first counts occurrences of L in state q_ℓ, then nondeterministically switches to q_r, and finally counts occurrences of R in state q_r. Thus, $\mathcal{T}$ has at most height(t) runs for each $t \in T_\Sigma$, which proves that $f = [\![\mathcal{T}]\!] \in \text{PA-RTL}(\mathbb{T})$. Additionally, we have

$$f(t) = \min_{i \in [n]} \left\{ |\{j \in [i] \mid C_j = R\}| + |\{j \in [n] \setminus [i] \mid C_j = L\}| \right\}$$

for a tree of the form $t = C_1[\cdots C_n[\sigma(\alpha, \alpha)] \cdots]$ with $C_1, \ldots, C_n \in \{L, R\}$ and $n \in \mathbb{N}$, and $f(t) = \infty$ otherwise.

It remains to show that $f \notin \text{FA-RTL}(\mathbb{T})$, which we prove by showing that f cannot be a point-wise recognizable minimum. For the sake of a contradiction, suppose that it is. Let N be the constant of Theorem 7 and consider the decomposition $C = (\square, L^N, \square, R^N, \ldots, \square, L^N, \square, R^N, \sigma(\alpha, \alpha)) \in D(t)$ of $t = (L^N[R^N])^N[\sigma(\alpha, \alpha)]$. Moreover, for every $j \in [N]$, let $\varphi^j \in \mathbb{B}^{2N}$ be such that $\varphi^j(2j-1) = \varphi^j(2j) = 1$ and 0 otherwise. Finally, let $\Phi = \{\varphi^1, \ldots, \varphi^N\}$. We first claim that $f(\mathcal{D}^h_\varphi) = N(N-1)$ for each refinement $\mathcal{D} \in D(t)$ of C, $\varphi \in \Phi$, and $h > N$. To see this, let $j \in [N]$ be such that $\varphi = \varphi^j$. Then $\mathcal{D}^h_\varphi$ only pumps one part of the j-th block of $L^N[R^N]$ to $L^{\ell_1}[R^{\ell_2}]$ for some $\ell_1, \ell_2 > N$. Thus for the minimum, the WTA $\mathcal{T}$ should switch from q_ℓ to q_r after processing the segment R^{ℓ_2}, which yields $f(\mathcal{D}_\varphi^h) = N(N-1)$. For the second item of Theorem 7, let $\varphi, \psi \in \Phi$ with $\varphi \neq \psi$ and $\phi = \varphi \vee \psi$. Since φ and ψ select different blocks, no matter where the WTA $\mathcal{T}$ switches from q_ℓ to q_r we will either count the pumped occurrences of L or the pumped occurrences of R in at least one block. Thus, $f(\mathcal{D}_\phi^h) < f(\mathcal{D}_\phi^{h+1})$ for all $h > N$. Thus, f is not a point-wise recognizable minimum, which together with Theorem 6 proves $f \notin$ FA-RTL($\mathbb{T}$).   □

The height and size of the input trees in Theorem 8, for which accepting runs exist, are linearly related, so we also obtain FA-RTL($\mathbb{T}$) $\subsetneq$ PAH-RTL($\mathbb{T}$).

In fact, using [5, Theorem 6.1] we are able to present similar results for the arctic semiring $\mathbb{A}$. Let $\mathcal{C} = (D_1, C_1, \ldots, D_n, C_n, s) \in D(t)$ be a decomposition of a tree $t \in \mathrm{T}_\Sigma$ and $f \colon \mathrm{T}_\Sigma \to \mathbb{A}$ be a weighted tree language. The decomposition $\mathcal{C}$ is *linear* if for all $\varphi \in \mathbb{B}^n$ there is a constant K_φ such that $f(\mathcal{C}_\varphi^{h+1}) = K_\varphi + f(\mathcal{C}_\varphi^h)$ for all sufficiently large h. Given a linear decomposition $\mathcal{C}$, a selector $\phi \in \mathbb{B}^n$ is *elementarily linear* for $\mathcal{C}$ if $K_\phi = \sum_{j=1}^n \phi_j \cdot K_{\mathbb{1}_j}$, where $\mathbb{1}_j = (0, \ldots, 0, 1, 0, \ldots, 0)$ with the 1 occurring in the j-th component.

Theorem 9 (Pumping Lemma for FA-RTL($\mathbb{A}$)). *Let $f \in$ FA-RTL($\mathbb{A}$). There exists a constant $N \in \mathbb{N}$ such that for each tree $t \in \mathrm{T}_\Sigma$ and decomposition $\mathcal{C} = (D_n, C_n, \ldots, D_1, C_1, s) \in D(t)$ of t with $n \geq N$ and $\mathrm{depth}(C_j) \geq N$ for all $j \in [n]$, there exists a linear refinement $\mathcal{D} = (D_n', B_n, \ldots, D_1', B_1, s') \in D(t)$ of $\mathcal{C}$ with $B_1, \ldots, B_n \neq \square$ such that for every subset $\Phi \subseteq \mathbb{B}^n$ with $|\Phi| \geq N$*

- *there exists $\varphi \in \Phi$ that is not elementarily linear for $\mathcal{D}$ or*
- *there exist $\varphi, \psi \in \Phi$ with $\varphi \neq \psi$ such that $\mathbb{1}_i \vee \mathbb{1}_j$ is elementarily linear for $\mathcal{D}$ for all $i, j \in [n]$ with $\varphi_i = 1$ and $\psi_j = 1$.*

Theorem 10. FA-RTL($\mathbb{A}$) $\subsetneq$ PA-RTL($\mathbb{A}$).

Proof. We reconsider the WTA $\mathcal{T} = (Q, \Sigma, \Delta, \mathrm{wt}, F)$ of the proof of Theorem 8 over the arctic semiring $\mathbb{A}$. Clearly, $f = [\![\mathcal{T}]\!] \in$ PA-RTL($\mathbb{A}$). Additionally, we have

$$f(t) = \max_{i \in [n]}\Big\{ |\{j \in [i] \mid C_j = R\}| + |\{j \in [n] \setminus [i] \mid C_j = L\}| \Big\}$$

for a tree of the form $t = C_1[\cdots C_n[\sigma(\alpha, \alpha)]\cdots]$ with $C_1, \ldots, C_n \in \{L, R\}$ and $n \in \mathbb{N}$, and $f(t) = -\infty$ otherwise. For the proof of $f \notin$ FA-RTL($\mathbb{A}$) we use the same technique as in the proof of Theorem 8. Since now the maximum is taken, each $\varphi \in \Phi$ is elementarily linear for $\mathcal{D}$. For the second condition, let $\varphi, \psi \in \Phi$ with $\varphi \neq \psi$ and $i, j \in [n]$ such that $\varphi_i = 1$ and $\psi_j = 1$. However, $\phi = \mathbb{1}_i \vee \mathbb{1}_j$ is not elementarily linear for $\mathcal{D}$ since $K_\phi = \max(K_{\mathbb{1}_i}, K_{\mathbb{1}_j})$.   □

6   Polynomially Ambiguous Vs. Recognizable

Our last pumping lemma will allow us to present a recognizable weighted tree language over $\mathbb{T}$ that is not recognizable by any PAH-WTA. To this end, we introduce some additional notation. Let $n \in \mathbb{N}$. A set $\Phi \subseteq \mathbb{B}^n \setminus \{(0, \ldots, 0)\}$ is called a *partition* of $[n]$ if $\bigvee \Phi = (1, \ldots, 1)$ and $\varphi \wedge \psi = (0, \ldots, 0)$ for all $\varphi, \psi \in \Phi$ with $\varphi \neq \psi$. We call $\psi \in \mathbb{B}^n$ a *cover* of Φ if $\sum_{j \in [n]} (\psi \wedge \varphi)_j = 1$ for every $\varphi \in \Phi$.

Theorem 11 (Pumping Lemma for PAH-RTL($\mathbb{T}$)). *Let $f \in$ PAH-RTL($\mathbb{T}$). There exists $N \in \mathbb{N}$ and a mapping $c\colon \mathbb{N} \to \mathbb{N}$ such that for each tree $t \in T_\Sigma$ and decomposition $C = (D_n, C_n, \ldots, D_1, C_1, s) \in D(t)$ of t with $\mathrm{depth}(C_i) \geq N$ for all $j \in [n]$, there exists a refinement $\mathcal{D} = (D'_n, B_n, \ldots, D'_1, B_1, s') \in D(t)$ of C such that for every partition Φ of $[n]$ with $|\Phi| \geq c(\sum_{j \in [n]} \varphi_j)$ for all $\varphi \in \Phi$*

- *there exists $\varphi \in \Phi$ such that $f(\mathcal{D}_\varphi^h) = f(\mathcal{D}_\varphi^{h+1})$ for all h sufficiently large or*
- *there exists a cover ψ of Φ such that $f(\mathcal{D}_\psi^h) < f(\mathcal{D}_\psi^{h+1})$ for all h sufficiently large.*

Now we give a recognizable weighted tree language $f \notin$ PA-RTL($\mathbb{T}$). We will actually show $f \notin$ PAH-RTL($\mathbb{T}$), but due to the special shape of f the height and size are themselves polynomially related, so $f \notin$ PAH-RTL($\mathbb{T}$) implies $f \notin$ PA-RTL($\mathbb{T}$). In contrast to the previous examples Theorem 11 operates directly on the tropical semiring.

Theorem 12. PA-RTL($\mathbb{T}$) $\subsetneq$ RTL($\mathbb{T}$).

Proof. We consider the ranked alphabet $\Sigma = \{\sigma^{(2)}, \tau^{(1)}, \alpha^{(0)}\}$, $s = \sigma(\alpha, \alpha)$, and the contexts $R = \sigma(\square, \alpha)$ and $L = \sigma(\alpha, \square)$ as before. Additionally, we consider the weighted tree language $f\colon T_\Sigma \to \mathbb{T}$ such that for every $t \in T_\Sigma$

$$
f(t) = \begin{cases} \sum_{\ell=1}^{k} \min(i_\ell, j_\ell) & \text{if } t = \tau\big(L^{i_1}\big[R^{j_1}\big[\cdots \big[\tau(L^{i_k}[R^{j_k}[s]])\big]\cdots\big]\big]\big) \\ & \text{for } (i_1, \ldots, i_k), (j_1, \ldots, j_k) \in \mathbb{N}^k \\ \infty & \text{otherwise.} \end{cases}
$$

Let $\mathcal{T} = (Q, \Sigma, \Delta, \mathrm{wt}, F)$ be the WTA over $\mathbb{T}$ with $Q = \{q_\ell, q_r, q_\alpha\}$, $F(q) = 0$ for each $q \in Q$, and the following transitions and weights

$$\{\alpha \xrightarrow{0} q_\alpha \qquad \sigma(q_\alpha, q_\ell) \xrightarrow{1} q_\ell \quad \sigma(q_\ell, q_\alpha) \xrightarrow{0} q_\ell \quad \sigma(q_\alpha, q_\alpha) \xrightarrow{0} q_\ell \qquad \text{(counting } L)$$

$$\sigma(q_r, q_\alpha) \xrightarrow{1} q_r \quad \sigma(q_\alpha, q_r) \xrightarrow{0} q_r \quad \sigma(q_\alpha, q_\alpha) \xrightarrow{0} q_r \qquad \text{(counting } R)$$

$$\tau(q_\ell) \xrightarrow{0} q_\ell \qquad \tau(q_\ell) \xrightarrow{0} q_r \qquad \tau(q_r) \xrightarrow{0} q_\ell \qquad \tau(q_r) \xrightarrow{0} q_r\}. \qquad \text{(reset)}$$

Clearly, $\mathcal{T}$ recognizes f and thus $f \in$ RTL($\mathbb{T}$). Assume now $f \in$ PAH-RTL, as mentioned above by the special shape of f, this implies $f \in$ PA-RTL. By Theorem 11 there exist a constant N and a mapping $c\colon \mathbb{N} \to \mathbb{N}$ with various properties. Let $m > c(2)$ and consider $t = (\tau[L^N[R^N]])^m[s]$ with decomposition $C = (\tau(\square), L^N, \square, R^N, \ldots, \tau(\square), L^N, \square, R^N, s)$. Additionally, for each $j \in [m]$ let $\varphi^j \in \mathbb{B}^{2N}$ be such that $\varphi^j(2j - 1) = \varphi^j(2j) = 1$ and 0 otherwise. Finally, let $\Phi = \{\varphi^1, \ldots, \varphi^m\}$. Clearly, $f(t) = Nm$. However, for every refinement $\mathcal{D}$ of C and $h > N$ we have $f(\mathcal{D}_\varphi^h) < f(\mathcal{D}_\varphi^{h+1})$ for every $\varphi \in \Phi$ as well as $f(\mathcal{D}_\psi^h) = f(\mathcal{D}_\psi^{h+1})$ for every cover ψ of Φ. $\qquad\square$

As before, we collect the corresponding results for the arctic semiring $\mathbb{A}$.

Theorem 13 (Pumping Lemma for PAH-RTL($\mathbb{A}$)). *Let $f \in$ PAH-RTL($\mathbb{A}$). There exists $N \in \mathbb{N}$ and a mapping $c\colon \mathbb{N} \to \mathbb{N}$ such that for each tree $t \in \mathrm{T}_\Sigma$ and decomposition $\mathcal{C} = (D_n, C_n, \ldots, D_1, C_1, s) \in D(t)$ of t with $\mathrm{depth}(C_i) \geq N$ for all $j \in [n]$, there exists a linear refinement $\mathcal{D} = (D'_n, B_n, \ldots, D'_1, B_1, s') \in D(t)$ of $\mathcal{C}$ such that for every partition Φ of $[n]$ with $|\Phi| \geq c(\sum_{j \in [n]} \varphi_j)$ for all $\varphi \in \Phi$*

 – *there exists $\varphi \in \Phi$ that is elementarily linear for $\mathcal{D}$ or*
 – *there exists a cover ψ of Φ that is not elementarily linear for $\mathcal{D}$.*

Theorem 14. PA-RTL($\mathbb{A}$) $\subsetneq$ RTL($\mathbb{A}$).

Proof. Reconsider the WTA $\mathcal{T}$ as well as the other infrastructure of the proof of Theorem 12 over the arctic semiring $\mathbb{A}$ and its recognized mapping $g = [\![\mathcal{T}]\!]$, which is essentially the mapping f with the minimum replaced by the maximum. It is straightforward to see that no $\varphi \in \Phi$ is elementarily linear for $\mathcal{D}$, but each cover ψ of Φ is elementarily linear for $\mathcal{D}$ since different selectors apply to different parts of t, separated by an occurrence of τ. $\square$

7   Conclusion

We investigated the expressive power of weighted tree automata with various amounts of ambiguity over the tropical semiring $\mathbb{T}$ as well as the arctic semiring $\mathbb{A}$. More precisely, we compared the expressive power of WTAthat are unambiguous (UA-WTA), finitely ambiguous (FA-WTA), and polynomially ambiguous (PA-WTA) and proved the strictness of the corresponding hierarchy UA-RTL(S) $\subsetneq$ FA-RTL(S) $\subsetneq$ PA-RTL(S) $\subsetneq$ RTL(S) for $S \in \{\mathbb{T}, \mathbb{A}\}$ using arguments corresponding to those of [5,19]. Moreover, we obtain a similar hierarchy UA-RTL(S) $\subsetneq$ FA-RTL(S) $\subsetneq$ PAH-RTL(S) $\subsetneq$ EAH-RTL(S) for the same ambiguity notions in the height of the input tree. Obviously it holds that PAH-RTL(S) $\subseteq$ PA-RTL(S) as well as EAH-RTL(S) $\subseteq$ RTL(S). It remains open, whether those inclusions are strict.

References

1. Berstel, J., Reutenauer, C.: Recognizable formal power series on trees. Theoret. Comput. Sci. **18**(2), 115–148 (1982)
2. Berstel, J., Reutenauer, C.: Rational Series and Their Languages, EATCS Monographs on Theoretical Computer Science, vol. 12. Springer, Heidelberg (1988)
3. Borchardt, B.: The theory of recognizable tree series. Ph.D. thesis, Technische Universität Dresden (2005)
4. Bozapalidis, S., Louscou-Bozapalidou, O.: The rank of a formal tree power series. Theoret. Comput. Sci. **27**(1–2), 211–215 (1983)
5. Chattopadhyay, A., Mazowiecki, F., Muscholl, A., Riveros, C.: Pumping lemmas for weighted automata. arXiv:2001.06272 arXiv (2020)
6. Comon, H., et al.: Tree automata techniques and applications (2007)
7. Doner, J.E.: Tree acceptors and some of their applications. J. Comput. Syst. Sci. **4**(5), 406–451 (1970)

8. Droste, M., Kuich, W., Vogler, H.: Handbook of Weighted Automata. EATCS Monographs on Theoretical Computer Science. Springer, Heidelberg (2009). https://doi.org/10.1007/978-3-642-01492-5

9. Ésik, Z., Maletti, A.: The category of simulations for weighted tree automata. Int. J. Found. Comput. Sci. **22**(8), 1845–1859 (2011)

10. Fülöp, Z., Vogler, H.: Weighted tree automata and tree transducers. In: Droste, M., Kuich, W., Vogler, H. (eds.) Handbook of Weighted Automata [8], pp. 313–403. Springer, Heidelberg (2009). https://doi.org/10.1007/978-3-642-01492-5_9

11. Gécseg, F., Steinby, M.: Tree Automata. Akadémiai Kiadó, Budapest (1984)

12. Gécseg, F., Steinby, M.: Tree languages. In: Rozenberg, G., Salomaa, A. (eds.) Handbook of Formal Languages, pp. 1–68. Springer, Heidelberg (1997). https://doi.org/10.1007/978-3-642-59126-6_1

13. Golan, J.S.: Semirings and Their Applications. Kluwer Academic, Dordrecht (1999)

14. Hall, T.E., Sapir, M.V.: Idempotents, regular elements and sequences from finite semigroups. Discrete Math. **161**(1–3), 151–160 (1996)

15. Hebisch, U., Weinert, H.J.: Semirings-Algebraic Theory and Applications in Computer Science. World Scientific, Singapore (1998)

16. Högberg, J., Maletti, A., Vogler, H.: Bisimulation minimisation of weighted automata on unranked trees. Fundam. Inform. **92**(1–2), 103–130 (2009)

17. Klimann, I., Lombardy, S., Mairesse, J., Prieur, C.: Deciding unambiguity and sequentiality from a finitely ambiguous max-plus automaton. Theoret. Comput. Sci. **327**(3), 349–373 (2004)

18. Krob, D.: The equality problem for rational series with multiplicities in the tropical semiring is undecidable. Internat. J. Algebra Comput. **4**(3), 405–425 (1994)

19. Mazowiecki, F., Riveros, C.: Pumping lemmas for weighted automata. In: Proceedings of 35th STACS. LIPIcs, vol. 96. Schloss Dagstuhl–Leibniz-Zentrum für Informatik (2018)

20. Paul, E.: On finite and polynomial ambiguity of weighted tree automata. In: Brlek, S., Reutenauer, C. (eds.) DLT 2016. LNCS, vol. 9840, pp. 368–379. Springer, Heidelberg (2016). https://doi.org/10.1007/978-3-662-53132-7_30

21. Paul, E.: The equivalence, unambiguity and sequentiality problems of finitely ambiguous max-plus tree automata are decidable. In: Proceedings of 42nd MFCS. LIPIcs, vol. 83. Schloss Dagstuhl–Leibniz-Zentrum für Informatik (2017)

22. Paul, E.: Finite sequentiality of unambiguous max-plus tree automata. In: Proceedings of 36th STACS. LIPIcs, vol. 126. Schloss Dagstuhl–Leibniz-Zentrum für Informatik (2019)

23. Rabusseau, G., Balle, B., Cohen, S.B.: Low-rank approximation of weighted tree automata. In: Proceedings of 19th AISTATS. JMLR, vol. 51, pp. 839–847. JMLR.org (2016)

24. Sakarovitch, J.: Rational and recognisable power series. In: Droste, M., Kuich, W., Vogler, H. (eds.) Handbook of Weighted Automata [8], Chap. 4, pp. 105–174. Springer, Heidelberg (2009). https://doi.org/10.1007/978-3-642-01492-5_4

25. Salomaa, A., Soittola, M.: Automata-Theoretic Aspects of Formal Power Series. Springer, Heidelberg (2012)

26. Simon, I.: Limited subsets of a free monoid. In: Proceedings of 19th FOCS, pp. 143–150. IEEE (1978)

27. Thatcher, J.W.: Characterizing derivation trees of context-free grammars through a generalization of finite automata theory. J. Comput. Syst. Sci. **1**(4), 317–322 (1967)

28. Yu, S.: Regular languages. In: Rozenberg, G., Salomaa, A. (eds.) Handbook of Formal Languages, pp. 41–110. Springer, Heidelberg (1997). https://doi.org/10.1007/978-3-642-59136-5_2

Boolean Kernels of Context-Free Languages

Martin Kutrib[1(✉)] and Luca Prigioniero[2]

[1] Institut für Informatik, Universität Giessen,
Arndtstr. 2, 35392 Giessen, Germany
`kutrib@informatik.uni-giessen.de`
[2] Dipartimento di Informatica, Università degli Studi di Milano,
Via Celoria 18, 20133 Milan, Italy
`prigioniero@di.unimi.it`

Abstract. While the closure of a language family $\mathscr{L}$ under certain language operations is the least family of languages which contains all members of $\mathscr{L}$ and is closed under all of the operations, a kernel of $\mathscr{L}$ is a maximal family of languages which is a sub-family of $\mathscr{L}$ and is closed under all of the operations. Here we investigate properties of the Boolean kernels of the family of context-free languages. Additionally, languages that are mandatory for each Boolean kernel and languages that are optional for Boolean kernels are studied. That is, we consider the intersection of all Boolean kernels as well as their union. The expressive capacities of these families are addressed leading to a hierarchical structure. Further closure properties are considered. Furthermore, we study descriptional complexity aspects of these families, where languages are represented by context-free grammars with proofs attached. It turns out that the size trade-offs between all families in question and deterministic context-free languages are non-recursive. That is, one can choose an arbitrarily large recursive function f, but the gain in economy of description eventually exceeds f when changing from the latter system to the former.

1 Introduction

Classical and well-developed concepts to represent (formal) languages are, for example, grammars, language equations, or accepting automata. Similarly, families of languages can be represented in several ways. For example, a language family can be defined to be the set of all languages represented by a certain type of grammar, automaton model, language equation, or by applying appropriate operations on other language families. From a practical point of view, there is often a considerable interest in language families that are robust with respect to language operations, that is, the families are preferably closed under the operations, and/or in language families that admit efficient recognizers. A good example are context-free languages, that are one of the most important and most developed area of formal language theory. However, the family is not closed under the two Boolean operations complementation and intersection. Moreover,

© Springer Nature Switzerland AG 2021
S. Maneth (Ed.): CIAA 2021, LNCS 12803, pp. 152–164, 2021.
https://doi.org/10.1007/978-3-030-79121-6_13

the known upper bound on the time complexity for context-free language recognition still exceeds $O(n^2)$. As an approach to characterize language families having strong closure properties and efficient recognizers but decrease the expressive capacity only slightly, closures of sub-classes of the context-free languages have been investigated. The Boolean closure of the linear context-free languages offers a significant increase in expressive capacity compared with the linear context-free languages itself. In addition, it preserves the attractively efficient recognition algorithm [10] taking $O(n^2)$ time and $O(n)$ space. The systematic investigation of the Boolean closures of arbitrary and deterministic context-free languages started in [12–14]. The closure of deterministic languages under the regular operations is studied in [1], while the regular closure of the linear context-free languages is considered in [9].

Here we are interested in language families with strong closure properties obtained as sub-families of a given family instead of closing and, thus, extending the family. To this end, we study Boolean kernels of the family of context-free languages. Basically, such a kernel is a maximal sub-family of the context-free languages that is closed under the Boolean operations.

The paper is organized as follows. After presenting the basic definitions and notions in the next section, Sect. 3 deals with the expressive capacities of Boolean kernels of context-free languages as well as with languages that are mandatory for each Boolean kernel and languages that are optional for Boolean kernels. For the latter, the intersection and union of all Boolean kernels is considered. The hierarchical structure of these families is depicted in Fig. 1. Section 4 is devoted to additional closure properties. In particular, the operations reversal, concatenation, and inverse homomorphism are studied. The results are summarized in Table 1. Descriptional complexity aspects are dealt with in Sect. 5. The size of a language is given by the size of its representation. Since, in most cases, no automata or grammar characterizations are known for kernels, here we use representations by context-free grammars which come with a corresponding proof attached. The proofs certify that the grammar generates a language belonging to the desired sub-family. The length of the proof is then added to the size of the grammar. It turns out that the size trade-offs between all families in question and deterministic context-free languages are non-recursive. That is, one can choose an arbitrarily large recursive function f, but the gain in economy of description eventually exceeds f when changing from the latter system to the former. Finally, we discuss some interesting untouched problems and questions for further research in Sect. 6.

2   Preliminaries

We write Σ^* for the set of all words over a finite alphabet Σ. The *empty word* is denoted by λ, and we set $\Sigma^+ = \Sigma^* \setminus \{\lambda\}$. The *reversal* of a word w is denoted by w^R, and for the *length* of w we write $|w|$. For the number of *occurrences* of a symbol a in w we use the notation $|w|_a$. Set *inclusion* is denoted by $\subseteq$ and *strict set inclusion* by $\subset$.

A subset of Σ^* is called a *(formal) language* over Σ. A *language operation* is an operation whose finite number of parameters are languages, and whose result is a language. For example, the *complement* of a language is defined with respect to the underlying alphabet Σ. That is, the complement of $L \subseteq \Sigma^*$ is $\overline{L} = \{ w \in \Sigma^* \mid w \notin L \}$. For all $k \geq 1$, a k-ary language operation $\circ$ is said to be *idempotent* if $\circ(L, L, \ldots, L) = L$, for all L in the domain of $\circ$. For easier writing, here we call even a unary language operation $\circ$ with the property $\circ(L) = L$ idempotent (so we do *not* require $\circ(\circ(L)) = \circ(L)$).

Let Ω be an infinite enumerable set of letters. The set $\mathscr{L}$ is a *family of languages* over Ω if for each $L \in \mathscr{L}$ there is a finite subset $\Sigma \subset \Omega$ such that $L \subseteq \Sigma^*$. In the sequel we tacitly omit Ω when it is understood.

Let $\mathscr{L}$ be a family of languages and $op_1, op_2, \ldots, op_k$, $k \geq 1$, be a finite number of operations defined on $\mathscr{L}$.

1. By $\Gamma_{op_1, op_2, \ldots, op_k}(\mathscr{L})$ we denote the $(op_1, op_2, \ldots, op_k)$ *closure* of $\mathscr{L}$. That is, the *least family of languages which contains all members of* $\mathscr{L}$ *and is closed under* $op_1, op_2, \ldots, op_k$. In other words, there exists no language family $\mathscr{L}'$ that is closed under $op_1, op_2, \ldots, op_k$ such that $\mathscr{L} \subseteq \mathscr{L}' \subset \Gamma_{op_1, op_2, \ldots, op_k}(\mathscr{L})$.
2. By $\gamma_{op_1, op_2, \ldots, op_k}(\mathscr{L})$ we denote the set of $(op_1, op_2, \ldots, op_k)$ *kernels* of $\mathscr{L}$. That is, the set of *maximal families of languages which are sub-families of* $\mathscr{L}$ *and are closed under* $op_1, op_2, \ldots, op_k$. In other words, for all kernels $\kappa \in \gamma_{op_1, op_2, \ldots, op_k}(\mathscr{L})$ there exists no language family $\mathscr{L}'$ that is closed under $op_1, op_2, \ldots, op_k$ such that $\kappa \subset \mathscr{L}' \subseteq \mathscr{L}$.

In particular, we consider the operations complementation ($^-$), union ($\cup$), and intersection ($\cap$), which are called *Boolean operations*. Accordingly, we write Γ_{BOOL} for $\Gamma_{-,\cup,\cap}$ and γ_{BOOL} for $\gamma_{-,\cup,\cap}$.

Since special attention is paid to sub-classes of context-free languages, we refer to the literature, for example to [3], for detailed definitions of context-free grammars and of the characterizing automata models. In particular, an automaton model for the recognition of context-free languages is the nondeterministic pushdown automaton. Its deterministic variant characterizes the deterministic context-free languages (DCFL).

It is known from [8] that the sets $\gamma_{\mathrm{BOOL}}(\mathrm{CFL})$ as well as $\gamma_{\mathrm{BOOL}}(\mathrm{DCFL})$ include infinitely many kernels, while the complementation kernel of the context-free languages is unique. Moreover, not all context-free languages belong to some Boolean kernel, while any deterministic context-free language belongs to some kernel $\kappa \in \gamma_{\mathrm{BOOL}}(\mathrm{DCFL})$.

3   Expressive Capability

In connection with the question of whether any language of a family belongs to some kernel based on given operations, or whether there are languages that do not belong to any of such kernels, the union of all kernels has been considered. Similarly, the question which languages belong to all kernels based on given operations raised the definition of the intersection of all of these kernels.

The union of all Boolean kernels of the context-free languages is denoted by $\mathcal{U}$, that is, $\mathcal{U} = \{\, L \mid L \in \kappa \text{ for some } \kappa \in \gamma_{\text{BOOL}}(\text{CFL}) \,\}$.

Similarly, the intersection of all Boolean kernels of the context-free languages is denoted by $\mathcal{I}$, that is, $\mathcal{I} = \{\, L \mid L \in \kappa \text{ for all } \kappa \in \gamma_{\text{BOOL}}(\text{CFL}) \,\}$.

It turns out that the union of all Boolean kernels of the context-free languages characterizes an interesting language family. Theorem 1 shows that it coincides with the unique complementation kernel in $\gamma_{-}(\text{CFL})$. That is interesting in itself but beyond that, the unique complementation kernel is also known as the family of strongly context-free languages [7]. A machine characterization of that family in terms of self-verifying pushdown automata is obtained in [2].

Theorem 1. *The family $\mathcal{U}$ coincides with the unique complementation kernel in $\gamma_{-}(\text{CFL})$.*

Proof. Let L be a language in $\mathcal{U} \subseteq \text{CFL}$. Then there is a $\kappa \in \gamma_{\text{BOOL}}(\text{CFL})$ with $L \in \kappa$. Since κ is closed under complementation, the complement $\overline{L}$ of L belongs to κ as well. We conclude that $\overline{L}$ belongs to $\mathcal{U}$ and, thus, to CFL. In particular, since L and $\overline{L}$ are context free, they belong to the unique kernel in $\gamma_{-}(\text{CFL})$.

For the converse, let L be some language over the alphabet Σ such that L and, thus, $\overline{L}$ belong to the unique kernel in $\gamma_{-}(\text{CFL})$. We consider the set $\nu = \{L, \overline{L}, \Sigma^*, \emptyset\}$ which is clearly closed under complementation, union, and intersection. Since L and $\overline{L}$ are context free, either ν is itself a Boolean kernel of CFL, or there exists a kernel in $\gamma_{\text{BOOL}}(\text{CFL})$ having ν, and thus $\{L\}$, as subset. So, L belongs to $\mathcal{U}$. $\qquad\square$

Since the family of context-free languages is not closed under complementation but by Theorem 1 the family $\mathcal{U}$ is, the inclusion $\mathcal{U} \subset \text{CFL}$ is strict. Moreover, since there are infinitely many different Boolean kernels in $\gamma_{\text{BOOL}}(\text{CFL})$, the maximality of kernels implies that any $\kappa \in \gamma_{\text{BOOL}}(\text{CFL})$ is strictly included in $\mathcal{U}$. For example, consider the two context-free languages $L_1 = \{\, a^n b^n a^m \mid m, n \geq 1 \,\}$ and $L_2 = \{\, a^m b^n a^n \mid m, n \geq 1 \,\}$. Their complements are context free as well and, thus, both belong to the unique kernel in $\gamma_{-}(\text{CFL})$ which coincides with $\mathcal{U}$. Therefore, by Theorem 1 both belong to some Boolean kernel from $\gamma_{\text{BOOL}}(\text{CFL})$. However, languages L_1 and L_2 cannot belong to the same Boolean kernel from $\gamma_{\text{BOOL}}(\text{CFL})$, since their intersection is the non-context-free language $\{\, a^n b^n a^n \mid n \geq 1 \,\}$.

In order to continue with the exploration of the hierarchical structure of Boolean kernels, we turn to consider the family $\mathcal{I}$ which is the intersection of all Boolean kernels of the context-free languages.

Proposition 2. *The family $\mathcal{I}$ is strictly included in any Boolean kernel $\kappa \in \gamma_{\text{BOOL}}(\text{CFL})$.*

It is shown in [8] that all Boolean kernels of the context-free languages include the regular languages and some non-regular languages. So far, we have the hierarchy $\text{REG} \subset \mathcal{I} \subset \kappa \subset \mathcal{U} \subset \text{CFL}$, for all kernels $\kappa \in \gamma_{\text{BOOL}}(\text{CFL})$, (see Fig. 1). Finally, we turn to compare the family of deterministic context-free languages with the hierarchical structure of Boolean kernels.

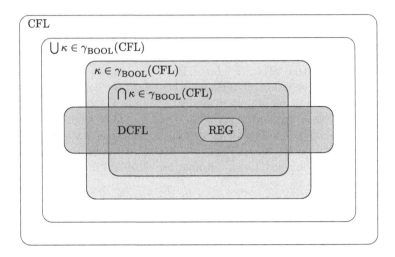

Fig. 1. Hierarchical structure of language classes. The class $\bigcup \kappa \in \gamma_{\mathrm{BOOL}}(\mathrm{CFL})$ denotes the union of all Boolean kernels of CFL. It coincides with the unique complementation kernel of CFL. By $\kappa \in \gamma_{\mathrm{BOOL}}(\mathrm{CFL})$ we denote an arbitrary Boolean kernel of CFL, and by $\bigcap \kappa \in \gamma_{\mathrm{BOOL}}(\mathrm{CFL})$ the intersection of all Boolean kernels of CFL.

First we deduce that the family DCFL is strictly included in the family $\mathscr{U}$.

Corollary 3. *The family* DCFL *is strictly included in the family* $\mathscr{U}$.

Proof. By Theorem 1, any context-free language whose complement is also context free belongs to $\mathscr{U}$. Since the family DCFL is closed under complementation and a subset of CFL, we obtain the inclusion DCFL $\subseteq \mathscr{U}$. Its strictness is witnessed, for example, by the context-free language $\{\, w \in \{a, b\}^* \mid w = w^R \,\}$ not belonging to DCFL whose complement is also context free (cf. [2]). So, it belongs to $\mathscr{U}$ but is not deterministic context free. □

Concerning an arbitrary Boolean kernel $\kappa \in \gamma_{\mathrm{BOOL}}(\mathrm{CFL})$ and the family $\mathscr{I}$ we obtain incomparability with DCFL.

Theorem 4. *For any* $\kappa \in \gamma_{\mathrm{BOOL}}(\mathrm{CFL})$, *the family* DCFL *is incomparable with* κ *and with the family* $\mathscr{I}$.

Proof. Both languages $\{\, a^n b^n a^m \mid m, n \geq 1 \,\}$ and $\{\, a^m b^n a^n \mid m, n \geq 1 \,\}$ are deterministic context free. Assume that they do belong to κ. Since κ is closed under intersection, the non-context-free language $\{\, a^n b^n a^n \mid n \geq 1 \,\}$ must belong to κ as well, a contradiction. So, there is a language in DCFL $\setminus \kappa$ and, trivially, in DCFL $\setminus \mathscr{I}$.

Conversely, it is known that the languages $L_1 = \{\, a^n b^n \mid n \geq 1 \,\}$ and $L_2 = \{\, a^n b^{2n} \mid n \geq 1 \,\}$ are included in any Boolean kernel of the context-free languages [8]. So, they belong to the family $\mathscr{I}$ and, trivially, to κ. We consider the union $L_1 \cup L_2$. Since L_1 and L_2 belong to any Boolean kernel of the context-free languages which, in turn are closed under union, also $L_1 \cup L_2$ must belong to any Boolean kernel of the context-free languages. In other words, $L_1 \cup L_2 = \{a^n b^m \mid m = n \text{ or } m = 2n, m, n \geq 1\}$ belongs to $\mathscr{I}$ and, trivially, to κ. But $L_1 \cup L_2$ is not deterministic context free. So, there is a language in $\kappa \setminus \mathrm{DCFL}$ and, trivially, in $\mathscr{I} \setminus \mathrm{DCFL}$. $\square$

So far we have derived the comparisons of DCFL with the other families in question. However, as shown in Fig. 1, its position in the hierarchical structure needs a finer adjustment. The first question is whether the union of some kernel κ and DCFL already characterizes the family $\mathscr{U}$. Proposition 5 gives a negative answer.

Proposition 5. *For any* $\kappa \in \gamma_{\mathrm{BOOL}}(\mathrm{CFL})$*, there is a language in* $\mathscr{U} \setminus (\kappa \cup \mathrm{DCFL})$*.*

To continue with the finer adjustment let us next ask whether the union of DCFL and $\mathscr{I}$ already captures the kernels κ. Again, the answer is negative.

Proposition 6. *There exists a* $\kappa \in \gamma_{\mathrm{BOOL}}(\mathrm{CFL})$ *such that there is a language in* $\kappa \setminus (\mathscr{I} \cup \mathrm{DCFL})$*.*

Proof. A language we are looking for has been considered in the proof of Proposition 5. There, it is shown that the complement of the context-free language $L_1 = \{a^n b^m a^m \mid m, n \geq 1\} \cup \{a^n b^{2n} a^m \mid m, n \geq 1\}$ is context free as well, and, thus, that L_1 belongs to $\mathscr{U}$. This implies that L_1 belongs to some kernel $\kappa \in \gamma_{\mathrm{BOOL}}(\mathrm{CFL})$.

Similarly, it is shown that $L_2 = \{a^m b^n a^n \mid m, n \geq 1\} \cup \{a^m b^n a^{2n} \mid m, n \geq 1\}$ belongs to some kernel from $\gamma_{\mathrm{BOOL}}(\mathrm{CFL})$, but L_1 and L_2 cannot belong to the same kernel.

So, we conclude that at least one of L_1 and L_2 does not belong to $\mathscr{I}$. Both languages are not deterministic context free. So, the assertion follows. $\square$

The last two areas to be considered in Fig. 1 are the intersection of DCFL and κ without $\mathscr{I}$, and the intersection of DCFL and $\mathscr{I}$ without REG. For the latter, we can utilize once more the non-regular but deterministic context-free language $\{a^n b^n \mid n \geq 1\}$ that is included in any Boolean kernel of the context-free languages [8].

Corollary 7. *There is a language in* $(\mathrm{DCFL} \cap \mathscr{I}) \setminus \mathrm{REG}$*.*

For the former, we have the following result.

Proposition 8. *There exists a* $\kappa \in \gamma_{\mathrm{BOOL}}(\mathrm{CFL})$ *such that there is a language in* $(\mathrm{DCFL} \cap \kappa) \setminus \mathscr{I}$*.*

4   (Non-)Closure Properties

The closure properties of the kernels from $\gamma_{\mathrm{BOOL}}(\mathrm{CFL})$ under the Boolean operations are trivial by definition. By Theorem 1, the properties of $\mathscr{U}$ can be derived from the results on strongly context-free languages obtained in [7]. In particular, it is closed under complementation but is not closed under union and intersection (see Table 1). For the family $\mathscr{I}$ and Boolean operations we have the following situation.

Proposition 9. *The family $\mathscr{I}$ is closed under complementation, union, and intersection.*

Since all $\kappa \in \gamma_{\mathrm{BOOL}}(\mathrm{CFL})$ include the regular languages and are closed under intersection, they are closed under intersection with regular sets. The same argument applies to the family $\mathscr{I}$.

We call a language that witnesses the non-inclusion of another language in some family by violating closure properties *toxic*. More precisely, let $\mathscr{L}$ be some family of languages not closed under an operation $\circ$, and L be a language belonging to $\mathscr{L}$. Then a language $L' \in \mathscr{L}$ is said to be *$\mathscr{L}$-$\circ$-toxic for L* if and only if $L \circ L' \notin \mathscr{L}$.

Lemma 10. *Let $\mathscr{L}$ be a family of languages that includes $\emptyset$ and Σ^*, for all alphabets Σ, and $\kappa \in \gamma_{\mathrm{BOOL}}(\mathscr{L})$. A language $L \in \mathscr{L}$ does not belong to κ if and only if either $\overline{L} \notin \mathscr{L}$ or there is a language $L' \in \kappa$ that is $\mathscr{L}$-$\cap$-toxic or $\mathscr{L}$-$\cup$-toxic for L.*

Proof. Let $L \in \mathscr{L}$ be a language not belonging to κ. Assume that $\overline{L} \in \mathscr{L}$ and all languages $L' \in \kappa$ are neither $\mathscr{L}$-$\cap$-toxic nor $\mathscr{L}$-$\cup$-toxic for L. Then we consider $\Gamma_{\mathrm{BOOL}}(\kappa \cup \{L, \overline{L}\})$. In particular, we have that L as well as $\overline{L}$ belong to $\mathscr{L}$, $L \cap L'$ and $L \cup L'$ do belong to $\mathscr{L}$ for *all* $L' \in \kappa$. Moreover, $L \cap \overline{L} = \emptyset \in \kappa$ and $L \cup \overline{L} = \Sigma^* \in \kappa$. Therefore, $\Gamma_{\mathrm{BOOL}}(\kappa \cup \{L, \overline{L}\})$ is included in $\mathscr{L}$. This contradicts the maximality of κ.

If $L \in \kappa$ then $\overline{L} \in \kappa \subseteq \mathscr{L}$, since κ is closed under complementation. Moreover, since κ is closed under union and intersection, for all languages $L' \in \kappa$, we have $L \cup L' \in \kappa \subseteq \mathscr{L}$ and $L \cap L' \in \kappa \subseteq \mathscr{L}$. We conclude that L' is neither $\mathscr{L}$-$\cup$-toxic nor $\mathscr{L}$-$\cap$-toxic for L. $\qquad\square$

Reversal. The family $\mathscr{U}$ is closed under reversal. Before we turn to the closure of the family $\mathscr{I}$, we show that the closure may get lost for fixed kernels $\kappa \in \gamma_{\mathrm{BOOL}}(\mathrm{CFL})$.

Proposition 11. *There is a kernel $\kappa \in \gamma_{\mathrm{BOOL}}(\mathrm{CFL})$ that is not closed under reversal.*

Theorem 12. *The family $\mathscr{I}$ is closed under reversal.*

Proof. Assume in contrast to the assertion that there is an $L \in \mathscr{I}$ such that $L^R \notin \mathscr{I}$. Then there is a $\kappa \in \gamma_{\mathrm{BOOL}}(\mathrm{CFL})$ with $L^R \notin \kappa$.

Consider the complement $\overline{L^R}$. Since complementation commutes with reversal we have $\overline{L^R} = \overline{L}^R$. Since $L \in \kappa$ we derive $\overline{L} \in \kappa$ and, since CFL is closed under reversal also $\overline{L}^R = \overline{L^R} \in \mathrm{CFL}$. Knowing this we apply Lemma 10 and conclude that there is a language $L' \in \kappa$ that is CFL-$\cap$-toxic or CFL-$\cup$-toxic for L^R. Since CFL is closed under union, L' must be CFL-$\cap$-toxic for L^R.

So, $L^R \cap L'$ does not belong to CFL. Since the family CFL is closed under reversal, we conclude $(L^R \cap L')^R \notin \mathrm{CFL}$ and, thus, $(L^R)^R \cap (L')^R = L \cap (L')^R \notin \mathrm{CFL}$. Since L belongs to *all* Boolean kernels of CFL, we derive that all Boolean kernels do not include $(L')^R$. Now Theorem 1 implies that either $(L')^R$ or $\overline{(L')^R}$ is not context free. Again, since complementation commutes with reversal we obtain that either $(L')^R$ or $\overline{L'}^R$ is not context free. However, $L' \in \kappa$ implies $\overline{L'} \in \kappa$. By the closure of CFL under reversal we obtain the contradiction $(L')^R \in \mathrm{CFL}$ and $\overline{L'}^R \in \mathrm{CFL}$. $\square$

Concatenation and Inverse Homomorphism. In order to prove the non-closure of the family $\mathscr{I}$ and *all* kernels $\kappa \in \gamma_{\mathrm{BOOL}}(\mathrm{CFL})$ under concatenation and inverse homomorphism, we consider semilinear languages that are subsets of a^*b^*, where the number of b's depends linearly on the number of a's. The dependency is given by linear functions $\varphi \colon \mathbb{N} \to \mathbb{N}$ with $\varphi(n) = c_1 \cdot n + c_0$, for some $c_0, c_1 \geq 0$. For such functions, we define $L_\varphi = \{\, a^n b^{\varphi(n)} \mid n \geq 0 \,\}$. In [8] it has been shown that all regular languages as well as all languages L_φ belong to all Boolean kernels of CFL. A generalization of the proofs reveals that this is true also for all reversals of the languages L_φ, that is, all languages L_φ^R belong to all Boolean kernels of CFL.

Theorem 13. *The family $\mathscr{I}$ and all kernels $\kappa \in \gamma_{\mathrm{BOOL}}(\mathrm{CFL})$ are not closed under concatenation, not even with concatenation of unary regular sets.*

Theorem 14. *The family $\mathscr{I}$ and all kernels $\kappa \in \gamma_{\mathrm{BOOL}}(\mathrm{CFL})$ are not closed under inverse homomorphisms, not even under length-preserving inverse homomorphisms.*

Proof. Let $\varphi \colon \mathbb{N} \to \mathbb{N}$ be the linear function $\varphi(n) = 2n$. We know that the languages $L_\varphi = \{\, a^n b^{2n} \mid n \geq 0 \,\}$ and L_φ^R belong to all kernels $\kappa \in \gamma_{\mathrm{BOOL}}(\mathrm{CFL})$. Furthermore, let $h \colon \{a, b, c\}^* \to \{a, b\}^*$ be the homomorphism $h(a) = a$, $h(b) = h(c) = b$ and $\hat{h} \colon \{a, b, c\}^* \to \{a, b\}^*$ be the homomorphism $\hat{h}(a) = \hat{h}(b) = b$, $\hat{h}(c) = a$. Then we have

$$h^{-1}(L_\varphi) \cap a^*b^*c^* = \{\, a^n b^m c^k \mid n \geq 0, m + k = 2n \,\} \text{ and}$$
$$\hat{h}^{-1}(L_\varphi^R) \cap a^*b^*c^* = \{\, a^k b^m c^n \mid n \geq 0, m + k = 2n \,\}.$$

Assume that the family $\mathscr{I}$ or some kernel $\kappa \in \gamma_{\mathrm{BOOL}}(\mathrm{CFL})$ is closed under inverse homomorphism. Since they include the regular languages and are closed under intersection, we derive that they include the language

$$h^{-1}(L_\varphi) \cap \hat{h}^{-1}(L_\varphi^R) \cap a^*b^*c^* = \{\, a^n b^n c^n \mid n \geq 0 \,\}$$

as well, a contradiction.   □

Table 1. Closure properties of the language families discussed. Symbol • denotes concatenation and κ stands for an arbitrary but fixed kernel from $\gamma_{\mathrm{BOOL}}(\mathrm{CFL})$. The properties shown for κ hold for *all* $\kappa \in \gamma_{\mathrm{BOOL}}(\mathrm{CFL})$ with the exception of reversal. For reversal, it has been shown that *some* kernels are not closed. It is currently open if there exists some $\kappa \in \gamma_{\mathrm{BOOL}}(\mathrm{CFL})$ that is closed under reversal. The non-closure under inverse homomorphism holds even for length-preserving homomorphisms.

	$^-$	$\cup$	$\cap R$	$\cap$	REV	$\bullet$	h^{-1}
CFL	✗	✓	✓	✗	✓	✓	✓
$\mathcal{U}$	✓	✗	✓	✗	✓	✗	✓
κ	✓	✓	✓	✓	✗	✗	✗
$\mathcal{I}$	✓	✓	✓	✓	✓	✗	✗
DCFL	✓	✗	✓	✗	✗	✗	✓
REG	✓	✓	✓	✓	✓	✓	✓

5   Descriptional Complexity

One topic in the field of descriptional complexity is to study the relative succinctness of different representations of languages by automata, grammars, and descriptional systems from a more abstract perspective. For languages that have more than one representation, the size trade-offs when changing the representation may be bounded by a recursive function or not. In the latter case we are faced with the phenomenon of so-called non-recursive trade-offs. In particular, whenever the trade-off from one descriptional system to another is non-recursive, one can choose an arbitrarily large recursive function f but the gain in economy of description eventually exceeds f when changing from the latter system to the former. See [6] for more details on descriptional complexity.

In order to deal with such questions for kernels, a descriptional system for languages from the kernel is necessary whose size can be measured. Since, in general, no automata or grammar characterizations are known for kernels, we take up an idea of Hartmanis [4] who raised the question whether the trade-off between two descriptional systems is caused by the fact that in one system it can be proved what is accepted, but that no such proofs are possible in the other system. For example, consider descriptional systems for the deterministic context-free languages. It is easy to verify whether a given pushdown automaton is deterministic, but there is no uniform way to verify that a nondeterministic pushdown automaton accepts a deterministic context-free language. So, one may ask whether the trade-off is affected if descriptional systems are considered which come with a corresponding proof attached whose length is added to the size of the system.

So, in the following we consider the representation of context-free languages by nondeterministic pushdown automata (NPDA) to which a proof is attached that the accepted language belongs to $\mathscr{U}$, $\kappa \in \gamma_{\text{BOOL}}(\text{CFL})$, or $\mathscr{I}$. We denote these automata as $\mathscr{U}$-NPDA, κ-NPDA, or $\mathscr{I}$-NPDA. The size of such an automaton is the length of the description of the automaton plus the length of the proof, say in binary. Then it is clear that, for any $c \geq 1$, there are only finitely many $\mathscr{U}$-NPDA, κ-NPDA, or $\mathscr{I}$-NPDA whose size is at most c.

It will turn out that the trade-offs between any of these three descriptional systems and deterministic pushdown automata (DPDA) are non-recursive. The proof is by reduction of the halting problem for Turing machines on empty tape. To this end, histories of Turing machine computations are encoded into strings. It suffices to consider deterministic Turing machines with one single tape and one single read-write head. Without loss of generality and for technical reasons, we safely may assume that the Turing machines cannot print blanks, can halt only after an odd number of moves, and accepts by halting. The size of a Turing machine is again measured as the length of its description. As for the NPDA, there are only finitely many Turing machines of the same size.

Let Q be the state set of some Turing machine M, where q_0 is the initial state, $T \cap Q = \emptyset$ is the tape alphabet containing the blank symbol, and $\Sigma \subset T$ is the input alphabet. Then a configuration of M can be written as a word of the form T^*QT^* such that $t_1 t_2 \cdots t_i q t_{i+1} \cdots t_n$ is used to express that M is in state q, scanning tape symbol t_{i+1}, and t_1, t_2 to t_n is the support of the tape inscription.

Dependent on M we define the language of valid computations. Let $\$ \notin T \cup Q$, $n \geq 0$, and $w_i \in T^*QT^*$, $0 \leq i \leq 2n+1$, be configurations of M. Then VALC(M) is defined to be the language of all words of the form

$$\$w_0\$w_1^R\$w_2\$w_3^R\$ \cdots \$w_{2n}\$w_{2n+1}^R\$,$$

where w_0 is an initial configuration of the form q_0, w_{2n+1} is a halting configuration, and w_i is the successor configuration of w_{i-1}, $1 \leq i \leq 2n + 1$. The language of *invalid computations* INVALC(M), is the complement of VALC(M) with respect to the alphabet $\{\$\} \cup T \cup Q$.

Corollary 15. *For any deterministic Turing machine M, the language INVALC(M) is a linear context-free language, such that its nondeterministic one-turn pushdown automaton can effectively be constructed from M.*

We denote the size of some system X by $|X|$.

Theorem 16. *The trade-offs between $\mathscr{U}$-NPDA and DPDA, κ-NPDA and DPDA, as well as between $\mathscr{I}$-NPDA and DPDA are non-recursive.*

Proof. Assume in contrast to the assertion that one of the trade-offs is recursive. We turn to show that in this case the halting problem for Turing machines on empty tape would be decidable, a contradiction.

So, let M be some given Turing machine of size $c \geq 1$. Then a Turing machine M_c with unary input alphabet $\{a\}$ is uniformly constructed as follows. On input a^x, first M_c enumerates all the finitely many Turing machines whose size is c. Then it simulates all these finitely many Turing machines on empty tape by dovetailing for exactly x steps (or up to halting if a machine halts before x steps). Machine M_c accepts its input a^x by halting if at least one of the simulations halts exactly after step x. If not, M_c does not halt. We conclude that the language $L(M_c)$ accepted by M_c is finite. Moreover, the length of the longest word in $L(M_c)$ gives the latest time step at which a Turing machine of size c halts on empty tape.

The finiteness of $L(M_c)$ is easily proved by a proof Π_1. The length of Π_1 can be bounded from above by $\varrho_1(c)$, where ϱ_1 is a recursive function.

Next, from M_c an NPDA N accepting $\mathrm{INVALC}(M_c)$ is constructed by Corollary 15. The corollary can be proved by a proof Π_2 whose length can be bounded from above by $\varrho_2(c)$, where ϱ_2 is a recursive function.

Since M_c accepts a finite language, $\mathrm{INVALC}(M_c)$ is a co-finite and, thus, regular language. This fact is easily proved by a proof Π_3 whose length can be bounded from above by $\varrho_3(c)$, where ϱ_3 is a recursive function.

Since all regular languages belong to all Boolean kernels $\kappa \in \gamma_{\mathrm{BOOL}}(\mathrm{CFL})$, the proofs Π_1, Π_2, and Π_3 reveal that N is a $\mathscr{U}$-NPDA, a κ-NPDA, as well as an $\mathscr{I}$-NPDA. The total length of this proof, which is attached to N, can be bounded from above by $\varrho(c)$, where ϱ is a recursive function.

Recall that we assume in contrast to the assertion that the trade-off between the size of N (including the attached proof) and the size of some equivalent DPDA D is given by a recursive function f, that is $|D| \leq f(|N|)$. Then $f(|N|)$ can be computed from N, and all DPDAs whose size is at most $f(|N|)$ can be enumerated. Since the family of deterministic context-free languages is effectively closed under complementation, each DPDA P in the list can be replaced by a DPDA accepting the complement of $L(P)$. Since finiteness of deterministic context-free languages is decidable, each DPDA that accepts an infinite language can be removed from the new list. The decision of finiteness of deterministic context-free languages includes the computation of an upper bound for the length of the longest word in the language. So, an upper bound for the length of the longest word accepted by any of the remaining DPDAs in the list can be computed. Moreover, among the remaining DPDAs there must be one that accepts the finite complement of $L(D)$. The finite complement of $L(D)$ is the language $\mathrm{VALC}(M_c)$. Clearly, the longest word in $\mathrm{VALC}(M_c)$ is longer than the longest word in $L(M_c)$. As before, an upper bound of the length of this longest word can be computed from D. But recall that the length of the longest word in $L(M_c)$ gives the latest time step at which a Turing machine of size c halts on empty tape.

Finally, it suffices to simulate the given Turing machine M for this number of steps in order to decide whether it halts on empty tape or not.   □

6 Untouched and Open Questions

We have started to study the properties of Boolean kernels of the family of context-free languages. Since little is known about kernels, many questions and problems remain open or untouched. Exemplarily, we mention some of them: (1) Is there a Boolean kernel $\kappa \in \gamma_{\text{BOOL}}(\text{CFL})$ that is closed under reversal or are *all* these kernels non-closed under reversal? (2) Further non-trivial closure properties of kernels are of natural interest. (3) A machine characterization of the complementation kernel of the context-free languages in terms of self-verifying pushdown automata is known [2]. Basically, the characterization is given by a machine for the underlying language family, where the acceptance condition is modified. Are there machine characterizations of other kernels? (4) In [5] an improved version of Earley's algorithm is adapted to context-free grammars which are extended by complement and intersection operators retaining cubic behavior. More generally, in [11] so-called conjunctive and Boolean grammars are studied. Can these techniques be applied to sub-families of context-free languages in order to find characterizations of kernels? (5) Alternative characterizations of kernels could be generators, where a generator is some smallest set of languages whose closure under certain operations is the kernel. Based on a generator, the languages in the kernel could be represented as expressions.

References

1. Bertsch, E., Nederhof, M.J.: Regular closure of deterministic languages. SIAM J. Comput. **29**, 81–102 (1999)
2. Fernau, H., Kutrib, M., Wendlandt, M.: Self-verifying pushdown automata. Fundam. Inform. **180**, 1–28 (2021)
3. Harrison, M.A.: Introduction to Formal Language Theory. Addison-Wesley, Boston (1978)
4. Hartmanis, J.: On the succinctness of different representations of languages. In: Maurer, H.A. (ed.) ICALP 1979. LNCS, vol. 71, pp. 282–288. Springer, Heidelberg (1979). https://doi.org/10.1007/3-540-09510-1_22
5. Heilbrunner, S., Schmitz, L.: An efficient recognizer for the Boolean closure of context-free languages. Theor. Comput. Sci. **80**, 53–75 (1991)
6. Holzer, M., Kutrib, M.: Descriptional complexity - an introductory survey. In: Martín-Vide, C. (ed.) Scientific Applications of Language Methods, pp. 1–58. Imperial College Press (2010)
7. Ilie, L., Păun, G., Rozenberg, G., Salomaa, A.: On strongly context-free languages. Discret. Appl. Math. **103**, 158–165 (2000)
8. Kutrib, M.: Kernels of sub-classes of context-free languages. In: Chatzigeorgiou, A., et al. (eds.) SOFSEM 2020. LNCS, vol. 12011, pp. 136–147. Springer, Cham (2020). https://doi.org/10.1007/978-3-030-38919-2_12
9. Kutrib, M., Malcher, A.: Finite turns and the regular closure of linear context-free languages. Discret. Appl. Math. **155**, 2152–2164 (2007)

10. Kutrib, M., Malcher, A., Wotschke, D.: The Boolean closure of linear context-free languages. Acta Inform. **45**, 177–191 (2008)
11. Okhotin, A.: Boolean grammars. Inform. Comput. **194**, 19–48 (2004)
12. Wotschke, D.: Nondeterminism and Boolean operations in PDA's. J. Comput. Syst. Sci. **16**, 456–461 (1978)
13. Wotschke, D.: The Boolean closures of the deterministic and nondeterministic context-free languages. In: Brauer, W. (ed.) GI 1973. LNCS, vol. 1, pp. 113–121. Springer, Heidelberg (1973). https://doi.org/10.1007/3-540-06473-7_11
14. Wotschke, D.: Degree-languages: a new concept of acceptance. J. Comput. Syst. Sci. **14**, 187–209 (1977)

Efficient String Matching Based on a Two-Step Simulation of the Suffix Automaton

Simone Faro and Stefano Scafiti[(⊠)]

Department of Mathematics and Computer Science, University of Catania,
Catania, Italy
{simone.faro,stefano.scafiti}@unict.it

Abstract. Automata play a very important role in the design of string
matching algorithms as their use has always led to elegant and very efficient solutions in practice. In this paper, we present a new general approach to the exact string matching algorithm based on a non-standard
efficient simulation of the suffix automaton of the pattern and give a
specific efficient implementation of it. To show the effectiveness of our
algorithm, we perform an extensive comparison against the most effective alternatives known in literature in terms of search speed and shift
advancements. From our experimental results the new algorithm turns
out to be very efficient in practical cases scaling much better when the
length of the pattern increases, improving the search speed by nearly 10
times under suitable conditions.

Keywords: Text processing · String matching · Automata based
algorithms · Suffix automaton simulation · Design and analysis on
algorithms

1 Introduction

The *string matching* problem consists in finding all the occurrences of a pattern x
of length m in a text y of length n, both defined over an alphabet Σ of size σ. The
first linear-time solution to the problem was the Knuth–Morris–Pratt (KMP)
algorithm [13], whereas the Boyer–Moore (BM) algorithm provided the first
sub-linear solution on average. Subsequently, the BDM algorithm reached the
optimal $\mathcal{O}(n \log_\sigma(m)/m)$ time complexity on the average [6]. Both the KMP and
the BDM algorithms are based on finite automata; in particular, they simulate,
respectively, a deterministic automaton for the language $\Sigma^\star x$ and a deterministic
suffix automaton for the language of the suffixes of x.

Beyond the theoretical results, from the practical point of view the efficiency
of such solutions is strictly affected by the encoding used for simulating the

---

This work has been supported by G.N.C.S., Istituto Nazionale di Alta Matematica
"Francesco Severi" and by Programma Ricerca di Ateneo UNICT 2020-22 linea 2.

S. Maneth (Ed.): CIAA 2021, LNCS 12803, pp. 165–177, 2021.
https://doi.org/10.1007/978-3-030-79121-6_14

underlying automata. One of the side effects of the BDM algorithm lies indeed in the use of the deterministic variant of the suffix automaton since the workload required to manage the individual transitions may be not negligible and, although its construction is linear in the size of the string, the proportionality factor hidden in the asymptotic notation is particularly high, making its construction prohibitive in the case of long patterns [11].

The most efficient solutions available in the literature are rather based on the simulation of the non-deterministic version of the suffix automaton by *bit parallelism* [1], an approach which takes advantage of the intrinsic parallelism of the bitwise operations inside a computer word, allowing to cut down the number of actual transitions on the automaton by a factor up to ω, where ω is the number of bits in a computer word. It is the case, for instance, of the Backward-Non-deterministic-DAWG-Matching (BNDM) algorithm [14] which is based on the bit-parallel simulation of the non-deterministic version of the suffix automaton of the reverse of the pattern.

However one bit per pattern symbol is still required for representing the states of the automaton, for a total of $\lceil m/\omega \rceil$ words. Thus, as long as the automaton fits in a computer word, bit-parallel algorithms are extremely fast, otherwise their performances degrade considerably as $\lceil m/\omega \rceil$ grows. Although such limitation is intrinsic, several techniques have been developed which retain good performance also in the case of long patterns [2,3,7,15].

A common approach to overcome this problem consists in constructing an automaton for a substring of the pattern fitting in a single computer word, to filter possible candidate occurrences of the pattern. However, besides the costs of the additional verification phase, a drawback of this approach is that, in the case of the BNDM algorithm, the maximum possible shift length cannot exceed ω, which could be much smaller than m.

The Long-BNDM [15] (LBNDM) and the BNDM with eXtended Shift [7] (BXS) algorithms are two efficient solutions specifically designed for simulating the suffix automaton using bit-parallelism in the case of long patterns. Specifically the LBNDM algorithm works by partitioning the pattern in $\lfloor m/k \rfloor$ consecutive substrings, each consisting in $k = \lfloor (m-1)/\omega \rfloor + 1$ characters. Similarly the BXS algorithm cuts the pattern into $\lceil m/\omega \rceil$ consecutive substrings of length w except for the rightmost piece which may be shorter. In both cases the substrings are superimposed getting a superimposed pattern of length ω. The idea is to search using a filter approach: first the superimposed pattern is searched in the text, then an additional verification phase is run when a candidate occurrence of the pattern has been located.

Cantone *et al.* presented in [2] an alternative technique, still suitable for bit-parallelism, to encode the non-deterministic suffix automaton of a given string in a more compact way. Their encoding is based on factorization of strings in which no character occurs more than once in any factor. It turns out that the non-deterministic automaton can be encoded with k bits, where k is the size of the factorization. As a consequence, the resulting algorithm, called Factorized-BNDM (FBNDM) tends to be faster in the case of sufficiently long patterns.

Finally, particularly relevant for this work is the Backward-SNR-DAWG-Matching (BSDM) algorithm, introduced by Faro and Lecroq in [10]. It is an efficient filtration algorithm based on a very simple encoding of the suffix automaton of a pattern x. The BSDM algorithm is based on the fact that a string where each character is repeated only once admits a deterministic suffix automaton which can be encoded with a simple integer.

In this paper, we present a new general approach to the exact string matching algorithm based on a non-standard efficient simulation of the suffix automaton of the pattern which avoids the construction of the full deterministic automaton, on the one hand, overcoming the drawbacks of the bit-parallel simulation of the non-deterministic automaton, on the other. The idea is to perform the first μ transitions in the suffix automaton all at once, where the value of μ is suitably chosen in order to simplify the simulation of subsequent automaton transitions.

We also give a specific implementation of such generic approach where the value of μ is related to the occurrence of unique factors in the pattern. The resulting algorithm, named Unique-Factor-Matcher (UFM) turns out to scale much better than any previous solution when the size of the pattern increases, improving the search speed by nearly 10 times under suitable conditions.

The paper is organized as follows. In Sect. 2 we briefly introduce the basic notions which we use along the paper. In Sect. 3 we introduce the new general approach and give its specific implementation in Sect. 4. Finally, in Sect. 5, we compare the newly presented solution with the best algorithms known in literature and draw our conclusions in Sect. 6.

2   Basic Notions and Definitions

Given a finite alphabet Σ, we denote by Σ^m, with $m \geq 0$, the set of all strings of length m over Σ. We represent a string $x \in \Sigma^m$ as an array $x[0..m-1]$ of characters of Σ and write $|x| = m$ (for $m = 0$ we obtain the empty string ε). Thus, $x[i]$ is the $(i+1)$-st character of x, for $0 \leq i < m$, and $x[i..j]$ is the substring of x contained between its $(i+1)$-st and the $(j+1)$-st characters, for $0 \leq i \leq j < m$. For any two strings x and x', we say that x' is a suffix of x if $x' = x[i..m-1]$, for some $0 \leq i < m$, and write $Suff(x)$ for the set of all suffixes of x. Similarly, x' is a prefix of x if $x' = x[0..i]$, for some $0 \leq i < m$, and write x_i to indicate the prefix of length i of x, i.e. $x_i = x[0..i-1]$. We write $x \cdot x'$, or more simply xx', for the concatenation of x and x', and x^r for the reverse of the string x. Given a string $x \in \Sigma^m$, we indicate with $S(x) = (Q, \Sigma, \delta, I, F)$ the non-deterministic suffix automaton with ϵ-transitions for the language $Suff(x)$, where $Q = \{I, q_0, q_1, \ldots, q_m\}$ is the set of automaton states, I is the initial state, $F = \{q_m\}$ is the set of final states and the transition function $\delta : \mathscr{P}(Q) \times (\Sigma \cup \{\epsilon\}) \longrightarrow \mathscr{P}(Q)$, where $\mathscr{P}(Q)$ is the set of parts of Q. Specifically, for any $Q' \subseteq Q$ we have $q_{i+1} \in \delta(Q', c)$ if $q_i \in Q'$ and $c = x[i]$, for $0 \leq i < m$. In addition we have $\delta(\{I\}, \varepsilon) = Q$. In all other cases we agree that $\delta(Q', c) = \emptyset$. For simplicity, in what follows, we will use the notation $\delta(q, c)$ instead of $\delta(\{q\}, c)$. The valid configurations $\delta^*(I, w)$ which are reachable by the automaton $S(x)$

on input $w \in \Sigma^*$ and starting from the initial state I are defined recursively as follows

$$\delta^*(w) := \begin{cases} \{q_0, q_1, ..., q_m\} & \text{if } w = \epsilon, \\ \bigcup_{q' \in \delta^*(I, w')} \delta(q', c) & \text{if } w = w'c, \text{ for some } c \in \Sigma, \text{ and } w' \in \Sigma^*. \end{cases}$$

3   The BTSM Generic Algorithm

From the analysis of the performance of the algorithms presented in the previous section [2,7,10] it turns out that the efficiency of a suffix automata based algorithms relies on the right trade-off between the encoding used to represent the underlying automaton and the size of the automaton itself. Regarding the first point it turns out that automata admitting simpler encoding are more efficient in practice. This is the case, for instance, of bit-parallel based solutions which limit the size of the automaton to the machine word size in turn of an efficient representation, like LBNDM and BXS. However, on the other hand, longer shifts are achieved when the size of the underlying automaton is close to the length of the pattern. This is the case of the FBNDM algorithm which trades a more complex representation in exchange for a higher size of the automaton.

In this section we present a generic algorithm, called Backward-Two-Step-Matcher (BTSM), for the online exact string matching problem based on a simplified and efficient simulation of the suffix automaton of the reverse of the pattern which, however, doesn't require its whole construction.

Before diving into the details of our solution, we introduce some additional useful definitions which will help to understand how the BTSM algorithm works.

Let x be a pattern of length m over an alphabet Σ of size σ. Given the suffix automaton $S(x) = \langle Q, \Sigma, \delta, I, F \rangle$ of x, we define the *minimum transitions function* $\gamma : \Sigma^+ \longrightarrow \{1, 2, ..., m\}$ which associates any string $w \in \Sigma^*$ with the length of its shortest prefix which must be read in order to reach a configuration containing at most one state. More formally, for each string $w \in \Sigma^+$, we have

$$\gamma(w) = \min\{1 \leq \ell \leq m : |\delta^*(w_\ell)| \leq 1\}.$$

Plainly, by the definition of δ, it trivially follows that if $\ell = \gamma(w)$ then $|\delta^*(w_\mu)| \leq 1$ for any $\ell \leq \mu \leq m$.

In addition, given a string w such that $|\delta^*(w)| \leq 1$, we define the *position function* POS $: \Sigma^* \longrightarrow \{0, 1, ..., m-1\}$ as the function which maps any string w to its eventually unique starting position inside the pattern x. Formally, for any string $w \in \Sigma^*$, we have

$$\text{POS}(w) = \begin{cases} m - i & \text{if } \delta^*(w) = \{q_i\}, 0 < i \leq m, \\ -1 & \text{otherwise.} \end{cases}$$

Assume, for instance to match the pattern $x = $ banana against the text window $w = $ anaban. Then, we have $\gamma(w) = 3$ and $\text{POS}(\text{ban}) = 0$.

We are now ready to present the generic BTSM algorithm. The main underlying idea is that the recognition process of a string w through the automaton $S(x^r)$ can be simplified by dividing it in two separate steps: a first non-deterministic step eventually followed by a deterministic step.

Specifically, as before, let x be a pattern of length m and let y be a text of length n, both strings over a common alphabet Σ of size σ and let $S(x^r) = \langle Q, \Sigma, \delta, I, F \rangle$ the suffix automaton for the reverse of the pattern x^r.

As in the case of the standard BDM algorithm, the searching phase of the BTSM algorithm works by sliding a window w of length m along the text, starting from the left end of the text and proceeding from left to right. At each iteration of the algorithm a new window position is attempted. For each attempt the recognition process of a string w through the automaton $S(x^r)$ is divided in the following two steps:

- *non-deterministic step:* during the first step an integer value μ is computed, depending on w, such that $\gamma(w_\mu^r) \leq \mu \leq m$ and $\mu+1$ transitions are performed all at once by computing $\delta^*(w_t)$. Then the position p corresponding to the unique active state q (if any) belonging to $\delta^*(w_\mu^r)$ is computed by means of the function Pos. If no active state q exists, i.e. if $p = -1$, the window is advanced to the right by one position, if $\mu = m$, by $m-\mu$ positions otherwise.
- *deterministic step:* If $p \geq 0$, then the computation proceeds with the subsequent transitions, which are simulated by comparing each character of the pattern, starting from position p, with its counterpart in the text, until a mismatch occurs or until p transitions have been performed. If a mismatch occurs then the window is simply advanced by $m - \mu$ positions to the right. Otherwise if p characters are read then a prefix of size $k + \mu$ of the pattern has been recognized. If $k + \mu = m$ then the pattern itself has been recognized and a match is reported, otherwise the window is shifted in order to align the first character of x with the starting position of the recognized prefix.

Denoting by $f(m)$ the computational effort related for computing μ and p, the worst case time complexity of the BTSM algorithm is $\mathcal{O}((m + f(m)) \cdot n)$.

The approach described above represents a generic way to avoid managing multiple states while simulating a suffix automaton for a given string at the cost of reducing the length of the shifts. Indeed, the only way to compute the exact shift value s consists in recognizing each suffix of x^r (i.e. each prefix of x), through the use of a full suffix automaton. Performing $\mu + 1$ transitions at once implies that only suffixes of length $\mu' \geq \mu$ can be recognized. However, provided that we can determine a value of μ which is close to $\gamma(w^r)$ and that $\delta^*(w_\mu^r)$ can be computed efficiently for any given text window w, overestimating the shifts values impacts less the efficiency than simulating the full automaton.

4   The UFM Algorithm

In this section we show how to turn the generic BTSM algorithm into a concrete efficient string matching algorithm. Our approach for estimating a good approximation for $\gamma(w)$ relies on the definition of *unique characters*, i.e. characters which occurs only once in the pattern. Although it can be rare for a given character $c \in \Sigma$ to occur only once, especially when m grows, we will show that, by convenient alphabet transformations, it could become very likely to happen. The resulting algorithm is called Unique-Factor-Matcher (UFM).

As before, let x be a pattern of length m over an alphabet Σ. For each character $c \in \Sigma$, we denote by $f_x(c)$ the number of occurrences of the character c inside x and we say that c is a *unique character* of x if $f_x(c) = 1$.

In addition, for each position of the pattern, we define the *unique distance function* $d : \{0, 1, ..., m-1\} \longrightarrow \{0, 1, ..., m-1\}$ as the function which maps each position i of the pattern with the rightmost position $j \leq i$ (if any) such that $x[j]$ is a unique character in x. If such a unique character does not occur in x we set by default $d(i) = i$. More formally, for $0 \leq i < m$, we have

$$d(i) = min(\{i - j \mid 0 < j \leq i \wedge f_x(x[j]) = 1\} \cup \{i\}).$$

Starting from the previous definition, we put $\bar{d}(c) := max\{d(i) \mid 0 \leq i < m \wedge x[i] = c\}$ for each character c appearing in x, while we set $\bar{d}(c) = -1$ if c does not occur in x. For instance, assume $x = \mathsf{pepsi}$ is a string over the alphabet $\Sigma = \{\mathsf{a}, \mathsf{b}, \mathsf{i}, \mathsf{e}, \mathsf{p}, \mathsf{s}\}$. Then, we have $\bar{d}(\mathsf{p}) = 1$, $\bar{d}(c) = 0$, for any $c \in \{\mathsf{e}, \mathsf{s}, \mathsf{i}\}$ while $\bar{d}(c) = -1$ for $c \in \{\mathsf{a}, \mathsf{b}\}$.

The following two technical lemmas define how unique characters of the pattern can be used to compute, for a given string w, a candidate value μ, such that $\gamma(w) \leq \mu \leq m$. Roughly speaking we prove in Lemma 1 that $\delta^*(w) \leq 1$ for any string w ending with a unique character. In addition we prove in Lemma 2 that if the second transition of the suffix automaton of x^r is performed on a character $c \in \Sigma$, then performing $\bar{d}(c) + 1$ transitions is enough to get (at most) a unique active state on the automaton.

Lemma 1. *Let x be a string of length m over Σ and let $S(x) = \langle Q, \Sigma, \delta, I, F \rangle$ be the suffix automaton for x. Moreover, let $c \in \Sigma$ such that $f_x(c) = 1$. Then for each $Q' \in \mathscr{P}(Q)$, $|\delta(Q', c)| \leq 1$ holds.*

Proof. Since c occurs only once in x, then $c = x[i]$ for some $0 \leq i < m$. By the definition of δ it follows that $\delta(Q', c)$ is nonempty if and only if $q_i \in Q'$. Specifically, when $q_i \in Q'$ we have $\delta(Q', c) = \{q_{i+1}\}$ and $\delta(Q', c) = \emptyset$ otherwise. In both cases $|\delta(Q', c)| \leq 1$ holds.

Lemma 2. *Let x, w be strings of length m, both over a common alphabet Σ, and let $S(x^r) = \langle Q, \Sigma, \delta, I, F \rangle$ the suffix automaton for x^r. Then, $\bar{d}(w[0]) \geq \gamma(w)$.*

Proof. Let $\mu = \bar{d}(w[0])$ and let $Q = |\delta^*(w_\mu)|$. Without loss of generality, we can suppose that $Q \neq \emptyset$. Then, there must exists at least one factor of the pattern $f = x[i..i + \mu - 1]$, for some $0 \leq i \leq m - \mu$, such that $f = w_\mu$. Moreover, by the definition of $\bar{d}$, f must contain at least one unique character of x. Let j the position of the first unique character of x inside f. By Lemma 1, $|\delta^*(f_j)| \leq 1$ must hold, and in particular $|\delta^*(f)| = |\delta^*(w_\mu)| \leq 1$ hold too, implying $\mu \geq \gamma(w)$.

In the following two sections we describe the preprocessing and the searching phase of the resulting UFM algorithm in detail (Fig. 1).

```
HASHINSERT(HT, x, s, μ)                    HASHGET(HT, x, f, μ)
  1. c ← x[s + μ − 1]                         1. c ← f[μ − 1]
  2. n ← NEWNODE()                            2. n ← HT[c]
  3. n.len ← μ                                3. while n ≠ NIL do
  4. n.start ← s                              4.    s ← n.start
  5. n.next ← HT[c]                           5.    if n.len = μ and x[s..s + μ − 1] = f
  6. HT[c] ← n                                6.       then return n.start
                                             7.    n ← n.next
PREPROCESSING(x, m)                          8. return -1
  1. for c ∈ Σ do
  2.    F(c) ← 0                            UFM(x, m, y, n)
  3.    D(c) ← −1                             1. (D, HT) ← PREPROCESSING(P, m)
  4.    HT(c) ← NIL                           2. j ← 0
  5. for i ← 0 to m − 1 do                    3. while j ≤ n − m do
  6.    c ← x[i]                              4.    s ← m
  7.    F(c) ← F(c) + 1                       5.    d ← D(x[j + m − 1])
  8. last ← −1                                6.    if d < 0 then
  9. for i ← 0 to m − 1 do                    7.       j ← j + m
 10.    c ← P[i]                              8.       continue
 11.    if F(c) = 1 then                      9.    μ ← d + 1
 12.       D(c) = 0                          10.    if μ = m then s ← 1 else s ← s − μ
 13.       last = i                          11.    p ← HASHGET(HT, x[j + m − μ..j + m − 1], μ)
 14.    else if last ≥ 0                     12.    if p ≥ 0 then
 15.       D(c) ← MAX(D(c), i − last)        13.       k ← 0
 16.    else D(c) ← i                        14.       while k < p and y[i − k − 1] = x[p − k − 1] do
 17. for i ← 0 to m − 1 do                   15.          k ← k + 1
 18.    c ← x[i]                             16.       if k = p do
 19.    μ ← D(c) + 1                         17.          if k + μ = m then
 20.    if i + 1 ≥ μ then                    18.             output j
 21.       HASHINSERT(HT, x, i + 1 − μ, μ)   19.       else
 22. return (D, HT)                          20.          s ← s − k
                                            21.    j ← j + s
```

Fig. 1. The pseudocode of the algorithm UFM and its auxiliary procedures.

4.1   The Algorithm

The preprocessing phase starts by computing the frequency of each character of the alphabet, in order to find the unique characters of the string x.

Then, function $\bar{d}$ is computed in the form of a table D. We recall that, given a text window w of length m, $\mu = D(w[m − 1]) + 1$ characters must be read in order to be sure that the suffix automaton for x^r contains at most one state. When this happens, we need to efficiently recover the starting position of the string $w[m − \mu..m − 1]$ inside x. In other words, we need an efficient method to implement the position function POS. To this purpose, a hash table HT can be used, storing the starting position of several unique factors of x. In particular, for each position i of the pattern x, factor $x[i − \mu..i]$ of length $\mu = D(x[i]) + 1$ is inserted into the table, whenever $i + 1 \geq \mu$. Note that, character $x[i]$ itself is used as the hash code of factor $x[i − \mu..i]$. In this way, each bucket HT[C] of the table contains exactly $f_x(c)$ elements, for each $c \in \Sigma$. The Preprocessing takes $O(m)$ space $O(m)$ time to be performed.

Regarding the searching phase, it follows the structure of the BTSM algorithm, specifically adapted to handle functions D and hash table HT. In particular, a window w of length m is slided along the text y. For each window, value $d = D(w[m − 1])$ is retrieved. If d is nonnegative, then the suffix of w of length

$\mu = d + 1$ is searched in the hash table, in order to get its starting position in the pattern, otherwise the window is instantly shifted by m characters to the right. The searching then proceeds as in the BTSM algorithm.

Regarding the time complexity of the search phase of the UFM algorithm, we observe that a single entry of table HT could contain up to $\mathcal{O}(m)$ factors, each of size equal to $k = \mathcal{O}(m)$. This means that a single call to procedure HASHGET could require in the worst case $\mathcal{O}(km) = \mathcal{O}(m^2)$ to be performed, leading to an overall complexity of $\mathcal{O}(m^2 n)$ in the worst case. Despite its worst case time complexity the UFM algorithm turns out to be very fast in practice, as shown in the following section.

4.2 Extension to Condensed Alphabets

In order to enlarge the number of unique characters of x it is convenient to use a condensed alphabet whose elements are obtained by combining groups of q characters of the original alphabet, for a fixed value q. A hash function $hash : \Sigma^q \leftarrow \{0, \ldots, \text{MAX}-1\}$ can be used for combining the group of characters, for a fixed constant value MAX. Thus a new condensed pattern x_q of length $m - q + 1$, over the alphabet $\{0, \ldots, \text{MAX} - 1\}$, is obtained from x. Specifically we have $x_q[i \mathinner{.\,.} j] = hash(x[i] \cdots x[i + q - 1]) \cdots hash(x[j] \cdots x[j + q - 1])$ for $0 \leq i, j \leq m - q$, where $x_q = x_q[0 \mathinner{.\,.} m - q]$. The set of unique characters is then computed on x_q.

The size MAX of the new condensed alphabet depends on the available memory and on the size of the original alphabet Σ. An efficient method for computing a condensed alphabet was introduced by Wu and Manber [16]. It computes the shift value by using a shift-and-addition procedure and in particular $hash(c_1, c_2, \ldots, c_q) = (\sum_{i=1}^{q}(c_i \ll (sh \cdot (q - i)))) \mod \text{MAX}$ where $c_i \in \Sigma$ for $i = 1, \ldots, q$. The value of the shift sh depends on MAX and q.

Table 1 shows the average number of the unique characters in patterns randomly extracted from a genome sequence, a protein sequence and a natural language text, for different values of q and m, and with $\text{MAX} = 2^{16}$. When $1 \leq q \leq 4$ we use the value $sh = 2$ for computing the hash value, while we use $sh = 1$ when $q > 4$.

From experimental results it turns out that the highest number of unique characters, though quite less than m in almost all cases, can be extremely larger than the size of a computer word (which typically is 32 or 64) exceeding this value by two orders of magnitude. This leads to larger shift in a suffix automata based algorithm. The highest value in the number of unique characters is obtained, in almost all cases, by the value $q = 10$. We notice however that for patterns of medium length ($m \leq 64$) the highest number of unique characters is obtained by smaller values of q, typically $q = 6$ or $q = 8$. This is also reflected in the practical performance of the corresponding algorithms.

Table 1. Average number of unique characters present in strings of increasing size, for several values of q. For display purposes all numbers have been rounded down. The three tables refer to random strings, extracted from a genome sequence, a protein sequence and a English text

q/m	32	64	128	256	512	1,024	2,048	4,096	8,192	16,384	32,768	65,536
1	0	0	0	0	0	0	0	0	0	0	0	0
2	4	1	0	0	0	0	0	0	0	0	0	0
4	25	44	66	77	62	28	6	1	0	0	0	0
6	25	53	99	165	234	264	232	155	74	23	4	0
8	24	55	114	223	410	686	986	1,153	1,090	817	492	229
10	22	54	117	240	476	914	1,660	2,775	4,009	4,742	4,528	3,477

(GENOME)

q/m	32	64	128	256	512	1,024	2,048	4,096	8,192	16,384	32,768	65,536
1	5	2	1	0	0	0	0	0	0	0	0	0
2	21	30	33	24	12	6	2	0	0	0	0	0
4	28	58	113	209	358	530	594	443	232	131	74	40
6	26	55	106	189	292	357	297	185	128	102	84	68
8	24	55	116	231	439	770	1,177	1,436	1,204	742	515	417
10	22	54	117	241	483	937	1,759	3,088	4,751	5,762	4,825	2,961

(PROTEIN)

q/m	32	64	128	256	512	1,024	2,048	4,096	8,192	16,384	32,768	65,536
1	8	8	8	6	6	5	5	4	4	3	2	1
2	22	32	40	42	39	34	31	29	29	27	25	21
4	27	54	95	164	256	377	502	604	654	649	607	565
6	26	55	106	192	325	508	701	824	798	684	581	503
8	24	55	113	221	411	743	1,278	2,006	2,813	3,362	3,340	2,877
10	22	54	115	232	453	855	1,582	2,891	5,051	8,039	11,237	13,306

(ENGLISH TEXT)

5   Experimental Results

In this section, we report the results of an extensive experimental comparison of the UFM algorithm against the most efficient solutions known in the literature for the online exact string matching problem, mostly focusing on those algorithms which make use of the suffix automaton. Specifically, the following 14 algorithms (implemented in 43 variants, depending on the values of their parameters) have been compared:

- BNDM$_q$: the Backward-Nondeterministic-DAWG-Matching algorithm [14] implemented with q-grams, for $1 \leq q \leq 6$;
- LBNDM: the Long BNDM algorithm [15];
- BSX$_q$: the Backward-Nondeterministic-DAWG-Matching algorithm [14] with Extended Shift [7] implemented using q-grams, with $1 \leq q \leq 4$;
- FBNDM: the Factorized variant [2,3] of the BNDM algorithm [14];

- BSDM$_q$: the Backward-SNR-DAWG-Matching algorithm [10] using condensed alphabets with groups of q characters, with $1 \leq q \leq 10$;
- UFM$_q$: the UFM algorithm presented in Sect. 4 implemented with condensed alphabets, using groups of q characters, with $1 \leq q \leq 10$.

For the sake of completeness, we also evaluated the following three string matching algorithms which are not based on automata but are considered among the most effective algorithm in practice in the case of long patterns:

- WFR$_q$: the Weak Factors Recognition algorithm [4,5], implemented using q-gram, with $3 \leq q \leq 7$;
- TWFR$_q$: the Tuned Weak Factors Recognition algorithm [5], implemented using q-gram, with $3 \leq q \leq 7$.
- EPSM: the Exact Packed String Matching algorithm [8,9] based on SIMD instructions;[1]

Table 2. Experimental results obtained for searching on a genome sequence, a protein sequence and an English text. Searching speed is reported in GB/s. Best results have been bold faced.

	q/m	32	64	128	256	512	1,024	2,048	4,096	8,192	16,384	32,768	65,536
GENOME	1	0	0	0	0	0	0	0	0	0	0	0	0
	2	4	1	0	0	0	0	0	0	0	0	0	0
	4	25	44	66	77	62	28	6	1	0	0	0	0
	6	25	53	99	165	234	264	232	155	74	23	4	0
	8	24	55	114	223	410	686	986	1,153	1,090	817	492	229
	10	22	54	117	240	476	914	1,660	2,775	4,009	4,742	4,528	3,477
	q/m	32	64	128	256	512	1,024	2,048	4,096	8,192	16,384	32,768	65,536
PROTEIN	1	5	2	1	0	0	0	0	0	0	0	0	0
	2	21	30	33	24	12	6	2	0	0	0	0	0
	4	28	58	113	209	358	530	594	443	232	131	74	40
	6	26	55	106	189	292	357	297	185	128	102	84	68
	8	24	55	116	231	439	770	1,177	1,436	1,204	742	515	417
	10	22	54	117	241	483	937	1,759	3,088	4,751	5,762	4,825	2,961
	q/m	32	64	128	256	512	1,024	2,048	4,096	8,192	16,384	32,768	65,536
ENGLISH TEXT	1	8	8	8	6	6	5	5	4	4	3	2	1
	2	22	32	40	42	39	34	31	29	29	27	25	21
	4	27	54	95	164	256	377	502	604	654	649	607	565
	6	26	55	106	192	325	508	701	824	798	684	581	503
	8	24	55	113	221	411	743	1,278	2,006	2,813	3,362	3,340	2,877
	10	22	54	115	232	453	855	1,582	2,891	5,051	8,039	11,237	13,306

---

[1] We notice that the EPSM algorithm is designed for simply counting the number of matching occurrences without reporting the corresponding positions.

All algorithms have been implemented in the C programming language[2] and have been tested using the SMART tool [12]. All experiments have been executed locally on a computer running Linux Ubuntu 20.04.1 with an Intel Core i5 3.40 GHz processor and 8 GB RAM. In all cases the patterns were randomly extracted from the text and the value m was made ranging from 32 to 65536.

Our tests have been run on a genome sequence, a protein sequence, and an English text (each of size 5MB). Such sequences are provided by the SMART research tool and are available online for download (additional details on the sequences can be found in Faro et al. [12]). In the experimental evaluation, patterns of length m were randomly extracted from the sequences, with m ranging over the set of values $\{2^i \mid 5 \leq i \leq 16\}$. In all cases, the mean over the search speed (expressed in Gigabytes per seconds) of 500 runs has been reported.

Table 2 summarise the search speed of our evaluations. Each table is divided into two blocks. The first block presents results relative to the most effective algorithms based on automata known in the literature. Best results among the first set of algorithms have been boldfaced to ease their localization. The second block concerns the speed search obtained by three algorithms among the best solution known in literature.

Many of the tested algorithms has been implemented using q-grams, for different values of the parameter q (including the UFM algorithm). For such algorithms we report only the best performance obtained among the variants.

Among the automata based algorithms the new UFM algorithm turns out to achieve the best results in almost all cases, showing considerable speed ups, especially in the case of long patterns. The only exception is in the case of natural language texts, where it is BSDM to achieve the best results for medium length patterns ($m = 32, 64$). Notice that as the length of the pattern grows, the performance of the UFM algorithm deviates more and more from that of the previous solutions, reaching a search speed up to 10 times higher than the second best solution, i.e. the BSDMq algorithm.

Extending the comparison also to non-automata-based solutions, it is interesting to note how the UFM algorithm scales better as the size of the pattern increases, outperforming all the remaining algorithms starting from $m = 512$, in the case of genome sequences, $m = 1024$ for protein texts, and $m = 8192$ for texts in natural language. Moreover, we also notice how the UFM algorithm is still very competitive also for patterns of medium size, since the search speed never deviates too much from the best results.

6   Conclusions

In this paper we introduced an efficient algorithm, called Unique Factor Matcher (UFM), based on a novel technique for simulating the non-deterministic suffix automaton of a string which separates the simulation into a non-deterministic and a deterministic part and turns out to be suitable for efficient string matching.

---

[2] Source code is available at: https://github.com/ostafen/unique-factor-matcher.

We showed experimentally how the new algorithm turns out to be very competitive when compared with the most efficient algorithms known in literature, and, under certain circumstances, the fastest in practice.

In our future works we intend to tune the algorithm in order to further improve its efficiency also for strings of medium size. This includes the use of fast loops and efficient hash functions for implementing the condensed alphabets and hash table operations. We would also investigate the possibility of finding alternative, more efficient strategies for implementing the BTSM generic algorithm.

References

1. Baeza-Yates, R., Gonnet, G.H.: A new approach to text searching. Commun. ACM **35**(10), 74–82 (1992)
2. Cantone, D., Faro, S., Giaquinta, E.: A compact representation of nondeterministic (suffix) automata for the bit-parallel approach. In: Amir, A., Parida, L. (eds.) CPM 2010. LNCS, vol. 6129, pp. 288–298. Springer, Heidelberg (2010). https://doi.org/10.1007/978-3-642-13509-5_26
3. Cantone, D., Faro, S., Giaquinta, E.: A compact representation of nondeterministic (suffix) automata for the bit-parallel approach. Inf. Comput. **213**, 3–12 (2012). https://doi.org/10.1016/j.ic.2011.03.006
4. Cantone, D., Faro, S., Pavone, A.: Speeding up string matching by weak factor recognition. In: Proceedings of the Prague Stringology Conference 2017, pp. 42–50 (2017). http://www.stringology.org/event/2017/p05.html
5. Cantone, D., Faro, S., Pavone, A.: Linear and efficient string matching algorithms based on weak factor recognition. ACM J. Exp. Algorithmics **24**(1), 1.8:1–1.8:20 (2019). https://doi.org/10.1145/3301295
6. Crochemore, M., Rytter, W.: Text Algorithms. Oxford University Press (1994). http://www-igm.univ-mlv.fr/%7Emac/REC/B1.html
7. Durian, B., Peltola, H., Salmela, L., Tarhio, J.: Bit-parallel search algorithms for long patterns. In: Festa, P. (ed.) SEA 2010. LNCS, vol. 6049, pp. 129–140. Springer, Heidelberg (2010). https://doi.org/10.1007/978-3-642-13193-6_12
8. Faro, S., Külekci, M.O.: Fast packed string matching for short patterns. In: Proceedings of the 15th Meeting on Algorithm Engineering and Experiments, pp. 113–121. SIAM (2013). https://doi.org/10.1137/1.9781611972931.10
9. Faro, S., Külekci, M.O.: Fast and flexible packed string matching. J. Discret. Algorithms **28**, 61–72 (2014). https://doi.org/10.1016/j.jda.2014.07.003
10. Faro, S., Lecroq, T.: A fast suffix automata based algorithm for exact online string matching. In: Moreira, N., Reis, R. (eds.) CIAA 2012. LNCS, vol. 7381, pp. 149–158. Springer, Heidelberg (2012). https://doi.org/10.1007/978-3-642-31606-7_13
11. Faro, S., Lecroq, T.: The exact online string matching problem: a review of the most recent results. ACM Comput. Surv. **45**(2), 13:1–13:42 (2013). https://doi.org/10.1145/2431211.2431212
12. Faro, S., Lecroq, T., Borzi, S., Di Mauro, S., Maggio, A.: The string matching algorithms research tool. In: Holub, J., Zdárek, J. (eds.) Proceedings of the Prague Stringology Conference, pp. 99–111 (2016). http://www.stringology.org/event/2016/p09.html
13. Knuth, D.E., Morris Jr., J.H., Pratt, V.R.: Fast pattern matching in strings. SIAM J. Comput. **6**(2), 323–350 (1977). https://doi.org/10.1137/0206024

14. Navarro, G., Raffinot, M.: A bit-parallel approach to suffix automata: fast extended string matching. In: Farach-Colton, M. (ed.) CPM 1998. LNCS, vol. 1448, pp. 14–33. Springer, Heidelberg (1998). https://doi.org/10.1007/BFb0030778

15. Peltola, H., Tarhio, J.: Alternative algorithms for bit-parallel string matching. In: Nascimento, M.A., de Moura, E.S., Oliveira, A.L. (eds.) SPIRE 2003. LNCS, vol. 2857, pp. 80–93. Springer, Heidelberg (2003). https://doi.org/10.1007/978-3-540-39984-1_7

16. Uratani, N., Takeda, M.: A fast string-searching algorithm for multiple patterns. Inf. Process. Manag. **29**(6), 775–792 (1993). https://doi.org/10.1016/0306-4573(93)90106-N

Approximate Hashing for Bioinformatics

Guy Arbitman[1], Shmuel T. Klein[1(✉)], Pierre Peterlongo[2], and Dana Shapira[3]

[1] Department of Computer Science, Bar Ilan University, 52900 Ramat-Gan, Israel
`tomi@cs.biu.ac.il`
[2] Inria, Univ Rennes, CNRS, IRISA, 35000 Rennes, France
`pierre.peterlongo@inria.fr`
[3] Department of Computer Science, Ariel University, 40700 Ariel, Israel
`shapird@g.ariel.ac.il`

Abstract. The paper extends ideas from data compression by deduplication to the Bioinformatic field. The specific problems on which we show our approach to be useful are the clustering of a large set of DNA strings and the search for approximate matches of long substrings, both based on the design of what we call an approximate hashing function. The outcome of the new procedure is very similar to the clustering and search results obtained by accurate tools, but in much less time and with less required memory.

1 Introduction

A particular form of lossless data compression is known as *deduplication*, which is often applied in a scenario in which a large data repository is given and we wish to store a new, updated, version of it. A case in point would be a backup system, which regularly saves the entire content of the digital storage of some company, even though the changes account only for a tiny fraction of the accumulated information. The idea is then to find duplicated parts and store only one copy P of them; the second and subsequent occurrences of these parts can then be replaced by pointers to P. The problem is of course how to define these parts in a useful way, and then how to locate them efficiently.

One of the approaches to solve the problem is based on hashing and can be schematically described as follows. The available data is partitioned into parts called *chunks*; a cryptographically strong hash function h is applied to these chunks, and the set S of different hash values, along with pointers to the corresponding chunks, is kept in a data structure D allowing fast access. These hash values act as *signatures* of the chunks, uniquely representing them, but requiring orders of magnitude less space than the original data. For each new chunk to be treated, its hash value is searched for in D, and if it appears there, we know that the given chunk is a duplicate and may be replaced by a pointer to its earlier occurrence. If the hash value is not in D, the given chunk is considered new, so it is stored and its hash value is adjoined to the set S [14].

An alternative has been suggested in [2] and is implemented in the IBM ProtecTIER Product [7]. The main idea there is to look for *similar*, rather than

© Springer Nature Switzerland AG 2021
S. Maneth (Ed.): CIAA 2021, LNCS 12803, pp. 178–189, 2021.
https://doi.org/10.1007/978-3-030-79121-6_15

identical chunks and if such a chunk is located, only the difference is recorded, which is generally much smaller than a full chunk. This allows the use of significantly larger chunks than in identity based systems. However, for similarity, a classical hashing function cannot be used to produce the signature, since one of the properties of hashing is yielding uniformly distributed values, regardless of regularities in the input, so that when changing even a single bit of the file, the resulting hash value should be completely different.

This lead to the design of what could be called an *Approximate Hash* (AH) function, a notion which seems bearing an internal contradiction, since unlike standard hash functions, their approximate variants should not be sensitive to "small" changes within the chunk, and yet behave like other hash functions as far as the close to uniform distribution of their values is concerned. The idea of AH functions is an extension of the notion of locality-sensitive hashing introduced in [9]. The approach of using similarity instead of identity has been adapted in [3] to applications in which the data is more fine grained, such as backup systems. The current paper is an extension, which applies similar techniques to string processing problems arising in Bioinformatics.

We concentrate in this paper on the following two problems, clustering and substring search, though similar ideas can be applied to a wide variety of other bioinformatic challenges. The first problem is that of *clustering* a large collection of DNA strings into sub-collections forming clusters, in the sense that strings assigned to the same cluster may be considered as similar for practical biological purposes (e.g., one may be obtained from the other by a limited number of mutations), whereas strings of different clusters are different enough to be judged not originating from the same source. Many clustering methods have been suggested, such as CD-HIT (CD) [12], or MeShClust^2 (MC) [10].

The second problem is that of locating a single string within a large collection on the basis of one of its fragments, or rather, one of its fragments that has undergone some limited number of mutations. We show how our notion of an approximate hash may be adapted to these and similar problems and report on the experimental setup and its results in the following sections.

2   Design of an Approximate Hash Function

Before trying to cluster a set of strings, one first needs some measure for the *distance* $d(\omega_1, \omega_2)$ between two given strings ω_1 and ω_2. If they were of equal length n, the *Hamming distance*, counting the number of corresponding positions in which the strings differ, would be a plausible candidate, and can be computed in $O(n)$. However, the Hamming distance is biased when insertions and deletions are allowed and is a reasonable choice only when ω_2 can be obtained from ω_1 by a series of substitutions. Therefore, in a general setting, one should rather use the *edit distance*, defined as the minimal number of single character insertions, deletions or substitutions necessary to transform one string into the other. Using dynamic programming, it takes quadratic time $O(nm)$ to compute the edit distance between strings of lengths n and m. The clustering problem is thus a difficult one: if a million (p) strings are given, each of length about one million (q), the time to evaluate the edit distance between all pairs of strings would be $O(p^2q^2) = O(2^{80})$, which is still too much for our current technology. We therefore suggest a more practical solution as follows.

2.1 Definition of the Signature

The idea is, given a collection $\mathcal{C}$ of DNA strings w, to produce a signature encapsulating the main features of the strings in as few as possible bits. A first approach could be to devise what could be called an *occurrence map* of the various substrings of length k, called k-mers, for $k \geq 1$, of all strings w in $\mathcal{C}$. Since our alphabet consists of just four nucleotides represented by the 4 letters, $\Sigma = \{A, C, G, T\}$, there are 4 1-mers, 16 2-mers, 64 3-mers and generally 4^k different k-mers. Depending on the available space, a general approach to devise a signature could include the following steps:

1. Fix lower and upper limits ℓ and u for the values of k we wish to include in the definition of the signatures, each of which will consist of a bitstring of length $4^\ell + 4^{\ell+1} + \cdots + 4^u$;
2. iterate over all the DNA strings w in the given set $\mathcal{C}$ and perform for each string:
   (a) Choose a threshold t_k for each of the values of k, depending only on k and the lengths of the given DNA string w;
   (b) sort, separately for each $\ell \leq k \leq u$, the 4^k k-mers according to some predefined order, e.g., lexicographically;
   (c) for all k in $[\ell, u]$, the bit indexed $i + \sum_{j=\ell}^{k-1} 4^j$, $0 \leq i < 4^k$, corresponding to the i-th ordered k-mer, will be set to 1 if and only if the number of occurrences of this i-th k-mer within the given string w is at least t_k. For example, AAAA is the first 4-mer in lexicographic order, so if $\ell = 2$, then the bit indexed $4^2 + 4^3 + 0 = 80$ will be set if the number of occurrences of AAAA in the string w is at least t_4.

A reasonable choice for the thresholds t_k would be the median of the number of occurrences of the 4^k k-mers within the given string w, for each k, which would yield signature strings in which the probability of a 1-bit is about $\frac{1}{2}$. Since this is only a heuristic, the median can be approximated by setting t_k as the expected number of occurrences, that is, their average, which is easier to evaluate.

As example, consider the input string

$$ACCTTGAAGTTGGGCCAACTGTTGCCC$$

of length $n = 27$ and set $\ell = u = 2$. The number of occurrences of the 16 possible pairs are:

AA	AC	AG	AT	CA	CC	CG	CT	GA	GC	GG	GT	TA	TC	TG	TT
2	2	1	0	1	4	0	2	1	2	2	2	0	0	4	3

There are $n - k + 1$ overlapping k-mers in a string of length n, so the average number of occurrences for each specific k-mer is $(n - k + 1)/4^k = 1.63$ on our small example. One could thus set the threshold to $t_2 = 1$, for which the resulting signature would be 1110 1101 1111 0011, where spaces have been included for readability. For $t_2 = 2$, one would get 1100 0101 0111 0011.

By concentrating on the distribution of the different k-mers within a string we try to catch underlying similarities, since DNA strings that are essentially different not just because of a limited number of mutations, will not tend to exhibit matching occurrence distributions. On the other hand, the proposed measure is flexible enough to allow some fluctuations, because the exact number of occurrences of a given k-mer is not given importance, only the fact whether or not this number exceeds the given threshold.

The idea of using k-mers to derive features of entire DNA strings is not new to Bioinformatics, and has been used in [5,8,16], to cite just a few, though, our approach is different.

2.2   Clustering

To extend the approach used for the deduplication of chunks, we shall apply here the clustering on the signatures rather than on the corresponding DNA strings, in order to obtain clusters from which the partition of the original set of strings can be deduced. There is obviously a significant reduction of the required time complexity, turning the clustering attempt into a feasible one. In particular, instead of using the edit distance between two strings, the appropriate choice for the distance between their signatures is the Hamming distance, as the signatures are of the same length and bits at the same index correspond to identical k-mers.

To check whether one can indeed identify clusters on the basis of using just the much smaller signatures, we report here on the details of a series of tests we have performed, first on artificially constructed sets, then real-life data. Even for the first set, we started with real DNA strings, downloaded from the website of the *National Center for Biotechnology Information*[1], and only the modified strings simulating data after mutations, were artificially generated. A sample of 50 different DNA sequences of various lengths and origins was randomly chosen, with lengths between thousands and millions of nucleotides. For each of the chosen strings, 15 variants, partitioned into three groups of 5, were generated, simulating various mutations. The first group consisted of strings derived from the given one by deleting some of their characters. More precisely, the heuristic used to produce the strings was:

1. Choose randomly an integer r between 1 and 50;
2. choose randomly a position t within the given string;
3. delete r consecutive characters starting from position t;
4. if the cumulative number of deleted characters does not exceed 7% of the length of the original string, repeat the process from step 1.

---

[1] https://www.ncbi.nlm.nih.gov/nuccore.

For the second group, a similar heuristic was applied, but instead of deleting, substrings of length r chosen randomly from the alphabet $\Sigma = \{A, C, G, T\}$ were inserted at position t. The five strings in the third group were obtained by allowing both deletions and insertions, more precisely, applying first the heuristic for the deletion and then that of the insertion on the output of the first, until the cumulative change reaches about 14%. The total number of strings in our set S was therefore 50 originals plus 50×15 variants = 800.

Generating artificial DNA strings by inserting or deleting elements is often used for simulations in Bioinformatics, as, e.g., in [13]. We wish to emphasize that there is no claim that the 50 chosen elements be representative of the entire NCBI database of more than 200 million sequences. We could have just as well started with arbitrarily produced strings.

The aim of the test was to check whether after applying our approximate hash function ah, the generated signatures $ah(\omega)$ for $\omega \in S$ carry enough information of the DNA strings ω they were produced from to identify the natural clusters, each consisting of one of the 50 randomly chosen strings and its 15 variants. We thus took the 800 signatures and calculated the Hamming distance between each of the $\frac{1}{2} 800 \times 799 = 319,600$ pairs. We used $\ell = 2$ and $u = 4$ on our tests, yielding signatures of length $4^2 + 4^3 + 4^4 = 336$ bits. Choosing $u = 5$ would already require 1024 more bits for each signature, a significant increase, for getting only moderately better results. As mentioned above, the thresholds t_k were chosen as the expected number of occurrences of a specific k-mer, which is $(n - k + 1)/4^k$, where n is the lengths of the string.

Table 1 displays a sample of these distances, showing, in the upper right triangle, only the results for the original strings indexed $j \in \{A, B, C, D, E\}^2$, and for each of these, two variants of each of the 3 groups, identified by $j.d.r$, $j.i.r$ and $j.di.r$ for the strings obtained by deletion, insertion and both, respectively, with $r \in \{1, 2\}$ giving the index of the variant within its group. For a pair $\omega_1, \omega_2 \in S$, the displayed value is the normalized Hamming distance between $ah(\omega_1)$ and $ah(\omega_2)$, that is, the number of 1-bits in $ah(\omega_1)$ XOR $ah(\omega_2)$ divided by the size of the signature 336, expressed as percentage. For visibility, cells containing values below 10% have been shaded in light green and the others in red. The lower left triangle contains, for each pair, a measure for the similarity of the original DNA strings. We chose the number of shared canonical 11-mers, as percentage of their total number, averaged for the two members of the pair.

One can see on this sample, which is representative for the entire 800×800 matrix, that while the distances between elements within the set of variants of the same original string are all small, all inter-set distances are much larger, so that one may conclude that using the signatures instead of the much longer original strings to perform the clustering process may be justified. A noteworthy exception are the sets produced by the strings indexed C and D, for which the pair-wise distances are only about 7–8%. This is in accordance with the

---

[2] The names of these 5 strings in the database are:

A - KV453883.1, B - NZ_DS996920.1, C - UPTC01000856.1, D - UPTC01000985.1, E - VAHF01000278.1.

Table 1. Sample of normalized Hamming distances between signatures.

	A	A.1.1	A.1.2	A.2.1	A.2.2	A.il.1	A.il.2	B	B.1.1	B.1.2	B.2.1	B.2.2	B.il.1	B.il.2	C	C.1.1	C.1.2	C.2.1	C.2.2	C.il.1	C.il.2	D	D.1.1	D.1.2	D.2.1	D.2.2	D.il.1	D.il.2	E	E.1.1	E.1.2	E.2.1	E.2.2	E.il.1	E.il.2
A	0.5	0.2	0.2	0.8	0.0	1.7	19.6	19.0	19.0	19.0	20.5	19.3	22.0	12.7	12.7	13.0	13.0	13.3	12.7	12.2	13.6	14.2	12.7	13.6	13.3	13.9	13.0	13.0	13.0	13.6	13.0	14.5	13.9	13.9
A.1.1		0.8	0.2	1.4	0.5	2.3	19.6	19.0	19.0	19.0	20.5	19.3	22.0	12.3	12.2	12.5	12.3	12.7	12.2	11.6	13.0	13.6	12.7	13.0	12.7	13.9	13.5	13.0	13.6	13.0	14.5	13.9
A.1.2			0.5	1.1	0.2	2.0	19.9	18.3	19.3	19.3	20.2	19.6	21.7	12.5	12.5	12.7	12.7	13.0	12.5	11.9	13.3	13.9	13.5	13.3	13.0	13.6	12.7	13.3	13.3	13.9	13.3	14.8	14.2	14.2
A.2.1				1.1	0.2	2.0	19.3	18.7	18.7	18.7	20.2	19.0	21.7	12.5	12.5	12.7	12.7	13.0	12.5	11.9	13.3	13.9	12.5	13.3	13.0	13.6	12.7	13.3	13.9	13.9	13.3	14.9	14.2	14.2
A.2.2					0.8	0.8	13.9	19.3	19.3	19.3	20.8	19.6	22.3	13.0	13.0	13.3	13.3	13.6	13.0	12.5	13.9	14.5	13.0	13.6	14.2	13.9	13.9	13.9	14.5	13.9	15.4	14.8	14.9
A.il.2						1.7	19.6	19.0	19.0	19.0	20.5	19.3	22.0	12.7	12.7	13.0	13.0	13.3	12.7	12.2	13.6	14.2	12.7	13.6	13.3	13.9	13.0	13.0	13.0	13.6	14.5	15.7	14.5	15.1
							20.8	20.2	19.6	19.6	21.1	20.5	23.0	12.7	12.7	13.0	13.6	13.9	12.7	12.2	14.5	15.4	13.9	14.8	14.5	15.1	13.6	14.2	14.2	14.2	14.2	15.7	15.5	15.1
B	2.89%							1.1	1.7	1.1	2.6	2.0	3.5	19.3	19.9	19.6	20.2	19.5	19.9	20.5	20.2	20.2	19.3	20.2	18.9	20.5	20.8	21.8	22.2	20.2	20.4	23.2	24.1	24.7
B.1.1									1.7	1.1	2.6	1.4	3.5	18.7	19.3	18.0	15.6	19.3	19.3	19.9	20.2	20.2	19.9	20.2	18.9	20.5	20.8	23.2	22.6	22.6	23.9	23.5	24.1
B.1.2										1.1	2.0	2.0	2.9	18.3	18.9	19.6	20.2	19.9	19.9	20.5	20.2	20.2	19.9	20.2	19.0	20.5	20.2	23.2	22.6	22.6	23.8	25.3	23.5	23.5
B.2.1											2.0	2.0	2.9	18.7	19.3	19.0	19.6	19.3	19.3	19.9	20.2	20.2	19.9	20.2	19.0	20.3	20.2	22.6	22.0	22.0	23.3	22.9	23.5
B.2.2												2.9	1.4	19.6	20.2	19.9	20.5	20.2	20.2	20.8	20.5	20.5	20.2	20.5	20.2	20.8	20.5	24.1	23.5	23.5	24.7	23.2	24.4	24.4
B.il.1													3.2	19.0	19.3	19.3	19.9	19.6	19.6	20.2	20.5	20.5	20.2	20.5	20.2	20.6	21.1	23.5	23.3	22.9	24.1	23.2	24.4	24.4
B.il.2														20.5	21.1	20.8	21.4	21.1	21.1	21.7	22.0	22.0	21.7	22.0	21.7	22.3	22.0	25.5	25.0	25.0	26.1	24.7	25.8	25.8
C	3.41%			3.31%										1.1	0.2	0.8	1.1	0.5	1.1	8.0	8.6	8.3	8.0	7.7	8.3	8.0	12.2	12.7	11.6	12.2	13.6	12.2	13.0
C.1.1															1.4	0.8	1.1	1.1	2.3	8.0	8.6	7.7	8.0	7.7	8.3	7.4	11.6	12.2	11.0	11.6	13.0	12.5	13.0
C.1.2																1.1	0.8	0.8	1.4	8.3	8.9	8.6	8.3	8.0	8.6	8.3	11.0	12.5	11.3	11.6	13.3	12.7	13.3
C.2.1																	0.8	0.2	1.4	7.1	7.7	7.4	7.1	6.8	7.4	7.7	12.5	13.0	11.9	12.5	13.9	13.5	13.9
C.2.2																		1.1	2.3	7.4	8.0	7.7	7.4	7.1	7.7	7.4	11.6	12.2	11.6	12.2	13.0	13.0	13.0
C.il.1																			1.1	7.4	8.0	7.7	7.4	7.1	7.7	8.0	12.7	13.3	12.2	12.7	14.2	13.6	14.2
C.il.2																				8.0	8.6	8.3	8.0	7.7	8.3	8.6	12.2	12.7	12.2	12.2	13.6	13.0	13.6
D	3.94%			3.47%					4.81%													0.5	1.4	0.0	0.2	0.2	1.7	13.6	13.6	13.6	14.2	14.5	14.5	15.1
D.1.1																							1.4	0.5	0.2	2.3	14.2	14.2	14.2	14.8	15.1	15.1	15.7
D.1.2																								1.4	1.7	1.7	1.4	13.3	13.3	13.3	13.9	14.2	14.2	14.8
D.2.1																									0.2	1.7	13.6	13.6	13.6	14.2	14.5	14.5	15.1
D.2.2																										0.5	2.0	13.9	13.9	13.9	14.5	14.8	14.8	15.4
D.il.1																											2.0	13.9	13.9	13.9	14.5	14.8	14.8	15.4
D.il.2																												12.5	12.5	12.5	13.0	13.3	13.3	13.9
E	3.28%			2.72%					3.50%						4.15%														1.1	1.1	0.5	1.4	1.4	2.0
E.1.1																														1.7	1.1	2.0	1.4	2.0
E.1.2																															1.1	2.6	2.0	3.2
E.2.1																																2.0	0.8	2.0
E.2.2																																	1.7	1.7
E.il.1																																		2.3

corresponding similarity measure of 4.81%, the only one exceeding a threshold of 4.5% (in green), and may be explained by the fact that the DNA strings were similar to begin with, being related to the same parasite.

As a control experiment, we also applied a real hash function instead of our approximate one. The choice was MD5 [15], for which all the values of the matrix were between 0.37 and 0.62, so that, as expected from a hash function, MD5 did not detect any of the clusters and would thus not be useful in this context.

To enable a fair comparison with alternative clustering methods, we took the same test collection as the one used for MC by [10] as second set of DNA strings: the top-level FASTA sequences containing one chromosome from Ensembl Genomes release 35 [6], a set of 3670 bacteria genomes taken from a collection of about 42,000. The size of the sequences varied from 114 KB to 15 MB, with an average of 3.5 MB.

We need a measure to compare the outcome of different clusterings A and B. Note that this measure is not symmetric: A is considered to be the base scenario, and we shall use MC as defining it, and B is a suggested new clustering method, one derived from *ah* in our case, and we wish to assess how much B deviates from A. It is acceptable that A should be a refinement of B, that is, every cluster in A is included in one of the clusters of B, but if a cluster of A is split over several different ones in B, we consider this as an error. Iterating over all the clusters *c* of A, we accumulate the *error counts* of *c*, defined as the difference of the size of cluster *c* with that of the largest intersection of *c* with one of the clusters of B. Finally, we define the normalized *error rate* by dividing the sum of the error counts by the number of sequences.

For example, consider 6 sequentially indexed strings. Figure 1 shows the clustering performed by a clustering A into clusters x, y and z, and by B into clusters

A Clustering

[1, 2], [3, 4,], [6]
x   y   z

B Clustering

[1, 2, 6], [3, 4], [ ]
a   b   c

Fig. 1. Comparing two different clusterings A and B

a, b and c. We see that B has merged the clusters x and z into a, but split the cluster y into b and c. Thus for clusters x, z, which are subsets of a, there is no error, but cluster y is not a subset of any cluster of B, and the largest intersection is with cluster b of B. This yields an error rate of $\frac{1}{6}$.

The reason for preferring such an asymmetric measure is that we intend using the clustering derived from our ah function in a preliminary filtering stage, on the outcome of which some other clustering can then be applied, with significantly reduced complexity. If several clusters of A are entirely included in a single cluster c of B, this is acceptable because the A clustering will anyway be applied on c after the filtering stage. Table 2 brings the comparative results. All tests were run on a Dell XPS 15 7590 with 32 GB RAM i9-9980HK @ 5.0 GHz, running Ubuntu 18.04.

Table 2. Comparison of clustering on 3670 strings from a Bacteria database

Method	Running tme (mm:ss)	Memory (MB)	Error rate	Number of clusters	Max size of cluster
MC	16:25	31744	–	1861	176
$ah - CC$	1:08	107	0.35%	861	1053
MC after ah	14:12	8200	2.02%	1862	177

We see that while there is a significant reduction in both time and required RAM when replacing MC by a simple Connected Component (CC) clustering[3] based on our ah signatures rather than the original DNA strings, this comes at a price of only marginally hurting the resulting clusters themselves, with an error rate of less than 1% of falsely assigned sequences. Even if we use ah only as a preliminary filter, the processing time is improved and the memory consumption is cut to a quarter, whereas the error rate is just 2%, and 96% of the clusters match those produced by MC alone. The table shows also that while most clusters are small, there are also some larger ones. The large difference in the number of clusters in spite of a low error rate implies that most MC clusters are entirely included in ah ones. We tried also to apply CD as alternative clustering, but had to abort its run after 24 h without results.

To enable also a comparison with CD to run in reasonable time, we limited the lengths of the strings in our third test set to be between 50 and 100K and

---

[3] Each string is a vertex, and vertices are connected by an edge if the distance between them is smaller than some threshold.

retrieved 4523 strings of viruses from the GenBank database[4]. The results appear in Table 3.

Table 3. Comparison of clustering on 4523 strings of a Virus database

Method	Running Time (mm:ss)	Memory (MB)	Error vs CD	Error vs MC	Number of clusters	Max size of cluster
CD	38:44	1500	–	–	3774	67
MC	00:54	2200	–	–	1934	208
ah – CC	00:04	160	0.71%	0.08%	1158	794
CD after ah	22:04	1115	0.75%	–	3804	67
MC after ah	00:45	265	–	0.80%	1945	208

The conclusions are similar to those for the set of bacteria DNA strings. CD is much slower than MC but requires only 1.5 GB of RAM instead of 2.2 GB and produces about twice as many clusters. If ah is used as a preliminary clustering, 99% and 98% of the original clusters are recovered for CD and MC, respectively.

2.3   Searching for a String Including Some Read

In the problem we consider here, a large collection $\mathcal{C}$ of strings is given, where both the size of $\mathcal{C}$ and that each of its individual elements may be of the order of millions and more. In addition, we are given a read R whose length could be in the thousands, and we wish to retrieve the subset of elements $C_i \in \mathcal{C}$ for which R is a substring of C_i. Actually, the notion of being a substring has to be understood in a broader sense, as we allow a limited number ℓ of mismatches. If $\ell = 0$, this is the *exact matching* problem that has been thoroughly investigated. For general ℓ, the problem is much more difficult; the best deterministic algorithm has a complexity proportional to $n\sqrt{\ell \log \ell}$ [1], which is not reasonable for large values of ℓ. A faster probabilistic algorithm, running in time $O(n \log n)$ can be found in [4], where n is the total length of the strings.

Our approach here is similar to the Karp-Rabin probabilistic algorithm for string matching [11], but using our approximate hash function instead of simple hashing modulo a large prime number. A brute force approach would be to compare R with the substrings $C_i^j = C_i[j]C_i[j+1]\cdots C_i[j+m-1]$ of length $m = |R|$ of C_i starting at position j, for all $C_i \in \mathcal{C}$ and all possible values of j, $1 \le j < n_i - m$, where $n_i = |C_i|$ is the length of C_i. This yields a complexity of mn, with n the total length of all the strings in $\mathcal{C}$, which may be prohibitive for the intended application. Instead, we suggest applying the approximate hash function ah to both R and the substrings C_i and compare the results. A Hamming distance *above* some threshold is a clear indication that the pattern R does not occur at the given position in C_i, yet being *below* does not guarantee that it does appear

---

[4] https://www.ncbi.nlm.nih.gov/labs/virus/vssi/#/.

there. Nevertheless, the function ah can serve as a filter, allowing us to restrict a full comparison of R with substrings of C_i only to indices at which a match has been declared.

At first sight, for calculating $ah(C_i^j)$ for all i and j, one needs $O(nm)$ operations, so there seems to be no gain by applying the approximate hash. Note, however, that the value of $ah(\omega)$ for a string ω is defined as a function of the statistics of occurrences of the different k-mers forming the string, and it does not matter where exactly they occur in ω. One can thus easily evaluate $ah(C_i^{j+1})$ as a function of $ah(C_i^j)$ in constant time, because of the large overlap of size $m-1$ they share, just as in the Karp-Rabin algorithm. The global complexity may therefore be reduced to $O(n+m)$.

The strategy of replacing comparisons between long reads by comparisons of the much shorter ah signatures will only be useful if, for DNA string fragments ω_1 and ω_2, there is a strong enough correlation between the edit distance $d(\omega_1, \omega_2)$ and the corresponding Hamming distance $HD(ah(\omega_1), ah(\omega_2))$. Note that we do obviously not expect a perfect match and that the edit distance between strings could be replaced by the HD between their signatures, so that

$$d(\omega_1, \omega_2) < d(\omega_3, \omega_4) \iff HD(ah(\omega_1), ah(\omega_2)) < HD(ah(\omega_3), ah(\omega_4)).$$

This is theoretically impossible because the signatures are shorter and thus cannot carry the same amount of information content. Even requesting just a weak inequality on the right hand side would not be realistic, and for a fixed edit distance, the corresponding HD values might fluctuate. We do, however, expect, that in spite of these fluctuations, the results may be partitioned into regions allowing to derive some cut-off points, that is, that d is small if and only if the corresponding HD is small, for some reasonable definition of smallness. The following experiment illustrates the validity of this assumption.

A sample of $s = 200$ strings has arbitrarily been chosen from the bacteria database, and the normalized edit distance has been evaluated for each of the $\binom{s}{2}$ pairs. The increasing purple line in Fig. 2 shows these values as function of their rank, after having sorted them in non-decreasing order. The blue line plots the corresponding Hamming distances between the ah values for the same pairs. Though these values are strongly fluctuating, one can still identify a clear cutoff point at about 3200, separating the plot into two regions with distinct and different extreme values for the Hamming distance. This fact enables the definition of thresholds for both edit and Hamming distances; in our case, we chose empirically 0.3 (in red) for the former, and 0.1 (in yellow) for the latter.

It will be convenient to describe our experiment borrowing the vocabulary of the Information Retrieval field. We are looking for *relevant* pairs, defined here as those for which their edit distance is below the chosen threshold, but we choose them by means of the Hamming distance between their signatures, so the *retrieved* pairs are those for which the HD is below the threshold. The outcome is color coded in Fig. 3 showing the matrix of all the pairs. True positive results are those for which both distances are below their thresholds and are shown in light green; true negatives (both distances above their thresholds) appear in blue.

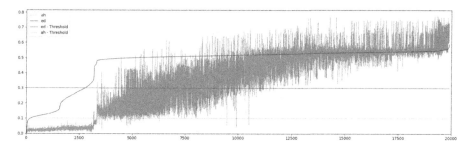

Fig. 2. Comparing edit distance between strings with Hamming distance on corresponding signatures, both normalized. The x-axis is the index in the sequence of 19900 pairs of strings, sorted by non-decreasing edit distance. (Color figure online)

Erroneous outcomes are false positives, shown in red, with a low HD in spite of a large edit distance, and false negatives (HD above in spite of edit distance below), which is not shown in this example—not a single pair fell into this category.

Table 4. Recall and Precision for various threshold settings.

ah threshold	Edit dist threshold	Precision	Recall
0.125	0.275	0.61	1
0.1	0.3	0.82	1
0.075	0.35	0.97	0.99

Table 4 displays the Recall/Precision values obtained for various settings of the two chosen thresholds. Recall is the fraction of the relevant items that have actually been retrieved, precision is the fraction of the retrieved items that are indeed relevant. We see that recall is very close to 1, as there are very few false negative results, and precision can also be very high for well chosen thresholds.

Our last experiment directly checked the applicability of the approximate hash approach to searching a long read in a DNA string. An arbitrary string C of length about 900K was chosen from the bacteria set, as well as a substring R of length $m = 5000$ starting at an arbitrary position (at about 650K), serving as pattern to be located. Figure 4 plots in green, as function of i, the normalized Hamming distance between $ah(R)$ and $ah(C_i)$, where C_i is the substring of length m of C starting at i. We see that there is only a very narrow region for which the distance is practically zero. As a control experiment, the search for the same pattern was repeated with a different DNA string C' of length about 1M, yielding the purple curve with not a single value even approaching zero.

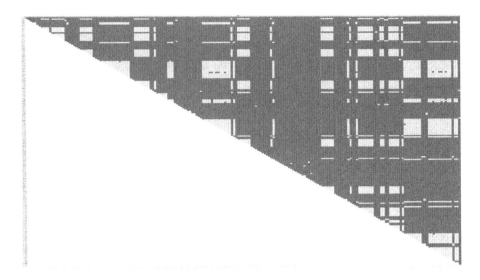

Fig. 3. Comparing pair distances: Blue – true positive; green – true negative; red – false positive; no false negative (Color figure online)

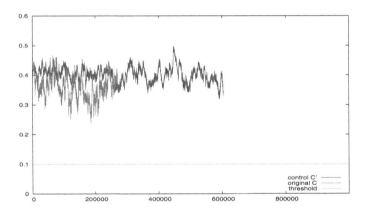

Fig. 4. Searching for a substring by comparing signatures. (Color figure online)

The search procedure will thus declare a match if the HD is below some threshold, symbolized in Fig. 4 by the blue line. It should be emphasized that if there are indeed matches, the procedure will find them all, and the possible errors are only to declare non-existing matches. However, the validity of the match can be verified, since we know where to check. We conclude that using the ah is a powerful tool significantly reducing the amount of work while only marginally affecting the quality of the results.

References

1. Amir, A., Lewenstein, M., Porat, E.: Faster algorithms for string matching with k mismatches. J. Algorithms **50**(2), 257–275 (2004)
2. Aronovich, L., Asher, R., Bachmat, E., Bitner, H., Hirsch, M., Klein, S.T.: The design of a similarity based deduplication system. In: Proceedings of SYSTOR, p. 6 (2009)
3. Aronovich, L., Asher, R., Harnik, D., Hirsch, M., Klein, S.T., Toaff, Y.: Similarity based deduplication with small data chunks. Discret. Appl. Math. **212**, 10–22 (2016)
4. Atallah, M.J., Chyzak, F., Dumas, P.: A randomized algorithm for approximate string matching. Algorithmica **29**(3), 468–486 (2001). https://doi.org/10.1007/s004530010062
5. Dubinkina, V.B., Ischenko, D.S., Ulyantsev, V.I., Tyakht, A.V., Alexeev, D.G.: Assessment of k-mer spectrum applicability for metagenomic dissimilarity analysis. BMC Bioinform. **17**, 38 (2016)
6. Kersey, P.J., et al.: Ensembl Genomes 2018: an integrated omics infrastructure for non-vertebrate species. Nucleic Acids Res. **46**(D1), D802–D808 (2017)
7. Hirsch, M., Bitner, H., Aronovich, L., Asher, R., Bachmat, E., Klein, S.T.: Systems and methods for efficient data searching, storage and reduction, U.S. Patent 7,523,098, issued 21 April 2009
8. Höhl, M., Rigoutsos, I., Ragan, M.: Pattern-based phylogenetic distance estimation and tree reconstruction. Evol. Bioinform. Online **2**, 359–75 (2006)
9. Indyk, P., Motwani, R.: Approximate nearest neighbors: towards removing the curse of dimensionality. In: Proceedings of the 30th STOC, pp. 604–613 (1998)
10. James, B.T., Girgis, H.Z.: MeShClust^2: application of alignment-free identity scores in clustering long DNA sequences. bioRxiv, 451278 (2018)
11. Karp, R.M., Rabin, M.O.: Efficient randomized pattern-matching algorithms. IBM J. Res. Dev. **31**(2), 249–260 (1987)
12. Li, W., Godzik, A.: cd-hit: a fast program for clustering and comparing large sets of protein or nucleotide sequences. Bioinformatics **22**(13), 1658–1659 (2006)
13. Morgenstern, B., Zhu, B., Horwege, S., Leimeister, C.: Estimating evolutionary distances between genomic sequences from spaced-word matches. Algorithms Mol. Biol. **10**, 5 (2015). https://doi.org/10.1186/s13015-015-0032-x
14. Quinlan, S., Dorward, S.: Venti: a new approach to archival storage. In: Proceedings of FAST 2002 Conference on File and Storage Technologies, pp. 89–101 (2002)
15. Rivest, R.L.: The MD5 message-digest algorithm. RFC **1321**, 1–21 (1992)
16. Wang, Z., et al.: A new method for rapid genome classification, clustering, visualization, and novel taxa discovery from metagenome. BioRxiv, 812917 (2019)

Author Index

Printed in the United States
by Baker & Taylor Publisher Services